GOLD SEEKING

Eugene von Guerard. 'I Have Got It!', oil on canvas, 23.7 x 18.4 cm.
Purchased 1928, La Trobe Library, State Library of Victoria.

GOLD SEEKING

Victoria and California in the 1850s

David Goodman

Stanford University Press
Stanford, California
1994

Stanford University Press
Stanford, California
© 1994 David Goodman
Originating publisher, Allen & Unwin, Australia
First published in the U.S.A. by
  Stanford University Press, 1994
Printed in Australia
ISBN 0-8047-2480-6
LC 94-67172
This book is printed on acid-free paper.

CONTENTS

ACKNOWLEDGEMENTS

Many people have assisted me in the writing of this book and the PhD thesis upon which it is based. Staff at the La Trobe Library in Melbourne and the Bancroft Library, Berkeley, were extremely helpful in enabling me to locate gold-rush material in their large collections, and to make the most of summer research spells. Friends and colleagues at the University of Sydney (1986–1989) and the University of Melbourne (1990–) have encouraged this work by asking after its progress, discussing issues, provoking anxiety and rekindling enthusiasm. Many people have read sections and offered important criticism and advice: Emie Aronson, Dan Beaver, Antoinette Burton, Bill Kunze, and Deb Rossum in Chicago; Barbara Caine, Peter Cochrane, Jim Gilbert, Richard Waterhouse, Richard White, and Shane White in Sydney; Leonore Davidoff, Kerryn Goldsworthy, Chris Healy, Katie Holmes, Jeanette Hoorn, Susan Janson, Susan K. Martin, Julie McLeod, Stuart Macintyre, Glenda Sluga, Christina Twomey, David Walker and Chris Wallace-Crabbe in Melbourne. Michael Roper in London and Robin Einhorn in Berkeley both read sections and kindly gave me accommodation. Neil Harris, Kathleen Conzen and Bernard Cohn in Chicago, my dissertation committee, gave crucial support and suggestion from a distance and on visits to Chicago in the winters of 1988–1989 and 1989–1990. Greg Dening set me working on the 1850s ten years ago, but more than that kept me studying history. Teaching in Richard Waterhouse's comparative Australian/American courses at the University of Sydney provided stimulus to my own comparative thinking. I am grateful for the award of the Harry Barnard Dissertation Fellowship at the University of Chicago in 1989, which was important in assisting further research in California, and for the earlier university fellowships and the Fulbright travelling scholarship which enabled me to begin my studies at Chicago in 1983–1984. Sections of this work have been published in earlier form in *Australian Historical Studies* (1988), *Australian Cultural History* (1991) and in the Melbourne History Department's festschrift volume for Greg Dening, and appear here by kind permission of the editors of those publications.

INTRODUCTION

On opposite sides of the vast Pacific Ocean lie two cities, Melbourne and San Francisco, which owed their original importance to the discoveries of gold in their extensive hinterlands in the early 1850s. In 1848, gold was discovered in California, a newly conquered territory of the United States. Between 1851 and 1860, the United States produced 41 per cent of the world's gold output, most of it from California. The population of California grew from 14 000 in 1848, to almost 100 000 by the end of 1849, and to 300 000 by the end of 1853.[1] The Native American population diminished from about 150 000 in 1848 to about 28 000 by the end of the 1850s.[2] California entered the Union in 1850.

In 1851 gold was discovered in the British colony of New South Wales, and some months later in the new southern colony of Victoria. Between 1851 and 1860, Australia produced 39 per cent of the world's gold output, the greater part of it coming from Victoria. In 1850 Victoria became a separate colony. Its population grew from 77 000 in 1851, to 237 000 in 1854, and 411 000 by 1857. The Aboriginal population of Victoria, at least 11 500, maybe more than 50 000 at the beginning of European settlement of the district in 1834, had diminished to 2700 by the census of 1851.[3]

For most Australians, school history moved from the decision to found Botany Bay, to convicts, to gold. No doubt teachers distilled from Geoffrey Serle's *The Golden Age* a broadly, cautiously, positive picture of the effects of gold on the development of Victoria, and from Russel Ward's *The Australian Legend* and other radical nationalist works a reflection of the nostalgia of the radical 1890s for the remembered freedom of individual mining. Reproductions of the comic images of S.T. Gill left a general impression of the gold rush as a rollicking good time. When discussed in universities, gold (like the other elements of the school Australian history curriculum) began to seem too exceptional, too much of an 'event', in the derogatory sense in which that term, after Braudel, came to be used. From Melbourne, social history as it had developed internationally by the 1970s, seemed most suited to the study of the internationally comparable cities of later nineteenth-century Australia. After a little flurry around the centenaries of the 1950s, and the stimulus of Geoffrey Serle's *The Golden Age* in 1963, the gold rush began to fall from favour as a serious historical topic.[4] Gold's comic inversions of the social order were considered by social historians too transient a phenomenon to be worth the extended attention

MAP 1

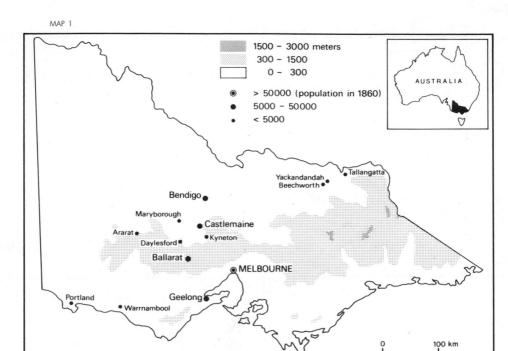

1500 – 3000 meters
300 – 1500
0 – 300

◉ > 50000 (population in 1860)
● 5000 – 50000
• < 5000

AUSTRALIA

Tallangatta
Yackandandah
Beechworth

Bendigo

Maryborough

Ararat
Castlemaine
Kyneton
Daylesford

Ballarat

MELBOURNE

Portland
Geelong
Warrnambool

0   100 km

social observers of the time and popular historians ever since had given them. The creation of Sovereign Hill historical park at Ballarat only confirmed a sense that interest in the gold rush was mostly for children and tourists. Sovereign Hill allows visitors to encounter some of the dust and noise of a gold-rush town and to see for themselves what tent life was like.[5] Historical tourism has become an important industry in the old gold towns, and brings with it an inevitable fixation upon the outward trappings of the gold era—the equipment, the 'look' of the buildings and the clothing of the miners.

By the 1980s, historical revisionism in Australia had almost completed the process of demotion of the gold rushes as events. The introductory essay to the catalogue to a 1982–83 exhibition at the La Trobe Library in Melbourne, *Dreams of a Golden Harvest: Gold Seekers in Victoria*, set out the themes which a new generation of history professionals found interesting about the gold period: immigrants and their ethnicity; failure at the diggings; the way in which the trials and tribulations of diggers were not recorded by goldfield artists; women and children on the goldfields; and, the physical devastation of the landscape.[6] The new environmental histories gave space to the gold rushes as instances of the general environmental destruction associated with mining history. The old heroic gold rush had

x

MAP 2

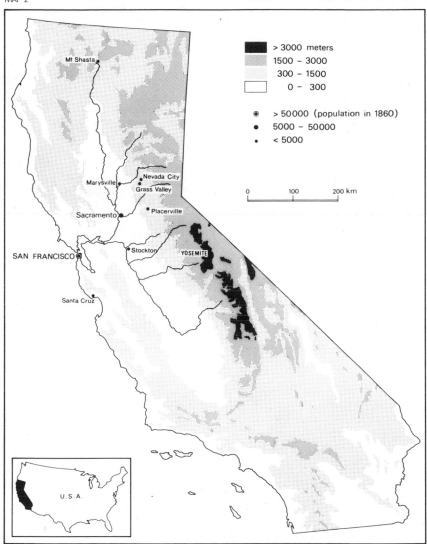

gone, but so had any sense of the gold rushes posing historically specific moral problems.

When I began researching the gold period, my image of it was thus unfocussed, beyond a general interest in the carnival-like atmosphere, the many recorded complaints of the privileged that their world had been turned upside down. I read through any contemporary material I could find—pamphlets, books, magazines, newspapers, sermons, letters, diaries— anywhere that people consciously reflected upon the effects of the gold

Photograph, Sovereign Hill

discoveries. I was drawn most strongly to the early 1850s, to the contents of initial hopes and apprehensions. There ideology seemed most clearly stated, substantial nuggets of ideologically informed social analysis, untempered by prosaic eventual outcomes, seemed most available for recovery. My interest was thus not in the actual outcome of the gold rushes—the disappointments experienced by the many, the declining average yields from the mines, the supplanting of the individual miner by the company aided by capital and science—but in the content of initial expectations; not in the gold rushes as events, but in what the events revealed of the constitution of the societies into which gold entered as a common factor.

I discovered two things about the arguments which gold provoked in Victoria. I found myself reading much more about the disruptions of gold, many more anxious and pessimistic accounts of the future which gold suggested, than optimistic celebrations of new freedoms. That must be partly because the literate classes were also the anxious classes, but one of my arguments will be that the optimistic accounts of gold come to us from later in the nineteenth century, tinged with nostalgia. What worried people in the 1850s about the gold rushes was not their outlandish or unusual character, but their conformity to existing trends. Gold-rush society seemed to many contemporaries to exhibit a comic exaggeration of the existing influence of the market on society back in Britain, but it was not an unrecognisable freak. Indeed to some, it seemed like a glimpse of the future. My second discovery was, unsurprisingly, that people in the 1850s argued about gold with the languages and ideas they had to hand. They thought about the disruptions of gold in terms of the positive categories of their own culture, which came to them from earlier periods of British history. In order to understand how gold was made sense of at the time, I had to look backwards from the 1850s.

That is where the idea of a comparison with California began to make sense. In the course of graduate work at the University of Chicago I had become interested in the possibility of a sort of micro-comparative history. How did the slightly differing common senses of Australians and Americans reveal themselves in small interactions on the street, in understandings of fundamental social categories, in formal argument? I decided to look at the Victorian and Californian gold rushes and to compare them close up, not from the macro perspective which has been the normal mode of comparative history, comparing structures and vital statistics from afar. I wanted to immerse myself in the arguments made in both places about gold, as well as study the day-to-day detail of local newspapers, the personal writing of private letters, the details of local religious controversies and political concerns. Did mid-century Americans bring the same categories to the comprehension of their contemporaneous gold rush?

Teaching in comparative Australian/American history courses at the University of Sydney, I had become aware of the importance of comparative approaches in tempering nationalist presumptions of unique development—on either side of the Pacific. The conclusions of this kind of comparative cultural history are instructive in their unremarkableness. Australians and Americans shared a great deal—the fundamental categories of response were the same in both places. But within these similarities there were different inflections, alternate emphases, which allow us to talk, in a way that historians have become wary of doing, of differing national cultures.

I hope the reading of this book is as subversive of a simple nationalist history of either gold rush as it is indicative of the importance of retaining some sense of a larger British history and its trajectory. The postcolonial societies often assert their nationalism in a rejection of the relevance of the history of the empire which spawned them. In reaction against the old order in which Australian history was taught simply as a footnote to imperial history, Australian historians turned to internal social history. But that social history makes sense only when placed within the context of a kind of historical anthropology of Englishness, of a study of the specificity and peculiarity of the dominant forms which were inherited from Britain. Within that study, similarities and differences with the experiences of other former colonies become instructive and important. If postcolonial studies have anything to do with the relatively privileged former settler colonies like the United States and Australia, it ought to be as a reminder of origins that nationalist history would like to forget.

In terms of the sweep of history, in terms of any kind of ethics of equitable attention from the present to the past, the gold rushes have had their due. And yet, there is surely more to be said. The existing historiography naturalises the decisions to seek for gold, does not see the need to ask how the gold rushes were understood at the time, as though it were the most natural thing that men should leave all that was valuable to them in one part of the world, to seek for precious minerals in remote regions about which they knew little. What could be more apparently self-explanatory than that men should risk a great deal for the prospect of enormous wealth swiftly gained? So arises the common-sensical tone of most of the historical accounts, and the employment of tropes (desire, lust) which naturalise the events. 'The men who mined for gold in those early days in Victoria were moved by an almost insatiable lust,' Molony argued, 'The very nature of large discoveries of minerals engenders disruption.'[7] Manning Clark's employment of the metaphor of 'madness' works in a similar way—the explanation is not to do with ideas but with uncontrollable drives. 'Gentlemen foamed at the mouth,' he wrote, 'women fainted; children somersaulted. Another great madness had begun.'[8] This book seeks to re-problematise the single-minded pursuit of wealth which lay at the heart of the gold rushes. One of the tasks of cultural history is to de-naturalise events. Self-interest may rule the world, but only in locally constituted forms. Why should men have had these priorities? That was a question, after all, which contemporaries in the 1850s asked themselves repeatedly. It was not human nature which led men to seek for gold, but a set of socially constituted ideas, and it was in particular social languages that the responses were framed.

CONTEMPORARY RESPONSES

If there was one thing that contemporaries agreed upon about the gold rushes, it was that they were a disturbance to the normal order of things. 'The close of the year 1851 found the whole country unsettled', P. Just wrote of Victoria.[9] Some of the reasons for this were obvious—people had left their homes and jobs, unprecedented immigration had led to homelessness and rapidly rising prices for all commodities. But there was also an ideological disturbance caused by gold.

Gold, the very definition of wealth, was apparently just waiting to be picked up by whoever reached it first. If a person, any person, could procure great wealth, perhaps without significant work, what would become of society as it was then constituted? If physical strength was now to be the greatest requirement for wealth acquisition, would the entire social order be turned upside down? Would the poor man at last have his day? Would society simply be randomly rearranged? Or would all starve in the frenzied but deluded pursuit of pure wealth? All were possibilities.

Some of them were frankly utopian. In California, the gold was understood by some as providing the means for a republican home for the starving millions: 'Never in the world's history was there a better opportunity for a great, free, and republican nation like ours to offer to the oppressed and down trodden of the whole world an asylum, and a place where . . . they can build themselves happy homes and live like freemen.'[10] Charles Thatcher, the popular Victorian balladist, celebrated the egalitarian consequences of the gold discoveries in some of his verse:

> On the diggings we're all on a level you know;
> The poor man out here ain't oppressed by the rich,
> But dressed in blue shirts you can't tell which is which.
> And this is the country, with rich golden soil,
> To reward any poor man's industrious toil;
> There's no masters here to oppress a poor devil,
> But out in Australia we're all on a level.[11]

In Australia and Britain, one of the strongest responses to gold was a fervently expressed hope that poverty might now be ended, and the lot of the working classes improved.

In Victoria and California, gold was dug or washed by individual miners, men who had left their homes elsewhere to seek their fortunes. In California the only licence system was a tax on foreign diggers—'foreign' here including, as Patricia Limerick points out, Sonorans and most Hispanics; the Anglo intruders had rapidly acquired the ability to cast themselves as the only legitimate natives.[12] The legal situation was confused by the transition from Mexican to American control, but the law in general deferred to the 'customs, usages, or regulations' established by miners themselves in cases of dispute.[13] By the mid-1850s, it had been decided that the owners of private land in California would have the rights to the precious minerals in them. Stephen J. Field wrote the opinion in the 1855 California Supreme Court case which found 'something shocking to all our ideas of the rights of property in the proposition that one man may invade the possession of another, dig up his fields and gardens, cut down his timber, and occupy his land, under the pretense that he has reason to believe there is gold under the surface'. The United States government, Field argued, had no right 'in derogation of the local sovereign, to govern the relations of the citizens of the State, and to proscribe the rules of property, and its mode of disposition'.[14] But on public land, California was 'literally without any law relating to the acquisition of mineral rights', and so, Umbeck argues, the miners were technically trespassers on federal land.[15] There was

California letterhead, 'Placerville'. Courtesy Bancroft Library.

discussion in California of imposing licence fees on diggers on public lands, but the early military governors lacked the troops to enforce any such tax. President Fillmore proposed selling off mineral lands in small parcels for mining, but was opposed in California, and agreed to a policy of 'non-interference' which remained in force in California until 1866—so that 'the government treasury did not derive any revenue of the hundreds of millions of dollars worth of gold extracted during this period by people from all parts of the globe'.[16]

In Victoria a licence system operated, whereby the right to dig for precious minerals, which were deemed the property of the Crown, could be purchased for a monthly and, later, yearly payment. The New South Wales government, which initiated the Australian gold mining licence policy, mistakenly believed that it was imitating a Californian practice.[17] The licence system brought with it an army of uniformed Gold Commissioners, who followed the rushes to each new field and regularly held licence inspections. The miner's licence gave the right to excavate private or public land, and to keep the resulting gold. Licensed miners gained access to private property on the argument that 'it is desirable for the public good that all lands found to be auriferous, whether public or private, should, under suitable regulations, be mined for gold'.[18] The size of mining claims allowed in California differed from place to place, but Australian regulations allowed only for small claims—enforcing, Blainey argues, a greater mobility among Australian diggers.[19] In California, where the new United States military government had little sway over the more stable, more distant, and almost self-governing miners' camps, self-constituted miners' courts settled disputes about claims; in Victoria, this was the job of the Gold Commissioners.[20] In both places, though, individual wealth seeking was allowed at the goldfields, which were generally on public land. Those who arrived first had the chance to stake legal claims giving, Limerick has argued of the American west, 'an almost mystical weight to the idea of getting there first'.[21] The gold finder was also the gold keeper. Miners could work for themselves, and the motivation for rushing to the new fields was individual enrichment.

The gold rushes of the 1850s were events with contradictory meanings. The prosperity and growth they produced in Victoria and California were satisfying to dominant ideologies of progress. Yet the ways in which that prosperity came about were troubling. Gold seemed to many to have brought about social decline rather than progression. Men had left their homes and families, and all the comforts and constraints of civilisation, for a wild life of wandering and seeking. It was difficult even for this pre-Darwinian generation, habituated as it already was to modes of hier-archical or evolutionary explanation of human history, not to think of the activity of gold seeking as regressive, a return to an earlier, less disciplined, and more primitive era. '[I]t is impossible to find persons here', William Walker wrote from Sacramento to his grandparents in New York. 'They are a wandering set: going from place to place, pitching their tents when night overtakes them: as the Israelites did in times gone by.'[22] Renouncing comfort in the speculative pursuit of comfort, leaving home for a restless wandering existence, the gold seeker seemed to have missed the point of many of the moral injunctions of the day. He had apparently failed to see the force of the arguments for the work ethic—that rapidly secularising cluster of beliefs which centred on the notion that work was not an irksome necessity but 'the core of the moral life'.[23] Further, it was fortune rather than virtue which governed the outcome of his quest, so that his work seemed to evade the moral improvement normally associated with steady labour. This opposition—fortune/virtue—came from a construction basic to western liberalism, and one vital to that sense of growing control over the conditions of life which was central to what the Victorians meant by civilisation. The terms of the unease with an individualised and uprooted society of disorganised wealth seekers were inherited and deep-rooted.

But there was a further, local, context for this kind of anxiety. 'In the land in which we live', Edward Stone Parker wrote of Victoria, 'the highest civilisation and almost the lowest barbarism dwell in juxta-position'.[24] The stated justification for the displacement of the indigenous populations, in

Victoria in particular, was that they were not settled peoples. They appeared to lack that diligent development of and attachment to a place which was taken to be the sign and index of civilisation; they were apparently not committed to wealth accumulation beyond the needs of the present. The Reverend Alexander Morison explained to a public meeting in Melbourne in 1851 that 'all savage races had been found destitute of the great principle that guided civilized man—the desire of accumulation'.[25] This indifference to accumulation could be portrayed as selfishness, as the absence of care for family and community. 'The civilised man', explained an article in the *Illustrated Australian Magazine*:

also is conscious of the indefeasible claims of children and relatives, yes, and of the common brotherhood of fellow citizens, upon his care and exertions; but the savage repudiates any such claim. He is selfish in the most exclusive sense. From these mental and moral defects results his habitual improvidence . . . .[26]

But how, it might have been asked, did this selfishness differ from that of the gold digger? In San Francisco, George Chalwill, in an 1854 temperance lecture, offered a portrait of the 'man of Nature' who 'roams at will among the fastnesses of his mountain home', and for whom the 'law of service to himself is measured by immediate appetite'. 'Yet if we compare this view with the reality of daily intercourse', Chalwill contended, 'shall we not find as apt similitude in civilized life demoralized by crime'.[27]

When a Committee of the Victorian Legislative Council asked, in a circular letter to settlers and officials in 1859, whether grants of land might persuade the Aboriginal people to 'more civilized and fixed habits'—as though the ownership of small parcels of land might impose civilisation more effectively than the ownership, still in living memory, of the whole country—the responses were almost entirely negative. 'It is their habit, and I believe their nature,' wrote Mr Synnot, 'to roam about.' 'The love of change,' opined Mr Lewis, 'appears engrained into their very nature.' Only Patrick Mitchell of Kangatong had a somewhat less essentialist explanation, arguing that it was the elders of the tribe who encouraged or enforced in their young men 'wandering habits'. 'Thus a passion for rambling grows up in these young men, and in many instances quite unfits them for steady employment.'[28] The language was the same as that used at the time about the settler population under the influence of gold. What if gold seeking imbued the European population of Australia with a similar 'passion for rambling'? What guarantees were there that men so unsettled would trade their rambling life for settled contentment at the end of their quest? And, if they constituted only a nation of wanderers, what moral claim would they have to the country they had taken? Doubts on that point were fundamentally disturbing.[29] 'We have taken their country on the principle that might is right', argued a letter to the editor of the Melbourne *Argus* in 1857.[30] That was clearly no moral basis for a New World civilisation meant to be free from some of the defects and injustices of the old.

If gold raised anxieties about a future undisciplined and wandering population, living outside the constraints and disciplines of the market economy, it also raised a contrary fear. The gold seekers, seen from a different vantage point, were men who had abandoned everything for the pursuit of wealth. Were they not, it was asked, too attuned to the work ethic? Had not these men left the possibilities of domestic comfort and fulfilment for a life often composed of nothing but arduous work? Much criticism of the effects of gold thus took the form of assertions of the limits to the place of work in civilised life. Work was not the whole of life, it was said. There was a justification of work in the conditions of life it created. Henry David Thoreau thought the rush to California a 'disgrace on mankind', for it seemed to him to represent and dramatise the tendency of the times to a concentration on getting a living rather than living itself: 'I know of no more startling development of the immorality of trade, and all the common modes of getting a living.'[31] Community, critics argued, was an important context for human life, and the wealth-seeking individual would have to curb his covetousness to find happiness. Melbourne's Anglican Bishop Perry lamented 'the great variety of nations and races, and the almost total want of any social intercourse of the people with one another' at the goldfields.[32] Eliza Farnham complained of the effect of California: 'it is one of the influences of the country to destroy confidence in friendship; in natural affection; in human sympathy'; there was a 'want of mutual confidence'.[33] What sort of a society would such isolated people bring into being? Thomas a'Beckett in Melbourne wrote of his hope that Victorian men would come at last to the conclusion that 'gold is not happiness, and that its pursuit is accompanied by a gnawing at the heart which they never knew when adding by their skill to the general comfort'.[34] The single-minded pursuit of wealth seemed to these critics to have created a society that was not worth living in.

Emigration officials in Britain worried about finding population for Australia which would continue to perform the necessary task of looking after sheep rather than excitedly rushing after gold. Where could emigrants be found who were so unentrepreneurial, so unoriented to profit maximising, that they would stay in steady but poorly paid employment rather than risk experiencing fortune or failure at the goldfields? Not among the success stories of industrialising Britain, clearly, but on its fringes, among those who were displaced and dispossessed by the transformations taking place. Colonial Secretary Pakington in London reported to Lieutenant Governor La Trobe in Melbourne in 1852 that the British Emigration Commissioners had 'entered into correspondence with some gentlemen connected with the Highlands of Scotland with a view to obtaining Emigrants accustomed to the care of Sheep and Cattle from Skye and the adjacent Country', as well as handloom weavers from Paisley, Carlisle and Kidderminster. 'These people,' he wrote, 'have been accepted under the belief that they are less likely to leave the constant and less arduous duties of Shepherds and Herdsmen for the more laborious though remunerative pursuit of Gold seeking.' Here perhaps were people for whom profit was not the only motive for action, for whom settled community would be a more important achievement.[35]

If the fear of an undisciplined population belonged to the spokespersons for an emerging industrial capitalist order, the reminder that there was more to life than work, that community was the necessary context for happiness, belonged to a bourgeois critical tradition which saw in domestic life a necessary retreat from the competition and strife of the world. This critical tradition, in valorising the domestic sphere, ascribed a dangerous competitiveness to men unchecked by family life. In the terms of this mode of thought, the largely masculine populations of Victoria and California were likely to be leading unbalanced lives, all work and no love. The critical tradition also questioned the innate value of gold, stressing its merely representative status. 'Intrinsic value is the power of anything to support life', wrote John Ruskin in 1862, arguing that a sheaf of wheat, a cubic foot of pure air, 'a cluster of flowers of given beauty', had intrinsic value, while gold, as money, expressed but a 'documentary claim to wealth'.[36] Karl Marx, too, saw gold as a sign, as 'the universal equivalent form of all other commodities, and the immediate social incarnation of all human labour'.[37] The rush to mine gold by large numbers of men seemed to critics with such understandings to indicate a general confusion of real wealth with its signifier.

The gold rushes raised moral questions for those still unprepared to admit the pursuit of wealth as the most important motor and regulator of human action in society. 'Gold must be sought secondarily in order to be sought safely', the Reverend Professor George Shephard warned the members of his Maine flock about to leave for California. The professor saw 'peculiar moral dangers' in 'this immediate searching and digging' for gold.[38] He, too, was part of the critical tradition which saw in gold-rush society but an exaggerated form of the commercial ethos of the times.

The criticism of gold-rush society necessarily involved the formulation of arguments about the limits to the government of social life by the market. Their formulation in the mid-nineteenth century is further evidence of what J.G.A. Pocock referred to as 'the singular persistence of early modern values and assumptions in American culture'; the comparative perspective allows us to observe their simultaneous persistence in other English-speaking communities.[39]

Much that was written about the gold rushes was of course celebratory and optimistic, talking up the possibilities of future greatness awaiting the societies in whose midst the gold had been found. Franklin Langworthy produced in 1855 a list of those in California who had an interest in such promotion: 'Shippers, Steamship Companies, Steamboat owners, Editors, Merchants, Grocery and Hotel keepers, Actors, Jugglers, Fiddlers, Gamblers, Thieves and Robbers, Teamsters, Butchers, Drovers, and even Gardeners and Farmers.'[40] One might compile a companion list of those in whose interest it was to criticise gold-rush society: ministers of religion, women, members of older social elites, radical critics of the commercial ethos. Recovering this curious alliance of conservatives and radicals against an emerging liberal capitalist orthodoxy is one of the chief interests of this study of responses to the mid-nineteenth-century gold rushes.

Gold, then, seemed to create conditions which were both encouraging to and corrosive of civilisation as it was understood at the time. The reactions to it in Victoria and California were thus deeply ambivalent. This is a comparative essay on that ambivalence. It is not a systematic comparison—the material is never symmetrical enough for that. A comparative study is inevitably more unwieldy than a study of one place. But thinking about a similar event in two places is at least potentially more illuminating than studying only one society. It is a paradox, which students of locality are always rediscovering, that we can only really understand the local by looking beyond it. Looking at two societies rather than one will always increase our sense of the contingent nature of the constitution of events—they might have been otherwise. It is unusual to have two such similar events in two societies at almost the same moment in calendar time, and the coincidence aids the comparative project.[41] Celebratory national histories are as endemic in new societies as in old. Claims of uniqueness are easily made when little checking is done beyond the borders.

When Victorians and Californians came to articulate their responses to the existence of gold among them, they drew upon a stock of arguments and cultural themes which were often held in common. When gold instantly assembled societies of men who had left their homes in pursuit of wealth, citizens of the two societies came to similar assessments of what was potentially wrong and disruptive about that. Although the questions were often the same, the balance of argument lay in different places in the two societies. In the end, from the largely common repertoire, Californians and Victorians constructed different responses to gold—responses that help us specify, in ways that studies of a single society cannot, something of the distinctive shape of their cultures.

(NO) FRONTIERS

Comparative frontier history has been one of the frames within which Australia and the United States' west have previously been compared by historians. Frontier historiography emphasises the changes brought about by the frontier environment, and sometimes makes claims for the uniqueness of the resulting experience. Billington saw in the Californian gold rush:

> an extreme example of the transition that occurred when men left their homes to grapple with the strange new world that lay beyond the borders of civilization. The changes wrought in their characteristics and institutions showed, even if in exaggerated form, the impact of the frontier on all who came under its influence.

In Australia, Russel Ward, in his 1957 *The Australian Legend*, argued that the gold rushes reinforced ideas and behaviours (collectivist rather than individualist) which had grown up on Australia's pastoral frontier amongst the itinerant rural labour force. While frontier historians were obviously describing something real in emphasising the process of adaptation to novel conditions on the frontier, recent historians concur in regarding as at least as significant the continuities with metropolitan experience. Men and women did not return to a state of nature in moving west or south.[42] A cultural history will always be unhappy with the implied environmental determinism of the frontier arguments, and will want to insist on the cultural constitution of even the most basic categories in any society, rather than assuming some evolutionary civilising path out from the frontier. Emphasising the received stock of metropolitan ideas and themes creates an argument in opposition to the established 'frontier' interpretations of the gold rushes.

Social historians since the 1970s have generally offered an anti-frontier account of the two societies—that is, they place much more stress on the process of reproduction of metropolitan forms than they do on adaptation to the new environment. Peter Decker concluded that San Franciscans in the nineteenth century carried with them 'from older communities in the East familiar habits and attitudes, political loyalties, economic forms, and social institutions which they modified hardly at all on the urban frontier'. Ralph Mann similarly argued that 'the California Gold Rush was not an aberration in nineteenth-century American history, nor were the forty-niners alienated from the values of their time'. This corrective to the frontier interpretation came most strongly from the urban historiography of the 1970s—for example, Gunther Barth's *Instant Cities* and, for Australia, Graeme Davison's *The Rise and Fall of Marvellous Melbourne* and Weston Bate's *Lucky City*. As social and urban historians, however, these authors do not give detailed attention to the content of the metropolitan ideas alive in the new societies, and the engagement of these themes with local conditions.[43]

A renovated frontier concept has more recently returned to historical inquiry however, and it would be a mistake to throw the frontier out with the westerns. While the old frontier thesis, which derived from the work of Frederick Jackson Turner, celebrated the encounter of white men and nature, a newer historiography has recognised frontiers as sites of conquest and culture contact. The drive to develop the American west, Donald Worster argues, 'was often a ruthless assault on nature and has left behind it much death, depletion and ruin'.[44] The American west, Patricia Limerick argues, was a 'meeting ground of Europe, Asia, and Latin America'—it was 'not where we escaped each other, but where we all met'. Limerick offers a more conscientiously multicultural version of Steffen's earlier suggestion that the mining frontiers of the American west be seen as 'cosmopolitan' frontiers.[45] Shorn of its old romanticism and innocence, the frontier returns as something more like a periphery—recognisably a part of the metropolitan culture of which it is the frontier. Bernard Bailyn argues in this way for an understanding of colonial American society as 'a periphery, a ragged outer margin of a central world, a regressive, backward-looking diminishment of metropolitan accomplishment'.[46] The mid-nineteenth century gold-rush societies were peripheries in this sense, but they were also beneficiaries of all the advanced forms of communication of the nineteenth century. There was more of the metropolis in these frontier societies than a Turnerian would have acknowledged—in their newspapers and libraries, in their sense of themselves. But these *were* also—in ways that matter more than nationalist histories are apt to acknowledge—frontier societies, founded upon conquest, in which metropolitan forms were embattled in significant ways.

But 'frontier' status was not all the two societies had in common. Contemporaries noted similarities in the appearance and climate of Australia and California—indeed Edward Hargraves, the recognised 'discoverer' of gold in New South Wales, attributed his discovery to his noticing, on his return from California, similarities in the appearance of the land in the Bathurst region to the gold-bearing districts of California. A writer in the *San Francisco Whig* in 1852 noted a 'striking similarity':

between the appearance of Australia and California. Vast plains, entirely naked, or presenting an orchard-like prospect of scattered trees—river channels that at one season are washed and worn by impetuous torrents, and at another dry, or basins or stagnant ponds—ranges of grass-covered knolls and lofty hills—a floral profusion—a bright sky and a balmy and health-conservative atmosphere, are characteristic of both.[47]

This comparison, argued from the landscape, led inevitably to others. The *San Francisco Whig* also saw Australia following a similar developmental path to the United States: 'Australia will become free, as she of right ought to be. That the achievement of her liberty is possible, our history is sufficient proof.'[48]

The two societies were well aware of each other. Many miners were to visit both places, and the metropolitan presses kept each informed of the dramatic developments in the other. We should not underestimate the extent to which in the mid-nineteenth century there was already a steady commerce of ideas and products around the world—even in outposts like Australia and California. Prince Albert told a banquet at the Mansion House in London in 1850, that the 'distances which separated the different nations and parts of the globe are rapidly vanishing before the achievements of modern inventions', and that the result would be the realisation of the unity of mankind—'not a unity which breaks down the limits and levels the peculiar characteristics of the different nations of the earth, but rather a unity, the result and product of those very national varieties and antagonistic qualities'.[49] To attempt to understand these societies outside the context of this commerce and communication, this heightened and informed sense of national difference, is to run the risk of misunderstanding the cultural expressions we find in them. Even the provincial presses of the two societies seemed somehow to keep in touch. The Victorian *Warrnambool Examiner* for example, ran a story in 1858 about the poisoning of a family in Grass Valley, California, citing as its sources the *Marysville Express* and the *Grass Valley Telegraph*—neither of them major urban newspapers.[50]

Australian ex-convicts were said to pose a crime problem in San Francisco, and many of the victims of the first Vigilance Committee (the self-constituted and business-led committee which took over the government of San Francisco for part of 1851) were Australian. After an 1849 fire in San Francisco, 48 of the 78 suspects arrested were from Sydney.[51] 'It is too bad', a San Francisco woman wrote in a private letter, 'that we must be cursed with such an influx of Sydney convicts for it is they who do all these things. But the citizens now are resolved to hang every one they catch if his guilt is plain.'[52] On the other side of the Pacific, the example of California hung over Victorians, as they apprehensively awaited the consequences of their gold discoveries—to be invoked as a dreadful lesson by conservatives, and as a republican model by radicals. Charles Dickens' *Household Words* repeatedly warned readers of the lawlessness and low morality of California. 'Bull, cock and bear fights are in full vogue', the companion *Household Narrative* claimed in April 1850, 'especially among the fair sex'.[53] Every contemptuous Californian reference to the criminals of Australia could be matched by a self-congratulatory Victorian comment about the wisdom of British institutions, and the awful example of lawlessness which California set before the civilised world.[54] The flow of information between the two societies was surprisingly strong, though so were the cultural stereotypes which shaped the understanding of it.

Comparative history is not a well-developed field in either Australian or American history. While certain subjects (the history of slavery for example) have had a significant body of comparative scholarship devoted to them, the number of explicitly comparative studies is not large.[55] Theoretical discussion of comparative history has generally been conducted in a social scientistic voice, with talk of controls, and holding variables, and systematic comparison. In the resurgent positivism around the new social histories of the 1960s and 1970s, comparison was recruited as one of the means by which history could at last make itself more scientific—'the comparative method is a method, a set of rules which can be methodically and systematically applied in gathering and using evidence to test explanatory hypotheses'.[56]

Writers without the utopian dream of a vast and systemic historical enterprise have detected further, short-term and polemical, uses for comparative history. In the American context, this has largely involved critics of the hypothesis of 'American exceptionalism'—the argument that American development has been quite unlike that of the countries of the Old World, and that its development has been immune from the social pressures, processes and conflicts that have shaped the histories of older societies. C. Vann Woodward introduced a 1968 collection of essays on *The Comparative Approach to American History* with the observation that the comparative studies therein worked to 'revise complacent assumptions of national exclusiveness, or excellence; to reconsider commonplace myths and flattering legends'.[57] Comparison here becomes a critical tool, the outsider's perspective a crucial corrective to national hubris. But the unit of comparison of most comparative history has still been the nation. Ian Tyrrell, calling for a new 'transnational' history, argues that comparative history written about the United States generally remains within a nationalist or exceptionalist frame—testing exceptionalism, not transcending its terms of argument.[58] My interest here is still in returning to the national frame, seeing what the comparative study can add to the respective national histories. It is not a 'transnational' study in Tyrrell's sense. Perhaps it is closer in spirit to David Thelen's call for an 'internationalised American history' which might 'begin with the recognition that people, ideas, and institutions do not have clear national identities . . . Instead of assuming that something was distinctively American, we might assume that elements of it began or ended somewhere else.'[59]

In Australia too, comparative studies have been few. Before the Second World War, membership of the empire and Commonwealth provoked some implicitly or explicitly comparative work. More recently, comparative studies of regions of recent settlement contrast Australia with other non-United States New World societies.[60] The current interest in placing Australia in a postcolonial context may add to this body of work further comparative studies with other former British colonies, or with countries of the Pacific region. But Australia still lacks a substantial body of comparative historical work. Perhaps this has something to do with the different nature of the 'whig' historiography in Australia, which has generally claimed, not unique-ness, but precocious progression down the liberal social democratic path.

Comparison raises questions of audience. The cosmopolitan or transna-tional perspective has certain intrinsic merits, but it is not the perspective of most people most of the time. I concur with John Higham when he writes that 'we would . . . do well to bear in mind the deep and rich significance that parochialism has for most historians who are the custo-dians of their own particular heritage'.[61] I see the benefits of comparison as accruing, not to some global community of social scientists eagerly working up the basis of a unified science of society, but to the local studies from which it grew and to which it returns. We may indeed only understand what is truly local by invoking comparison. Our knowledge of the broader careers of the ideas we meet locally may enable us to hear accurately the particular inflections of the home enunciation of a more universal dis-course. But in the end, as historians, we turn home, front up to our local audience to explain to them what we have found that is new. The aim of comparison should be a more cosmopolitan and sophisticated parochialism.

In this book I have tried to show some of the reasons why *gold seeking* (the term so often used in the 1850s) was widely considered a morally troubling activity. From the published and unpublished writings of the period, from pamphlets and sermons, newspapers, letters, poetry and polit-ical debates, I have tried to abstract the underlying themes of the response, to get at the categories which organised and informed social thought in Victoria and California through the gold era. In chapter 1, I examine the Victorian and Californian historiographic traditions, and more generally the contrasting ways in which the self-interest that drove the gold rush has been remembered in the two societies. There is a need, I argue here, to disentangle late nineteenth-century nostalgia for the gold period from the more pressing fears and anxieties which dominate the record of the 1850s, as well as to recall the effects of the gold rushes on the indigenous populations of the areas they affected. My central argument here is that those contemporaries who approved and who were optimistic about the gold rushes were necessarily subscribers to one or another form of laissez faire philosophy: they believed that the best social outcomes would be achieved when events were left to unfold without governmental interven-tion. Doctrinaire laissez faire liberals, for example, the followers of political economy, had faith that the self-seeking individuals who made up the gold rush would in the end constitute a governable society. Most others had doubts. From a range of conservative and radical positions, moral critiques were offered of gold rush society. To those who felt, for a range of reasons, that the old moral bonds were no longer holding, the gold rushes and the tens of thousands who were drawn to them were signs of a new, more purely self-interested and materialistic future. The gold-seeking men who rushed to Victoria and California seemed to the critics to be not frenzied oddities but harbingers of the future.

In the second chapter I compare the languages available in the two societies to discuss both the nature of wealth and its effects on society and individuals. In California, while pointing to the dominance of liberal individualism, I notice the presence of classical republican thought about the cyclical nature of the history of nations. Republican thought was often pessimistic about the consequences of widespread affluence, looking gloomily beyond prosperity to inevitable softening and decline. While this kind of republican thinking gave Californian critics of the gold rush a language with which to talk about the dangers of prosperity and the uncontrolled pursuit of wealth, it was open to some obvious objections. More radical republicans saw in the apparently randomly distributed gold the possibility of a more egalitarian and democratic future, a republic built around the hard-working miner, in which wealth would be available to all. In Victoria, such republican thinking was rare. Elites there criticised materialism, and feared the effects of gold's redistribution of wealth on the apparently natural hierarchies of class, wealth and taste upon which they thought society depended for its very existence.

The third chapter examines ideas about order in the two societies, so as to get closer to understanding the disorder that gold was said to have caused. Here I contrast the Victorian faith that order could be brought about by institutions—such as the law and police, religious and educational institutions—almost regardless of the morality of the population, with the dominant Californian belief that institutions and laws were useless without a virtuous population. A more detailed look at the Victorian police, and at the social thought of Judge Redmond Barry, develops this theme. In California, I notice the way the episodes in which 'respectable' business-led Committees of Vigilance took over the elected city government of San Francisco in 1851 and 1856 led elites there to separate law from order in their arguments. Liberal individualism was seen to be put to the test in California, where individuals were left to pursue their own interests more or less ungoverned—a debate ensued about what Californian conditions would reveal about human nature. The rituals of the law were as important in California as in Victoria, but there seemed to be a greater difficulty in separating issues of personal honour from the demonstration of the law's impersonal majesty—an issue I take up by examining an incident in the early career of Judge Stephen J. Field.

Chapters 4 to 6 examine some of the most important themes in the contemporary criticism of gold-rush society. Agrarianism and pastoral provided one of the most pervasive and profound languages which could be used in Victoria and California to criticise the disruptions of gold. In contrasting gold digging unfavourably with the practice of farming, the agrarians were drawing upon existing discourses about the virtues of the agricultural society and applying them to novel circumstances. In looking to the hills and seeing the possibility of a more natural and less laborious life, Californian authors in particular drew the ancient themes of the pastoral into service as more immediate social criticism. Agrarian and pastoral responses to gold have not fared well in the popular memory of the gold rushes—they have indeed been almost entirely eclipsed by what I term the 'colonial narrative', the comic story of a society turned upside down by gold, which formed the staple of travellers' anecdotes about gold-rush society, and which has been retold ever since in popular histories.

Ideas about the importance of domesticity—the home and the family—formed another important shared frame of reference, another set of positive values to assert against the disruption for critics of gold-rush society in both Victoria and California. Those who rushed to seek gold were overwhelmingly men, and a set of preconceived expectations about what a masculine society untempered by the feminine would be like contributed to critics' anxieties. Victoria and California seemed to provide disturbing demonstrations of what would happen if masculine competitive individualism came to completely dominate society. Much nineteenth-century social thought was about balance—city and country, masculine and feminine, world and home—and gold-rush conditions brought forth all the conventional warnings about a society dangerously out of balance. Celebrants of masculine freedom and independence revelled in gold-rush conditions—though more often, I think, in nostalgic retrospect than at the time. Women, as recent Californian studies in particular make clear, found good markets in gold-rush societies for services such as cooking, washing, housekeeping, sewing and, of course, prostitution—but again few positive statements about gold-rush opportunities can be found written by women at the time.[62] The dominant tone was critical. Informed by contemporary ideas about the importance of domesticity and about the complementary differences between men and women, many Victorians and Californians held grave fears about the kind of society gold seemed to be creating.

The gold was most commonly said to have caused excitement. A debate ensued in both Victoria and California about the levels of excitement which were desirable in society. Critics of the masculine excitement of the gold rush argued that the problem was that, once excited, men might never settle down again into quiet contentment. For these critics, gold seemed only to add to the excessively stimulating life in the new societies—the warm climates, the prevalence of alcohol and the expectations, uncertainties and disappointments of Victoria and California seemed designed to excite men beyond the levels their bodies and minds could sustain. There was much anxious discussion of madness in both places, and the lunatic asylum was seen by many critics as the inevitable destination of the over-excited individual. Quietness was understood in contemporary discussions as the opposite of excitement. My argument here is that, while both Victoria and California produced articulate critics of the excited society and of the life which was possible within it, the fantasy of a quiet society was more dominant in Victoria. There were indeed influential Californian advocates of excitement who argued quite explicitly that a degree of excitement was necessary in an active, expanding and ambitious society. This defence of excitement was strongest among the Protestant clergy of California, among them men like the Reverend William Anderson Scott who warned in 1856 of 'the quietness of dejection, the sullenness of despair, and the lethargy of death'.[63] In arguments over excitement, we see the clearest divergences between the Victorian and Californian responses to gold.

My aim throughout is to show that ideas were important even in such 'frontier' histories. Apparently simple ideas—like those to do with agrarianism and domesticity and excitement—underlay the always complicated ways in which actual people made sense of their participation in the gold rushes. For many of these people, goldseeking in the early 1850s was the biggest most significant experience of their lives, and they would recall it ever after—creating, around firesides and in letters and journals, a memory of the events inevitably shaped by subsequent histories, ideas and stories. My project here is to reconstruct, from contemporary sources, as much of the understandings of the events of the early 1850s as I can, in the languages of the time. It is a contextual cultural history, reliant on giving readers enough of the writings of the time that they can begin to see the categories of understanding I am emphasising at work in the language and thought of the Victorian and Californian men and women of the 1850s. Some individuals are given extended treatment, if I think that the sources allow it and that the demonstration of the coherence and creativity of one individual's thought will say more than the scattered reconstruction of other less well-documented people's concerns. But many others are here without much introduction, important more for what they said than for who they were. I am more concerned here with underlying patterns of discourse than with the individuals who happened to speak them—not because of some old-fashioned post-structuralist feeling that it doesn't ever matter who speaks (it clearly does), but because I think historians in particular have not yet done enough of this kind of work, the historically particular mapping of the languages that were available to actors. It is work which inevitably ends up showing that their commonsense was not ours, but it should also give a feeling for the intellectual landscape within which people thought and acted.

CHAPTER 1

UNDERSTANDING THE GOLD RUSHES

Gold is the most potent lever, the
very connecting rod of power.
*Reynell Coates, 'The Golden Future', **Sartain's Magazine** 1850*

Gold! Supreme is thy dominion
God of church upon whose creed
Every nation is agreed;
Where's another one on which
Holds mankind the same opinion . . .
*William a'Beckett, **The Earl's Choice and Other Poems***

It is to be hoped that the Australian gold-shit
will not hold up the commercial crisis . . .
Friedrich Engels to Karl Marx, 23 September 1851

And Australia and California and the Pacific Ocean! The
new citizen of the world won't be able to comprehend how
small our world was.
Karl Marx to Joseph Weydenmeyer, 25 March 1852[1]

The gold discoveries and the societies they created were among the wonders of the age—sensational occurrences. 'The circumstance of being able to pick up gold like common dirt is,' James Ward noted in his 1852 *History of Gold*, 'in itself, of so extraordinary a nature, so completely opposed to all our own experience, that its first announcement was received with something like a doubting reservation.' The Whig *American Review* described the Californian discovery as an event with 'stupendous, world-embracing historical consequences', and thousands of contemporaries agreed. Reformer Eliza Farnham wrote from California in 1856 of her millennial expectation that the 'islands and continents of the Pacific' would 'bring their treasures to redeem the millions, and their light shall spread abroad, and the millions shall receive both the treasure and the light'. In Melbourne, the lawyer Thomas a'Beckett wrote even more explicitly that:

> [i]t may seem fanciful and visionary to imagine any connection, however remote, between these discoveries that are now startling the world, and the great event which the Christian believer expects one day will be developed; but we cannot help feeling that they are calculated to bring about a state of things which is likely to precede it.

Even the cautious London *Times* commented of the Australian gold discoveries that 'they will certainly be ranked among the most curious and surprising phenomena in the history of mankind'. To an historically and religiously literate age, the discovery of vast treasure was full of possible meaning and importance. Publishers rushed to both create and satisfy public curiosity about the gold-seeking adventure—Barclay and Co. in St Louis, Missouri, for example, had *The Dreadful Suffering and Thrilling Adventures of an Overland Party of Emigrants to California: their terrible conflicts! with savage tribes of Indians!! and Mexican bands of robbers!!!* on the market by 1850.[1] The impact of the gold rushes would be the subject of much discussion, in part because they physically disrupted the lives of so many. The population centre of the United States moved 180 kilometres west between 1849 and 1853. 'Well, I have seen a great deal,' a character in a contemporary book is made to say, '—magnetic telegraphs, railroads, women's rights, crystal palaces, California, Australia.'[2]

In popular memory, the gold rushes survive as a good and yet fantastic time—the concentration of events of wealth accumulation and loss exercising great fascination for the inhabitants of quieter places and times. Historians of both societies have noted the very early appearance of nostalgia for the days of gold. In both places, many of the gold towns have never known such prosperity since. Keeping alive the memory of those few heady years, in all its antiquarian detail, has been a kind of defence against the contemplation of the rest of their history.[3]

The commemoration of the gold rushes began soon after the event. 'Still,' wrote *Hutchings' California Magazine* in 1856, 'there is a fascination in the memories of that time, which those of us who mingled in its whirl and excitement, call back with delight and intense longing for such days again.' Even recollecting from 'amid this quiet, this comfort, this happiness', the writer observed, 'I feel a pang, almost amounting to pain, at the thought that I shall never see their like again'.[4] The memory of those extraordinary events has been self-consciously kept alive in Victoria and California ever since. The 'pioneers' in both places were revered by themselves before their descendants had a chance to pay their homage. Something about the mobility and questing of the gold seekers (and of the small number of 'pioneers' who preceded them) allowed them swift admittance to a hall of masculine national heroes. The Society of California Pioneers was an organisation open to those men who had arrived in California during 1849 (second-class pioneers) or before 1849 (first-class pioneers). Its celebration of the pioneer was representative of the veneration in which that entrepreneurial figure was held throughout the American west.[5] At their annual commemorations of the admission of California to the Union, the Pioneers celebrated their own centrality to the new polity, and the founding character of their own activities. Their biographies had become instantly historical in a public manner unusual in the modern world. Gold, John Hittell told the Pioneers' celebration in 1893, 'developed California from rudeness, poverty, obscurity and semi-barbarism, into brilliant, complex, and wealthy enlightenment, under our eyes, in the midst of our labors and as part of our personal consciousness'.[6]

The pioneers' privations and sacrifices, as the necessary prelude to their subsequent wealth and good fortune, became a crucial and legitimating part of the legend. As Earl Pomeroy has noted, 'if anything is clear about the forty-niners it is that most of them had no intention of founding anything other than their own fortunes', yet 'soon their admirers, including themselves, were comparing them with the founders of colonial New England'.[7] The pioneers' personal qualities grew with the passage of time. 'The Pioneers were handsome men,' Henry Childs Merwin wrote in 1912:

> archaic men, not quite broken in to the modern ideal of drudging at one task for six days in the week and fifty weeks in the year. Who does not know the type! The hero of novels, the idol of mothers, the alternate hope and despair of fathers, the truest of friends, the most ideal and romantic, but perhaps not the most constant of lovers.[8]

But the pioneers were also perceived to have political lessons to teach. During the California Pioneers' New Year's celebrations in 1851, a toast was proposed to the first pioneers, 'the heralds on the shores of the Pacific of that grand principle of civilization and republicanism, that man is best governed when he governs himself—and of that other principle of social progress, that the interests of society are best protected when most let alone by government'. Was that to be the meaning of it all? Certainly the *Alta California*, San Francisco's most important newspaper, was already generating a kind of nostalgia for the early gold-rush period as a heyday of laissez faire. 'When we had no law, or only the law of necessity,' the paper argued, 'we were comparatively safe. The people then protected themselves . . . With State laws we are in the midst of chaos.' The history of the pioneers quickly became a lesson in laissez faire. The celebration of their energy and manhood became an argument that amid frontier harshness only the fittest and best would survive. 'It was a driving, vigorous, restless population in those days,' Mark Twain reported, 'not simpering, dainty, kid-gloved weaklings, but stalwart, muscular, dauntless young braves, brimful of push and energy, and royally endowed with every attribute that goes to make up a peerless and magnificent manhood—the very pick and choice of the world's glorious ones.'[9]

The later literary depiction of the California gold rush was probably most influentially shaped by Bret Harte (1836–1902) in short fiction and poetry written from the early 1860s. Harte's was a sentimental gold rush, all about the goodness in the hearts of men left to themselves. 'It was a land of perfect freedom', he recalled, 'limited only by the instinct and the habit of law which prevailed in the mass. All its forms were original, rude, and picturesque.'[10] In Harte's fiction, the most unlikely miners displayed hearts of gold—Dick Bullen in 'How Santa Claus Came to Simpson's Bar', for example, who upon hearing little Johnny ask 'Wot's Chrismiss anyway? Wot's it all about?', rides all night through great danger to bring him a present. Kevin Starr argues that Harte saw the gold period as 'already possessing the charm of antiquity'. Josiah Royce accused Harte of 'perverse romanticism'.[11] There is also in Harte much celebration of masculine camaraderie. 'In Bret Harte's stories,' one later critic wrote, 'woman is subordinated to man, and love is subordinated to friendship.'[12] In 'The Luck of the Roaring Camp', one of his most loved stories, a male baby arrives in the camp and brings about its 'regeneration'—the rough community of men acquires the nurturing and renovating qualities that nineteenth-century ideology ascribed to Woman. But Harte's stories were also direct in depicting the harsher aspects of frontier life. He openly confronted racism several times during his career. His stories dealt with death and violence—the deaths of all of the protagonists in 'The Outcasts of Poker Flat', the death of the baby Luck and his guardians in 'The Luck of the Roaring Camp'—in a way less common in later Australian representations of the gold rush.

The subsequent memory of the Californian gold rushes has become entangled with the general form of the western, with its preoccupations with law and order, violence and community. Western film makers were generally pessimistic about the possibility of real community in the gold-mining towns.[13] In the western, the gold rushes become the setting for the conventional western moral drama of corruption and regeneration, strangers riding in to town and then into the sunset when their work is done. The 1954 western, *The Forty Niners* fitted this pattern—the corrupt gold-town sheriff and his hotel-keeping partner are finally brought to justice by the alliance of the good federal marshal and the drifting cardsharp. In Clint

Eastwood's 1985 *Pale Rider*, the conflict is between the individual miners and a rapacious mining company—product of a very different kind of western history, but still making the California gold-rush towns of the 1850s the site for a moral drama about law and order. In popular fiction, too, the conventions of the western have shaped the memory of the California gold period. Robert W. Broomall, author of the popular western novels *Dead Man's Town*, *Dead Man's Canyon*, *Dead Man's Crossing* and *Texas Kingdoms*, published in 1992 the gold-rush novel *California Kingdoms*: a 'gripping story of high adventure, brazen courage and the passionate desire of three friends with dreams of gold'. Here the conventions of popular romance and the western intersect, as the hero, Wade Rawson, 'ruggedly quiet in the full vigor of his manhood', embarks 'on a quest for gold that leads him on a wilderness adventure where danger lurks in the darkness and death may come with dawn', a quest which sees him finally united with the 'radiantly lovely' heroine, Kathy Beddoes.[14] The existence of the western genre has thus allowed space for the continued telling of gold-rush stories in American popular culture—it has produced a popular history.

The memory of the Australian gold rushes had no such popular cultural form to carry it. But there was in nineteenth-century Australia a rapidly growing nostalgia for the freedom of the digger, once the great, legendary time of the early rushes was over. By 1854, the popular balladist Charles Thatcher was singing his song 'Two Years Ago' at goldfields theatres:

The light of other days burns dim,
And in the shade is cast,
You'll own I'm right, if you will just
Look back upon the past;
Its glories are all faded,
And each of you must know
That times ain't what they used to be
About two years ago.[15]

Nostalgia for the early gold-rush years was also fostered by the emerging labour movement, interested in recalling a time when working men were at least temporarily free of the master–servant relationship. By the late nineteenth century, the 1850s began to seem like a lost heroic age. W.E. Adcock published his *The Gold Rushes of the Fifties* in 1912, announcing that he had spent more than thirty years collecting the 'personal experience of participants in the exciting scenes upon the early goldfields', promising a future, more comprehensive book 'embodying copious details of the golden era in the memorable years 1851–1859, during which our pioneers were founding a nation'. But twentieth-century Australia has not had an equivalent popular genre to the western which might have allowed greater circulation of gold-rush histories. Even the historically-minded and nationalist film revival of the 1970s showed little interest in the gold period.

Cyrus Mason, Eng. & Lith. 35, Swanston St

George Strafford engraving, 'The Gold Digger of Victoria'. From Thomas Ham,
The Gold Digger's Portfolio: consisting of a series of sketches of the Victorian
Gold Fields *Melbourne: Cyrus Mason, 1854.*

By then the interest was not in pioneering and the establishment of order on the frontier, but in images of established bourgeois colonial life—an innocent past, with the harmless colonial overturning of respectable English norms the main narrative concern.[16]

Bret Harte was a major influence on nineteenth-century Australian writers' depiction of the gold rush. Here, as elsewhere, the delineation of discrete cultural traditions becomes impossible. Marcus Clarke in 1871 reviewed Harte's *The Luck of the Roaring Camp* enthusiastically. Harte's characters, he said, were not unreal beings: 'We have met them, or men like them, at Ballarat, Bendigo, or Wood's Point.' Henry Lawson too read Bret Harte, at the age of thirteen, and, like Harte, read Dickens. Lawson later recollected that Harte's stories 'seemed to bring a new light, a new world into my life, and this with Dickens still fresh'. And though at times Lawson became annoyed by continued comparison of his work with Harte's, he wrote once that the 'grandest stories ever written', were two stories of men's mateship—Dickens' *A Tale of Two Cities* and Harte's 'Tennessee's Partner'.

Henry Lawson (1867–1922), thirty years younger than Bret Harte, had perhaps most to do in Australia with articulating a nostalgia for the gold period. Lawson's pessimism about the Australian present was elaborated in relation to a dimming collective memory of the golden years. There was in his fiction a sense that there was something incommunicable about the experience of that time, something which older men shared but could not pass on: 'But how was it they talked low, and their eyes brightened up, and they didn't look at each other, but away over sunset, and had to get up and walk about, and take a stroll in the cool of the evening when they talked about Eureka.'[17] Some of Lawson's earliest published literary works described the landscape of the abandoned goldfields of New South Wales. 'Golden Gully', published in the *Bulletin* in 1887, evoked an empty and melancholy scene: 'No one lives in Golden Gully, for its golden days are o'er.' The short story 'His Father's Mate', published the following year, was also set in an abandoned Golden Gully: 'The predominant note of the scene was a painful sense of listening, that never seemed to lose its tension—a listening as though for the sounds of digger life, sounds that had gone and left a void that was accentuated by the signs of a former presence.' Another early poem, 'The Roaring Days' opens:

The night too quickly passes
And we are growing old,
So let us fill our glasses
And toast the Days of Gold;
When finds of wondrous treasure
Set all the South ablaze,

7

And you and I were faithful mates
All through the roaring days!

These comradely diggers were hailed by the young Lawson as pioneers, fathers of the nation: 'Oh, they were lion-hearted/ Who gave our country birth!'

The 1893 Lawson story, 'An Old Mate of Your Father's', looks back on the mining days from the settled domesticity of small farming life. Father's heart was never really in farming—'the old man was always thinking of putting down a shaft'. Visits of old digging mates set him off into moody nostalgia—'and when the visitor had gone by the coach we noticed that the old man would smoke a lot, and think as much, and take great interest in the fire'. The gold rush in Lawson was mostly a memory, a contrast with the smallness of the present—it had all come down to this. In part this was radical condemnation of the loss of independence suffered by the working man since the roaring days, and in part a critique of the agrarian ideal of quietness which had been so influential a response to gold in mid-century Australia.

Edward Dyson's poetry, first published in the *Bulletin*, contained memories of boyhood among worked-out mines:

By yellow dams in summer days
We puddled at the tom; for weeks
Went seeking up the tortuous ways
Of gullies deep and hidden creeks.[18]

Dyson also contrasted the confinement of city life with the remembered freedom of the diggings:

I'm stewing in a brick-built town;
My coat is quite a stylish cut,
And, morn and even, up and down,
I travel in a common rut;
But as the city sounds recede,
In dreamy moods I sometimes see
A vision of a busy lead,
And hear its voices calling me . . .
An easy life we lived and free.[19]

As in Lawson, the memory of the gold rush becomes a half-secret masculine longing for a time of greater independence and freedom, a lost pastoral age when work had been scarcely necessary.

The dominant memory of the Australian gold rushes was and is still the one shaped by the masculinist 'Australian legend' between the 1890s and the 1950s, a set of stories about the freedom of the digging life and the egalitarian spirit of the gold diggers, which culminated in their 'fight for freedom' at the 1854 Eureka Stockade. The later nostalgia in Australia was thus only in part for the laissez-faire freedom of the days of individual mining. It was also for 'mateship', that fraternal 'bond between equal partners or close friends' so celebrated in Australian legend, and supposed to have particularly flourished on the goldfields.[20] The 'Australian legend' has drawn upon an optimistic interpretation of the gold rushes, one which saw the activity of gold seeking as liberating, conducive to an independence and freedom which only the anti-democratic imperial officials sought to crush. But this optimistic interpretation reads back some of the nationalist concerns of the 1890s into the 1850s. In bequeathing to us a memory of the gold days as great and glorious, the late nineteenth-century literary tradition has left a false idea of the way gold was actually understood in the 1850s. To a surprising extent, contemporary reaction to gold, from most points on the political spectrum, was pessimistic, worried about the kind of society which the gold rush was threatening to bring into being, and dismayed at the chaos of self-interest which gold seemed to have unleashed. In the pessimistic view, the separate world created by the diggers—the goldfields world in which there was no past and little prudent thought of the future—was not simply a space of freedom. 'Drink! why, we all drink!', a digger remarks to a young girl in Mrs W. May Howell's *Reminiscences of Australia—The Diggings and the Bush*, 'What else do we have to care for? It excites us, and drowns the memory of the past'.[21]

The pessimistic view of gold-rush society became a part of the conservative memory of the gold rushes, but was gradually obliterated from radical memory. Rolf Boldrewood's conservative *The Miner's Right*, published in serial form in 1880, saw the goldfields primarily as posing a set of challenges to order and authority. The ability of men to shed their past on the fields was a part of this threat. The heroes of the novel are the officials—police and commissioners—whose job it is to maintain order, and the orderly miners who support them. The administration of justice, the novel records, was 'backed up by the whole force of genuine diggers', men who were 'prompt and decided in action' and who 'fully appreciate these qualities in their rulers'.[22] Conservative memory of gold is thus not about a moment of freedom, but about disorder. One of the most lyrical and disturbing expressions of a more conservative view of the gold rushes, one which remembered them as a vast delusion, a kind of madness which lured and trapped a multitude in exile in an alien and hostile land, is in the opening pages of Henry Handel Richardson's 1917 *Australia Felix*, the first volume of the Richard Mahony trilogy, based on the life of her father. 'They became prisoners to the soil,' she wrote of the gold diggers:

> Such were the fates of those who succumbed to the 'unholy hunger'. It was like a form of revenge taken on them, for their loveless schemes of robbing and fleeing; a revenge contrived by the ancient, barbaric country they had so lightly invaded. Now, she held them captive—without chains; ensorceled—without witchcraft; and, lying stretched like some primeval monster in the

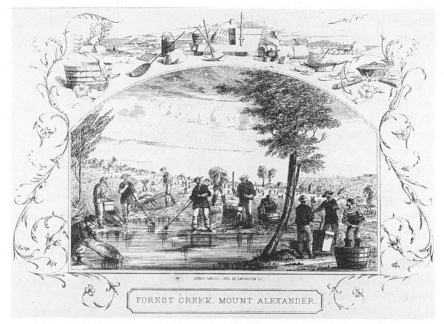

FOREST CREEK, MOUNT ALEXANDER.

David Tulloch, engraving: 'Forest Creek, Mt. Alexander'. From Thomas Ham,
The Gold Digger's Portfolio: consisting of a series of sketches of the Victorian
Gold Fields Melbourne: Cyrus Mason, 1854.

sun, her breasts freely bared, she watched, with a malignant eye, the efforts
made by these puny mortals to tear their lips away.[23]

Richardson's diggers were greedy marauders who became exiles unable to
return home, condemned to a restless and unhappy existence. This tragic
conservative vision of the gold rushes is closer to the tone of much of the
contemporary reaction than the later celebration of mateship on the fields.
For gold in the 1850s posed a series of interrelated moral problems, and
contemporary reaction was most often pessimistic or deeply ambivalent.
Only doctrinaire believers in laissez faire could manage complete enthusiasm for the gold rushes at the time.

THE HISTORIOGRAPHY OF THE GOLD RUSHES

The older historiography in Victoria and California, preoccupied above all
with the nation and its development, saw the gold rushes as important, if
slightly problematic, events. The story was of temporary disruption and
confusion giving way to solid nation-building results: satisfying increases
of population, impressive urban structures, sound political development.
Gold, though morally troubling at first, rapidly became the cornerstone,
the foundation, of new societies built in the image of the old, and in

astonishingly rapid time. Mainstream history has in general celebrated the achievements of the gold period.[24] The gold seekers, Billington argued, transformed California from 'a half-tamed wilderness to a settled commonwealth'.[25] 'In ten years,' Serle wrote, 'gold had transformed Victoria from a minor pastoral settlement to the most celebrated British colony.'[26]

In the larger narratives of Australian history, the self-interest of the gold seekers, redescribed as initiative and enterprise, came to seem admirable to the historiographical tradition in comparison to the qualities their convict and assisted immigrant predecessors had to offer as nation builders. This theme was strongly articulated in the 1930s, in a context of concern about the quality of the racial stock. W.K. Hancock's 1930 *Australia*, praised the gold diggers in almost eugenic terms. Later generations of Australians, he reported, 'have acclaimed the diggers as their Pilgrim fathers, the first authentic Australians, the founders of their self-respecting, independent, strenuous national life, the fathers of their soldiers'—and the legend, Hancock argues, 'does not greatly distort the facts'; the diggers were 'predominantly vigorous, independent, law-abiding Britishers'.[27] G.V. Portus, writing in the 1933 volume on Australia in the *Cambridge History of the British Empire*, similarly viewed the gold rushes in terms of their effects on the racial stock. The most significant result of the gold discovery, he argued, was a 'change in the quality of the population'. The gold rushes selected out a specialised type, 'resourceful and vigorous, yet impatient of control; and that type has been perpetuated by the Australian environment'. W.P. Morrell's history of all the nineteenth-century gold rushes concluded that 'tens of thousands of men took part, and though many faltered or fell by the wayside, the best of them evolved a new type of self-reliant character, a new free, careless social life'. The theme was thus well established by 1963. Serle's *The Golden Age* contains an index entry for 'Immigration, high quality of', which guides the reader to four places in the book where this 'quality' is discussed. The gold immigrants, Serle argues, were 'magnificent economic material with educational qualifications and professional and industrial skills superior to any other group of migrants to Australia, at least in the nineteenth century'.[28] Here the stress on population 'quality' marks the place of the gold rushes in a story of national development.

The only qualification on the radical nationalist historians' approval of the nation-forming tendencies of gold was that the very high numbers of immigrants lured by gold swamped the Australian-born population in the colonies, delaying, it has been argued, the rise of nationalism until the end of the century.[29] This recognition that Australian nationalism played very little part in the consciousness of the 1850s has not prevented the popular reading of the gold rushes into a story of emerging national consciousness.

Because the desire for great individual wealth is no cultural universal, in different societies it will be constructed and mediated in different ways.

Californians and Victorians remember their gold rushes differently, tell themselves other stories about these shaping, founding events. In each case the historians have found, in their reading of the gold rushes, evidence of distinctive national traits.

Geoffrey Serle, in what is still the major work on the Victorian gold rushes, noted that 'this was certainly a society in which material values were almost unchallenged and the speculative instinct was almost unbridled'. But, he continued, 'in the end, perhaps the most significant aspect of life on the goldfields was the degree to which the traditional restraints—the acceptance of fair dealing, consideration for one's neighbour and desire for order—were preserved, and how much the fraternal spirit developed and prevailed in such an atmosphere'. Here the story is of newer forms of competitive individualism, encouraged by the activity of gold seeking, partially but not completely displacing older forms of 'restraint' and cooperation. Serle detected equality and fraternity on the goldfields, but found in the digger that 'interplay of the mercenary and the fraternal' which made his contribution to Australian society so difficult to assess. Russel Ward found the Australian gold miners to have embraced the same 'faith' already adopted by the pastoral workers, convicts and other significant working-class groups in Australian society—'mateship, and that curiously unconventional yet powerful collectivist morality', a kind of early-Victorian socialism without doctrine. More recently, Weston Bate has similarly concluded that, while gold stimulated the development of capitalism in Victoria, it was a 'democratic mineral', and its pursuit was 'frequently more valued for itself than its outcome'. He stresses the 'unusual public spirit' of the gold towns.[30] Since the Second World War, then, the Australian historiographic tradition has seen the gold rushes as encouraging, or further encouraging, the development of a distinctive Australian ethos, one of collectivism, 'mateship', and a rejection of competitive individualism. This historiography refers back to the nostalgia of the literature of the 1890s, and to the racial concerns of the 1930s—celebratory both of the freedom of the individual digger, and of his involvement with the fraternal doctrine of mateship—and shares with them an almost wholly positive attitude towards the gold rushes of the 1850s.

The American stories about California are somewhat different and the Californian rushes have a much less significant place in the American national history than the Victorian ones in the Australian. California, historian Kevin Starr has written, remained through the gold-rush period, 'a land characterized by an essential selfishness and an underlying instability, a fixation upon the quick acquisition of wealth, an impatience with the more subtle premises of human happiness'. These, Starr continued, 'were American traits, to be sure, but the Gold Rush intensified and consolidated them'.[31] Ralph Mann similarly argues that: 'The Gold Rush

David Tulloch, 'Golden Point, Mt. Alexander'. From David Tulloch, Ham's Five Views of the Gold Fields of Mount Alexander and Ballarat in the Colony of Victoria *Melbourne: Thomas Ham, 1852.*

granted young men access to opportunities and experiences approved by their society—even identified by it as uniquely American.'[32]

The American historiography sees individual wealth seeking as cultural, evidence of a 'value' or a national 'trait'. This can be contrasted with Serle's representative Victorian text, which describes the greed manifested in the gold rushes as an 'instinct', a natural tendency that it was the task of social institutions and higher ideals to restrain. His characteristic Australian story is one of a struggle to overcome temptation. In the dominant American liberal historiographical tradition, the competitive individualism of the gold era does not have to be resisted, for it of itself gives way to social and national results.

Lotchin's history of San Francisco, for example, tells of a people who 'had come to get rich . . .' unless government contributed to that end, they ignored it. San Francisco was at first unlike other American cities, Lotchin concludes, and 'greater liberty constituted the main explanation of this divergence'. Only gradually, but inevitably, did 'society's bonds creep in where the freedom had been'. Gunther Barth, too, has a story of the inevitable transformation of what he calls the 'instant city', characterised by its unplanned development and individualist temperament, into an 'ordinary city', regulated by custom and tradition. This transformation took place despite the intentions of the actors involved: 'In their single-minded pursuit of riches, these settlers, who seemed bent on destruction, came up with dynamic urban environments and were themselves turned into citizens.' 'Weak and corrupt government,' Barth optimistically concludes, 'left each of the residents free to exploit the egalitarian premise of the instant city to his own ends.' The achievement of the gold era in San Francisco was that of 'a minimum of order with a minimum of coercion'—a mixture Barth describes as 'freedom'.[33] Out of this freedom, Barth wants us to conclude, came an ordered society. The theme is an old one in American thought. Josiah Royce's 1886 study of *California, from the Conquest in 1846 to the Second Vigilance Committee in San Francisco* had similarly argued a development from self-interest to community. The 'irresponsible freedom of the gay youth' who had flocked to San Francisco turned to more constructive ends—'Even while they organised their private schemes their camp became a town, and themselves townsmen.' Out of self-interest came social order, the 'meanness and good order of an Anglo-Saxon community of money-seekers'.[34]

Different metanarratives are appealed to in each case. Behind the American histories is a story about the self-regulating propensities of a society driven by individual greed and ambition. Despite themselves, and out of the chaos of self-interest, the Californians built a society and a civilisation. The Australian historiographical tradition is less about an invisible hand than about the emergence of an ethos. It is this ethos which made possible a kind of order, a distinctive settlement of the political and social questions—yet another new England freed from the defects of the old. The Australian historiography institutionalises the memory of an admirable collectivism which triumphed over baser motives, and the American that of an individualism which turned social despite itself. In the American tradition, self-interest has its own logic and discipline; in the Australian, self-interest is to be overcome by nobler and more social attributes. But in both places, the historiography of gold has drawn a generally optimistic picture of the gold period.

THE INDIGENOUS POPULATIONS

Like all histories, these stories left out a great deal. It is only recently, in both California and Victoria, that the history from the other side of the frontier has begun to be written. From the point of view of the indigenous peoples of both regions, the gold rushes have never been susceptible to triumphal interpretation. Even within the context of their societies' histories of invasion, the gold rushes facilitated dispossessions of a peculiarly concentrated and brutal kind.

The very success and rapidity of expansion of settler society seemed in both places to provide ready arguments for those who sought to justify the dispossession. It was a difficult question, a Californian writer argued, 'how far a weak, ignorant, indolent and sluggish people have claim to dominion over wide regions in the vineyard of the earth', which they left in 'waste and uselessness': 'If men stand ready to plough, and delve, to reap and build, to navigate and legislate, to fight and protect a portion of God's land, must they wait the slow process by which a willful and stubborn race doom themselves to dishonourable and certain decay?'[35] A Californian doctor observed in 1850, writing of the shooting of Indians, that 'Christian maxims and precepts are naught with the frontiermen'.[36] The arguments used to justify imperial adventures abroad were just as useful at home—the spread of 'freedom' and energy was inevitable. 'Our American experience has demonstrated the fact,' Governor Burnett told the California Legislature in 1851, 'that the two races cannot live in the same vicinity in peace.' He went on to argue that 'a war of extermination will continue to be waged between the two races, until the Indian race becomes extinct'.[37]

Californian newspapers did record the killing of the Indian population. 'Terrible Slaughter of Indians', the Alta California reported in 1849: 'every man was instantly shot down, and the women and children taken into captivity'. The same paper admitted, on another occasion, that 'in nine cases out of ten it is to the wantonness of the whites more than to the criminality of the Indians that difficulties and outbreaks are owing'. E. Gould Buffum reported, under the heading 'Indian Outrages', an attack by Indians upon a party of five gold diggers, which was followed by extensive retribution—'several expeditions were fitted out, who scoured the country in quest of Indians, until now a redskin is scarcely ever seen in the inhabited portion of the northern mining region . . . the whole race is fast becoming extinct'. Buffum was writing in 1850. Indigenous population decline in both California and Victoria was dramatic, yet the belief in theories of inevitable extinction meant that the killings, while not ignored, received little serious ethical discussion. Californian writers described massacres of Indians, sometimes lamenting excesses, but rarely doubting that extinction was anyway inevitable.[38]

The amnesia on this point may have been deeper in Victoria. The Californians, with a national history of war and treaty-making behind them, took it for granted that the Californian Indians had a claim to their land, albeit one which had to be 'extinguished' as expeditiously and cheaply as possible. Federal Indian Commissioners were sent to California to attempt to establish reservations in return for cession of the bulk of the land. 'Their intentions are peaceable treaties and the extinguishment of Indian titles, if it can be peaceably effected,' the Alta California reported.[39]

The treaties were rejected by the United States Senate in 1852, and the final outcomes may have been little different from those in Victoria, but the open recognition of prior ownership meant in California at least some franker public discussion of the issue. The Federal Commissioners wrote to the people of California in 1851 about the Indian population:

> They were the original owners and occupants of those beautiful valleys and mountain ranges. Their fishing and hunting grounds, and acorn orchards, surrounding the graves of their fathers for many generations, were long unclaimed by others. Until the discovery of the golden treasures . . . the white and red man lived together in peace and mutual security. Since that period . . . the Indian has been by many considered and treated as an intruder, as a common enemy of the whites, and in many instances shot down with as little compunction as a deer or an antelope.

There was no 'farther west', the Commissioners pointed out, into which the Indian could be displaced. The stark alternatives were extermination or assimilation.[40]

In the United States, Indian affairs had long been managed by the War Department. Both volunteer militia and regular army units were used in California up until the 1870s, though the Indian wars were generally carried out by volunteer militia companies. The historian of these companies comments that perhaps this was because 'the volunteers had the philosophy of the settlers they represented—that the Indians should be exterminated or removed to a remote location where they would not be troublesome'. 'Indians, boys, Indians!' shouts one of the more admirable characters in Grass Valley merchant Alonzo Delano's 1857 play, *A Live Woman in the Mines*, 'Hurrah for a fight! Fun, boys, fun—drop your tools, and run, boys, run.'[41]

The acknowledged 'Indian wars' were fought in California in the later 1850s—'the north became California's dark and bloody ground'.[42] California's war debt at the close of 1853 was already $924 259.[43] These expensive campaigns were eventually paid for by the United States government. There were always some in California who contested the idea that 'war' was the appropriate term for the violence that all acknowledged. The majority of the committee of the California Legislature investigating the Mendocino War in 1859 reported that they were 'unwilling to dignify, by the term war, a slaughter of beings, who at least possess the human form, and who make no resistance, and make no attacks, either on the person or residence of the citizen'. The series of Indian wars in California were mostly 'simply sadistic massacres', argues James Downs. But the press of California was not embarrassed about the word. 'Every little while,' the *Alta California* remarked in 1851, 'war panics break out in new places.'[44]

There was here a clear acknowledgement of the effects of gold on the indigenous population, and of the violence which characterised the

California frontier. Frontier conflict in Victoria was less often understood and remembered as warfare in this direct way.[45] The ideological attachment there to an idea of peaceful settlement was stronger, and the denial of what actually took place was deeper.[46] In Australia, there was the pernicious official assumption of 'terra nullius', that the land was empty. 'We seem to have come to inhabit only', the *Mount Alexander Mail* observed complacently in 1854, 'there being nothing to conquer'.[47]

Some isolated public acknowledgements of prior claims on the land did take place, and some recognition of the violence of the mining frontier. In 1851, the *Victorian Christian Herald* observed that 'the race is rapidly becoming extinct. It is but too well known that many have perished by the hand of violence, by the bullet, and by the poisoned cake. The cry of blood riseth from many parts of this land; and think you not that it will enter into the ears of the Lord of the Sabbath?'[48] Edward Wilson, editor of the *Argus*, lamented of the Victorian Aborigines (Kooris) in an editorial in 1856 that:

> In less than twenty years we have nearly swept them off the face of the earth. We have shot them down like dogs. In the guise of friendship we have issued corrosive sublimate in their damper and consigned whole tribes to the agonies of an excruciating death. We have made them drunkards and infected them with disease . . . [49]

Conservative pamphleteer R.L. Milne argued that Britain had won Australia, 'shed blood, seized the territory, and poured her people upon it with the commission of banditti'. 'You have taken possession of a country that is not yours,' Milne insisted, 'Ye have disinherited and slain its owners.' Edward Stone Parker in 1854 also acknowledged that, in some regions of Victoria, 'a fearful sacrifice of human life has unquestionably taken place'. These were lone voices, but their views arose from a time when interaction—trade, exchange, conversation—between the Koori inhabitants and the white invaders was still common. W.J. Wills, the future explorer—despite his view that the Aboriginal people around Deniliquin were a 'lazy set'—could express admiration for their skills. 'They will dive under ducks in a pond and catch them by the legs. They will also dive into a pond with a spear and turn on their backs so as to see the fish above them and spear them.' The written record of the 1850s contains some reminders, such as this, that whites and blacks in this period were often in close contact. The visual record, too, contains some such material—Eugene von Guerard's painting of diggers trading with Aboriginal people on the road to the diggings is one of the best examples.[50]

The first official post-gold enquiry into the reasons for the decline in the Aboriginal population came to an ambivalent conclusion. The Select Committee of the Victorian Legislative Council on the Aborigines reported

Eugene von Guerard. 'The Barter' 1854. Oil on canvas, 46.0 x 75.5 cm. Collection: Geelong Art Gallery. Gift of W. Max Bell and Norman Belcher, 1923.

in 1859 that 'great injustice has been perpetrated on the Aborigines', a 'great moral wrong'.[51] The Committee argued that the:

> great and almost unprecedented reduction in the number of the Aborigines is to be attributed to the general occupation of the country by the white population; to vices acquired by contact with a civilized race, more particularly the indulgence in ardent spirits; and hunger, in consequence of the scarcity of game since the settlement of the colony; and, also in some cases, to cruelty and ill-treatment.

The 'great cause', though, the Committee added, was the 'inveterate propensity of the race to excessive indulgence in spirits'.[52] Here we see a mixture of the frankness of an older humanitarian discourse mingling with the newer justificatory rhetoric of racism. As time passed in Victoria, less would be heard of the injustice of a people deprived of their traditional sources of food, and more of the 'propensity of the race' to this or that vice or weakness. The discovery of gold, William Thomas, the Victorian Guardian of Aborigines reported in July 1852, had 'greatly affected' the moral condition of the Aboriginal people. Those in the counties around Melbourne had, he claimed, in part because of the 'prodigal liberality of the gold diggers', 'generally speaking . . . become habitual drunkards'.[53]

By the later 1850s, overt Aboriginal resistance in Victoria was largely broken.[54] 'As a colony of but seventeen years standing,' William Thomas reported in January 1853, 'we may congratulate ourselves that the weapons of opposition between us and our sable fellow subjects are laid aside . . .

We may safely state that loop holes in huts are no more needed.' When the Legislative Council Select Committee of 1859 enquired into the condition of Aboriginal people in the colony, settlers from the various districts almost unanimously reported that the Aboriginal population had been pacified. The question on the official circular asked whether the Aborigines in the district were 'quiet', and the replies almost all indicated that they were now quiet—'very quiet' reported some, with obvious satisfaction; 'perfectly quiet' stated the reports from the Wimmera district and from Colac. From many areas, especially the goldfields, the settlers and officials from whom information was sought replied that no Aborigines were known in the district. They had 'long since disappeared', William Lavender wrote from Kyneton. W.H.F. Mitchell, Justice of the Peace in Kyneton, added that 'since the diggings opened the native race has entirely disappeared'.[55] This was only, it has to be remembered, twenty years after the first European intrusion into the land.

The 1859 Committee's report contained some pointed descriptions of a despair felt by Aboriginal people at their prospects in their own country. The humanitarian Dr Thomas Embling recalled of his travels in the colony in 1851 and 1852 that: 'Hopelessness is their prevailing feeling.' 'They felt themselves to be a dying race,' he wrote, 'and that no effort they could make would avert their destiny.'[56] There were low birth rates in Aboriginal populations in the 1850s. Diane Barwick concludes that venereal and other disease were responsible for extremely high infant mortality rates.[57]

The indigenous peoples, in both California and Victoria, were for a number of years valuable to the invaders as a workforce. In California, through the 1850s, Native Americans remained a very important part of the labour force in agriculture, cattle ranching, wheat farming and domestic service—though in each case the demand for their labour diminished over the decade.[58] Historians have suggested some initial mitigation of the severity of treatment of the Californian Indians as a legacy of the paternalist models of the Hispanic system of colonisation, which had fostered the indigenous labour force. For many expansionist and nationalist Americans of the 1840s too, argues James Rawls, the 'docile, tractable Indians joined the other features of California, such as its salubrious climate and fertile soil, which made the land so eminently desirable'.[59]

A Californian law of 1850 allowed Indians found to be without work ('vagrant') to be given into the care of a white person—often this happened at public auction. The law also established a system of Indian 'apprenticeship', which allowed a Justice of the Peace to give the 'care, custody, control, and earnings' of an Indian child to a white person wishing to obtain their labour. This meant that, in addition to other hazards, the indigenous population was subject to kidnapping by whites. The 1850 law, strengthened in 1860, was widely understood as a system of involuntary servitude, and Indians were, under its provisions, openly being bought and sold in California. Heizer and Almquist argue that the system 'can only be termed slavery'.[60] The laws under which this system operated were repealed in 1863, in the context of Civil War embarrassment at the existence of something so very like slavery in a free state.

California Indians did participate in the gold rush as miners. One government report in 1848 estimated that more than half the diggers at the mines at that early stage were Indians. Most of these were working for white men, but some were digging and trading for themselves. 'Indians were at work for miners and others', James H. Carson reported, 'receiving in payment for their week's work an old shirt or handkerchief.' The demand for Indian labour in mining, even at these rates, declined rapidly in the face of white competition, and the shift to hydraulic and quartz mining later in the decade. There was also a breakdown of the stability of the older paternalist, semi-feudal models inherited from the Spanish period, and Rawls argues that it was this loss of continuity with the Hispanic systems that led rapidly to open hostility and a kind of warfare on the California frontier. Now Indians began retreating from mining districts in fear of their lives.[61]

In Victoria, Aboriginal labour also became important to the white population during the labour scarcity of the early 1850s—one of the few moments in Victorian history when this has been the case. 'There is scarcely a station which the natives are in the habit of frequenting,' Edward Bell reported in 1853, 'where they have not been more or less employed.' '[I]t is a fact I should like to state, well known to me,' stated former Assistant Protector of Aborigines in Victoria, Edward Stone Parker, 'that, at the time when the country was in a state of universal excitement on the outbreak of the gold mining, there were several stations where no shepherds were left but aboriginal shepherds.'[62] Temporarily, Aboriginal men in Victoria had something to bargain with. 'The dearth of European labour occasioned by the discovery of the Gold Fields,' Charles Tyers wrote from Gippsland, 'has no doubt led to improvement in their position in relation to the Europeans.'[63] Money wages were sometimes paid, though more commonly food and clothing served instead.

In neither Victoria nor California was the testimony of indigenous persons admissible in court.[64] The first Californian legislature restricted the suffrage to white citizens; in Victoria, Aboriginal people were not granted full citizenship until the twentieth century. For the invaded and colonised peoples upon whose land the gold was found, gold proved a fatal commodity.

THE CHINESE

'The question of the influx of such large numbers of a pagan and inferior race', the 1854 parliamentary Victorian Gold Fields' Commission of

Enquiry reported, 'is a very serious one'.[65] The Chinese were the group, in Victoria and California who, after the indigenous populations, suffered the most from the hard edge of colonial racism. It was on its own terms a puzzling racism. The arguments against the Chinese were always put with some anxiety, and a consciousness of the contradictory nature of the case. Chinese miners were acknowledged generally to be hard working, clean and law abiding. There was an objection to their not bringing women with them—'under which conditions', the Victorian Gold Fields' Commission argued, 'no immigration can prove of real advantage to any society'. But Victoria was of course also being swamped by European men without women. '[T]heir proceedings on the Gold Fields are certainly such as may occasion inconvenience to the general population,' the Commission continued, 'if not strife and collision with the European laws. The Chinese are content with very small earnings acquired under the rudest modes of mining.' But thrift and diligence were generally admired characteristics in this society. Their disposition was 'remarkably quiet', the Commission admitted, and this was a society which prized quietness. The Commission had received testimony on this point from several witnesses. Mr Henry Gibson, a surgeon, testified that the Chinese were a 'most quiet, inoffensive class of persons'. Mr Charles James Kenworthy reported that he found the Chinese to be 'sober, industrious, and quiet'. Yet, the Commissioners decided, their 'degrading and absurd superstition', their 'incurable habit of gaming and other vicious tendencies', their 'low scale of domestic comfort', would 'tend to demoralise colonial society'.[66] A hundred years later, the history of the Chinese on the goldfields was still being posed as a question of their moral character. In the Victorian government's centenary history of the gold discoveries, the Chinese were similarly commended for their 'industrious and orderly' behaviour, but 'some were thieves' it was alleged, 'and frequently brought trouble to their camps by stealing gold from sluice boxes and machines.'[67] Racism against the Chinese worked in this way by posing as a question the morality of the Chinese population. Humanitarian defenders and racist critics of the Chinese thus occupied the same discursive terrain—their common demand was that the Chinese population be open to the scrutiny of the dominant society. What was unacceptable to them was not in the end any particular set of practices or beliefs, but the threat they saw in a self-enclosed community, one which which was not open to the inquiring, judging, governing gaze of the majority.

By 1859, the Chinese made up about eight per cent of the Victorian population. An 1855 Act limited the number of Chinese passengers allowed on any vessel, levied a £10 tax on each Chinese arrival, and confined Chinese diggers to segregated camps under official Protectors. An 1857 Act added a £6 yearly licence for Chinese men. Racial violence arose on many Victorian goldfields, most seriously at Ararat, where the six thousand

Chinese at times comprised almost one-third of the diggers on the field, and the Buckland, where on 4 July 1856, European diggers attacked the Chinese camp, destroying 750 tents, driving the Chinese miners off the field and stealing their gold. Chinese in Victoria endured not only this abuse, but also the mental strain of racial tension. Madness afflicted them in unusual proportion. They had to pay a punitive tax to support the 'protectorates', which provided some protection but with it supervision and subjection to official and unofficial scrutiny. The 1856 regulations allowed the Protector of the district to remove any Chinese camp 'for sanitary or other purposes' on seven days' notice.[68] Thousands of the Chinese had left for home by the end of the decade.

The churches faced particular difficulties in gold-rush society when they attempted to undertake missionary work. How to persuade others, in the midst of so much rushing after gold, that in a Christian society there were higher goals and sterner tests than the achievement of great wealth? A Church of England missionary to the Chinese miners at Beechworth and Yackandandah in Victoria encountered blank and comic incomprehension:

> They have a picture of an idol, and I ask them 'Do you worship these?' and they said 'Yes.' I said, 'Can this god do you any good?' They answered and said, 'Our gods has protect us to get plenty of gold.' And I said, 'Can he forgive your sins?' They replied, 'We have no sins.' I said, 'Can he save your soul?' They replied, 'We have no soul.' I then replied, 'You did not understand at all.'[69]

Clearly from the missionaries' point of view the Chinese miners did not understand at all, but they had posed some difficult questions for the apologists for Christian other-worldliness. The Geelong and Western District Chinese Evangelization Society stated in 1858 that the entire efforts of the committee had only managed to support one teacher at Ballarat, and that there were 'no positive cases of conversion to report'.[70]

In Victoria, Chinese people could offer evidence in court—though practical issues of translation and ideological issues to do with accepting a Chinese oath discouraged judges from seeking it. Markus argues that, although there was active prejudice in both places, the Victorian Chinese were at least given some protection for their tax payments.[71] The inability of California Chinese to offer testimony in court stemmed from an 1854 ruling by Chief Justice Murray that Chinese should be considered as 'Indians' for the purposes of the law, and so be unable to act as witnesses against whites. This became the main civil grievance of the Chinese in California.[72]

The largest waves of Chinese immigration to California came in 1852 to 1854, and then again in 1860 to 1863. Foreign miners in California paid a special tax of $3 a month from 1852, raised to $4 a month from 1853, $6 from 1855, and down to $4 again from 1856. The revenue from this tax, which was often farmed out to private tax collectors, was an important part of the income of the Californian state government: nearly one-quarter of its revenue in the years 1854 to 1870.[73] Miners' conventions in the early 1850s passed anti-Chinese resolutions, threatening to drive the Chinese from the mines. In Columbia county in 1852, and then in Shasta county, the majority of the Chinese left after such resolutions were passed—though Markus argues that it was the sporadic use of force rather than regulation which established the subordinate place of the Chinese.[74] From the conventions, the issue passed to the state legislature. A committee of the California Assembly deemed 'the question of the migration of the people of China to California as the most important which can possibly engage the attention of the Legislature and the country', and argued in favour of immigration restriction. 'However true it may be in theory, orthodox in morals, or sound in philosophy,' the committee argued, 'that all men are by nature free, equal and independent, yet the imperfections and fallibilities of human nature are such, and so great, that all human wisdom has failed to reduce such theory to living reality, or a practical truth.'[75] A committee of the California Senate argued in 1855 that 'we find, from our own experience and acquaintance with the customs, manners, language and religion of this people, that they have no feeling or interest in common with us', and advocated immigration restriction.[76] The Californian press seemed especially virulent in its anti-Chinese sentiment. The *Alta California* wrote in 1854 of the 'vicious and disgustingly filthy' Chinese arrivals: 'Were they an industrious, laboring people we might permit their peculiar appearance, their jaw-breaking jargon and even their filthy habits; but being as they are wholly useless and unproducing, and beside that an eyesore and a stench in the nostrils of the community, they are entirely unbearable within our city limits.'[77]

By the late 1850s in California, there were campaigners for the civil rights of the Chinese population. John Archibald defended the general superiority of the Caucasian race, while arguing that depriving the Chinese of the right of giving evidence was 'an extreme of barbarism'. The Reverend William Speer, missionary to the Chinese in California, wrote extensively in their support. Denying the Chinese the right to testify in court, he observed, made them 'a tempting prey to all the depraved classes with which a new country . . . must abound'. They should not be taxed, he argued, if they were not protected by law. The Chinese, he claimed, were the 'Yankees of the East', diligent and ingenious, and were needed in California to occupy the poorer diggings 'where Americans would not consider their labor remunerated'.[78]

In both California and Victoria, then, the large Chinese populations were subjected to discrimination and ultimately to violence. A history of gold from their perspective would not be one full of nostalgia for the roaring days. Clearly, actual Chinese people often found ways to cope with conditions in these societies, became more than victims of white racism. My intention here has been only to describe some of the dimensions of that racism, not to enter into argument about what they or their experiences were really like.

OPTIMISTIC RESPONSES TO GOLD: ENDORSING LAISSEZ FAIRE

In responding to gold, Victorians and Californians drew upon a common stock of arguments already available to them. What seemed remarkable about gold was also what seemed remarkable about the changed conditions of life back home. The conditions of the gold rush seemed to present to contemporaries, in heightened form, the dilemmas posed by the spread of capitalist social relations. In examining conscious arguments made about the impact of gold, I am also studying attitudes within the two societies to the idea that the individual pursuit of wealth was the best possible basis for social life.

The gold rushes presented the spectacle of a society made up of men pursuing wealth to the neglect of all else. 'It must be borne in mind,' Hinton Helper told his readers, 'that all the adventurers to this country have come for the express purpose of making money, and that to this every other consideration is sacrificed.' 'The whole community,' wrote Franklin Langworthy, ' . . . are engaged in one perfect scramble for gold. This one motive absorbs and swallows up every and all other considerations.' 'Money, money, is the all-absorbing object . . .' J.D.B. Stillman noted, 'Whatever depravity there is in a man's heart now shows itself without fear and without restraint.' 'The love of gain, the master passion of the human heart', James Ward wrote of California, 'has drawn that heterogenous assemblage here, and what they earn they will enjoy, each according to his desires . . .' [79] Here was an opportunity for some practical testing of contemporary social theory.

Gold-mining society might appear the exact antithesis of capitalist-industrial society, in that it took men out of the discipline of the cities into raw and unformed settlements, to work for a time outside the wage nexus. This perception of a regression from civilisation and discipline was an important part of the response to gold. But gold was primarily disruptive because it introduced an explosion of market forces—seesawing prices and wages, inflation and then depression, poverty and then riches, riches then poverty—into societies which had previously been considerably less volatile. 'The sudden and extreme fluctuations of prices in San Francisco have occasioned a great deal of surprise . . .' reported the *Alta California* in February 1850. 'Every new or great discovery in any of the Colonies,' noted C. Rudston Read, a Victorian Crown Lands Commissioner, 'causes a great fluctuation in the labour markets.' 'There are few events that have occurred in the history of our civilisation,' Kinahan Cornwallis opined, 'which in proportion have been the cause of greater extremes of prosperity and calamity than the discoveries of gold in California and Australia.' These fluctuations could be seen to be merely exaggerations of the characteristics of developed capitalist society. 'One could not pass through the city,' wrote the Reverend Daniel B. Woods of San Francisco, 'without being impressed with the sentiment which seems to describe the whole thing, "Enterprise run mad" '. When G.W. Rusden, who had lived through the Victorian gold era, came to write his conservative *History of Australia*, it was the control of social life by the market which he remembered:

> An unsettled population, the lust for gold, a culmination of the Manchester theory of the highest good for men and nations—a belief that 'the infinite celestial soul of man is a kind of hay-balance—for weighing hay and thistles, pleasures and pains'—so afflicted Victoria that for a time she was an object for pity or regret.[80]

This was how contemporaries most often understood the gold rushes: as dramatisations and exaggerations of the social theory that the individual pursuit of wealth was the best possible basis for a social order, and that laissez faire was thus the best social policy. For critics, gold seeking seemed a grotesque exaggeration of individual wealth-seeking behaviour, which served usefully to display to the world what would happen if men were to become motivated only by wealth. But, preoccupied with other issues, particularly the development of the nation and national consciousness, twentieth-century historians have seldom interpreted the response to either gold rush in these terms. These mining men of the 1850s were the true subjects of the new liberal ideologies. Self-seeking, self-regulating, morally and emotionally autonomous, transnational, the gold diggers were the citizens of nineteeenth-century liberal modernity. The great question was— how could they be governed? One had to be very modern indeed in 1851 to have complete confidence in the governability of such a diverse, mobile, independent population. Michel Foucault and his followers have studied the nineteenth-century reformers who had confidence that an ethically autonomous and mobile population could be governed. In arguments about gold-rush society we meet the many provincial or old-fashioned thinkers of the time who were not so sure. The gold diggers were limit cases, boundary riders of modernity, and the educated classes at home read about them with great interest and concern. That is one of the reasons why the gold rushes were such great publishing events, why the details of all the journeys after gold needed to be so carefully recorded in thousands of curiously similar individual journals and letters, why the learned journals debated the 'effects of gold' for years after.

Colonial governments in Victoria evinced continuing anxiety about the population they had to govern. Population statistics were regularly produced and nervously scrutinised, and Australian colonial statisticians were 'ambitious and able' practitioners.[81] There were times in the 1860s, records the historian of the Victorian police, when almost the entire force of mounted constables was employed circulating agricultural statistics forms.[82] If a diverse and mobile population was somehow to be governed, much information about it would be needed.

Laissez faire is the concept which best helps categorise the responses to gold. Those responses fall into two broad groups: those which expressed, in the political-economic, imperial or providential ideologies of the day, confidence that the market would provide, and that the outcome of all the individual wealth-seeking which constituted a gold rush could not be bad; and those which sought some grounds from which to offer a critical perspective. Of course in new societies laissez faire had a different meaning than it did in old ones. In Victoria and California, markets had still to be made, and, as Wells has argued of Australia, 'the formation of markets is neither spontaneous nor necessary'—the state had an important role in constituting property relations, creating a market in land and labour.[83] But social criticism did not necessarily reflect the general necessity of state constitution of markets in newly capitalist societies—on this topic as on others, the languages of debate came from the metropolis, and the argument about laissez faire or management proceeded more or less as at home.

The critical arguments were inevitably more complex than the optimists' assertions, often looking back rather than forward in the attempt to formulate some alternative to the pure pursuit of wealth. These critics of gold-rush society *might* be seen, on the contrary, as the modernisers, for their project after all was one of civilising and domesticating a labour force which had temporarily broken its bounds. Ian Tyrrell's work on American temperance movements argues this case—that temperance reform was not reactionary but modernising, that temperance reformers sought 'to create a society of competitive individuals instilled with the virtues of sobriety and industry'.[84] In Ralph Mann's study of two California gold-rush towns, the argument is developed that it was the merchant elite of the towns who supported the various reform movements there, because they sought to normalise and Americanise the town, realising that the 'perpetuation of Gold Rush attitudes and conditions was unthinkable'.[85] So foreigners, drinking, gambling and prostitution all became the targets of reform activity. But as Mann notes, reformers disagreed as to whether 'the pursuit of wealth or an anticipated freedom from restraint was paramount in shaping Gold Rush society', though they agreed, he says, that both created social chaos.[86] Either way, the reformers were pessimistic about gold-rush society. It was only those who accepted unambivalently the pursuit of wealth as a proper basis for a social order that could confront gold-rush California or Victoria with unmixed optimism. Reformers, almost by definition, were not advocates of laissez faire—they believed that interventions, such as their own, in social processes could be beneficial. Though the intended or unintended consequence of the actions of the reformers may have been a more disciplined and settled labour force, this complicity with the modernising project must always be set against the profoundly anti-modernist arguments which they actually articulated. These critics of gold-rush society were the ones who lacked the liberal, laissez-faire confidence that radically individualised populations could be governed. In this they were clearly, in metropolitan terms, old-fashioned.

There was little doubt in the 1850s that the market was becoming more determining of social life, and in this way the gold rushes seemed to observers like a glimpse of the future. 'Their civilisation,' a contemporary wrote of California, 'is a peculiar one, and not at all unlike all others, but in some respects in advance of all others.' In Britain, free trade and protection were still, in the aftermath of 1846, among the most crucial and most divisive of political and social issues, for the tensions they articulated (commerce and agriculture, north and south) were fundamental and unresolved. In the United States, the Democrats and Whigs divided on similar questions. The Democratic belief was that government should relinquish its control over the economy and almost everything else, and that self-interest would provide all the regulation which society needed. Their Whig opponents favoured protection, internal improvements, and government oversight of the economy.[87]

Observers in the 1850s who had any knowledge of or involvement in these fundamental debates, could not help but read the gold rushes as commentary upon them. To approve of the effects of the discoveries of gold, to look with equanimity or even approbation upon the unplanned movement of so many men around the globe in the pursuit of their own enrichment, one had to be whole-heartedly committed to some form of laissez-faire belief, to some version of the doctrine that what happened of its own accord, or as the spontaneous result of the aggregation of individual self-interests, must be the best possible outcome. W.E. Hearn, Professor of Political Economy at Melbourne University, argued confidently that Victoria, as 'heir to all the ages', was 'free from all those obstacles by which men, in their ignorance of the laws which regulate society, hampered their progress'.[88] P. Just in Victoria argued the same case, with a confident sense of his own modernity, distancing himself from some of the pessimistic older settlers in the colony who 'predicted nothing but ruin and disaster' from gold. These pessimists, Just argued, 'did not see that, according to the unerring operation of natural laws, all this irregularity would in time adjust itself, and that the gold would soon attract that labour they were so anxious to obtain'. If the gold caused disorder for a time, 'it in due course brought about the usual regularity of a well ordered community'.[89] Thomas Hart Benton told the United States Senate that, although he disapproved of gold mining on moral grounds, his faith in laissez faire meant that he had no serious concerns about the outcome: 'It is no matter who digs up the gold or where it goes. The digger will not eat it, and it will go where commerce will carry it.'[90] This appeal to commerce and the 'unerring operation of natural laws' was characteristic of optimistic thinking about gold. It belonged to a mode of thought which was emergent but not yet uncontestedly dominant. It had some influential proponents but also, and in particular in Victoria, some influential opponents.

Laissez faire was not just an economic doctrine. There were three major ways in which the gold discoveries could be approved by contemporaries. They could be used in various combinations, and were probably, for some individuals particularly well attuned to the times, all ultimately compatible. All implied some kind of laissez-faire doctrine. If one wanted to argue that the discovery of gold was unambiguously a good thing, the available means were: to argue within an imperial discourse about the good to be expected from a gold-funded expansion of empire; to argue within a religious discourse that Providence intended the discoveries to happen at just that moment, for a number of possible reasons; to argue within a discourse of political economy that the market would order all for the best, and that no great economic event such as the gold discoveries, particularly one so stimulating of economic activity, could have ultimately negative effects. These arguments had a common desire to legitimate gold seeking, and by implication the kinds of societies which the gold seeking promised to create; they shared, that is, an optimism about the outcome of all the questing for gold.

The first argument, then, was imperial. The task of imperial apologists for the gold rushes was to assimilate the individual seekings for fortune which constituted the rushes, to a history of racial and imperial destiny. Edmund Randolph marvelled to the Society of California Pioneers in 1860 at the prospect of:

> California in full possession of the white man, and embraced within the mighty area of his civilisation! . . . We see in our great movement hitherward in 1849 a likeness to the times when our ancestors, their wives and little ones, and all their stuff in wagons, and with attendant herds, poured forth by nations and in never-ending columns from the German forests, and went to seek new pastures and to found new kingdoms in the ruined provinces of the Roman Empire.[91]

The *American Review* looked forward to 'the beginning of a great American epoch in the history of the world', a new imperial prospect:

it seems no less clear that God intends to give here, on this continent, a scope for human energies of thought and will such as has never yet been seen since the days before the flood; to let there be seen the freest, widest, most diversified and powerful display of what man's science and skill can accomplish in subduing the elements . . . in overcoming and annihilating the old limitations of human endeavour.[92]

The *Democratic Review*, equally optimistic, saw the discovered gold as 'the great instrument of that national progress so compatible with the genius of the people', as the 'motive power which will put in operation the already-prepared vast machinery of American enterprise, and be but a means of accelerating the march to national supremacy'. Martial imagery was here combined with a celebration of American energy, as usual at the expense of the 'indolent Spaniards', who had used their wealth, it was said, merely as a means of 'indulging an inglorious ease'.[93] Looking to the east, the *Review* imagined a new American and commercial empire spreading across the Pacific, replacing a fading Britain:

The uncertain and criminal possession which English satraps hold of the Indian peninsula, is becoming relaxed through the declining vigor of the Imperial country; and the friendly hand of American commerce will soon supplant the mailed glove of British oppression. The sums now extracted from the wretched ryot to feed the pomp of British officials, will soon swell the profits of American dealers in exchange for the products of industry.[94]

Some Californians looked rather to the south seeing, as C.E. Havens argued it, room for expansion in the 'tropic solitudes' of South America:

Our fancy beholds its unploughed wastes and immemorial woods—its mountain ranges, girdled at the base by banana, palm and cycas, and the gloaming in the skies . . . its imperial streams, whose monotonous music is only broken by the whistle of the 'shrill cicadas' and locusts . . . transformed by the magic innovation of Republicanism and civilization, into farms teeming with the golden grain of plenty, its rivers filled with argosies of commerce, and the whole continent busy with the restless activity of modern progress.[95]

In London, more soberly and complacently, the *Times* told its readers that a 'new state has been founded on the Pacific, and a new empire is struggling into being at our antipodes'. The *British Quarterly Review* thought the discoveries would raise Australia from a 'dreaded penal colony' to a 'mighty empire'. Examples could be multiplied, but in both places the gold discoveries were understood to strengthen the existing reach of empire, and possibly to extend it. There was much rhetoric in both places about bringing Anglo-Saxon civilization and the Christian religion to, and just as much about the wonderful possibilities for trade with, the East. In this optimistic imperial discourse, much was made of the fact that there had never been such gold found before in Anglo-Saxon societies, and arguments that gold inevitably created disorder and immorality were rejected on the grounds that the experiences of other nations were inapplicable. Imperialists could view the gold discoveries optimistically because they promised to supply the motive force which would expand the blessings which their nation had to offer the world. 'It is impossible to doubt,' observed W.R. Greg in the *North British Review*, 'that the progress and welfare of humanity in its highest phase will be best served by the spread of English civilization over the globe.'[96]

The second major mode of optimistic explanation of gold was religious. Although many clergy condemned the gold rushes as a short-sighted pursuit of merely earthly riches, there was always a tension in their pronouncements. To condemn the events unreservedly could appear as a doubting of Providential design. Charles Perry, evangelical Anglican Bishop of Melbourne, was greatly exercised on this question. Despite many apprehensions, he had in the end to approve of gold, and this placed him at odds with some of his most prominent church members, notably the a'Beckett brothers, who sometimes spoke as if they saw the discoveries as an unmitigated evil. 'We should be guilty,' Perry wrote in January 1852, 'of unpardonable ingratitude and unbelief, if we were to regard so remarkable a providential event as sure to be productive of evil to the country. God has hitherto been peculiarly gracious to us.'[97]

The gold, Perry maintained, was the Lord's, and he had brought it forth 'in such abundance out of the bowels of the earth, in this country, and at this particular period' for 'some wise and good purpose'. Perry, his wife recorded, speculated at home that the gold might be 'a providential appointment for the speedy peopling of these colonies'. The gold discoveries, he argued, did not represent a divine punishment:

> we can see in this circumstance none of the marks of a national judgement. To the mass of the people, although it will too probably exercise a most injurious influence upon their religious and social character, and so upon their real happiness, it is the immediate source of immense pecuniary gain. It can scarcely therefore be regarded as a divine judgement upon them . . .

Perry wrote a prayer for use in Anglican churches, which expressed his ultimate optimism about the gold: 'We should remember that it is Thou, O God, who hast stored up so vast a quantity of gold in this land, and hast brought it forth at this particular time; and we would therefore confidently hope, that this discovery will eventually prove conducive to Thy glory and to the welfare of mankind.'[98]

Even if they were not construed as positive evils, events like the discoveries of gold could have easily appeared as merely chance occurrences, accidents of fate. This illusion had to be dispelled by the spokesmen for Christian religion. Thomas a'Beckett in Melbourne, himself a proponent of the pessimistic and critical interpretation of the gold rushes, allowed his faith to triumph when he wrote that 'while the ways of Providence are inscrutable, they are planned by infinite wisdom, and will inscrutably lead, though it may be in a way we wot not of, to the ultimate happiness of man'.[99] 'Many will ascribe the settlement of this country to accidental causes', the Reverend Charles A. Farley warned his San Francisco congregation in 1850, 'but Christianity knows no such thing as accidents or chances. She recognises God in all history'.[100] In England, D.T. Coulton in the *Quarterly Review* argued for the happy coincidence of Providential design and the spread of all the virtues which Manchester associated with free trade and expanding commerce:

> In the expansion of our trade, the increasing commerce of the world, the rapid growth of our colonies, we hope to reap the fruits of this latest gift of Providence. Whenever we see movements of great masses of men, as lately towards California and now towards Australia, we think we can recognise Divine design more plainly than in other facts of history. The singular manner in which the gold is spread over certain tracts of the earth, the ease with which it can be collected by individual effort, and the universal opinion entertained of its value, seem to point it out in an especial manner as one of the agencies by which intercourse between nations is to be promoted, and the social condition of man raised.[101]

Of both California and Victoria, it was said often that Providence had held the gold in readiness for just the right historical moment, and that a great age in the history of the world was undoubtedly imminent. The Reverend William Speer believed that 'Ophir has been hidden until the time had come, and the men were ready' for America to be the agent of regeneration of 'the two dark continents of heathenism'.[102] Even Ralph Waldo Emerson shared a kind of providential view. He noted in his journal that events only happened when the world was ready for them, and that the California gold rushes were a good illustration of this rule. 'Such a well-appointed colony as never was planted before arrives with the speed of sail and steam on these remote shores.'[103]

In California in particular, providential argument often also had an imperial dimension to it, as the observation was made that the Spaniards had had the country for three hundred years and not found the gold, while the enterprising Anglo-Saxon had needed only three months. 'Such is the difference of the races!' Archibald Alison observed in *Blackwood's Edinburgh Magazine* on this point, 'It is easy to see to which is destined the sceptre of the globe.' Anglo settlement had a religious significance, particularly for American Protestant clergy. 'Does it not seem as if Providence had been keeping these regions from the attention of the great nations', the Reverend Professor George Shephard asked his parishioners in Maine, 'until a thoroughly *Protestant* people would occupy them?' California Catholics were much less likely to see anything providential in the discoveries. The Catholic archbishop there, fearing for the established Spanish missions, wrote that 'the great emigration brings Protestantism and immorality'.[104]

Many other providential intentions were discerned in the discoveries. In Victoria, the *Australian Gold Diggers Monthly Magazine* thought the gold supplies had been opened up as an act of 'a gracious Providence' for the 'starving millions of the Old World'. A writer in the *New Englander* saw, 'thanks to the discovery of the gold mines', an effective end to the westward spread of slavery. 'Surely, then,' he asked, 'it is not in vain that an overruling Providence has so long withheld the treasures of the extreme West from human grasp, and just at this crisis has revealed them in all their extent and attractiveness?'[105]

The Providential interpretations of gold were laissez faire in implication—whatever had happened must have happened for some wise purpose; there was a plan, the argument went, though we may have trouble discerning it. It is with some relief that one turns to the more acerbic opinion of Henry David Thoreau. He found the flight to California a depressing and futile thing, yet one more indictment of the dominant American ethos: 'It makes God to be a moneyed gentleman who scatters a handful of pennies in order to see mankind scramble for them. The world's raffle! A subsistence in the domains of nature a thing to be raffled for! What a comment, what a satire, on our institutions!'[106]

The third major context of optimistic interpretation was economic. British and American political economists were typically sanguine about the effects of the discoveries. William Newmarch told the 1853 meeting in Hull of the British Association for the Advancement of Science that 'generally, we are justified in describing the effects of the new gold as almost wholly beneficial':

> It has led to the establishment of new branches of enterprise, to new discoveries, and to the establishment in remote regions of populations carrying with them energy, intelligence, and the rudiments of a great society. In our own country it has already elevated the condition of the working and poorer classes; it has quickened and extended trade; and exerted an influence which thus far is beneficial wherever it has been felt.[107]

Political economists such as Newmarch saw in the gold discoveries a stimulus for the British and world economies, through the creation of new markets and the increased circulation of money. The new gold was generally acknowledged to stimulate activity, and to awaken desire for gain and self-enrichment—which, the political economists argued, could only be for the good of all. In the hands of some political economy writers, the arguments about the extension of trade, and the arguments for empire, became one. So the *Economist*, in an unusually lyrical but typically free-trade fervour, argued that:

The consequence of finding gold in California and Australia is to quicken and extend amazingly the commerce between Europe, America, Asia, and the islands in the Pacific, bringing all the old and well-peopled, and the new and fast-peopling countries of three-fourths of the globe to nearly the same level of civilisation, with as large a want of the precious metal as ourselves, and extending the demand for them probably quite equal to the produce. There is happily but one opinion as to the ultimate effect of the discovery of great quantities of gold, that, like all things not of human contrivance, it cannot fail to promote the civilisation of the species, and contribute to the progress and power of man.[108]

This belief was just as strong across the Atlantic. The *Western Journal* thought that the gold would at once open up an 'immense commerce' between 'this country and the continent of Asia, Australia, and the rich Islands of the Indian Ocean', that the mines would become 'an important element of national wealth, and of national greatness; calculated to quicken the development of the vast resources of this country; to enlarge our intercourse with all the nations of the earth, and advance the cause of civilization throughout the world'.[109] In Australia, the Sydney merchant T.S. Mort expressed the optimistic laissez-faire position most clearly at a dinner held in Sydney in 1853 to celebrate the anniversary of the discovery of gold: 'Gold is the mainspring of commerce,' he said, 'commerce is the forerunner of civilization; and civilization is the handmaiden of Christianity.' There were loud cheers from the mercantile audience, and the band struck up the 'Railway Gallop'.[110]

The gold discoveries were thus widely seen as both vindication and enhancement of the operation of laissez faire. They set in train vast movements of population and capital, movements which were, observers pointed out, quite beyond the control of governments. 'Governments do not determine the progress of population, the extension of trade, the value of gold, the rewards of labour,' argued the free-trade *British Quarterly Review*, 'and must not fancy therefore that . . . they can have any great influence over the consequences of these great discoveries. They lie beyond the scope of all ordinary legislation.' The *Review* therefore argued that the 'newly discovered gold, like most other events in modern times, is a forcible argument in favour of perfectly free trade'.[111] The free market was also perceived to extend to emigration. 'It is neither by forethought nor counsel of governments that men are impelled to fill up the void places of the habitable earth', John Chapman pointed out in the *Westminster Review*, '. . . nor is it by deep calculation for the public good that individuals so seek each his own advantage, however in so seeking each may really advance, as he could not otherwise advance, that public good'. Gold had, he argued, hastened into being a free market in population, and this laissez faire in citizenship would create freedoms, 'Now that, to a considerable extent, men can practically choose under what government they will live, it will be madness in those who affect to govern to blind themselves to the necessity of conforming, however unwontedly, to the new conditions of the market.'[112] Gold thus seemed to true free-trade political economists, as it did to true Democrats, a perfect example of an enormously beneficial, and purely self-interest driven, social and economic event.

Some economists were of course less optimistic.[113] Opponents of complete laissez faire were at a loss to suggest a remedy. 'Here, then, is a state of things pre-eminently calling for the interference of a Government,' argued John Lalor of Australian gold, 'if Government can interfere to any purpose. It must be admitted, however, that there was never a case which appeared to present greater difficulties.' Lalor, an admirer of Carlyle, feared national decay among the British people, a decline in 'moral courage and frankness' in public life:

> National corruption, then, may be said to consist of two things—a dispropor-
> tionate development of all the impulses leading to personal gratification, and
> a loosening or destruction of numerous traditional restraints, by which indul-
> gence was more or less controlled, and individual wills held habitually in
> subjection.

In rejecting conventional political economy, Lalor looked for a moral solution to the national problems which he saw the gold discoveries as only compounding, one which would 'subordinate the all-engrossing passion for wealth to the nobler inspirations of the soul'.[114] His response was typical of the critics of gold, in that it was argued in terms of restraint and self-subjugation.

There was lively debate about whether the new supplies of gold would lead to a fall in its value, and a consequent rise in the price of other goods.[115] James Ward argued that there would be little change in the relative value of gold, because the desire for gold was 'uniform, constant, and inappeasable'. There was no limit to the desire for gold because there was 'no assignable limit to human desires'.[116] The French political economist Michel Chevalier took the position that a fall was inevitable and perhaps not entirely beneficial. His English translator, Richard Cobden, also warned that there would be 'innumerable shocks and sufferings' as a consequence, that would 'derange and convulse the relations of capital and labour'.[117]

But optimists in Britain and America who accepted the argument that the value of gold would fall, saw that as a good thing. 'The opinion that the depreciation will be a benefit to the whole community,' said the *North American Review*, 'is not expressed by M. Chevalier so decidedly as we would wish.' The inflationary tendencies of a fall in the price of gold could only be applauded in a professedly egalitarian society. 'In this democratic country, also, we may be permitted to consider it as an advantage,' the *Review* observed, 'that the gain will be very widely diffused—will be shared by the great bulk of the community.'[118] The decline in the value of money, thought the journal, might be so great as to reduce it to a quarter or a third of its current value—but that would be 'a blessing', for it would alleviate debt and stimulate industry. The English economist W. Stanley Jevons, looking back from 1863, similarly thought the rise in prices of other commodities would be permanent and beneficial, and that 'hardly a person in the kingdom' could remain unaffected.[119] Unlike Cobden, though, he thought the effects of the inflation had been and would be ' gradual and gentle'. 'Far from taking place with sudden and painful starts, flinging the rich headlong down to a lower station, and shaking the groundwork of society, nothing is more insidious, slow and imperceptible.'[120] Jevons produced a list of occupations and classes of persons who would be adversely affected by a general rise in prices—these included bond and debenture holders, creditors, owners of leasehold property, 'goldsmiths, bullion dealers, misers, or others who hold any considerable quantities of gold', 'the Royal Family, officers of state, judges, government employees and others upon the civil list', and all professionals whose charges were fixed by 'law, custom, or convenience'. Those whose incomes were entirely independent of the value of gold, and who would consequently not suffer at all, included 'manufacturers, farmers, contractors, mine-owners, ship-owners . . . merchants, brokers, agents, commercial travellers, hawkers, and dealers generally . . . artisans, skilled workers, labourers, porters, domestic servants'. Jevons could thus look forward with equanimity to the changes portending. He thought that the rise in prices would have a positive effect: 'It loosens the country, as nothing else could, from its old bonds of debt and habit. It throws increased rewards before all who are making and acquiring wealth, somewhat at the expense of those who are enjoying acquired wealth. It excites the active and skilful classes of the community to new exertions . . .'[121]

This opinion seems to have been widely held at both ends of the political spectrum. The British Quarterly Review expected that the rise in wages consequent upon the discoveries would be permanent, and looked forward to 'the beginning of a very great and permanent improvement in the condition universally of the labouring classes'.[122] While radicals and liberals could applaud what they expected would be a redistribution in favour of the productive classes and of commerce and trade, there was also a kind of Tory paternalism, an echo of eighteenth-century country thought, which looked forward to a redistribution away from the merely moneyed towards the productive and, particularly, the agricultural classes. Archibald Alison in the staunchly Tory and protectionist Blackwood's Edinburgh Magazine thought the influx of gold would diminish the burden of taxes and debt, and that 'the unjust monopoly of realised capital will be arrested'. Blackwood's looked to gold to mitigate, though it could not cure, 'the dreadful evils of Free-Trade'.[123]

These, then, were the major stands of approving interpretation of the meaning of the gold discoveries. They were, in general, common to the two societies. Although there were obviously different inflections to the imperialist rhetorics, they shared a common stock of racial and racist arguments about the virtues of the Anglo-Saxon. The specific issues differed, and the concern about the relief of poverty in the home country seemed stronger in Australia, but exponents of the theory of an omniscient and omnipresent Providence were equally inventive in the two societies at discerning the reasons why they had been so especially rewarded with extraordinary amounts of worldly riches. And although laissez faire had importantly differing constituencies in the two societies, the heritage of free-trade ideas was a common one—the arguments of Adam Smith and his heirs were common currency on both sides of the Atlantic and the Pacific. In California and Victoria, only those with great faith in the results of unimpeded individual wealth seeking could offer whole-hearted approval of the gold rushes. The optimists posited some mechanism—imperial destiny, Providential design, or an invisible hand—which would order and control an apparently chaotic series of events.

Australia and the United States were headed in different directions on the question of state intervention in the economy. By the late nineteenth century the Australian colonies, and Victoria in particular, had the reputation for being something of a 'social laboratory' for experiments in state activity—pensions, wage arbitration, factory legislation—and even in the 1850s they can be seen to be moving in that direction. By 1850 in Britain, Serle argues:

> elementary legislation on public health, industrial conditions and education had been passed in the face of strong resistance of principle and self-interest. The long road to the welfare state was open and if 'laissez faire never had a chance in Victoria', it was largely because the question had already been decided before Victoria was created.[124]

The United States in 1850 was heading in the opposite direction, away from Commonwealth and further in the direction of laissez faire. There were indications in the late ante-bellum United States, Fine argues, that 'state activity was on the wane', although actual laissez faire ideology was not common.[125] Gold mining in California proceeded with little regulation, and was a practical explication of laissez faire principles. Hydraulic mining, the use of running water to tear the topsoil off a hillside, set up a sharp conflict of interest in California between miners and farmers. By 1853, Californian miners were using hoses with nozzles to direct pressured water, enabling the demolition of whole hillsides with relatively little human labour. Kelley argues that hydraulic mining, destructive as it was, 'was a process that expanded rapidly in conditions of absolute and complete laissez faire'. Both California and Victoria in the 1850s inherited laissez-faire ideologies, and in both parent societies those ideologies were associated with the reformist side of politics of a decade or two earlier—the English radicals, the Jacksonian Democrats. At some point in the mid-nineteenth century there is a change of positions on this issue, for by the later nineteenth century in the United States it is the Republicans who come to stand for laissez faire, just as it is the conservatives in Australia and Britain. Kelley's study of water management in California shows how Democratic state governments in the 1850s relied on laissez faire in flood control, in effect abandoning the problem to individual farmers. But, he argues, after the Civil War, California's political culture shifted toward 'corporate, team-spirit, and community-centred attitudes'.[126] Only so far though. David Alan Johnson stresses, that even for the later nineteenth-century Workingmen's Party in California, 'the heart of the republic rested in access to market opportunities by individuals'.[127]

Contemporaries and later nineteenth-century historians understood something about the gold rush that has to some extent been forgotten— that it was experienced as an invasion of market forces. Contemporary response was framed in those terms, and took the form of the assertion of a set of alternate, older and less competitive values. The legacy of gold may have had something to do with heading Victoria down its later protectionist path. 'Undoubtedly the problem of putting ex-miners to work, which was more onerous in suddenly populous Victoria than in New South Wales', Brian Fitzpatrick argued, 'was largely responsible for the protective system; Victoria's relative freedom from obligation to overseas capital was one of the conditions in which the colony struck out along a fiscal line of its own.'[128] Perhaps the post-gold direction of Victoria and California away from laissez faire had something to do with the perception of the gold rush as a time of unfettered individual enterprise, and the memory of the dislocations which accompanied it. Nostalgia for the individualism of the early gold rushes could not arise generally in Victoria until the 1890s, by which time economic depression and reduced expectations made even the lottery of gold seeking seem alluring.

CRITICISING GOLD: VICTORIA

This convulsion has unfixed everything. Religion is neglected, education despised, the libraries are almost deserted; nobody is doing anything great or generous, but everybody is engrossed by the simple object of making money in a very short time. I know that you can write the truth clearly, Gilbert . . . Put it to the good sense of our people and our government if, in circumstances like these, this colony is to be trusted to *supply and demand* for its moral and religious regeneration.

Catherine Helen Spence, **Clara Morison**

Californian engraving, 'The Hydraulic Method of Mining'. Courtesy Bancroft Library.

Radicals and conservatives in Victoria generally disapproved of gold-rush society because they could not in the end endorse a laissez faire social policy. Radicals, it is true, sometimes held out hopes that gold would bring about great and beneficial social transformation. For the Sydney radical John Dunmore Lang, the discoveries only confirmed the inevitability of Australian independence from Britain. He saw nothing inherently evil in

·the search for gold, and predicted a 'brilliant and glorious future for Australia'. A 'Constant Reader' wrote to the Melbourne *Argus* to express his opinion that 'when the news of the discovery reaches home . . . every person will be anxious to get away. The poor people, ground down with poverty, will now have a golden opportunity'. In London, too, there were radically utopian expectations. An Anglican minister wrote to the *Times* appealing to his fellow clergymen to 'organise an English Exodus' to the new 'Promised Land, overflowing with means of sustenance—a realized El Dorado' where 'the poor man, after a few months' labour' would be 'transformed into a prince'. 'Why should not,' he asked, 'this rich inheritance descend to the children of those labourers, mechanics, soldiers, sailors, who created that imperial power which won it?'[129]

Radicals sometimes also saw the improvement in the lot of the working people which gold promised as the last chapter in the decline of feudalism. Gold promised the chance to procure land in a new country, unburdened by the aristocratic monopolies and corruptions of the old world. English radicalism still often rhetorically opposed itself to the remnants of feudalism, rather than the coming industrial capitalist order. Thus 'An English Radical', writing in 1853, complained of the 'deadening and stiffening effects of the feudal system' which: 'still remain visible in our every-day life, in our habits, and our modes of thought . . . it still rests like an incubus on all our social state, still vitiates our laws, and still haunts the ideas, and festers in the minds of the men who, for the most part, rule over us'. The writer saw the colonies as places where the people could emancipate themselves from the remnants of the feudal system, and particularly from the aristocratic monopoly of the lands, and achieve at last an independence:

> The Anglo-Saxon population in leaving England . . . have shaken off the last links and fetters of that feudal mail, have freed themselves at length from Norman conquest and aristocratic rule, and have reverted, in all their thoughts and aspirations, to their old Anglo-Saxon habit, that of self-government. . .[130]

Liberals, too, tended to celebrate Victoria's liberation from English feudalism ('here no slavery . . . exists—no state church—none of the relics of feudal times—of an ancient aristocracy—of a military dominancy—of an enslaving priestcraft' wrote Frederick Vines in his *A Glorious Future for Australia*), while radicals often saw in colonial government policy covert attempts to reproduce the aristocratic dominance of the land familiar in England.[131] The prosperity which gold would bring to ordinary people could thus seem a chance to bring to an end historical injustices.

But despite such hopes, Australian radicals were ultimately uneasy about the sort of society gold seemed to be creating. They were unlikely to connect the free market to the achievement of equality, as California Democrats would. And their ideal of independence was the yeoman farmer, who seemed to them to embody the independence they sought. Rapidly in Victoria, the distribution of the land emerged as the leading item on the radical agenda, and the radical argument was precisely that there should not be a free market in land. It was only with government regulation, radicals argued, that monopoly of land by capitalists could be avoided. From the later 1850s, liberal and radical forces in Victoria united on a policy of economic protection. The Melbourne *Age* was their organ, regularly linking the cause of protection with that of progress. 'The laissez faire system will not answer in this country', the paper declared in 1857.[132] C.J. Don, a radical member of the Victorian parliament, looking back in 1864, gave an account of the gold rush highly critical of laissez faire. 'The people', he told a public meeting, had come from Britain and overwhelmed the generally wealthy squatters' undemocratic hold on the land, 'and very soon all their attempts to keep the people from "rushing" the gold fields proved ineffectual. In vain were the attempts of Crown rangers to turn them off; wages got higher, and the poor man at length got practical possession of this nuggety land. (Loud cheers).' But the people, he pointed out, had not triumphed entirely. They, the 'young, healthy, and hard working sons of the old country', still lacked access to the land for farms, had still not broken the squatters' monopoly on ownership. They were forced to live in the towns in poverty and misery. 'This was what free trade was doing,' Don declared, 'it had produced this abundance of misery, and it was slowly, but surely, defeating all other attempts to make Victoria a prosperous country.'[133] This was the dominant radical analysis in Victoria— thankful for the prosperity gold had briefly brought to the ordinary man, but sure that laissez faire was not the policy of the people in the long term.

The evidence of radical response to gold is fragmentary, but at a public meeting held in Melbourne on 10 June 1851 to discuss the effects of the New South Wales rush on Victoria, and to consider offering a reward for gold found in Victoria, there occurred a surprise intervention. A man, identified only as 'A WORKING MAN' (the anonymity, in a newspaper account which named each of the other speakers, is telling) rose from the body of the hall to put a dissident point of view:

> he believed he had as good a right to speak, as a working man, as anybody else. He would tell them that he came from Yorkshire. (Great confusion and cries of order). He wanted to know why they had not taken steps before now to find these mines and minerals? He could tell them—why all had had gods of their own, but for all that there was one God in whose worship they all agreed, and that was—gold. (Applause). Well, he was perfectly prepared to go with them and worship gold too, but he was not to be carried away by the gold mania. He had occupied the same situation for three years, indeed ever

since he had come to the colony, and he would most earnestly impress upon his fellow men that they should not leave their work and run away after gold finding. He did not believe that that meeting was really called for the advantage of the working classes. If those who had called it had wished to serve the working classes, they would have done something during the last three years, to remedy the dirty lanes and alleys, and the stagnant pools of Melbourne, for he could tell them health was always gold to the working man. He saw many of the corporation coming forward now, but why had they not come forward to remedy these evils? (Cries of order). He protested against the whole of the proceedings; the meeting was merely to enrich the rich and oppress the poor man. (Hisses and applause).[134]

Such voices are rare in the surviving record. This speech, with its key assertion that 'health was . . . gold to the working man', gives a hint of a respectable radical argument against gold, and of a continuing belief in a moral economy in which government had a crucial role to play in ensuring the welfare of the people.[135]

Australian historians have debated for decades the question of the radical political views of the gold diggers—the Left historians of the 1940s and 1950s celebrated the egalitarian and democratic qualities of the miners, while their conservative opponents disputed these qualities or minimised their significance. But because the target of much radicalism was feudal relics, aristocratic dominance of the land, Victorian radicalism in the 1850s seems not to have been so much concerned with defending the values associated with individual gold seeking as with articulating a right to the land, to a settled domestic life, and to peace and prosperity. It is for this reason that I count most radical responses to gold, although in some ways enthusiastic and even utopian, among the critical or pessimistic responses. Radicals did not see the social order prefigured in the gold rushes as any kind of proper basis for a new society. Theirs was not a purely individualist vision, because it held that the good society could not be realised without government control and protection—that is, crucially, that there should not be free trade in land. Victorian radicals, then, sometimes approved of gold, but not of the laissez-faire future that it seemed to presage.

British and Australian conservatives, like radicals, generally disapproved of gold because they too had an ideal of active and paternal government. Australia inherited the politics of nineteenth-century Britain, and Victorians habitually and unselfconsciously used the language of class to analyse the state of their society. Democracy was something to be agitated for, though great faith was still generally placed in the mixed form of government in which the popular voice was balanced by other and more stable interests; the power of the great landed elites was something to be curtailed or defended. As Asa Briggs has noted, mid-Victorian Britain 'prided itself not on its equality but on its balance, on its nuances of social status'.[136] Elites in Victoria usually posed the problem of gold in terms of a threat to a stable hierarchy, to the influence of persons appropriate to dominance and governance. 'It is sad,' lamented the *Melbourne Morning Herald*, 'that the gentleman should change places with the lucky black-guard.'[137] Much humour was generated by dramatising the absurdity of working men and women being suddenly enriched.[138] In Britain the *Quarterly Review* observed: 'These discoveries altered the conditions of society. Those on the lowest rounds of the ladder suddenly found themselves at the top of it . . . It is contrary to all our notions that a policeman or a scavenger should be entitled to as high wages as a government clerk.'[139]

The Chief Justice, William a'Beckett, was throughout the 1850s one of the most explicit defenders of an hierarchical and classed society. 'Distinctions and grades', he told the Melbourne Total Abstinence Society in 1851: 'there will always be in any constitution of civilized society . . . "Equality", as has well been said, "is the dream of a madman, or the passion of a fiend" '.[140] a'Beckett worried that gold would erase the distinctions so necessary, in his conservative view, to a civilized community. His 1852 pamphlet, *Does the Discovery of Gold in Victoria, Viewed in Relation to its Moral and Social Effects, as Hitherto Developed, Deserve to be Considered a National Blessing or a National Curse?*, articulated the concern that the erosion of the external signs of class and distinction would eventually also erode the substance of civilisation:

> The general contempt of dress and personal appearance, the crowding together of numbers in places where decent accommodation can hardly be provided for one—the smoking and drinking and swearing . . . all this might have a tendency to weaken that regard for external decencies, and to impair that sense of self-respect, which lies at the foundation of the manners, not to say the morals, of civilized and domestic life. Certainly these are not the substantials of existence; but they are most valuable accessories, and without them we should speedily relapse into a state of barbarism.[141]

Manners were crucial to civilisation because they were part of the preservation of a civil public life. Thomas a'Beckett, William's brother, insisted on the role of government in controlling and regulating the gold rush, and argued that government should be the beneficiary of some of the wealth, that it might be used for public purposes like roads, harbours and railroads, as well as 'Religion, Education, water supply, well-lighted streets, public promenades, parks and gardens'—the construction of a public sphere. 'All I ask,' he wrote, 'is the assent of the community to the proposition that the Government shall have the power of regulating the amount of labour to be bestowed upon the discovery of Gold, and that a portion of the Gold when discovered shall be applied to the public service.'[142] Conservatives in Victoria were far from happy with the unleashed individual wealth seeking which was the gold rush.

For some Victorian liberals, especially for members of the successful mercantile class, gold had brought only beneficial changes to the colony. Paul de Serville, historian of Melbourne's upper class, writes of the swamping of the old elite by the new wealth of the 1850s.[143] Those who owed their wealth to gold were less likely to criticise its other social effects. 'The discovery of the apparently boundless richness of our gold fields has given an immense impetus to this country,' wrote Melbourne merchant James Graham in June 1852, 'and increased the value of property very much.'[144]

Social upheaval, however, did concern some prominent liberals. William Westgarth, Melbourne merchant and a true free-trade liberal of the most optimistic laissez faire school, confessed to the Melbourne Chamber of Commerce in his 1853 anniversary address that 'we must all admit that the colony has suffered as well as gained by her recent developments'. Even Westgarth was arguing that 'the accustomed relations and gradations of society have been too suddenly upset'.[145] The British Quarterly Review, too, expressed some concern at the conditions of production at the goldfields where gold was gained by labour 'not under the direction of masters, and without the intervention of capital':

> Civilized man is thus again placed as it were under the primaeval laws of nature, which bestows on its labour all its produce . . . The 'Diggers', independent of capitalists in an extraordinary manner, considering the general relations of society, and little liable to the multiplied exactions of government, acquire, possess, and enjoy the produce of their own mere manual toil.[146]

The loss of the surplus value of the labour might, the Review warned, make the cost of production of the gold very high. Even for liberals in England and Australia, there was something very anomalous about the idea of masterless labour. There were very few in Victoria so committed to laissez faire that they could entirely approve of the gold rushes as events.

CRITICISING GOLD: CALIFORNIA

These were not the ways in which Americans talked critically about the dislocations of California. The United States was a republic, and one in which white adult male suffrage was already almost a generation old. Its official ideologies spoke of equality of opportunity, celebrated both national and personal independence, and the fluidity of social life. In the United States, the discussion of gold was not to do with its upsetting the natural order of society, but rather with the limits of individualism, and the republican themes of the dangers of wealth and the necessity of keeping government small. The Democratic Review, in its initial response to the Californian discoveries, made this clear. It rejected suggestions of licences to dig for gold: 'all idea of force or restraint would seem to be to the last degree puerile', it argued, for 'the worst possible evil which could befall the country would be for the government to command any considerable portion of the money. The guarantee of republicanism is governmental poverty.' But the *Review* went further. It foresaw gold making a more perfect republican system possible:

> The gold deposits in the new territory may now offer the means, without resorting to direct taxation, to abolish all customs duties, discharge 10,000 officers from the pay of government, and from interference with the elective franchise; and also to abolish all postages, and defray the whole expense of the department from the same source, *carrying all letters and newspapers free to all parts of the Union*. By this means we may present to the world the glorious spectacle of a free people, governed absolutely without taxation, or the creation of any machinery like the pernicious protective system, contrived to fleece the many in order to pamper the wealth of the few.[147]

Here gold was expected to fund a republican utopia: free and extensive communication and trade, almost no government, no taxation.

On the other side of American politics there was less faith in the beneficence of the republican system on its own, and more concern about controlling the rampant individualism which California seemed to have unleashed. The Whig *American Review* wrote that:

> It is not in mere forms of government; not in the fullest, world-wide development of democratic institutions, to save and regenerate the world. Men must learn to reverence something higher than money and themselves; they must learn that the spirit of self-will is not the genius of true freedom.[148]

This was not the plea of the Victorian conservative for rank and distinction in the public sphere, but a distinctly American argument for some limitation on individuals and their independence from control and responsibility. 'The state cannot be a mere aggregate of individuals', argued the Reverend Laurens P. Hickock for the American Home Mission Society. 'SELFISH-NESS is the tyrant foe to our happiness', preached the Reverend William Scott in San Francisco, 'SELF must be crucified'.[149] To a considerable extent, this argument *was* American conservatism. For American Whigs, Ashworth argues, 'the ultimate evil in the all conquering ethos of democracy was its enthronement of the individual as an autonomous, self-sufficient unit'.[150] But the solution often proposed was self-regulation, rather than government. That was the liberal discovery. There were more positions on the Californian political spectrum from which gold might be approved than there were in Victoria.

EXPERIENCING GOLD

San Francisco's charismatic Reverend W.A. Scott, called to San Francisco from New Orleans, carefully distinguished the 'moral evil' of self interest from the 'mutuality of self interest' which made of commerce a moral good.

He was on balance optimistic about the effects of gold, and though he warned against the over-valuing of worldly riches, he devoted himself to providing a legitimating synthesis of the Bible and free trade.[151] 'The danger to our country from the rapid increase of wealth,' he argued, 'is in a great degree neutralised by the rapidity with which it changes hands.'[152] In Scott's paradigmatic optimistic thought, it was commerce which would save California from the perils of gold.

It was men like Scott, the economic rationalists of the period, who could happily approve of gold. They took the larger view, imbued with an ideological faith in ultimate outcomes, and the wisdom of laissez faire. The good-hearted ordinary diggers about whom Harte and Lawson wrote were unlikely in the 1850s to have been so enthusiastic or so optimistic. 'To people intending to come out here,' David Matthew Watson wrote home to Edinburgh from Forest Creek, 'I would say, read no books, they all tell lies, and believe very few old settlers, for they mostly become brutes.'[153] 'My thoughts often wander from this land of gold and misery,' Albert Lyman wrote from California, 'to that cherished home of loved beings.'[154] Ordinary men of the gold period have left us writings which complain about the heat and the flies, the extraordinary cost of basic provisions, the frauds and swindles, the sickness and the disappointments. They wrote to their friends at home imploring them not to throw up good jobs to join them at the diggings. They complained of the emptiness of life in a society in which the shared scramble for wealth was the only common bond. Ordinary diggers were generally pessimists about gold-rush society.

CHAPTER 2

WEALTH AND
REPUBLICANISM

CALIFORNIA

> The gold-digger is the enemy of the honest laborer, whatever
> checks and compensations there may be. It is not enough to
> tell me that you worked hard to get your gold. So does the
> Devil work hard.
>
> *Henry David Thoreau*

The nature of wealth was one of the issues underlying almost all of the
discussions generated by the gold discoveries. Russell Nye, in his general
study of *Society and Culture in America*, found the 1850s to be a time of
particular concern about the too urgent love of worldly gain, a materialism
feared to have blunted the nation's idealism.[1] Fred Somkin, too, discovered
that in the decades before the Civil War 'a wide-spread uneasiness reflected
the fear that American success had poisoned the springs of the national
spirit'.[2] California, and those who rushed to it, were obvious targets for
this kind of critique. Gold did not pose a novel problem for many
Americans, merely an exaggerated instance of an old one. 'This gold fever
is not a new disease', H.T. Tuckerman observed in *Godey's Magazine*, 'it is
one of the most familiar and well defined'.[3] Gold presented, in heightened
and exaggerated form, an issue which had been at the centre of social and
religious thought for some time—what would be the consequences of
allowing to come into being an entirely individualised society, in which
each was preoccupied solely with the project of acquiring his own individual fortune?

Analysis of the problems associated with the gold rush thus merged into
older and larger discourses about the materialist nature of American society

as a whole. Californians believed themselves to be an unusually wealth-hungry people. 'Here,' a California writer argued, 'more than in any other land, the lust for wealth is the all-absorbing passion of society'.[4] The Unitarian Reverend R.B. Cutler in his 1856 Thanksgiving sermon in San Francisco observed that although the love of money was an affliction by no means peculiar to Americans, 'never, perhaps, was the appetite so active, so urgent and keen in any entire nation, as it is, at this moment, in our own'.[5]

Eliza Farnham wrote despairingly of California that the 'mercenary spirit is a more despotic tyrant in this land of freemen than czar or sultan could be in a land of slaves'. She could only hope that an awareness was growing that there were 'truer purposes in human existence than the accumulation of wealth'.[6] Others were less hopeful. The Episcopalian Reverend Flavel S. Mines told his congregation in San Francisco in 1852 that: 'when I saw Mammon in his gorgeous trappings, pouring his legions from the caves and hills, and waters laden with gold, so that our very priests that bear the ark were tempted to trail their snowy vestments in the miners' dust, I saw the day was lost'.[7]

For Henry David Thoreau, the pursuit of wealth in California was further evidence of the American propensity to devote all of life to business and money making: 'we are warped and narrowed by an exclusive devotion to trade and commerce and manufactures and agriculture and the like, which are but means, and not the end'. Gold digging was objectionable to him because it seemed a pure form of wealth seeking: 'To have done anything by which you earned money *merely* is to have been truly idle or worse.' He criticised devotion to any activity for its own sake: 'I see advertisements for *active* young men, as if activity were the whole of a young man's capital . . . I wish to suggest that a man may be very industrious, and yet not spend his time well.'[8] For Thoreau too, gold did not pose a new problem; it was but a further and exaggerated instance of a prevalent confusion of the means and ends of life.

But what was to be added to money making to constitute a full life? Some advised more attention to leisure and recreation. R.B. Cutler used his 1856 Thanksgiving sermon to call for more 'public days of pastime' and 'release from toil and anxiety':

> The hard crust of materialism . . . should be broken up more frequently, by the insertion here and there of appointed days of amusement and recreation. Throughout the whole country, and most eminently true is it here, where visions of gold dazzle every eye, there is an eager haste and excitement over the great matter of becoming *rich*.[9]

Another minister similarly defined the problem as an unhealthy *concentration* on wealth seeking at the expense of other activities:

47

Photograph: Portsmouth Plaza San Francisco, looking north. Graves collection, Courtesy Bancroft Library.

a man's energies become concentrated in a burning focus, on one single point—money; and this absorbing idea is strengthened by the obstacles and obstructions it meets in the way of its realization until it draws within its sweep all other considerations and rides over them, reckless of the consequences to character and influence.[10]

Such clerical and critical discussions of wealth had their counterparts in Victoria. What was more distinctive to California was the use of the ideology of republicanism, with its theme of civic virtue and its preoccupation with the rise and fall of nations, as a resource by critics of gold. The debates among historians over the past two decades about the dimensions and longevity of the influence of republican ideology in the United States go to the heart of the issues of individual wealth seeking and its merits as the basis of a social order. For the arguments about republicanism are arguments about the transition to liberal and capitalist modernity. The very idea that there *was* a transition in the United States is in some ways new to American historiography. Historians now debate the timing of the transition—when and in what terms the capitalist values of liberal individualism triumphed in the United States over the older communitarian or republican values. If a consensus is already appearing it is that republicanism, in the form that J.G.A. Pocock and others described it, persisted for much longer than previously thought, and that through the nineteenth century there were competing ideological formations in American public life.[11] Banning points to ways of thinking that were 'moving toward an ultimate predominance of liberal and democratic values' yet in which 'liberal ideas were so entwined with concepts coming from a different tradition that the consequence would never be the liberal monolith that scholars once described'.[12] In the United States at mid-century, then, we would expect to find both liberal individualist and republican languages, strategically competing and combining as explanatory and justificatory rhetorics.

Californian gold created the spectacle of men abandoning all for the individual pursuit of wealth. Some approved their actions in the language of laissez-faire individualism, and others disapproved them, drawing upon the older language of republicanism. In a recent study, David Alan Johnson has contrasted the republican ideology apparent in Oregon politics with the greater hold of liberal individualism in California and Nevada. He notes that gold-rush migrants to California carried with them 'an exaggerated sampling' of attitudes dominant in the United States at the time, especially 'an idealisation of self-seeking within a market society'— 'Although they never used the term, *laissez faire* captures a central conviction amongst them'.[13] Liberal individualism certainly predominated in California. In a comparison with Victoria, however, the persistence of republican thought in California, as a residual tradition, becomes more visible.

Classical republican ideology promoted, first of all, anxieties about wealth and the corrupting effects of luxury. The pessimistic republican account of the effect of gold on California stressed the dissipation and surrender to the passions which might be expected when wealth spread throughout society, and gloomily depicted the national decline which would inevitably follow. The Reverend William Scott knew the theory well. If there were no checks on the accumulation of wealth, he argued: 'Effeminacy, dissipation, luxury and crime would know no bounds.'[14] The republican idea was in part that a virtuous citizenry was essential to the survival of the republic. Economic conditions threatened that virtue from two directions—from the servile dependence that came with poverty, and from the luxurious living that was the inevitable concomitant of wealth.

Republican ideology entailed a cyclical view of history. The cycle which led nations from primitive conditions through barbarism to agricultural society, then to commercial society and empire, and thence into decline, could be learned from classical sources, but it had been systematised and popularised by the eighteenth-century Scottish thinkers who were so influential in America.[15] The Scottish account of the 'four stages' of civilization served merely to reinforce republican anxieties about wealth, and the prosperity of the highest stage. For in republican thinking, the theme of decline was ever present. What Pocock has called the 'Machiavellian moment' was the moment when the republic confronted itself in time, recognised its own finitude and the certainty of its own eventual decline.

American Protestant religion proved quite able to combine its own Christian themes of the dangers of wealth and worldliness with republican anxieties on the same subjects, skilfully blending the vocabularies of secular virtue and spiritual salvation. The Reverend Laurens P. Hickok preached a sermon in both New York and Brooklyn in May 1853 on behalf of the American Home Missionary Society, which was already actively engaged in mission work in California. His text was 'it is easier for a camel to pass through the eye of a needle'. He began by declaring unequivocally that 'riches exclude from heaven', and arguing that this applied as much to nations as it did to individuals. His understanding of history was therefore pessimistic, as corruption seemed unavoidably to follow wealth: 'The natural course of a rich nation is to destruction. It will trust in its prosperity, and boast of its destiny, and lose its integrity, and bring upon itself its own ruin . . . Its very abundance will corrupt its own members'. The lessons from the classical world were clear. Rome's wealth 'was also her ruin': 'Luxury and venality and anarchy prepared the way, and the great . . . metropolis of the world was sacked by hordes of northern barbarians.' The position led Hickok into a critique of laissez faire, for his republican determinism seemed to suggest that to leave man alone was to condemn him to decline: 'From the great facts which history teaches, we thus confirm the truth . . . take man as he is, and as he makes states to be, and give him wealth and power, and let him take his own course, and he will dig the grave of any nation.'

This diagnosis led Hickok to a particularly gloomy assessment of the future of the United States. All the conventional grounds for celebrating American success came to seem, on this strict republican assessment, only further reasons for pessimism. 'Never was such progress made,' he observed, 'in the attainment of all that ministers to the material greatness of a nation, among any people as in our nation.' America was endangered by nothing except its own prosperity: 'our danger of death is only from plethora. Should our grand experiment ultimately fail, it will doubtless be because our prosperity is greater than our virtue can bear.' This was for Hickok a peculiarly American problem only to the extent that American prosperity was peculiarly great. The social criticism was based on a reading of all history, not on an argument about the special characteristics or destiny of the Americans:

An increase of luxury, dissipation, prodigality, inducing popular effeminacy and frivolity; a growth of ambition, ostentation, vain-glory, begetting national self-conceit, arrogance and insolence; all bringing in venality and corruption

... destroying the very life of all patriotism and public liberty, this is common everywhere to the rapid acquisition of national wealth.[16]

It was a characteristic of republican thinking that it was universalistic, and even when merged, as here, with American Protestantism, it retained its universalist character.[17]

American Home Missionary Society ministers were active in California from 1848. By 1858 there were 28 New School Presbyterian and Congregationalist ministers in California, 'nearly all of whom had been sent there by the American Home Missionary Society'.[18] These ministers' often gloomy analyses of the prospects for Californian society illustrate the hold which some of these republican themes had upon them. The all-absorbing pursuit of wealth was their greatest complaint, and the participation of church members in the general stampede their greatest embarrassment. 'The great body of Christians . . . it is well known', the Reverend J.W. Douglas wrote back to headquarters:

> come expressly for gold, and with very little idea of remaining longer than time sufficient to amass it. Their main object, their chief, some may say, only motive in coming here is to get rich in the shortest possible time . . . Why, talk to an impenitent man about making wealth his idol, and he has an answer always ready for you. 'Sir, those Christians!', 'How earnest to get rich!', 'What do *they* chiefly desire now but gold?', 'As much absorbed in its pursuit as any of us.' [19]

Douglas explained that in these conditions he had been able to accomplish 'but little' in California. Other AHMS ministers shared his pessimism. W.W. Brier wrote from Marysville that 'the golden mountain has great power to draw the Divine electricity from the souls of men'.[20] He also believed that the prosperity of California was responsible for its resistance to the Christian message. Behind the Christian complaints about the all-absorbing pursuit of wealth, or concerns about the indolence that might arise in an arcadian environment, lay a republican theory about the growth and inevitable corruption and decay of societies. Our civilization 'can not sustain itself at this high pitch very long', wrote J.A. Benton, 'Its own vices will destroy it'.[21] This republican language could thus be used both for congratulation and warning, a reminder of the splendour and fragility of the achievements of civilisations.

The republican theme of wealth and decline was thus prominent in commentary on Californian society. The links between wealth, luxury and decline had become sufficiently part of the common currency of social and political thought that a fairly brief invocation of the key terms of the argument was sufficient. The Reverend Orange Clark, addressing his congregation in San Francisco, observed that: 'Wealth enervates and causes the progeny of the rich to degenerate and sink downward in influence.'[22]

The Whig *American Review*, in discussing California, offered a warning about the future:

> Grandeur and wealth, luxury and corruption, dissolution and ruin, this is the brief but accurate summary of the history of the extinct, but once most powerful empires of the ancient world . . . without some adequate conservative moral power, our national history will sooner or later be summed up in the same words.

The Whig response was a call for restraint: 'What a hell upon earth, if the boundless lust of gold be unrestrained, unsanctified by better influences. Pandemonium was built of molten gold.'[23] Reynell Coates wrote in *Sartain's Magazine* that it was: 'a wise law of the Omniscient, written in glaring capitals upon the page of history, that wealth abused inevitably leads through luxury to weakness and ultimate slavery.'[24] C.E. Havens argued that there were no bounds to the Californian and American future, unless 'we . . . corrupt our manhood and sink into premature decay'. But, he argued, 'if we austerely guard our virtues, time will ever lend us a helping hand'.[25] Republican thought could be used to construct timely and culturally resonant warnings to Californians that, not only would wealth of itself not guarantee individual happiness, but society itself might decay if the pursuit of wealth became the sole motivation for action.

Gold also posed questions about work. The search for gold was wealth seeking shorn of any intermediary transactions or exchanges. The gold hunter was conceived as a solitary, indeed a selfish figure, who had no necessary contacts with the society around him, unlike the labourer, the merchant or the farmer. He seemed, in terms of the thought of the day, to threaten a reversion to an earlier 'stage' of civilisation. Guardians of the moral order in America were troubled specifically by this direct nexus between the individual and wealth, and it was in part a republican vocabulary they drew upon to make their criticisms. Work normally involved mediation of some kind, labour at the production of goods or services which subsequently and consequently had an exchange value. Gold digging was anomalous in these terms because the product was money itself. H.T. Tuckerman, writing in *Godey's Magazine*, went so far as to posit a law of nature ('one of the most universal, occult and inexorable of natural laws') which he termed the 'indirect method'. The law, Tuckerman reported, stated that 'nature does not yield her choicest gifts except, as it were, incidentally'. Wealth, he assured his readers, was only really available indirectly, through labour, invention, patience or care. Wealth picked up directly from the earth would be necessarily inauthentic, 'like a stolen badge of honor or a forged passport—a facility, not genuine, authentic or capable of realizing the good of which it is the illegitimate sign'. The anxiety reflected here was about the necessity of work and the discipline attached to waged labour in preserving social order and control, but it was expressed in moral economic terms, as an argument about the nature of real wealth, which derived ultimately from the celebration of the producer which was at the heart of republican thinking. Tuckerman's concern was both about gold digging as an apparently illegitimate form of work, not productive of real wealth, and about the possibility that in California fortune, rather than virtue or diligence, would come to govern rewards gained. On the goldfields, the quantity of labour bore no necessary relation to the magnitude of the reward—months of diligent labour might bring no reward, a lucky swing of the pick might bring comfort for life. It was rather too vehemently that Tuckerman sought to reassure his readers that 'moral causes lie at the basis of all enduring good fortune'.[26] The Reverend Charles Farley was expressing the same concerns when he argued in his 1850 Thanksgiving sermon that 'so far from complaining, every true man should rejoice that gold cannot be picked up on the surface, and everywhere, but requires, like everything else worth having, hard and patient toil'.[27] The threatened disappearance of labor as the necessary and controlling mediator between the individual and wealth was a problem in republican thinking, at the same time as it obviously posed problems of social control—how could the working population be persuaded to lead diligent and obedient lives if the belief that hard work was the basis of wealth were to be undermined?

These arguments were clerical and moral/paternal uses of the republican arguments, uses with which a Whig would have been happier than a Democrat. They formed a significant framework of response to Californian gold, and one relatively easy to locate in the historical record. Protestant ministers were among the most prominent and vocal commentators on the Californian rush, and their views were often recorded in print. The pessimistic republican argument on the effects of gold came most loudly from the churches, as ministers sternly denounced the short-sighted pursuit of worldly riches—though of course most were careful to qualify their criticisms of wealth seeking in general.

More fugitive are the radical uses of republican thought which draw attention, not to the sweep of history and the decay of empires, but to the distribution of wealth within society, for religious pessimism about the enrichment of the populace was open to some obvious democratic objections. 'We find,' wrote 'Oliver Outcast', 'that those who have most delighted to philosophize on the vanity of riches have been those who literally rolled in wealth. King Solomon was one of the earliest to discover that "all was vanity", and there is no reason to suppose he ever suffered for the necessaries of life.'[28]

The shoemaker Samuel McNeil put the optimistic and democratic case about gold:

Some preachers have asserted from the pulpit . . . that the straightest way to California is the nearest road to hell; but as fanaticism never can be right, I must believe that the discovery of California gold will be a general blessing to the earth, aiding in extending religion, philosophy, and commerce—not only benefiting the public generally, but shining gladness into many a private circle.

McNeil wrote an account of his travels in California in 1849 in proudly egalitarian voice. He criticised those who were doubtful of the outcome of the gold rushes, arguing that the gold could fund an ideal republic: 'God has placed those golden placers in our way, saying unto us: "Yea, verily I say unto you, ye shall take of the gold I have provided, and therewith build on the sacred mount of republican principles the Temple of Liberty".'[29] Eliza Farnham argued that the thousands of men who had come to California had: 'aided throughout the world, more powerfully than any contemporary laboring class, the growth of that republican sentiment whose rugged justice threatens the throne and smiles upon the hovel'.[30]

To these authors, gold seemed to have democratic and republican implications. Their optimistic republicanism was articulated against the patrician gloom of the clerical denunciations of the social effects of gold. Samuel McNeil told an anecdote typical of those which also abounded in descriptions of the Australian goldfields:

> A sailor was at my tent. The captain of a vessel wished to hire him to accompany the former to Oregon. The captain offered him $250 per month. The sailor asked $300. The captain observed that that was too much, and he could not give it. The sailor then retorted, that if this captain would accompany and help him at the mines he would give him $300 per month and board. This is the only country where I have seen true democracy prevailing.[31]

This is a story about the overturning of deference and hierarchy. In Australia, as what I term the 'colonial narrative',[32] it formed the staple of travellers' accounts of gold-rush society. In democratic and republican California, such an equality of manners was already supposed to exist, and the story was less common as a narrative about class. It had other uses there though. The Virginian James Carson recorded a story in his *Life in California*:

> I remember the captain of a brig on the beach at San Francisco, who had a crew, with the exception of a cook. He met a negro, and asked him if he wished to go as cook on his brig. The negro, after cocking his hat on the side of his head, and bringing his arms akimbo, coolly inquired the wages offered. The captain informed him that ten dollars a day was as much as he could afford. The negro, at this offer, burst into a loud laugh, and informed the captain 'Dat if de *capten* wished to hire heself out for *twenty* dollars a day to fill dat occupation, jes walk up to de restaurant, and he would set him to work immediently.'[33]

The narratives of inversion were made for metropolitan entertainment—
they emphasised the absurdity of the inversions which occurred on the
fringes. Alonzo Delano, a Grass Valley merchant and writer, evoked in his
1857 play, *A Live Woman in the Mines*, a happily open and egalitarian world
in which the markers of class and region remained, but with only comic
consequences, as their irrelevance to the new world was shown. All could
be enriched; the overturning of an older social order was available as matter
for comedy.[34] In California, more commonly than in Victoria, there was a
radical republican belief that classes and social hierarchies were unnatural
things, sustained only by the intervention of corrupt governments. Laissez
faire, in California, was for a time a radical doctrine.

At the Constitutional Convention in Monterey in 1849 which drafted
the first Californian constitution, Democrats offered republican arguments
of an egalitarian kind against banks, corporations and paper money in
California. 'The people of California are peculiarly a laboring people,'
argued Rodman Price, 'they are miners, sir, who live by pick and shovel,
and "by the sweat of their brow, earn their bread."' As a Democrat, Price
endorsed laissez faire as the means by which equality of condition would
be achieved: 'Our people, sir, will be most happy to abide by the laws of
trade, and require no false credit or artificial regulation. In short, sir, I
believe the broad doctrine of free trade and free banking as most applicable
to their condition.'[35] William Gwin, soon to become one of the first United
States senators from California, put similar laissez-faire arguments to the
convention. He argued that banks would only enrich those 'who live by
their wits' at the expense of the 'hard-handed gold digger, who by his labor,
enriches the country'. He defended the miners, as the legitimate producers
of wealth, as 'the people': 'Let us guard against infringing on the rights of
the people, by legalising the association of capital to war upon labor. This
is the only country on the globe where labor has the complete control of
capital. Let it remain so if we would be free, independent and prosperous.'[36]
Although the Convention, as David Alan Johnson argues, 'effectively
legalised banks', it did so in the midst of a 'torrent of invective' against
them.[37] And that invective was full of republican arguments about the real
producers of wealth, and their need to be free from the interference of
corrupt governments.

When a Miners and Settlers Convention met in 1852, it recommended
'most earnestly' to the mining communities that they not sanction the
making of any new claims to men who 'already have enough', and it argued
that there was a danger of a 'mining aristocracy' growing up in California.
In supporting the 'real and actual miner', against the 'spirit of speculation',
the Miners and Settlers Convention was expressing a republican and radical
sense that the gold rush was supposed to create and support a society of
equals, and that the speculation and profiteering characteristic of the world

outside should have no place there.[38] But they departed from the analysis of the Democratic politicians in that they began to argue that intervention was necessary to prevent monopoly and unrepublican elites.

This equalitarian republicanism was quite a different thing from the patrician classical republicanism articulated by the ministers of California, yet they derived from the same sources, and shared a vocabulary of concern about the moral and social implications of the accumulation of wealth. These republican doctrines could be used to argue for equality or opportunity for enrichment, or alternatively for the importance of establishing or strengthening a public sphere and of civic virtue—a public orientation which might lead to a patrician criticism of an excessive preoccupation with individual wealth seeking among the populace. This republicanism was a major ideological resource in California, and its existence there marks one of the important differences between the two cultures.

VICTORIA

Although one can find isolated expressions of concern about the cyclical histories of nations and the corrupting effects of wealth and luxury, these were not common in mid-nineteenth-century Australia.[39] There are, however, arguments about the importance of the public sphere as more than the site of struggle between competing individual interests, and arguments about the importance of the private and domestic sphere and its values in an increasingly market-governed world. It was in general the barrenness of materialism that troubled Victorian conservatives, rather than the corrupting effects of wealth and the moral career of the wealthy nation. And Victorian radicals tended to argue that laissez faire would increase inequalities of wealth rather than diminish them, as they focussed their attention on the land and the people's right to it.

Redmond Barry, delivering the Inaugural Address to the Victorian Institute, spoke approvingly of the formation of libraries, societies and the new university which was taking place in Melbourne. 'All this points,' he said, 'to prove that the barren acquisition of money does not satisfy the cravings of a people who possess a comprehension beyond that of the method of acquiring it.'[40] Barry was a tireless exponent of the view that culture could be recognised by its detachment from the utilitarianism and materialism of the age. He also, like other conservative critics, dwelt upon the decline of the public sphere and its values in the frenzy of the private pursuit of gold. The theme was a common one, and could be articulated in travellers' books with comic exaggeration:

> society, in the common acceptation of the term, there is none; for the heterogenous mass thrown together in Melbourne, have no interest in common. Intercourse is restricted to buying and selling whenever men are

gathered together . . . for salutations you have bids; and the answer to inquiries are taken from the price list.[41]

Education in Victoria was intended to help overcome the materialist and selfish tendencies of gold rush society. The first Report of the Commissioners of National Education argued that National (public) schools at the goldfields would be 'conducive to the encouragement of the higher social feelings of that numerous body of our countrymen who occupy the Gold Fields of the Colony'.[42] In Victoria, 'higher' meant 'social'—that was simply part of the commonsense of the period.

Criticism of the excessive pursuit of worldly riches was of course a standard Christian theme, but it was one used to good effect by gold-rush clerics in Australia. The Catholic Bishop Polding in Sydney worried at Lent in 1852 about the children of the gold-rush generation. The children would suffer, he warned, if 'the world and its follies are made by you the subject of praise and of admiration, if the possession of wealth and the means of sensual enjoyment be continually spoken of, as above all other things to be coveted and sought after'. Children had somehow to be taught, in the midst of what the Bishop clearly imagined as excessive material success, to 'esteem a life of industry—to love honest labour, to hold in utter contempt that miserable existence made up of idleness, vanity, and arrogance, of sensuality and foppishness, which frequently is met with in the present day'.[43] The possibility of a society in which work would no longer be necessary for all, animated, as threat or fantasy, much gold-rush rhetoric.

The eagerness of the gold seeking, the energy it drew forth, seemed almost an affront to Christian critics of the period in Victoria. Earthly possessions, George M. Hardess reminded his readers, were 'but vain illusions'.[44] 'Man searches diligently for the gold that perisheth', the Mayor of Melbourne told a meeting in 1858, 'but what criminal apathy does he not evince when admonished to seek the everlasting treasures of heaven'.[45] The Reverend Adam Cairns, prominent Presbyterian minister, warned in 1856 of all 'being swept away in the engrossing current of worldliness, which forms a conspicuous feature in the constitution and habit of colonial life'.[46] Other ministers struggled to imagine a holy society which would have a place for great wealth. The Reverend Robert Hamilton, of the Melbourne working-class suburb of Collingwood, spoke in a sermon of the streets of gold in the kingdom of Christ, 'with its golden treasures, its stainless purity, its matchless legislature, its ennobling employments, its blissful inhabitants'.[47]

Bishop Perry's writings for the Melbourne *Church of England Messenger* during these years articulate his concerns about the likely effects of gold. They can stand as a well-articulated statement of conservative concerns about wealth in gold-rush Victoria. Perry's first extended article on the

'Ballarat Gold Fields' was published in November 1851. When the Bishop asked himself whether gold would be a force for good or evil, the alternatives were stark—gold could act 'for the increased prosperity of this Colony, and for the happiness of its people; or for the destruction of social order, and the introduction of an age of barbarism amongst us'. Perry had many reasons for contemplating the pessimistic assessment:

> The employment of so many hundreds, we might say thousands, in searching for gold, with the prodigious profits which many of them make, in our opinion, naturally tends to demoralise those who are engaged in it, to exercise a pernicious influence upon others, and to derange the whole system of Society.

The only example he could see before him of the effect of gold on a society was contemporary California, and 'the picture which California presents is indeed a frightful one'.[48]

There were three main reasons that Perry offered for fearing the effects of gold. The first was that gold threatened to make the poor rich. This was troubling to the Bishop because he thought the poor would not have any legitimate use for their new wealth. The 'actual wants', he wrote, 'of one, who has not been accustomed to the refinements of the educated classes, are exceedingly few, and satisfied at a very small cost.' There was a problem when the excitable lower classes were too suddenly enriched— with the 'large amount of money suddenly put into the hands of men, who know no other enjoyment than the gratification of their appetites', members of the 'lower—we mean the uneducated, unreflecting, and sensual portion of the community'.[49] The sudden acquisition of wealth by members of the labouring classes would 'destroy that sobriety of mind which is essential both to real happiness, and to a consistent Christian course of conduct'.[50] Gold threatened the settled order of society, and the acceptance of their place by those at the bottom of it. Perry was moved by the threat he perceived to a full articulation of his social philosophy:

> We know that there are many, who exult in the expectation that the poor will now have their rights; and there is no one who desires more heartily than we do, that every man, whether he be rich or poor, should have his rights. But we are convinced, that the happiness of the labouring, as well as of those who are called the higher classes, will be most securely promoted by the preservation of a sound social system; with a gradation of rank, based upon morality, education, natural abilities, refined tastes, and gentle manners.

Perry's second objection to gold was that it made the acquisition of wealth an arbitrary process, unrelated to work or worth, to 'integrity, good judgement, and diligence'. He wanted a way to exclude from the upper class 'those, who have nothing but their suddenly acquired riches to recommend them to it; and we therefore tremble at the consequence to a small community like this of the accumulation of wealth by many through mere good fortune'. Gold thus threatened to de-naturalise the order upon which Victorian society was instituted, to create a society in which rank was seen to be arbitrary. Perry pointed to the precariousness of the returns to be expected from gold seeking:

> This uncertainty gives to the occupation the character of a lottery, in which some draw large prizes, and the rest draw only blanks. There will therefore be naturally produced the feverish excitement, and all the evil passions which are engendered by gambling.

Perry's third objection to gold was that it weakened domestic ties by 'withdrawing the husband and father from his wife and children'. At stake was the morality of the rising generation and beyond them of the whole society. Here Perry feared 'the diminished enjoyment of home comforts, the ignorance and want of subordination in the rising generation, and the derangement of the whole social system'.[51] The linking of home comforts to the welfare of the whole social system is a clue to the solution Perry had to offer to the unsettlednesses of gold-rush society. His prescription at this moment of cultural crisis was for quietness—for the masculine imagination of the time linked the home with quietness and retreat from the world. Perry wrote of the necessity, the 'special obligation', of maintaining a 'calm and quiet mind'.[52]

Excessive devotion to the pursuit of wealth often troubled Victorian critics of the gold rush. Here the colonial response was able to draw upon languages and arguments developed in different circumstances in Britain. Adam Cairns explained in a pamphlet in 1856 that the worst of the evils which affected Britain was 'the sinking and demoralisation of the masses': 'Commerce was eagerly plied, speculation grew . . . men were dealt with as machines, their strength was rated as a brute force, their value was represented by a piece of money, the relation between the employer and the employed was not of a moral, but strictly of a mercenary kind.'[53] With this kind of social analysis from home, it was no wonder that Adam Cairns began to promulgate trenchant criticisms of the pursuit of wealth in Victoria. 'Wealth desired for itself,' he warned, 'shrivels up the mind into a lump of clay. It extinguishes every spark of good feeling, turns the heart into a stone, recoils from generosity as a dreaded foe.' The common good would suffer as 'in the headlong strife to obtain wealth, public virtue will decay, honor and magnanimity be cast to the winds'.[54] Other ministers in Melbourne were even more alarmed than Cairns. 'The plague is indeed in our camp', the Reverend M. Mackay told his flock in Melbourne:

> The hand of that Providence has been seen, as if writing upon the wall, before the eyes of revelling idolaters of gold, recording the vanity of all their drudgeries and their dreamings, and the utter deceitfulness of that which they worshipped.[55]

The Reverend F. G. Barton, returning to his congregation in Kyneton in 1858 after a serious illness, nominated 'acquisition, aggrandisement, sensuality, selfishness' as the false gods of the time. He, too, obviously saw prosperity as the enemy of a properly Christian spirit, and argued for the importance of affliction and suffering, 'the manifold interruptions of earthly ease, satisfaction, prosperity, are for the very purpose of introducing into minds darkening and hearts hardening *thoughtfulness* as to those higher than earthly interests'.[56]

In an 1854 lecture in Melbourne, George Rusden linked the critique of the pursuit of wealth to an argument about selfish individualism. 'The danger is lest the absorbing pursuit of gold should dull the finer energies of our adventurous Colonists.' The solution was a collectivist one: 'Peculiarly in this country do we need the aid of institutions which have for their object the improvement of our social condition, which tend to gather us together for good purposes.'[57] This conservative response to gold-inspired avarice was a prescription for collective and institutional action.

Gold did not necessarily accrue to those who laboured hardest, or those whose birth or education had marked them for the inheritance of elevated social station. 'Gold hunting is not, *per se*, a desirable occupation', Thomas a'Beckett wrote in a Melbourne magazine, 'Its success is not dependent upon moral worth, and it has a tendency to destroy rather than promote the observance of those rules of conduct which, while they contribute to worldly welfare, elevate the individual who practises them, and promote social happiness.'[58] The concern was at the detachment of wealth acquisition from steady labour and abstemious habits. As William Westgarth noted to the Melbourne Chamber of Commerce, 'Our auriferous soil is not the creation of enterprise or genius'.[59] Nor were the rewards distributed with regard to these qualities, and that was cause for concern to liberals as much as conservatives.

The colonial elite often found it important to argue that the class hierarchy was a natural, inevitable and functional feature of society, particularly when they felt it to be threatened by a random redistribution of wealth. When the Reverend John Symons spoke to the young men at the gold town of Beechworth, he reminded them that rank, wealth and office, the outward signs of gradation, 'arise from the constitution of our natures, and the fitness of things, and must therefore be regarded as the ordinance of God'.[60] Symons probably had in mind actual political challenge to the class hierarchy when he made this appeal at Beechworth. But there were also more random and carnivalistic challenges to the classed order. Visitors to Melbourne in the 1850s never tired of repeating stories of the behaviour of newly wealthy diggers revelling in the theatre of their socially anomalous position, lighting their pipes with banknotes, shoeing their horses with gold, refusing all offers of work. 'I have been assured,' recorded George

Butler Earp, 'that several of them have *eaten the bank notes* which have been given them in payment for gold, the notes having been *asked for* for that purpose.'[61] 'A digger upon one occasion,' recalled Dr John Shaw, 'ate a five-pound note as a sandwich—placing it between two pieces of bread and butter, as a substitute for ham or beef.'[62] Stories of the eating of money appealed to middle-class observers as one of the ultimate scandals (and satires) of the gold rush. Such stories expressed the futility of enriching the working classes, but also embodied a Midas-like moral about the uselessness of money in a world where all was gold.

Middle-class observers expressed the fear that society was being effectively turned upside down, because what was now rewarded was the labourer's strength, rather than any more certificated or cerebral talents. Henry Brown observed in his *Victoria as I found it during five years of adventure* that 'what I had learnt was not of the character, in a new colony, either to produce money or pleasure to me, and that many around me, who could neither read nor write, were better educated for the circumstances in which we all stood than any man who possessed mere book learning'.[63] So the helplessness of the upper classes in the new environment was as much a matter for comment as the antics of the poor made wealthy. Earp's litany of disruption was typical: 'the flocks and herds were left straying in the bush for want of tendance; ships lay useless in every harbour, no man to navigate them; shops were shut up; ladies cleaned their own shoes, made their beds, and cooked the dinners; judges had to groom their own horses, and fetch water from the well, or the meat for their dinners from the butcher's shops; all order in the towns was at an end'.[64] While some undoubtedly enjoyed this carnivalisation of all social relations, they were generally not the ones who have left written accounts of the situation. Hugh Culling Eardley Childers, minister in the Victorian government from 1853, wrote in some distress to his sister: 'We, the unfortunate *gentle people* are reduced to a most subservient state. As an instance of what we are coming to our friend, Mr. Were, went into a shop the other day to buy some bread, his cook having refused to bake. There was none to be had, excepting some *pieces*; so with these he was obliged to content himself for the whole of his large family!'[65] In the countryside too, the high price of labour was causing distress to the employing class. 'It is utterly impossible for you to conceive the state the country is in for want of labour; and if there is not an immense assignation sent out shortly the country will be ruined', Arbella Cooke wrote to her brother in 1852. She hoped the recent floods would 'have the effect of starving out the gold diggers', for 'it is not exactly agreeable to have servants in these times going and coming as they choose'. In her anger is some measure of the disturbance gold created for the Victorian upper classes. The worst of the diggings, she wrote, 'is that it unsettles the men's minds for steady work and the working men have generally been very fortunate'.[66]

An incident from a Melbourne newspaper in 1852 provides another hint of the disruption that gold brought to this classed society. 'A gentleman appeared before the City Bench yesterday', the *Argus* reported:

> to answer a charge made against him by two of the mounted police for 'cooying' in Bourke St. at twelve o'clock on Tuesday night. The defendant proved the incident to have taken place in Lonsdale St. and not in Bourke St. as stated by the constables, and was discharged. Mr. Hull remarked that it was to be regretted that the police were not better acquainted with the persons of the citizens, as it was unnecessary to arrest a person of the defendant's respectability, if he gave his address. He, however, did not approve of the practice of 'cooying', and would not 'cooy' himself.[67]

There is a great deal going on in this complex fragment of interaction—the alliance of the gentleman defendant and the magistrate Hull against the slow-witted constables, who cannot even get the facts of the case right, the public definition of the bounds of respectability ('and would not "cooy" himself'). But the message the magistrate, and presumably much of the *Argus'* respectable readership, drew from the incident had to do with the regrettable difficulty of maintaining the links between respectability, decorum and a universally acknowledged station in life, in a rapidly expanding society in which wealth was being distributed in unpredictable ways. That a gentleman should cooy in the city, that he should have been arrested by the constables even though willing to offer them his address, that the constables should somehow have lost their sense of the denotations of the social hierarchy—these were but signs of the disturbed nature of the times. In a society in which the police were not 'acquainted with the persons of the citizens', display and appearance became crucially important. And yet in a society in which great wealth seemed to be almost randomly distributed amongst the classes, appearances became deceptive, and the constables could scarcely be relied upon to read the signs of respectability aright. Gold, in the words of Mary Stawell, wife of the first Victorian Attorney General, led to the 'complete disorganisation of society'.[68]

Moral reformers stressed the crucial connection between legitimate wealth and work. In Catherine Helen Spence's novel, *Clara Morison*, the female characters have the role of articulating criticisms of the wealth which can be acquired at the goldfields. 'I prefer a life of labour and activity', Margaret Elliot tells her brother, when he laments that he has not brought enough back from the fields to be able to offer her a life of leisure, 'and the position you ought to hold is one you will have risen up to by slow and painstaking steps, and not one that you can mount to on the back of a bag of nuggets'.[69] Gilbert Elliot comes in for some further criticism from Clara herself:

'You know that I only go in the hope of returning with gold enough to increase my influence, and to improve my prospects.' 'But that is very commonplace,' said Clara. 'Everybody looks for advancement by means of money: it would be much more distinguished—much more striking—to trust to prudence and talent. And I am sure it would be pleasanter, when you grow old, to have people date your rise from the time when you made an eloquent speech or an important reform, rather than from the day when you brought home a large bag full of nuggets from the gold-fields.'[70]

Money should follow success, it was argued, not precede it. Reformers in Australia were troubled by the consequences of what seemed to them to be gold's threat to randomly redistribute wealth in their societies, obliterating all the fine calibrations of the social order.

In both Victoria and California, influential voices were attempting to argue that there were dangers to the unmitigated pursuit and the possible redistribution of wealth. But the intellectual resources available were significantly different. These concerns about wealth in Victoria were elaborations of the work ethic or Christian denunciations of worldly materialism. Wealth and its distribution during the gold period were problems in Victoria for the established colonial elite and for the Christian reformers. There was little of the grander republican anxiety about the cyclical history of nations and the corruptions that came with wealth. As Victorians discussed the life hereafter and the importance of the public sphere, Californians continued an old American argument about the dangers or possibilities great wealth posed to society as a whole.

CHAPTER 3

ORDER

What land is like ours for the future? Even now our hills are
dotted with countless herds; our immense valleys will
speedily be covered with vineyards, and fields of wheat,
cotton and rice; our plains wave with the mulberry and
olive; our swarthy laborers be drawn from the inexhaustible
hordes of the children of the East; while our very rocks and
mountains are speckled with gold. More than all, and above
all, for order and law we have the glorious standard of
American freedom . . .
Rev. Sylvester Woodbridge, **Benicia, California,** 1851

While the anxiety of the Government to act justly and
rightly towards the large mining population will be
admitted by the great majority, I am aware that no
concession and no practicable arrangement will meet the
views of the class who aim at nothing short of Californian
freedom from all control . . .
Lieutenant Governor C.J. La Trobe, **Melbourne,** 1853

The first interest of many contemporary observers of the gold rushes in
Victoria and California was in how order could be maintained in a society
in which all were rushing, madly, after their own fortunes. 'The main thing
every where to be attained is order, that honest men may do their work
in peace and quietness,' wrote Hinton Helper in California.[1] Josiah Royce,
the philosopher, writing later in the nineteenth century, also regarded the
achievement of order as the most important 'philosophical' theme of the
California gold rush, observing that the pioneers there had to deal with

'forces, both within themselves and in the world beyond, that produced an exciting and not bloodless struggle for order'.[2] With the Californian experience of gold continually in mind, observers of the Victorian gold rush earnestly and repeatedly addressed the question of order. Contemporaries in both places tended to argue that their countrymen had an innate instinct for order, and that the creation of a new society was striking testimony to it.

But what did they mean by order? 'Order' is not a cultural universal, nor can it simply be measured on some generally valid scale. Understanding the constitution of the notion of order at a particular time can take us a long way towards comprehending the dynamics of a particular society. What *is* orderly will also at any time be the subject of dispute, or elaboration—for order is always a contested category. It was with regard to questions of order and disorder that observers in the 1850s most often argued about the differences between the Californian and the Australian gold-rush societies. The theme of the relative degree of order on the mining frontiers of the nineteenth century is one which has also preoccupied later historians, who have contrasted experiences in the United States and those in Canada or Australia—not always free from some of the assumptions of their nineteenth-century predecessors.[3]

VICTORIA

A Gentleman is acknowledged as such more readily here than in England, and I have always found the greatest respect and consideration payed to such even when working on the diggings amongst the greatest ruffians the world can produce.

James Prendergast, letter to his father from Melbourne, 1852

In Britain and Australia, gold-rush commentators were continually praising the natural love of order which, they held, characterised the British peoples. 'The discoveries, so far, have proved the strong hold which lawful order has on a British population', Charles Dickens' *Household Words* observed approvingly. 'The contrast is very great between the orderly behaviour at the goldfields in Australia, and the disorders of California', the same journal noted a few months later.[4] The gold rushes provided a wonderful opportunity to expand upon this theme and, in criticising California, to offer some implicit warnings about democracy. 'Just transport yourself, reader', James Ward wrote from London:

from the foot of the Sierra Nevada to that of the Blue Mountains, from the banks of the Sacramento to that of the Macquarie, and you will perceive a similar scene of activity . . . At the first blush the Australian group will appear as like that of California as one swarm of bees is like another, or as one rope of onions resembles its fellow; nevertheless, upon closer examination, you will

soon perceive a difference . . . Here you have more quietude among the
diggers—indicative of a higher social discipline than you can observe in the
Californian group—and a marked absence of the predominant feature of the
latter, that reckless, rollicking, devil-may-care, desperado character . . .[5]

Victorian publications devoted to the cause of settlement, in elaborating
the idea that there was a natural propensity for order among the British
peoples, often equated the maintenance of order with the persistence of
deference:

> The fears of those in power as to the maintenance of order, were proved to
> be without foundation. Britons are a law-respecting people, and whether it be
> within the precincts of soldiers and policemen, or in the wild bush of Australia,
> they are ever found willing to obey the reasonable commands of constitutional
> authority.[6]

In part, this was a self-interested theory, whose aim was to promote
emigration to British colonies rather than to the United States. It was
much cheaper to travel to North America, so emigration to Australia
needed some special pleading. The settlers of the American west, readers
of the *Dublin University Magazine* were warned:

> do not bring with them the nucleus of an organised society, as Englishmen,
> Irishmen, and Scotchmen do, when they land in fresh spots in Australia . . .
> far better therefore, to plant one's stakes where the licence of democracy is
> tempered by the restraints of common sense, where no class or colour is
> proscribed or enslaved, and where religion is not subject to such vagaries as
> those of Mormon.[7]

The virtue of the British colonies, the writer continued, was the 'stability
of British institutions, and the thorough identification of every educated
subject of Queen Victoria with their spirit'.

In Victoria, law and order could generally remain conjoined, in part
because defences of order by the privileged classes were usually also
defences of a stable class hierarchy. The celebration, by so many observers,
of the maintenance of order in Victoria, was often a half-surprised recognition of the tenacity of class distinctions and the culture of class in the
face of colonial challenges and confusions. Lord Robert Cecil, later the
British Prime Minister, kept a diary during his 1852 tour of the Victorian
goldfields. In it he noted all the signs of the tenacity of order, all the
indications that the alarmists were wrong when they predicted that a gold
colony must be a revolutionary and unstable place. He watched the
superintendent of police empty two sacks of earth collected by two diggers
working illegally on a Sunday: 'They neither made resistance nor showed
any discontent. One of them only said, "Well, Sir, I hope I never to do it
again." I at first stood quite aghast at this specimen of submissiveness in
Anglo-Saxons and colonists, especially after all I had heard of their

independent and unruly dispositions.' Cecil decided that 'turbulence' belonged not to the lower but to the middle classes, and that the goldfields would thus be safe.[8] Lieutenant Colonel Thomas Valiant, commanding the 40th Regiment, observed the crowd at Bendigo receive the news of the government's decision to reduce the licence fee, and was gratified to discover deference on the fringes of Empire: 'when His Excellency's intention was read to them . . . they received the intelligence with their hats off, and in the most orderly manner expressed their satisfaction, and they gave three cheers for the Lieutenant Governor. There was no exultation at having gained their point . . . but simply the expression of their gratitude.'[9] The discovery of deference and order at the Victorian fields was a matter for imperial and conservative pride, for it seemed also to signal the safety of class society at home.

Beyond national self-interest connected with emigration destinations, comparative statements about order on the goldfields articulated cultural characterisations which were extremely pervasive in the 1850s, and which eventually shaped behaviour as much as perception. National characteristics are cultural not social facts—they exist only in commonly repeated stories, narratives that serve to explain and eventually form social life. Characterisations of other societies serve purposes at home—they help define what ought to be the case, they articulate official stories and so legitimate individual actions. The Dublin author offered a statement of the case against the Americans and their new societies—they lacked the institutionally-created calm and solidity of the British colonies:

> When adventurers go forth from beneath the folds of the star-gemmed banner, it is not to rear a fabric having even the measure of excellence and the fair pretence of the structure which they vacate. Loosely attached to the slipshod system of their government, their minds on a level with the discontent and capricious politics of their nation, they carry to fresh territories no defined plan of action in their social capacity.[10]

Victorian conservatives, in particular, returned often and publicly to the theme of the disorder of California. It became a kind of touchstone with which they could remind themselves and others of what their society ought not to be allowed to become. Thomas a'Beckett, drawing upon the story of Midas as well as the common British characterisation of the Americans as a fickle, restless, passion-governed people, wrote luridly of the danger that the Victorians would become a 'lawless and disorganised race such as we see in California, where amid heaps of Gold, men have been known to die of starvation in their thrice destroyed city, and where the only emotions of which men appear susceptible, are miserable alternations of fear and frenzy'.[11]

The terms of the contrast recur again and again in the sources: American restlessness and capriciousness are opposed to British stability, patience and

David Tulloch, 'Great Meeting of Gold Diggers, Dec. 15th 1851'. From David Tulloch, Ham's Five Views of the Gold Fields of Mount Alexander and Ballarat in the Colony of Victoria *Melbourne: Thomas Ham, 1852.*

peace. For the governing classes of Victoria, America meant disorder, haste, and democratic disregard of class and respectability. 'They pride themselves on fast assuming the American type', wrote William Howitt of the Victorian colonists, 'and in that they are not mistaken. They go ahead in everything excepting order, cleanliness, effective police, good taste, and security of property.' Himself a radical in England, Howitt's Victorian experience led him to think that radicalism and republicanism could go too far. Clara Aspinall wrote approvingly of Collins Street, commenting that: 'No lady ever ventures into the other streets, excepting on urgent business . . . There is an American, go-a-head spirit pervading them, very objectionable to the well-regulated minds of our sex.' The tone was ironic, but the irony could work only because the mythic and gendered oppositions were well embedded in the minds of readers: America, men, commerce, bustle, and rule-breaking on one hand, against England, women, the home, quiet, and rule-observance on the other.[12]

Victorians thus had a strong sense of how the law and order of their society was supposed to differ from that of California—a sense which may have been part of the folk wisdom of the day, but which was certainly reinforced by most of the newspapers and journals which a Victorian might have read. Private writings too develop the theme of the British love of law and order, and regard for institutions, and the Californian disregard for them. Lord Robert Cecil recounted a story of sitting in a coach opposite an archetypal American: 'He wore a pair of pistols in his belt, and the words "put a bullet through his brain" were constantly in his mouth.'[13] Henry Mundy, writing up the diary of his life decades later, told a story of his experience on the Victorian goldfields with a Californian. The story had no doubt sharpened and improved with many tellings over the intervening years. The man, the story went, had been accused of robbing a claim. A crowd gathered:

> There was silence for a while, when someone spoke. What are we going to do with him, there are no police here to give him in charge. A voice came out of the crowd which unmistakably from its nasal drawl proclaimed itself to be Yankee, 'do as we do in California. Lynch him'. There was silence for half a minute. The accused man turned green. Then a man, a noble earnest looking fellow he was, enquired, 'Where is the man who spoke last?' Then a tall lean looking fellow stepped forward 'here I am gov., it was me I reckon, Hiram Jones, late of Californy and California born'. The previous speaker said in a quiet earnest way, 'Look here, Hiram Jones late of California, California born. We are law abiding subjects of the British Queen Victoria, if a man is accused of breaking the laws of the Realm, if caught, he is handed over to proper judicial authorities to have a fair trial, if found guilty he has to suffer the penalty. We have no sympathy with mob law in the Queen's dominions nor do we, Hiram Jones, tolerate Californian ruffianism in this land.'[14]

This may have been only the way Mundy thought it ought to have happened, but the story illustrates the way culturally-shared characterisations made their way into individual life stories.

The Americans were dangerous not only for their supposed addiction to violence, but also for their republicanism. Those who feared the Americanisation of Victoria saw personal as well as political effects. There was always discussion of a growing spirit of personal independence. 'The general aspect of the town and river is decidedly Yankee', Philip Prendergast wrote bitterly to his father, 'The men have a lank, greedy look—I mean of course those who have been here some time'.[15] It was to the United States (as well as to continental Europe) that Victorian radicals looked for democratic and republican ideas.[16] R.L. Milne, conservative pamphleteer, witnessed an open-air meeting on the land question in 1852, at which 'to my astonishment, was a republican flag, the stars and stripes of North America, waving in prognosticating triumph, right over the British ensign, in full view of the city of Melbourne'. One of the speakers, he reported 'is in the habit of taking off his hat to the multitude at public meetings, stating that in doing so he pays them a compliment which he would not pay to the Queen; thereby intimating that the right of sovereignty is in them, and not in the

Crown of England'.[17] Americans, from the consul down, were active in the political struggles around land in Victoria, which culminated in the Land Convention of 1857.[18]

Californian vigilantes served negatively as a point of definition of disorder for Australian liberals and conservatives. The conservative *Melbourne Morning Herald* complained somewhat helplessly late in 1851 of the 'gold mania': 'If something is not done, and that instantly . . . Victoria will in all probability be a second California within another month; robbery and murder will be rife on every side, and Judge Lynch will take his seat among us.'[19] The *Mount Alexander Mail* agreed that lynch law was to be avoided at all costs, and argued that 'the "Vigilance Committees" in California could not be emulated on the Gold Fields of this colony without disorganising our whole social system'.[20] After the violence at Eureka in 1854, the *Argus* blamed foreigners, including 'our kinsmen from America', in whose 'traditional feelings, and ignorance of British customs, there was found reason of the ready appeal to arms'.[21] Judge Redmond Barry, sentencing a black American, claimed somewhat implausibly that the use of the knife was 'quite unknown amongst British subjects'.[22] The American journals, Captain H. Butler Stoney assured his readers, 'abound with instances of lawless violence, and tales of savage customs unknown in Australia'.[23]

Although Victorian miners did improvise their own procedures to some extent, they were officially governed by a body of Gold Fields Commissioners, usually 'young men of good family', who were relatively highly paid, and who lived near the mining camps in government compounds, with servants.[24] Lord Robert Cecil regarded the affluence of the commissioner's establishment as crucial to the maintenance of control, and he was relieved to find at Bendigo that the 'feebleness and meanness' of the establishment there (no tablecloths, he noted) did not seem to have weakened the diggers' respect for 'constituted authority'.[25] There was inherent in the system, the more critical William Howitt observed in his novel *Tallengetta*, 'a great deal of pretence, and a morbid love of gold lace and parade dreadfully demonstrative of the *parvenu*'.[26] It was the commissioner's job to settle disputes, and to enforce the laws. 'They distrust each other's arbitration', Lord Robert Cecil claimed, articulating the rationale for the system, 'but have full reliance on that of one above them.'[27] Gold Fields Commissioners had, in particular, to ensure that all those who dug for gold had a licence. The licence, initially thirty shillings a month, sought to regulate more than the right to dig. It was a token of the moral oversight granted to the commissioners. It enjoined its holder to 'maintain and assist in maintaining a due and proper observance of Sundays'. The commissioner, according to the regulations, could only issue a licence to a person once they had proved that they were not 'improperly absent from hired service'. And the commissioner had the responsibility of ensuring 'by all means in his power . . . that Sundays are properly observed, and that all persons in public employment attend Divine Service when means of doing so are afforded them.'[28] The assistant commissioner had the task of 'settling disputes, keeping order among the people'. He was to maintain a level of surveillance of the affairs of the community of diggers he governed, and a position of arbitration above them—'all complaints made by them, either one against another or against different persons, are to be particularly enquired into, and adjusted as far as possible'.[29]

The colonial state attempted to normalise the labour involved in gold mining, to fit it to the rhythms and rules of ordinary social life. The licence fee policy did this, by refusing to recognise any distinction between the work involved in successful and unsuccessful gold seeking. Miners' protest movements argued that a tax should only be levied on gold found, not on labour expended—that is, that it should only be paid by successful miners. Governor La Trobe described the argument:

> the broad objection seems to have been that it made no distinction between the successful and the unsuccessful adventurer, between the man who raised his shovelful of gold per week and the man who threw away all he possessed in the world on his venture without any fruit . . . in short that the revenue raised was not a fair percentage upon the actual yield of the Gold Fields but upon the labour employed, whether successfully or unsuccessfully.

This was a point that La Trobe could not concede. If the tax were only upon yields, the state might be seen to be encouraging speculation. Besides, the unsuccessful miner looked to the state for 'similar facilities' and protection to the successful miner.[30] The licence was a tax to pay for the services which the state was obliged to provide for the speculators.

Order in Victoria was widely understood by liberals and conservatives to involve respect for law and established institutions, among them the hierarchical nature of society. Chief Justice a'Beckett was presumably not the only Victorian conservative who believed that equality was 'the dream of a madman, or the passion of a fiend'—the interesting thing is that it was still acceptable for major public figures to say so.[31] Order in Victoria was understood to be crucially dependent upon the maintenance of class harmony. So when the newly-appointed Governor Charles Hotham wished to assure the inhabitants of the gold town of Castlemaine of his good will, he told them that he was interested in promoting the welfare of all classes equally, 'and I trust that there will be no arraying of class against class, but that all classes will determine to do their duty'.[32] There was no suggestion of transcending or abolishing class. The vision was rather one of achieved class cooperation and harmony.

Governor Hotham's inference that order could best be achieved through the maintenance of a classed society was of course questioned by radical observers, for whom the possibility of an ordered and equal society was an

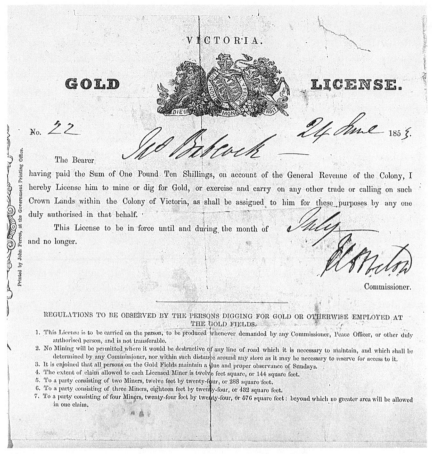

Victorian Gold Licence, 1853. From Geo. McArthur scrapbook, Special Collections, Baillieu Library, University of Melbourne.

article of faith. The *Bendigo Advertiser* argued, in an 1854 editorial, that 'the peace and good order generally prevailing on the gold-fields, is unquestionably attributable to the independence of the mass'. The Victorian radical position was thus in some ways similar to Californian orthodoxy. It could have been any Californian Democrat organ which explained that:

> Where every man is working for himself, all are interested in the preservation of social order, and the protection of mutual rights, and the most stringent police regulations in the world cannot effect half so much for the general well-being of society, as the influence of the universal exercise of the great principle of self-protection.[33]

This was a part, in Bendigo, of an emerging defence of the virtues of the individual miner, working for himself, against the encroachments of company mining, in which the miner was an employee. In this radical discourse, independence and self-interest were the best police. Victorian radicals, though, seldom embraced complete laissez faire. On other occasions the *Bendigo Advertiser,* too, joined in the general celebration of British freedoms, a celebration which saw the origins of those freedoms in institutions rather than in individual virtues—'even in the United States', the paper observed in 1855, 'there is yet wanted the profound and consolidated liberty which is found enshrined within our own constitutional privileges'.[34]

Only for those Victorian radicals for whom the status quo embodied a state of injustice so severe that order could not be expected to be sustained within it, were order and law dissociated. The Eureka rebels, protesting the licence fee, adopted the language of the American revolution—they refused, they said, taxation without representation. The government blamed foreigners, but privately was deeply worried about the spread of republican ideas, particularly after receiving a message from the British consul in Philadelphia warning that parties of Americans in Victoria were planning to foster a republican revolution. 'It is unquestionable,' Governor La Trobe wrote to London, 'that this period of excitement has been attended by the . . . almost open anticipation of the subversion of the Queen's authority.'[35] The disorder that the Victorian government most feared was a concerted attempt to change Victorian institutions. Detective police were sent to spy on small meetings of radicals earnestly drafting new constitutions for the colony. If order was lawfulness, then attempts to change the laws or the system of laws were among the most dangerous of actions.

Stress on the wisdom, stability and balance of British institutions often implied a faith that the forms and institutions would create order almost of themselves. The morality of the population was not a major theme in Victorian discourse. Former Melbourne *Argus* editor Edward Wilson, in an 1857 debate in that newspaper, made a particular point of refuting the view that 'a nearly perfect form of government is hopeless, except in the case of a nearly perfect people'. For the formation of a 'nearly perfect form of government', he wrote, 'I am quite contented to take people as they are'. [36] It was not upon the commonsense of the people that Wilson rested his confidence in Victoria's future, but on a political system which would represent interests rather than population. When the more democratic liberal George Higinbotham responded, he returned to the question of the nature of the population, arguing that the peculiar situation of Victoria meant that education rather than wealth was the only appropriate measure of the qualities of the people. While 'in most countries the wealthy class is also the educated class', this was 'not generally the case in Victoria', where the 'enormous fortunes which some persons have amassed have been not unfrequently acquired suddenly, and with little trouble by their owners'.[37] For Higinbotham, the moral state of the population was a particularly important precondition for the construction of a democratic polity. His was not, though, an influential position in Victoria, for radicals tended to take the virtue of the populace as a given, while liberals and conservatives expected that institutions would render virtue irrelevant to the construction of order.

When Francis Nixon wrote in 1862 in defence of the quality of the Victorian population, it was not its innate morality that he dwelt upon, but its diligence in reproducing British institutions. 'Let us at least this credit to ourselves as British colonists,' he argued, 'that we have, in the heat even of struggles, as individuals . . . modelled our adopted country in most essential particulars on the plan of that which we formerly abandoned: that we have not neglected to foster, even to excess, all the institutions, ecclesiastical, judicial, scientific, intellectual, educational, charitable, and otherwise, for which Great Britain is justly renowned'. In some misinformed quarters, Nixon observed, Victorians were known as 'a crowd of vulgarians and gambling traders; besotted revellers in all that is gross and animal', but in fact, he argued, 'in ratio to the number and classification of the population in Victoria, . . . there is no one portion of Her Majesty's possessions that can compare favourably with us in the possession and observance of the acknowledged amenities, and in the encouragement of all those humanizing institutions from which society derives its most admired attributes'.[38]

Faith in institutions creating order led to a belief in a moral and supervisory role for government, producing virtue where none might have been, providing official means by which virtue would be seen to meet its reward. R.L. Milne, an old soldier who claimed he was 'not quite a stranger' to the Duke of Wellington, was something of an eccentric. But he shared with other conservatives a view of the role of government which, though he exaggerated, he did not distort. His main theme was the need for government oversight of all aspects of social life—'moral supervision is the one, the great, the all-essential requisite of human polity'.[39] 'Can any *reasonable* objection be made to the introduction of the practice of generally certifying character?' Milne asked, arguing that everyone, not just servants and candidates for office, should be certified as to respectability. This was a conservative fantasy and a response to the disorder of gold. But it was a fantasy grown out of a particular political culture. Nothing but moral supervision, Milne argued, would 'save Australia from the gambling, stilletting, vile abominations, and desecrated Sabbaths of assassinating Italy, infidel France, and republican America'.[40]

The police in Victoria took on some of this supervisory role. In September 1853, the Colonial Secretary wrote to the Chief Commissioner of Police requesting that police attend political meetings on the goldfields—'it is very desirable that intelligent men should attend all public meetings to watch the proceedings and to take down accurately such words used as may appear to them desirable'. This intelligence was then to be efficiently and centrally processed: 'The Police Magistrate at each Gold Field should instantly despatch an account to you transmitting the words, which I will cause to be immediately laid before the Law Officers and should they recommend such a course, orders will at once be issued to arrest the speaker of them.'[41] It is very doubtful that such efficient surveillance would have been possible with the resources at hand, but a way of thinking about order is strikingly evident here. The population should be always within sight and hearing of the officers of the state; government was seen to be crucially dependent upon observation and knowledge about population.[42]

In Victoria, one of the key institutions involved in this work of making the population transparent to official gaze was the police. Victorian belief in the importance of institutions was no idle theory. The colony in the 1850s was policed to an extraordinary degree. Policing was an instrument of government, and colonial governments were happy to expend large amounts on the force. The Victorian police grew under the influence of two competing models of policing. The crime-preventative model of the London Metropolitan Police, with its beat system and uniforms, was adopted in the city of Melbourne. Here the aim was to make police visible to the population, as a friendly deterrent to crime. The other model came from the Royal Irish Constabulary—it provided for a more militaristic police force, one that could be used against a hostile or subservient population. This model was closer to that adopted on the goldfields, and it aroused the hostility and ultimately rebellion of diggers.[43] In the strength and importance of the police lies one of the clearest contrasts between Victoria and California. By June 1853, the total strength of the Victorian Police Force was 875—'great as the force is', the Superintendent reported, it needed to be further extended. He thought 2000 men would be adequate.[44] By mid-1854, the police had 1639 men, making a police to population ration of 1:144 for the colony as a whole. But, Haldane's calculations show, those police were heavily concentrated in the goldfields areas—Castlemaine had, on official figures, a police to population ratio of 1:56.[45] The sheer number of police in Victoria compared to California has a great deal to do with the different understandings of order in the two places. In 1853, at the gold town of Bendigo in Victoria, there were 66 mounted and 105 foot police, as well as 127 foot and 27 mounted soldiers, for a population which was estimated to have peaked that year at 23 000 adult males.[46] Between 1850 and 1856, the city of San Francisco itself, which had a population of 34 000 in 1852, had a police force which was never above 80 men in strength, and often only around thirty.[47]

One key to the disorders the police were there to combat is the legislation they had to enforce. The most relevant Acts were the 1838

NSW *Towns Police Act*, and later, the *Victorian Town and Country Police Act* of 1854. There were some differences between the Acts, but in general terms they seem to have been designed to preserve the order of the city, by permitting movement, communication and exchange; they consistently prohibit blocks and interruptions, as well, of course, as nuisances, indecencies and blasphemies. The NSW Act provided for the apprehension of drunks and loiterers, for the regulation and licensing of publicans, for the keeping of the Sabbath free from games; it prohibited the damaging of public buildings, the fouling or obstruction of water courses or the injuring of public fountains, beating carpets, flying kites, breaking horses or slaughtering any animals in public places. It prohibited the obstruction of footways by persons washing barrels or stacking timber or bricks, the letting off of fireworks or firearms, bathing within view of a public place between six am and eight pm, indecent exposure, the keeping of swine, allowing rain to drop on the footpaths, the carrying of nightsoil during the day, negligent careless or furious riding, the leaving of dead animals on the roads, and the malicious breaking of lamps. The later Victorian Act dealt with the symptoms of disorder in the towns in considerably more detail. A number of offences connected with horses and vehicles were added—they had to be driven on the left side of the road except when overtaking and they could not be driven while intoxicated. Turning loose cattle, horses or swine on the public roads and thoroughfares of the town was forbidden; skittle grounds had to be registered, and selling adulterated food was not allowed.

These Towns Police Acts embraced the central concerns of the police in the city, but much other legislation had to be enforced. In 1856 the Victorian police published a little handbook of *Extracts from Colonial Acts for the Use of the Police Force in Victoria*, which must represent the police view of the circumstances most likely to require policing. It reproduced Acts requiring stage coaches to be licensed, dogs to be registered, forbidding the carrying of firearms on Sundays, lengthy regulations concerning the licensing of public houses and the procedures for gaining permission to allow billiard games therein, forbidding illegal meetings or the sale of liquor to Aborigines in public houses, requiring the licensing of hawkers, peddlers, pawnbrokers and public entertainments, and providing regulations concerning gaols, fires, bakers, electric telegraphs, post offices, the influx of criminals, auctioneers, gold duty, the pollution of the Yarra, cruelty to animals, Chinese immigration and thistle prevention. Particularly important were the vagrancy laws, which provided the classifications and grounds for arrest of the unhoused and the unemployed. The idle and disorderly (no visible means of support, lodging or wandering with Aborigines, habitual drunkards or common prostitutes, begging, being armed at night, having an article of disguise or a deleterious drug) could be sentenced to gaol for twelve months with or without hard labour, while rogues or vagabonds (second offence idle and disorderlies, exposing obscene books or pictures, obscene exposure of person, playing unlawful games, imposing on a charitable institution or person on false pretences, possessing instruments of housebreaking, or being found at night with face blackened wearing felt slippers and a felonious intent) could receive up to two years gaol with or without hard labour. A rogue or vagabond who recommitted any of these offences could be sentenced as an Incorrigible Rogue for three years hard labour.

The police superintendent in Victoria was involved in processes of licensing and regulation. Licences were required, not only to dig for gold, but also (among other things) to run a public house, to distill spirits, to work as a hawker, and to hold public entertainments. Those who sought such licences had to write to the Colonial Secretary in Melbourne, who seems often to have consulted with the police superintendent. The police were active agents of an interventionist and morally-regulatory state.

There was considerable fear of civil disturbance, even in Melbourne. 'Society is now in such a state', the Melbourne Town Clerk told a Parliamentary enquiry into the Victorian police in 1852, 'that if there be not speedily a sufficient Police force there will soon be an overturn of all government and order'.[48] The Victorian Police Force was greatly reduced in 1851 and 1852, as men resigned to try their luck on the goldfields. Those that remained in the force were, the superintendent explained in 1852, becoming demoralised and confused:

> They witness the Theatres and places of Public Amusement crowded by elated and successful Gold diggers, their wives bedecked in the most costly finery, and the Cabs employed by day and night driving them about . . . They cannot but notice the utter disorganisation of the domestic arrangements of every private establishment, to the extent that the Master becomes his own Groom— The discharged Policeman returning to Melbourne, there to astonish his former comrades by the Golden results of his labors at Mount Alexander; all these are circumstances of reality which cannot but tend to disorganise any body of men, subvert all discipline, and paralyse the most strenuous efforts to maintain efficiency in the Police.[49]

The police chief was clearly pessimistic about the chances of maintaining order in a society in which the natural hierarchy was upset. Social inversion would 'disorganise' even the guardians of order, leaving them with no clear sense of just what it was they were protecting. Worse, difficulties were experienced in securing uniforms for the police that remained. 'I have no hesitation in saying that unless in uniform, the moral effect of a Police is lost.' Not only was the behaviour of un-uniformed police difficult to control, there was a problem with members of the public impersonating police.[50]

In a society in which the class of people seen as requiring policing might be wealthy rather than impoverished, special difficulties and temptations confronted the police. The minds of the police were 'continually excited', their superintendent reported in August 1852, by evidence of the extravagant success of others on the goldfields. Daily they arrested 'drunkards and street brawlers' who often had money or gold about their persons, 'to my own knowledge, in many instances exceeding in value five hundred and six hundred pounds'.[51] William Hull, the magistrate, told an illustrative story to the 1852 Parliamentary enquiry. A constable was pursuing a man, who jumped into the river to try to escape: 'He there, whilst swimming, offered to give the constable 12 pounds to let him go free; but the policeman refused the bribe, jumped into the river, and at the expense of a ducking, secured the offender. Now this, I conceive to be a case calling for some token of approbation from the Government.'[52] The dependence of dominant notions of order on an established and stable economic hierarchy is made clear in these difficulties. How could order be maintained if the criminal classes were to be permanently and substantially wealthier than the police—if the nexus between wealth and respectability was entirely broken?

The difficulties of the police, though, were temporary. The pay of police was increased, a body of 130 military pensioners was brought from Van Diemen's Land, and 50 London Metropolitan policemen were recruited. Soon the turn in the economy of the colony meant that the force was swamped with applicants for positions from men of all classes, and could afford to be extraordinarily selective. To take advantage of these changed conditions, the Victorian police force set up a special mounted cadet corps for gentlemen recruits. The superintendent of the City Police explained the idea in October 1852, when he reported to the Colonial Secretary that a 'class of young men are now seeking employment in the Police, who will rapidly change the character of the service, with their education and feelings of principle and honour. They enter the force as cadets, in no way losing their position as gentlemen, they look forward to promotion in the Force.' They would act as a moral leavening, 'above the influence of temptation which have hitherto paralysed our efforts. I look forward with confidence to their instilling an "Esprit" which, I trust, will have the effect of shortly raising the character of the Police, and constitute themselves as a safeguard to the community.'[53] Though the cadets would initially only have the rank and pay of lowly constables, they had the comfort of working with men of their own class, and the lure of rapid promotion. In August 1853 barracks were opened in Collins Street for twenty mounted men of the cadet corps. The Chief Commissioner explained to the Colonial Secretary that 'having been brought up in a superior sphere of life, more orderly conduct and more active exertion will be expected', and that, while the corps would be expected to perform the duties of ordinary constables, they 'will be required to observe the conduct of Gentlemen'.[54] Their pay was deducted to provide linen, glass, and other essentials.

Admission to the cadet corps was extraordinarily difficult because of the number of respectable young men left stranded in Victoria by the gold rushes. 'I am well aware at the present time,' wrote T.B. Dymock, 'of the hosts of applicants whose priority of application in this province render my obtaining any other appointment a remote contingency.' He felt though that he was well qualified for a position in the cadet corps by 'my knowledge of horses, my strength of body, my understanding of military exercises' and service in the army of an unspecified European king. He offered testimonials from 'my Masters and Tutors at Eton and Oxford', from Lord Kenyon, the Bishop of New Zealand, and the Victorian Attorney General. Nevertheless, the Chief Commissioner felt that, at twenty five, he was really too old to be considered. Other applicants included a scholar from the Paris polytechnique, a Captain from the Royal Artillery and one from the Bengal army, a graduate of the King of Hanover's riding school, a judge's advocate, a process server, a graduate of Trinity College Dublin, a surgeon, a man who had seen service in the Danish army and the Appellant Surgeon from the Royal Berkshire Yeoman Cavalry. One gentleman explained that 'having always been brought up with the idea of inheriting from my family a sufficient competency if not a fortune, I cannot turn my attention to any profession . . . my family are highly respectable being connected with some of the first families in England, nothing but sheer necessity and a lot of disappointment of my hopes would have prevail'd upon me thus to intrude upon your kindness and interest'.[55] Even Edward Mayne, barrister nephew of Richard Mayne, Chief Commissioner of the London Metropolitan Police, equipped with letters of recommendation from his famous uncle, the British Secretary of State for the Colonies, and the Irish Attorney General (who was moved to write that 'there is not at either Bar, English or Irish, a finer young man, liberal and enlightened, sound and conservative, well-educated and sober-minded') could not secure a position in the Victorian police force in 1853. It was no wonder that narratives of inversion, of a world turned upside down, were circulating in this society.

Gold, then, was seen to pose problems for the maintenance of order. In seeking to answer the question of just what order meant in the two places, consciously articulated statements may not be the best source. Ideas about order *are* sometimes written down, argued in a formal way in discursive texts. More often though the definitions have to be found in behaviour and ritual. Actions and events also embody crucial meanings. The ethnographic approach allows moments of social action to be read for what they reveal of more enduring patterns of social meaning, for what they can tell us about the construction of key social categories such as 'order'. A mood of anxiety on the part of the governing classes meant that displays, enactments, of the orderly and lawful nature of the society were of unusual importance.

The rituals of the law provide societally central opportunities to analyse the enactment of dramas about order and disorder. What follows is an attempt to reconstruct some of the social thought of Redmond Barry, Supreme Court judge in Victoria during the gold-rush period, Chancellor of the University of Melbourne, founder of Melbourne's Public Library, patron of almost all of its organised cultural activities, 'a man of the old-gentleman John Bull's stamp' according to Raffaello Carboni.[56]

As the junior of the two Victorian Supreme Court justices, and as a new judge—he had been appointed in January 1852—Redmond Barry had, perhaps, an exaggerated sense of the importance of the outward show of the majesty of the law, the symbolic display of the dignity of the office he held. Douglas Hay and many others have argued that the theatre of the law was not peripheral to its functioning, but rather one of the central means by which the people at large were to be convinced of the legitimacy of the decisions reached within the courtroom, and of the fair and merciful nature of the legal system as a whole.[57] Barry was perhaps an unusually proud and pompous judge—he was mocked unmercifully for his hubris by the Melbourne *Punch* from early in his colonial career—but he was also an unusually astute one in his unerring sense of the importance of the ritual dimension of judging. In comparative context, ritual moments are of peculiar interest in enabling us to understand how order was constructed and understood in each community, what influential men like Barry meant when they spoke of an ordered society.

It was on 4 May 1852 that Redmond Barry sent a letter to the Colonial Secretary, concerning his planned trip to Portland and Geelong on circuit, later that month. He wrote requesting 'that you will have the goodness to direct the necessary preparations to be made for my being conveyed thither at that season'. Barry would not be travelling alone: 'I shall require the services of my Clerk to act as Clerk of Arraigns and Associate and of my Messenger to act as Crier of the Court, and the attendance of Two of the Law Officers of the Crown will also be necessary to conduct the prosecutions.' Because the party was to be so large, Barry felt a carriage would be expensive and unreliable, and suggested a sea voyage, advising the government that it should charter 'a *Steam Boat*' for his use.[58]

There was to be a protracted correspondence between Barry and the Colonial Secretary about the trip. On the 13 May, the government agreed to fit out the government schooner with cabins for the law officers.[59] On 29 May, Barry wrote asking that two-hundred pounds credit be assigned to him, for expenses in Portland and Geelong. When the Colonial Secretary

Redmond Barry, portrait, 1866. Batchelder and O'Neill. La Trobe collection, State Library of Victoria.

offered one hundred pounds and requested in response that Barry keep the receipts for his expenses and present them to the Colonial Treasurer for reimbursement, Barry protested strongly: 'I have the honour to inform you that I will respectfully decline to produce any vouchers for my expenditure.' On 5 June, having received confirmation that he would only be allocated one hundred pounds for expenses at Portland, Barry wrote again to the Colonial Secretary, insisting that he be given open credit for any further expenses. It was not, as he explained it, merely a matter of money: 'As Judge of Assizes I do not proceed on circuit as an ordinary Traveller might do. I submit therefore with deference to His Excellency that I am the person to estimate what may be requisite for me'. He hoped that the Governor would: 'entertain such consideration for me as not to render my disagreeable expedition still more unpleasant by proposing that I should be compelled to calculate prospectively each item of daily expenditure, and retain vouchers for every trivial disbursement.'

Governor La Trobe acceded to his terms, and raised the amount to one hundred and fifty pounds, though with some acerbic remarks about the 'demands' made on government by the judge: 'H.E. cannot do otherwise than remark that on the part of your Honour there has not been shown that disposition to facilitate matters for which H.E. has always given you credit.'[60] 'I demanded nothing to which I was not justly and strictly entitled', Barry responded.[61] The Melbourne *Argus* heard of the government restrictions on Barry's expenditure for the Portland journey, and came out on the side of public ceremony: 'we know that, in England, when the judges travel on circuit, there is a good deal of display allowed, the expense of which is invariably borne by the Crown. We like to see every man uphold the dignity of his office, from the Governor downwards.'[62] It was Barry's idea that judges should progress in lordly fashion through the countryside, a retinue in tow. The penny-counting precautions of the colonial government and its bureaucratic procedures were inimical to such a progress. 'I do not proceed on circuit as an ordinary Traveller might do'—was it not extraordinary that these elementary facts of British juridical symbolism had to be explained to the Governor himself?

The details of the journey settled in advance, Barry and his party left for Portland, and there, on 15 June, the Circuit Court was opened. Never one to let an important ritual event go unremarked, Barry opened the session with a lengthy address to the jury which was reported by the local newspaper, and later published as a pamphlet. 'On an occasion like the present,' he began, ' . . . it would evince an indifference to the importance of the event, and an insensibility to the honor which devolves on me, were I to omit to address to you some remarks.'[63]

Barry took the opportunity to outline the roles of the judge, the jury, and the witnesses in criminal trials, articulating for his audience some of the orthodox wisdom of the British legal system. He stressed the difficulty and importance of the judge's function:

> He defines the nature of the issue joined on the record, and removing from consideration all extraneous topics calculated only to confuse and needlessly occupy the public time, confines the evidence strictly to that; declares upon whom the burden of proof is thrown, what facts are indisputable, and how those in dispute may be affected by the rules relating to the quality of testimony, whether of accomplices or other suspected or interested persons; how certain facts may [be] proved by one witness or may require to be substantiated by more than one, or by one and corroborative circumstances, or may require or dispense with a certain description of proof; pointing to that which is direct, or circumstantial—positive or merely presumptive, distinguishing such presumptions as are in their nature, conclusive from such as may be rebutted by counter evidence—whether a sufficient case be made to call the opinion of the jury, or whether a substantial variance in a material point between the statement and the proof occur.[64]

These were formal and technical skills to which claim was being laid. The judge, as master of the laws, was able to discern the relevance of information, its proper bearing on the question at hand.

Barry then turned to the role of the jury. Their task was to:

> weigh with anxious and careful attention the evidence of the different witnesses. It is here their interesting province to sound the motives which may appear to actuate the bias, to influence, the interest to sway, or the passions to stimulate them; and in this regard not only the words which fall from their lips, but by their united discernment to sift their sincerity and the accuracy of their memory, to scrutinize their behaviour, to detect by the voice, the gesture, the readiness, the flippancy, the reluctance with which they narrate facts, their inclination to state, distort, exaggerate, diminish, or conceal the truth, to separate the improbable, irreconcilable, or seemingly incredible statements from those to which credit may with safety be attached, and then applying to the facts upon which they resolve, the law as expounded by the judge, to deduce therefrom a rational and sound conclusion.[65]

These were the skills of the street—reading the semiotics of respectability, the theatre of sincerity, the denotations of honesty. Only a local knowledge was required of the jury—a sense of what would pass on the street as normal, expected, credible behaviour. Barry warned the jurors, though, that their task had the largest of implications: 'the principle upon which they base their verdict will vibrate through the whole social fabric of the state'.[66]

The crucial issue was separation of the judicial and jural functions. It was on that separation that the British constitution depended for its peculiar virtues. 'Should we,' Barry warned, ' find the judge invading the jury box, or the jury usurping the judgement seat, it is hopeless to expect that the antient landmarks of that constitution can be preserved.' Juries, he warned them, should be 'content to walk in the useful vocation assigned to them'—theirs were artisanal virtues, 'a graceful, mutual deference, a cordial good understanding', a 'ready and steadfast cooperation' without 'any concession of their independence'.[67]

This separation was not a purely theoretical matter. Barry expected to see the constitutional separation enacted in the very space of the courtroom. On his return to Melbourne, he wrote again to the Colonial Secretary, complaining of the conditions of gaols and courthouses at both Portland and Geelong. It was the promiscuous mixing of judges, barristers and jurors which disturbed him. At Geelong, he explained:

> the room to which a jury retires to deliberate is that used on ordinary occasions by the Clerk of Petty Sessions, and is filled with books and papers which are exposed to the risk of annihilation and abstraction. It is also used as a robing room by the Gentlemen of the Bar and much delay and unseemly Interruption of the Public business occurs when a jury retires in consequence of those things which the Gentlemen of the Bar may require being removed from the room.[68]

It was not just the suspicion that the jurors were liable to turn to petty thieving, the importance of keeping the public in its place, that animated Barry's concern; there was also his abiding sense of the importance of spatial discriminations and the particular importance of establishing and maintaining meaningful spatial boundaries in new and unformed societies.

That this was Barry's message was not lost on his Portland audience. The *Portland Guardian and Normanby General Advertiser*, under the heading 'What Did You Think of the Judge's Address?', began to contest his definition of the space of judging. 'The usual attempt was made', the paper observed, 'to bring the jury under a feeling of subjection to the Judge or his legal opinion'. 'Judges always have been fond of trying to keep this illiberal hold upon juries', but the principle of the separation had, the paper maintained, long been disputed. The *Guardian*, though, implicitly conceded the theatrical function of judging, and began assessing Barry's appearance in the town, his speech, as performance. His speech was deemed '*very suitable to the occasion*'. The paper concluded that it was too early to pass judgement on the performer: 'this one exhibition we cannot consider sufficient for a just inference regarding talent and ability'.[69] If the function of the jury was to be a street-wise scrutiny of their peers, the function of judging was held on both sides to be one of performance—and difficult performance at that.

Performance about what? Judicial theatre was about the maintenance of the law and of order, of the settled and hierarchical nature of society. In 1852, Victorian society was anything but settled, and its hierarchy was threatened by the redistribution of wealth portended by the discovery of gold in its fields. The problem Barry saw, as he expressed it to the Colonial Secretary in August 1852, was the 'repression of crime' at a 'season of wealth without example'. The normal sanctions of wealth and rank were failing; at such a time it became the function of the law to provide 'example'. Barry's correspondence with government in 1852 is one long series of recommendations that leniency *not* be shown in remission of sentences imposed, that the exemplary functions of punishment be retained at all costs.

When Barry asked himself why Victoria had not suffered the anarchy and violence so widely understood in Australia to have been the Californian experience of gold-rush society, he was clear about the answer. It was British law and the British constitution which had protected peace and good order. The goldfields population was, he informed his Portland audience, 'orderly and well-disposed'. 'To what, then, is this condition of things to be ascribed? Gentlemen, I reply that it is to the blessings of that Constitution which makes you the arbiters of the nation's tranquillity— which places you as a bulwark against the oppressor, and a shield against the marauder and assassin.'[70]

There was a tension at the heart of Barry's, and many of his conservative contemporaries', constitutional and political thinking. On the one hand, there was this professed belief in the genius of the British constitution, and the egalitarianism perceived to be at its core—trial by a jury of one's peers, the people as a bulwark against aristocratic or monarchical tyranny— and on the other hand, there was the instinctively hierarchical thinking of men of Barry's class, for whom order was both rank and calm, both example and acknowledgement. When gold seemed to threaten the very roots of deference, it became important to emphasise again the orthodoxies about the limits of the understandings of jurors, the need for the special knowledge of the judge. Trial by jury had at its core an equalitarian belief in equal knowledges; Barry, while acknowledging the principle, was anxious to assert the importance of higher expertise.[71]

The paradox was in the assertion of an equal independence as the guarantee of an unequal order. The Victorians were part of a people, Barry assured his audience at Portland:

which revere the ordinances of pure religion—which maintains the decencies of law and order—which bases its franchise not on notional theories or abstract undetermined generalities respecting the 'rights of man', but with one which esteems and cultivates such sentiments as will instil a manly morality, and cause itself to be respected and honored amongst the nations.[72]

It was in the courtroom that Barry could show what he meant by a 'manly morality', could enact the principles of the British constitution, show its realised operation, quite distinct from the 'abstract undetermined generalities' of the democratic agitators outside.[73] In the space of the courtroom, the public had its place. That place was not everywhere, nor was it unbounded; and yet it was on them, of course, that the whole system was based.

Barry envisioned a society held together by a complex web of rights and obligations, one in which the social contract was regarded:

in. another light than that of a mere casual aggregation of human beings employed in one absorbing pursuit of delving in the hills for ore, held together by the fragile bonds of occasional interest, a partnership of mutual distrust to be dissolved at pleasure, or when the sordid object of its initiation has been accomplished.[74]

Barry occupied a particular position, of course, on the spectrum of colonial social and political thought. His views on the fragility of 'bonds of occasional interest' mark him as a critic of liberal faith in the market and self-interest, that is, as either a conservative or a radical; his belief in the necessity for hierarchy in society further marks him clearly as a conservative. Although Barry's views on hierarchy and deference were at the conservative end of the political spectrum, open to frequent challenge and contestation, his belief in the virtue of a quiet society, I would argue, put him somewhere near the centre of Victorian thought on that question. His belief in the important role of institutions, such as the law, religion and education, in both encouraging and demonstrating order, was also widely shared among the Victorian elite. Interestingly, this belief did not extend to restrictive views on personal conduct—from 1846 Barry openly conducted a relationship with a married woman, with whom he had four children.[75]

Barry spoke at Portland of gold mining as an 'exciting and wonderfully remunerative employment'.[76] Later in 1852, opening another circuit court at Castlemaine, he spoke of the 'wild excitement' caused by gold, and looked forward optimistically to its diminution:

The wild excitement which prevailed has in a great measure subsided; reflection is permitted to resume its dominion, and those who yield to its sway acknowledge that gold, however lavishly showered upon them, will be but a sordid acquisition if unaccompanied by the decencies, the proprieties, the charities, and the refinements which distinguish that great nation with which we are affiliated.[77]

Gold for Barry raised questions of social control, for the maintenance of order was understood in metaphors of restraint and control. The critical question raised by the gold, he suggested at Castlemaine, was:

whether the restraints of principle, education, and example drawn out and self imposed by the particular juncture, would so come in aid of the law as, with it, to maintain the equilibrium of tranquillity, or whether the worst human passions, seizing on the occasion, shaking off those bonds, and inflamed by the sudden acquisition of the means of the amplest gratification of depraved desire, would force their way in defiance of all control.[78]

The good society was possessed of the 'equilibrium of tranquillity', was marked by quietness and the settled acceptance of role and place. The 'principle, education and example' which would help preserve this tranquillity were the prerogative and responsibility of a class, but could also be promulgated by institutions.

Tranquillity and quietness were of course more often rural than urban virtues. As early as 1840, Barry had delivered a lecture in Melbourne in praise of agriculture, which described the British perfection of the art, and argued that the colonists had a duty to 'render this a noble territory', by developing its agriculture.[79] If agriculture was most likely to create the kind of settled and quiet society that Barry desired, it was the discovery of gold which moved him to articulate more clearly the virtues of quietness in society, and the importance of social bonds more substantial and more settled than those of mere 'occasional interest'. That was what he meant by order. It was the antithesis of a belief in laissez faire, for it was for Barry only institutional intervention and example which could persuade people away from the frenzied pursuit of self-interest to quieter occupations, only the constitution and the laws and a classed order in society which could preserve British freedoms.

Institutions were central to the attempt by elites to reassert order in gold-rush Victoria. Barry himself was instrumental in the establishment and supervision of most of the cultural institutions of the city of Melbourne, each of which had a 'civilising' and ordering mission. The University of Melbourne was founded in 1854. Redmond Barry was its first Chancellor, and he conceived its role explicitly as a counter to the disturbingly materialist tone of the times. In a young society, 'where material wealth is so engrossing an object of pursuit', only practical and scientific knowledge, he lamented, was valued at all. Writing to Herschel and Airy, the English astronomers who were members of the committee charged with selecting four professors for the new institution, Barry sought four men 'not in holy orders, of approved worth and moral standing', exhibiting a 'total abstraction from political or sectarian interference', preferably graduates of Oxford, Cambridge, London, Edinburgh or Glasgow, and 'of such habits and manners as to stamp on their future pupils the character of the loyal well-bred, English gentleman'.[80] The committee in England, sifting through the couple of hundred applicants, seemed acutely aware that they were to make a selection on moral as well as academic grounds. There was a scare when the provisional choice for the chair in Classics was discovered to be quite unsuitable. 'Mr. D has this evening called on me', Herschel wrote to Airy, 'to tell me that he has been informed from 2 quarters both dependable that our provisional man (upon inquiry into character) *will never do* . . .

there are stories about him playing cards with *pupils*'. Airy is shaken by the incident—can the testimonials they have been collecting be trusted? 'I cannot help feeling all along that this proceeding is taking a leap in the dark, without knowing what spikes there may be for us to spit ourselves upon.' In another incident, a German scholar of the Bunsen family applied for one of the chairs. Airy wrote that 'if we wanted a professor in England, he might do well. But our instructions point emphatically to the "English Gentleman". He is to know the politics, the tastes, the social feelings, and is even to partake of the prejudices, of an Englishman. And with the view of securing this we are to take if possible, not only a learned man, but also a man who has felt the social influence of a British University.'[81] This university at Melbourne was conceived not just as an academy, but as a machine for the production of loyal English gentlemen, and hence as an instrument of social control in a disordered society.

Similar concerns surrounded the establishment of the other key cultural institutions of Melbourne—the public library, the mechanics institutes, the botanical gardens, the museum. Each sought to bring more order and rationality into the lives of Victorians. Institutions were the key to hopes for a quieter, less materialist and less self-interested society.[82] Order in Victoria was to be institutionally established. Those who sought to establish it looked to government, the law and institutions of public improvement to work their magic on a population of whose qualities and loyalties they remained rather unsure.

CALIFORNIA

Tens of thousands voluntarily rush forward, unaided by any national treasure and unprotected by any political power; each one acts as his own sovereign, directs his own time and mode for travel, and feasts or starves at pleasure . . . he is actuated solely by his love of adventure, and his love of gold.

Dr C. N. Ormsby, letter from the overland trail to California, September 1849

What was your name in the States?
Was it Thompson, or Johnson or Bates?
Did you murder your wife and fly for your life?
Say, what was your name in the States?

The Gold Rush Song Book

Confronted with the same problems of a rapidly assembled and anonymous population, Californians dramatised in their behaviour and pronouncements different understandings of order. Order there could not be reduced unproblematically to lawfulness, even for the ruling elites, nor could it easily be thought of as a static quality, or as something which could be created by institutions of themselves. In a discursive situation both older and more modern than the Victorian, the individual was central to the Californian construction of order. The situation was older in that it referred back to pre-modern concepts of individual honour protected outside the public and institutionalised law, and more modern in that it suggested a world of sovereign individuals whose rights were prior to those of the society as a whole, or the law as inherited. From the importance of the individual, the Californian discourse on order moved to consideration of the question of the morality of the population, for it was from the virtue of the people that good government and good order was thought to flow. As one observer put it, 'the rapidity with which society was organized, order restored, and law and equity resumed the balance between man and man, shows the inherent good qualities of the early emigrants'.[83] This was the Californian ideology of order—not external constraints, but the morality of the individual, and hence of the population as a whole, was to be the bedrock of order.

The rapidity of change in California allowed little room for faith in the unchanging wisdom embodied in institutions. 'The ordinary processes of law are not adapted to this community,' wrote a San Francisco woman, 'they are too slow and criminals escape.'[84] Metaphors of speed were common. California was held to be simply too fast for conventional institutional processes. This rhetoric of restlessness emphasised that change was the price and condition of progress. 'The immutability of the various systems of religion, of government, of science and of art', wrote Edward Pillock in the San Francisco *Pioneer*, 'is being daily called into question'. The source of all knowledge, he argued, the 'centre of all excellence', was the 'inexhaustible, the inexplicable human heart'.[85]

So it was with the virtue of the people that hopes for order in California rested. Governor John Bigler articulated orthodoxy when he told the California legislature in 1855 that the 'intelligence and virtue of the people, nearly allied as they are, may be justly esteemed the main stay of our republican government, and the perennial spring whence issue the streams of enduring prosperity and happiness'.[86] The virtue of the people was thus understood to be primary, the source of order rather than its consequence. One of the more patriotic characters in John Ballou's novel *The Lady of the West* boasts that: 'No law, no politicians, no priests, no courts—no none of the binding said-to-be-indispensibles existed among the miners, and yet all moved along in more harmony and morality than any other collection of men since the days of history began.'[87]

That this was ideology is shown by its usefulness in times of crisis—a political crisis such as the 1856 rule of San Francisco by the Vigilance

Committee, for example. When a revolutionary force of respectable business men took over the allegedly corrupt city government, their apologists
had to sever discussion of law from that of order, and to elevate the morality
of the population above the eternal wisdom of institutions.

The Reverend B. Brierly justified the actions of the San Francisco
Vigilance Committee the same year with the argument that the Committee
consisted of good and orderly men:

> It was not a lawless mob, nor a body of hasty, impulsive, ignorant or revengeful
> men; but orderly men, men of intelligence and great social and moral worth—
> the bone and sinew of the goodness and business of the city—men who in
> the various relations of life, and the possession of those excellencies which
> constitute men great and good, have not often been surpassed. These men had
> no love for excitement . . .

For Brierly, the goodness of these men justified them transcending institutional methods, in falling back on 'rights older than legislatures and
courts'.[88] The political crisis of 1856 was an exceptional time, but it brought
forth arguments which were usually latent, rather than causing new theories
to be invented. The morality of the population, collectively and individually, was understood to be the true basis of order in society. 'Laws are
dead,' the Reverend W.A. Scott observed, 'without a vigorous public
sentiment.'[89]

To point out this appeal to popular will, and ultimately to the individual
conscience, is to return to some very old terrain in American history—the
1950s argument that the ante-bellum period in the United States was
dominated by an anti-institutionalism which found its highest expression
in the Transcendentalist celebration of the individual. The individual,
argued Stanley Elkins, 'had become an almost mystical symbol of promise';
the very success of American society, 'of capitalism, of religious liberalism
and political democracy', made it unnecessary for the American to be
concerned with institutions.[90] George M. Fredrickson's 1965 study *The Inner
Civil War* argued that the 'dominant American belief' in the ante-bellum
period was that 'the individual could find fulfilment outside of institutions'.
The millennial optimism of the period, he argued, led many to believe that
institutions were merely constraining and limiting, and they strove for 'a
society of free individuals operating without institutional restraint'.[91]

This older historiography was most interested in the consequences of
anti-institutionalism for abolitionism and the Civil War. It overstated the
national and popular influence of New England Transcendentalism, and of
intellectuals in general. It neglected rival intellectual traditions, such as
the more recently re-discovered tradition of republicanism. But these
historians nevertheless describe a real trait in the thought of American
elites in the 1850s, one which becomes even clearer in comparative focus.
This emphasis on American individualism also came, in the historiograph-

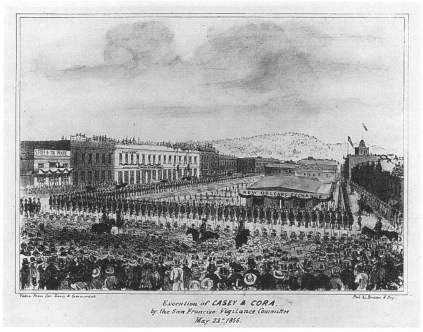

Engraving: 'Execution of Casey and Cora' (San Francisco). Courtesy Bancroft Library.

ical tradition, from the enduring frontier thesis. So Ralph Henry Gabriel argued in 1940 that the frontier, Transcendentalism, and eastern industrialisation all contributed to the strength of American individualism—the mining frontier in particular reinforced American individualism because there it was 'normal for the individual to outlast the community'.[92] Rejection of the old frontier argument, with its romantic epistemology and environmental determinism, should not lead us to underestimate the importance of individualism as ideology among American frontier elites in the 1850s. John Patrick Diggins has reasserted the importance of the liberal individualist tradition as the 'natural ideology for nineteenth-century America'.[93] In comprehending the meanings attributed to the gold rush in California, particularly in understanding its differences from the meanings in Victoria, liberal individualism and anti-institutionalism remain extremely important.

The California gold rush provided a test case for the anti-institutionalists. If that chaotic and individualising event could resolve itself without strong institutional intervention, then the faith of the anti-institutionalists would be triumphantly confirmed. In the writings of gold-rush California, we find many elaborations of the idea that society and its institutions were and should be constructed around the questing individual, rather than the individual being shaped by existing or inherited institutions. 'We Californians', argued a writer in 1854, 'enjoy to the full our present opinions . . . with almost rash confidence in our final success, we give our passionate energies full scope in carrying out their impulses, until our laws, literature, commercial relations, and educational systems have been indelibly stamped with a character for energy and progress unequalled throughout the world'.[94] The future lay with individual passion and energy, rather than with institutional control. Out of this individual energy would somehow come an order.

California also provided a test case for the study of human nature in its unsupervised state, particularly important for those grappling with the Puritan legacy of pessimism about human nature. Reformers back east had been propounding a doctrine of the innate goodness of human nature, and the great potential of each individual. 'When you tell me of the ineradicable evil of human nature', Henry James senior told an audience in New York city in the winter of 1850–51:

> I point you to these United States for an illustration on the largest scale of its uncontrolled tendencies. Here you will doubtless see individual corruption and disorder as well as elsewhere . . . But you will not see . . . any of that wilfulness, disorderliness, and ferocity which the theories in question charge upon humanity when left to itself.[95]

This optimism about human nature characteristically expressed itself in a scepticism about the necessity for institutions. Institutions, James claimed, only quenched the 'genial spirit' in man from which they sprang. James was also optimistic about the materialism inherent in human nature: There was no sheerer fallacy, he argued, than that man valued property above all things—this was only a morbid appetite which arose during scarcity.[96]

These arguments could be seen to be put to the test by conditions in California. 'In the regions whence we came', J. A. Benton wrote in his moral and didactic *The California Pilgrim*, 'there has been, for some years, a growing disposition to think too well of our common nature, its innocencies, excellencies, capabilities, and susceptibilities to good. Human nature there is not so free to show its worst features as here.' Even a pessimist like Benton, though, had little faith in institutions. Civilisation, he wrote, 'is not sufficient of itself, to renovate humanity, to cultivate, refine, purify, and ennoble man's moral nature'.[97] Order had to come from within.

The sermon provides a societally central ritual occasion, upon which ideas about order were articulated. The Reverend Charles Wadsworth was not to emigrate to California until 1862, replacing W.A. Scott, who had to leave for Europe because of his Confederate sympathies. In 1856 Wadsworth was back east in Philadelphia, minister at the Arch Street Presbyterian Church, but his views at this period give a sense of the ideological resources which Americans brought to California.[98] 'For what is America', he asked at Thanksgiving, 'and where? . . . Does she abide in great cities? or voyage in great ships? The simple fact is, that each American is America. You, and I, and all of us, are the American nation.'[99]

Questions of national morality, Wadsworth argued, were really only questions of individual morality magnified: 'there is no such thing as national character apart from individual character'. This was anti-institutional thought. Yet, on Wadsworth's own account, nations did have collective characters. For, articulating the republican argument that nations rose and fell in cyclical fashion, Wadsworth presented, alongside his cheerful moralism of the individual, a gloomy republican determinism. 'To the philosophic eye', he explained:

> history is but a roll of defunct nations, all essentially alike in career and destiny. Unto Chaldaea, Tyre, Greece, Rome, unto all, as if by an inevitable law, there came, after the day of civilization and empire, the deep night of barbarism and slavery. This has been repeated again and again . . . [T]he race in its struggling progress, can be successful only up to a certain point, which having been reached, all the fruits of past labor, all the accumulation of legislators, philosophers, statesmen, warriors, must be swept away, and the race begin again, the laborious process—upward from the same gulf, to be overtaken by the same disaster.[100]

What was it that ensured that all future history would also follow these repetitive 'ever recurring cycles'? It was above all the corrupting and debilitating influence of wealth: 'Men philosophize upon the process as inevitable in nature—power begetting wealth—and wealth, luxury—and luxury, feebleness—so that to complete civilization, is only to develop the germ of destruction.'[101]

The individual was the basis of national success, yet national success would inevitably manifest itself in prosperity, which ate at the individualism that had enabled it. Wealth and luxury, Wadsworth explained, created in society 'crusts of distinctive caste', which were destructive of the 'culture, and development, of *Individual Man*'.[102] Custodians of the culture like Wadsworth were thus caught in a difficult double bind. They had on the one hand to assert the importance of the individual and his enterprises, while on the other to limit carefully the scope he would be allowed. Republicanism and anti-institutional individualism conflicted here within the one person.

Wadsworth was preoccupied with the proper limits of masculine selfhood. The issues were to do with the individual man and the bounds to be placed upon him; he was seen as an enterprising and energetic profit seeker, whose restlessness was both the chief source of vitality within, and the chief threat to the nation. This comes out in Wadsworth's illuminating discussion of the respective qualities of men and gentlemen:

A *man* may be only a rugged plateau of rock—*a gentleman* is that same rock beautified into rich landscape; he is a patient man; a gentle man; he is courteous and forebearing, and pitiful; he does not bluster, nor blaspheme, nor carry weapons, nor practice pistol-shooting; nor talk loudly of his honor.[103]

But a gentleman was not merely gentle, 'for such a creature may be a gentleman with only *THE MAN left out of it*'. The gentleman possesses manly energies, but curbs them for the good of the whole, 'governs himself; conquers his passions and prejudices'.[104] This self-governing quality becomes particularly important in restless times:

Enthusiastic excitement is the law of the generation. In trade, what rage of competition and speculation! In pleasure, what a quickening of sentimental taste into a fierce appetite, clamorous, and craving! Alike, in little things, and great things, mean things, and mighty; from the weaving of a shoe tie, to the conquest of an empire; the whole race is in a furore; and the tides of life are boisterous and white as an advancing deluge.[105]

The excitement had origins in wealth-seeking activity, but it developed beyond it into a whole culture of frenzy.[106]

This excitement was not, from Wadsworth's point of view, entirely a bad thing. Excitement was energy ('in times like these, intense energy is the true inspiration'), and the energetic individual was the basis of the culture ('we are partial to boyhood; its flashing eyes; its hot blood; its fresh senses; its high impulses; we are enamoured of all of them') even though he had always to be careful to keep his energy within sociable limits.[107] It was in the dialectic between the man and the gentleman that the good society would develop. And it was crucial for the culture as a whole that the two extremes be avoided: 'Between the extremes of self-negation, and self-sufficiency, lies the golden mean of self-respect and reliance.'[108]

When he arrived in California, Wadsworth proselytised on behalf of the quieter and more domesticated, but also more disciplined and collectivist, qualities of the 'gentleman', through organisations such as the Young Men's Christian Association (YMCA). Wadsworth welcomed the Civil War, as providing a chastening check to overdeveloped American individualism, self-seeking materialism, and democracy.[109]

Order for Wadsworth was constituted as the correctly balanced relationship between individual masculine energy, and a more socially oriented concern. Order was not quietness, but rather lay in some restraint of excitement. This was the problematic within which many of the guardians of American culture were to understand the event of gold in California. The question was how to retain the energy of manhood, and yet combine it in some way with the order that followed the gentleman.

In California, the usually coupled 'law and order' had to be separated in debate. The frequent recourse to vigilante justice on the goldfields, and the two San Francisco experiences of Vigilance Committees, meant that order in California had to be established by its defenders as something which might be of more importance than the law. Californians interpreted the improvised and extra-legal judicial practices of the 1850s in the context of a legacy of republican and revolutionary political thought. Law could not be allowed to stand as an unqualified good, even in conservative discourse, for on both sides of politics the lessons of the revolution had to be acknowledged. Conservatives thus rallied around order, which was argued for in moral or overtly economic terms. In this separation we can see, as David A. Johnson has suggested, the 'moral authority that Californians, like other Americans of their era, gave to the "people" over the coercive power of the state'.[110]

When Vigilance Committees temporarily took over the government of San Francisco in 1851 and 1856, in what Josiah Royce later dubbed a 'Business Man's Revolution', almost all the Protestant ministers in the city endorsed their actions.[111] The decision was often not an easy one, as the contorted arguments offered publicly on the subject suggest, because support for the committees involved arguing for the necessity of going outside the law to maintain the laws, or of setting aside the laws to maintain order. The justifications offered for this were in terms of the qualities of the persons effecting the 'revolution'—their orderliness (and wealth) guaranteed, their apologists argued, the orderly outcome of their intervention.

Timothy Dwight Hunt, minister in San Francisco successively to Congregationalist and Presbyterian churches, offered qualified public support in an 1851 sermon for the hanging of John Jenkins by the Vigilance Committee.[112] He began by vigorously arguing the extraordinary importance which respect for law and authority had in the maintenance of order: 'Law secures to us all we value in society. We owe to it the inviolability of our homes . . . On this we rest for the security of our possessions. In this we hope for the continuance of life and liberty. He trifles with all that is sacred who speaks evil of dignities, and scorns the restraint of wholesome law.'[113] But after praising obedience, Hunt turned to a somewhat perfunctory account of the right of rebellion against 'arbitrary and oppressive rule'. Bad rulers have no right to rule, he reminded his hearers, and bad rule is 'just cause for revolution': 'Especially is this true in republican forms of government. The relation, among us, of officers to the people, is that of servants. Power emanates from the people.' But the people, Hunt stressed, should not rise up in revolution at every offence. Here his language again became more vivid: 'No. This would result in constant revolution. In such a case, no community would be at peace. Every populace would be a wave of the sea, driven into fury by the breath of any demagogue . . . No. Put us under the iron rule of a despot, rather than deliver us over to the reckless fury of a blind and angry multitude.' Having set up the points between which a stable society must steer, Hunt maintained that the committee's

actions were justified for 'there are circumstances that require a transcend-
ancy of the laws . . . for the purpose of an impressive example, and the
intimidation of the desperately wicked'.[114]

The contortions of a public figure such as Hunt, firmly committed to
the status quo and the maintenance of law *and* order, but prepared to
sacrifice law to order in certain solemn circumstances, illuminate something
of the definition of order in California. *'Justice is always sacred'*, the
Reverend B. Brierly explained, 'and no hallowed hand may meddle with
it; law is sacred for it subserves the ends of justice, and it is not worth a
straw beyond this. The stupid cry of the *"sacredness"* and *"majesty"* of law
. . . is as senseless as the ancient cry of the *"divine right of kings"*.'[115] Once
outside the law, it was only moral judgement or economic interest which
allowed one to decide when and how far to take matters into one's own
hands.

Defenders of the vigilantes' actions, whether in San Francisco or the
mining areas, always stressed their attachment to the *form* of legal process,
even if the performance was not by legally constituted authorities. Jan
Nicholson has argued that process rather than person granted legitimacy
in the American, as against the British colonial context, where authority
derived from the person of the official, who had to be visibly invested with
the dignity of office.[116] Although the observation of the emphasis on
procedure by the American vigilantes is a significant one, the contrast will
not quite hold—the stress the vigilantes placed on process was precisely a
sign that they knew and their audience knew that they were not the proper
people to be performing the actions they were undertaking, but that they
could be accepted as proper because of who they were—respectable men.
Procedure was so important to them because they knew that their observance of due process was not the same as process followed by the elected
authorities, and that their acceptance would ultimately depend upon their
status as persons. The San Francisco Vigilance Committees in particular
had to demonstrate symbolically that their extra-legal actions were not
those of a mob. Approving observers often praised the silent determination
which characterised the actions of the vigilantes and their supporters—for
mobs were by definition noisy. Frank Fargo's admiring description in the
Daily Alta California of the silent movement of Vigilance Committee men
through San Francisco in 1856 is typical: 'the whole living throng moved
forward with scarcely an audible voice, save that of the officers in command. A solemnity and stillness pervaded the whole party that at once
was significant of the might and power in those brave hands.'[117] The
vigilante compensated for his extra-legal status by a greater, rather than a
lesser, degree of observation of solemnity, of form and process. Order, he
implicitly argued, was compensating for law. His own person—purposeful,

respectable, orderly, silent—compensated for abbreviation or alteration of legal form.

Horace Bushnell spent most of 1856 in California for reasons of health.[118] Observing the vigilante events of that year, he delivered on 6 July a 'Sermon for California', in which he undertook to argue that true religion was 'the only sufficient spring of civil order and social happiness'.[119] This might seem an unremarkable theme for a Protestant minister, but it led him to a significant stress on the 'character of the people' as the foundation of the state, without which there would be inevitable breakdown into 'anarchy and irredeemable barbarism'. Bushnell carefully distinguished truly Christian revolutions, such as, presumably, that of the Vigilance Committee, from 'all that rioting for justice and liberty which is the froth of unbelief and vice and mere natural passion'. He warned particularly against putting too much faith in the state or the republican political system on its own: 'The civil state is a mere repressive agency; a law for transgressors, not a power to cure the spirit of transgression.' The republic of itself could not be a positive moral force, and 'were all virtue extinct, it would, as a republic, be a mere system of checks and balances'. 'Public morality' was all that could really redeem a society. 'No external checks and balances,' Bushnell argued, 'can suffice if there be no checks of principle and virtue within.' The problem of the age was that men were too adept at discovering rights: 'abundance of rights, too fantastic ever to be named with sobriety— the right to have a farm, the right to be made happy, the right of individual sovereignty, the right of free love'.[120] Order was crucially dependent, in Bushnell's thinking, not on a system of government, but on the morality of the population. Moral people might have to override the laws. This was a particularly striking conclusion in Bushnell, who was at the pro-institutional end of the American spectrum.[121]

The only Protestant clergyman to oppose the Vigilance Committee in 1856 was the Reverend W. A. Scott, and he too argued that order in the state depended upon the morality of the people: 'it is . . . plain that the framework of society rests upon the masses . . . if they are corrupt and in an unhealthy state, then the social edifice is like a stately home on the edge of a slumbering volcano'. Asking himself why there was such continued 'violence and blood . . . suffering, depression and consuming want' in California, he found the answer in human depravity and immorality, and looked despairingly to the future of California: 'And is this demon thirst for blood never to be slaked? Has our community become like the herds of wild beasts in a Roman amphitheatre . . . Is our history henceforth to have but two chapters, gold and blood, and blood and gold?' Scott could not countenance the actions of the Vigilance Committee in these circumstances, and urged a return to the laws—'our fundamental laws are good. They embody the highest wisdom and the vast experience of the wisest and best men that have ever lived.'[122] Scott was hanged in effigy in San Francisco for making public these views.[123] While he was a dissenter on the question of law in California, he was right in the mainstream in his view of the prior importance of a moral population. It was immorality, in his view, which made men turn away from the law, and the laws themselves could not create morality.

Turning to the theatre of the law in California, we can see some of these themes enacted. There was perhaps more difficulty in establishing the majesty of the law above or apart from issues of individual honour and personal senses of justice than in Victoria. The theatre of the law was as important in California as in Victoria, and it is important not simply to contrast the makeshift pomp of the colony with the rough informality of the republican frontier. In both places the law had crucial demonstrative as well as regulatory functions. But in California individual persons had more to do with legitimation than did institutional forms of themselves.

Stephen J. Field was a Californian lawyer, legislator and judge, who spent most of his career on the United States Supreme Court. But in 1850 he was newly arrived in Marysville, California with, as he writes it in his autobiography, only twenty dollars to his name. On arrival he signed up for 65 town lots, for a total of $16 250, as a consequence of which 'the proprietors of the place waited upon me and showed me great attention'. Soon after he succeeded in being elected *alcalde* (magistrate) of the town—'the main objection urged against me was that I was a newcomer. I had been there only three days; my opponent had been there six.'[124] Field began to practice law in the town.

In a case heard before District Judge Turner in Marysville in June 1850, Field rose to make an objection to the judge's preliminary ruling, and began reading to the court from a statute he considered relevant. Turner, angered, ordered Field to resume his seat and, after some altercation, imposed a fine and 48 hours imprisonment for contempt of court. Field was arrested and brought before Judge Haun of the County Court, who decided that there were no proper grounds for arrest and released him. A crowd which had gathered outside gave three cheers for Field and three groans for Turner. That evening, Judge Turner was burned in effigy on the public plaza, a 'spontaneous act of the people' according to the pro-Field Sacramento *Daily Transcript*.[125]

When Turner's court resumed on Monday, he ordered the sheriff to rearrest Field and to arrest Judge Haun, whom he ordered to be fined $50 and imprisoned 48 hours for releasing Field. Turner also ordered that Field and two other attorneys be expelled from the bar.

The sheriff, Buchanan, arrested Field and Haun, but left them in the charge of another man, who became 'alarmed at some idle threats' and discharged them both. When the sheriff went to rearrest Haun, the judge drew a pistol on him and threatened his life, according to the *Sacramento Transcript*, or paid his fine and left, according to the *Daily Transcript*.[126] Judge Haun then proceeded to his own house, where he opened the Court of Sessions of Yuba County—and there Field sued out a writ of habeas corpus, and began an address to the court 'touching the cause of his confinement'.[127] Turner, hearing of this tactic, 'ordered a posse to be summoned and appealed to gentlemen in his court room to serve on it; and ordered the sheriff to take Field and Haun by force from the court of sessions and put them in confinement'. When the sheriff arrived 'at the head of fifty men' to rearrest Field and Haun, he was told that the court was in session, 'and that order must be preserved while it was in session'. The sheriff and his party left, but returned five minutes later, saying that Haun must leave the court and go with him. Haun told Sheriff Buchanan that he was violating the laws of the land. Buchanan said that he 'could not be trifled with', then seized Haun and attempted to drag him from the court. Haun imposed a fine of $200 on Buchanan for contempt of court. Buchanan 'then and there called upon the fifty persons ordered out by him as his posse to take hold of the said H.P. Haun', but they refused to assist, and the court adjourned.[128] The *Daily Transcript* commented that: 'These proceedings aroused a feeling of indignation such as I have never seen exhibited in any community, and I am grateful to Almighty God that no violence was committed . . . if there is any right that Americans hold sacred, it is the great right of the writ of habeas corpus.'[129]

There are varying reports of what took place that evening. The pro-Turner *Sacramento Transcript* has it that Field's friends gathered at his house, and heard an 'inflammatory address' from Field. Turner himself wrote that Field and attorney Goodwin made:

> the most vile and slanderous speeches against me to an armed mob, thereby inciting a riot, and causing the mob to attack me in the night, while I stood alone in the doorway of my office. Field advised the mob to throw me into the Yuba, and told them that he would be with them in anything they did to me, and that if they would sink me to the bottom of the river, he could go to bed and rest contented.

The crowd proceeded to Turner's house, the *Sacramento Transcript* reported:

> Judge Turner . . . being alone and seated in his doorway, dispersed the 'mob' by that indomitable moral power which some men are known to possess and exert upon others. The Judge bade them come on! They obeyed the invitation by firing 10 or 12 shots at him . . . The mob became panic-stricken at their own firing, and, as a friend in company with me remarked, if these are the persons we are to expect to protect and defend California, the 'Digger Indians have got us sure!'[130]

The pro-Field *Daily Transcript* had a less heroic story to tell—the crowd had merely delivered three groans in front of Turner's house, and then, as it was dispersing, 'several of the gentlemen fired in the air, as a sort of finale to the whole'. Turner was not in his office at the time, the paper said, 'and all the stories about pistols being fired at him, and his daring the crowd *to come on*, are sheer fabrications'.[131] Field and Goodwin wrote to the *Placer Times* and, in a letter published on 23 July, contested Turner's description of the crowd of Monday evening as a 'mob'—'what he chooses to call a mob was a peaceable assembly of the citizens of Marysville'. They further alleged that Turner had recently been to the mines—'Judge Turner is paid by the state $7500 a year, and the law supposes he is either at his chambers or in court. It is not supposed that he is in the mountains hunting for *claims*.'[132]

The three men expelled from the Bar applied to the California Supreme Court which, on 4 July, ordered Turner to vacate his order of expulsion, and to restore them to the Bar. Turner refused; the Supreme Court was appealed to again, and made a second order, with which Turner complied. Field had his final revenge when he won soon after a seat in the California legislature, and had a bill passed which reorganised the state judiciary in a complex way which entailed, among other things, Turner being sent to a remote north-western region of the state.[133]

What was at stake in this encounter? There are some commonsense explanations for the series of seeming over-reactions which set off this spiralling feud—careers, and possibly lives, were at stake. Turner seems to have been a particularly bad and arbitrary judge; Field was an ambitious young man with a career to make. Turner was from Texas, pro-slavery, and part of his dislike of Field and his associates was a distrust of northerners ('witnesses there can be procured to prove anything', Turner said of New York, 'I have learned that S.J. Field and J.O. Goodwin are from New York, where they may have had, for aught I know, much experience in matters of this sort.')[134]

But we can also derive from this episode some ideas about the presentation of judicial performances in California. Field's 1930 biographer saw the whole controversy as evidence merely of the 'rough, unformed character of California in the early days'.[135] Yet despite the threats of violence, and the apparent violations of decorum, this is really a drama in which the form and appearance of legal process is of great importance. The incident began with Turner's sensitivity about the questioning of his judicial pronouncement. The charges being bandied about all had to do with contempt of court, and the dignity of their courtrooms was obviously much of the issue for both Haun and Turner. The editor of the *Sacramento Transcript* wrote to Turner supporting his actions, and stressing the 'necessity of upholding and maintaining the majesty of the law, and the dignity of the bench, particularly in a country like this'; Turner collected and published many other testimonies from judges and lawyers who all testified to the dignity, the despatch of business, and the order ('so much order and general satisfaction rendered') which they said characterised Turner's court.[136] Order and dignity were acknowledged on both sides to be the issues at stake.

If the partisan newspaper accounts have any truth to them, the crowd which gathered to play a part in these events responded to suggestion or direction, but also had ideas of its own about fundamental legal issues such as habeas corpus, formal legal ideas that is, which went beyond mere partisan loyalty to one of the big men in town. The crowd was crucial in this story—forming a posse, but holding back from dragging Haun from his court; groaning in front of Turner's house but not, its defenders argued, actually threatening him with violence. The definitional line between the good crowd (the people's voice), and the bad mob, was also obviously a key issue here.

Underlying the whole story is the theme of masculine self-assertion, and those questions of honour and manly dignity which still had life in a society in which duelling, although it had been specifically outlawed in the state constitution, was still rife.[137] 'As a *matter of fact*', the evangelical *Pacific* argued in 1851, 'dueling is a *relic of barbarism* . . . These ruling passions, when embodied, constitute the savage.'[138] In the published verbal exchanges between Turner and Field, this is the barely submerged context. Turner went out of his way to taunt Field about alleged cowardice. Field was the first to run, Turner said; he did not respond to insult.

Field, Goodwin and Mulford published an article in the *Placer Times* for 27 July 1850. In it they attacked Turner's character. He had been seen in the streets 'in a state of beastly intoxication, uttering the most blasphemous oaths'; he had had seated by his side during a session of his court 'a keeper of a brothel' and then 'talked and laughed with her to the great scandal of the court and of the county', and subsequently he visited her brothel and she was let off charges; he had traversed the streets day after day applying epithets 'too low and obscene to be repeated' to the citizens of Marysville. Field and his friends described Turner, in conclusion, as a man of 'depraved tastes, of vulgar habits, of an ungovernable temper, reckless of truth, when his passions are excited, and grossly incompetent to discharge the duties of his office. It is a sad thing that such a man should ever be clothed with Judicial Ermine.'[139] This was the article which caused Turner to attempt to have all three removed from the Bar. Turner wrote a letter 'To the Public' which attacked the editor of the *Placer Times* for publishing the letter, and said that his contempt for the editor 'has no adequate form of conveyance through the ordinary channel of words, and can only find suitable expression in the application of a different mode of reasoning'.[140]

Field got up a petition to Californian Governor Burnett, which alleged that Turner was incompetent, that he exhibited 'ignorance of the most elementary principles of the law', that he exercised his power in 'an arbitrary and tyrannical manner', that he 'frequently went into court with revolving pistols upon his person, to the great scandal of the court and of the county'. Turner was 'guilty of oppression in office which has no parallel in the history of the country':

> He consorts with the low and disreputable . . . A conservator of the peace, under the Constitution, he is heard almost every day swearing that he will cut off 'the damned ears' of this and that gentleman who may happen to incur his enmity. An example to the rising generation, he is often seen in the streets reeling from intoxication.[141]

Turner published a description of Field as a 'perjured, damned villain', and attempted to 'chastise' him in the street with a switch. Field, Turner said, 'had no courage to resent the former, and just speed enough in his system to avoid the latter'. He further described Field as a man 'whose life, if analysed, would be found to be one series of little-minded meanlinesses, of braggadacio, pusillanimity, and contemptible vanity'.[142] Field published a card on 21 December in Marysville in response, describing this assertion as 'a shameless lie':

> I never, to my recollection, saw Judge Turner with a switch or a whip in his hand. He has made . . . many threats of taking personal vengeance on myself, but he has never attempted to put any of them into execution. I have never avoided him, but on the contrary have passed him in the street almost everyday for the last four months . . . Judge Turner says he holds himself personally responsible in and under all circumstances. This he says in print; but it is well understood in this place that he has stated he should feel bound by his oath of office to endeavour to obtain an indictment against any gentlemen who should attempt to call him to account. Shielded behind his oath of office he has displayed his character by childish boasts of personal courage and idle threats of vengeance.[143]

The issues here are complex. Both men apparently routinely carried weapons into court, and about town.[144] The exchange of insults is, among other things, the somewhat ritualised prelude to a duel, one which never quite came about. The issues of personal, masculine honour intersect obliquely with those of legality.

Dueling was illegal, and that illegality had to be upheld by public figures like Field and Turner. At the same time, the code of honour, to which both more or less subscribed, required that one hold oneself 'responsible' at all times for one's statements and actions. This amounted to an alternate, and older, system of dispute resolution.[145] One of the objections to dueling was that in fact it usurped the position of the law. 'In this State it is an open violation of the Constitution', observed the *Pacific*, 'More than this it assumes the right of private jurisdiction over the constituted courts. The duelist usurps the judgement of his own cause.'[146] Defenders of dueling argued merely that it was functional in resolving disputes and keeping the peace. Judge David Terry wrote in 1856 that:

> I believe no man has the right to outrage the feelings of another, or to attempt to blast his good name, without being responsible for his actions . . . My own experience has taught me, that when the doctrine of personal responsibility obtains, men are seldom insulted without good cause, and private character is safer from attack; that much quarrelling and bad blood, and revengeful feeling is avoided.[147]

In the Turner–Field controversy, the participants were attempting to satisfy the demands of honour and to keep up the display which that required (the personal bearing, the insults), while also keeping up the different displays required of the upholders of the forms of the law, the dignities of the court. The accusation that Turner was hiding his honour behind his judicial oath brings this conflict into the open.

At least in Marysville, the institution of the law could not be clearly separated from issues of personal honour, and older and more individual codes of dispute resolution. This story of frontier justice, while not 'typical', provides insights into tensions in the Californian attempt to establish institutions perceived as legitimate. The Victorian stress on institutions, the public resources devoted to developing them, reflected the trajectory of British government towards greater central control and intervention. Macdonagh characterises the nineteenth-century 'revolution in government' as the 'transformation . . . of the operations and functions of the state within society, which destroyed belief in the possibility that society did or should consist of contractual relationships between persons'.[148] Institutions and state bureaucracies were to be the instruments of collective rather than individual goals in Victoria.

This incident in Marysville provides illustration of some of the tensions in dominant ideas about order in California. The issue was the proper balance between individualism and control. It was not that the laws would generate order, but that moral individuals, with all their energy, would behave in ways just social enough for the society to maintain an appearance of order. Stephen J. Field, in a later judgement, stressed that order in California had grown from the qualities of the people rather than from institutional forms. 'Wherever they went, they carried with them that love of order and system and of fair dealing which are the prominent characteristics of our people.'[149] This individualism, which sought order in the characteristics of the people, looked back to pre-modern codes of dispute resolution by individuals, but also forward to dominant forms of liberal individualism.

As Victoria moved into a more institutionally oriented future, it was only the most old fashioned of conservatives who argued that order was best maintained by individuals who could inspire deference. Thus J.F.L. Foster argued in the Victorian Parliament in 1854 that the great difference between English and American institutions was that the English were still based upon the 'idea of a gentleman'—'a man respecting himself, courteous to others, with truth in his acts, and honour in his heart; and I cannot help thinking that the fact of the Crown selecting for high office and political position, has a great deal to do with this'.[150] The more common Victorian argument was rather that institutions had the best chance of inspiring order in society. The story of Field in California is some evidence that the 'idea of a gentleman' still had life within American political culture. The elite and masculinist individualism it embodied intersected and reinforced to some extent the growing dominance of liberal individualism as the dominant American ideology.

It is possible, then, to differentiate something of what was meant by 'order' in the two societies. In Victoria, order was institutionally backed, its goals were social peace and, often, the maintenance of hierarchy. In California, order was understood in more individualised terms. Order was understood to be inseparable from the morality of the population in general and the dignity of prominent and powerful men in particular. In confronting the chaos of gold, Victorians and Californians turned in different directions in the hope of finding order.

CHAPTER 4

AGRARIANISM AND
PASTORAL

The following chapters examine strands of the critical response to gold. They deal with those observers who had arrived at a pessimistic assessment of the possibilities of gold-rush society. If order was not to be attained through laissez faire, where did one turn? For many Californians and Victorians the answer was clear—they turned to the possibility of another kind of social order, that of the agricultural society. And some looked further than this, to the natural world in its uncultivated state—what these invaders called 'wilderness'—and to the values they associated with it. In both places, they seemed to see a possible context for social forms not governed by self-interest alone.

VICTORIA

> I recommend men to dig for gold, wherewith to purchase lands and settle (Applause) . . . .
>
> Caroline Chisholm at the Castlemaine Hall, November 1854

Samuel Sidney, the English writer and publicist of emigration, one of the most eloquent theorists of the agrarian view of the possibilities of the Australian colonies, celebrated the discovery of gold in Australia in his 1852 emigrants' manual, *The Three Colonies of Australia*. Gold, he assured his readers, had transformed Australia from a mere 'sheepwalk tended by nomadic burglars' into:

> the wealthiest offset of the British crown—a land of promise for the adventurous—a home of peace and independence for the industrious—an El Dorado and an Arcadia combined . . . where every striving man who rears a race of industrious children, may sit under the shadow of his own vine and his own fig tree—not without work, but with little care—living on his own land,

looking down the valleys to his herds—towards the hills to his flocks, amid the humming of bees, which know no winters.

As it happened Sidney had never been to Australia, but it was not mere distance which lent an air of unreality to his claims. He was, after all, dealing with a set of highly conventional arcadian images, which enjoyed just as frequent use in Australia as in England. The implausibility came rather from the attempt to argue that Australia could be 'an El Dorado and an Arcadia combined'.[1] To almost everyone in the 1850s the two states seemed profoundly opposed; how *could* a land at once offer promise to the adventurous and peace to the industrious?

Was it even possible to imagine a tranquil and pastoral scene of gold digging? James Bonwick, editor of the *Australian Gold Digger's Monthly Magazine*, writing in 1853, made the most sustained and lyrical attempt. 'In the neighbourhood of Ballarat', he wrote:

> is one of the sweetest little valleys in Victoria. The prettiest of bush flowers dotted the green carpet with beauty. The yellow Buttercup, so endeared to British feeling, the little white Pimelia, the gorgeous red and massive flowering Kennediae, the deep blue Indigo, the modest Everlasting, with other offspring of the soil, throve beneath the deep shade of the towering Eucalypti. Two streams mingled their transparent waters, and lightly glided through the valley. In the midst of this sylvan scene a few families of diggers had pitched their tents. The rosy cheeks of the little ones, the contented smiles of the matrons of the camp, and the aspect of comfort presented within the canvas, satisfied the observer that in such quarters one might expect to find a happy home. One could not help contrasting such a view with that of a tenement in the crowded and odorous streets of Melbourne. The fret and fever of life have little place in this Diggings station.[2]

Bonwick's journal failed after a year. His project, the depiction of an arcadian El Dorado, was a forlorn one. The sylvan tranquil diggings, in complete harmony with a picturesque landscape, remained a hopeful but increasingly unconvincing fiction. What is striking about the responses to the gold rush that have survived, is the extent to which contemporaries were preoccupied with exactly the issue of the tension between Arcadia and El Dorado, the tension between the life of cultivation of the soil and that of extraction from it. To most observers it appeared that the discovery of gold in the garden would lead to some very profound disturbances.

The pastoral, with its evocation of a golden age always just passed, when labour was unnecessary and nature was spontaneously fruitful, and carefree shepherds could devote themselves to the pursuit of love, has a long history in English literature.[3] By the 1850s we are dealing with a late, rather earnest and Victorian version of pastoral ('not without work', Samuel Sidney hastened to assure his readers, 'but with little care'), but the conventions are still clearly visible beneath the more sober advice given to prospective emigrants, or the more 'realistic' descriptions offered by travellers. One emigration manual, Sidney Smith's *Whether to go and Whither?*, argued that one of the virtues of the more natural life possible in the Australian colonies would be escape from endless labour: 'who can believe that starvation, endless unendurable toil, wretched, slavish dependence . . . are normal dispensations of Providence? Industry is a virtue, but not labour.'[4]

The fantasy of a society in which work might be unnecessary was fostered both by the early expectations of gold, and by the pastoral expectations of the countryside. The *Mount Alexander Mail* felt it necessary to refute the idea that work would be unnecessary in Victoria by reminding its readers that 'the immutable decree has gone forth—that labor is man's destiny—and . . . success will, in the main, attend only the enterprising and industrious'.[5] As influential a Victorian as J.F.L. Foster, later Colonial Secretary, observed in his *The New Colony of Victoria* that in Victoria 'meat is produced, and beasts of burden maintained by the pastoral class, with little or no effort'.[6] William Howitt, writing for children, was at pains to point out that the Australian shepherd was not quite the reflective character of poetry: 'They wander through the woods and among the hills after their sheep and bullocks without anything to employ their thoughts; they are not like the jolly shepherds of old as represented in . . . the pastorals of the poets.'[7] Even where scepticism such as this was expressed, it was the pastoral story which provided the frame within which the Victorian experience was placed. When James Daniel was speculating in a letter to his brother in England about what he would do if he found gold, his answer was the conventional one within his society, balancing pastoral expectations with the necessity for work : 'If I am successful I shall take to farming—it's a splendid occupation . . . occasionally toilsome but healthful and even romantic from the scenery and I may say the immensity of the place.'[8]

The colony of Victoria, in particular, was appropriated to agrarianism and pastoral; it was celebrated as a scene of cultivation or of grazing, a garden and a farm, in which the labour of humankind was necessary, morally as much as horticulturally, gently to tend the *almost* spontaneously fruitful soil. Sidney Smith explained in his emigrants' manual, writing of Victoria, that agriculture was the 'happy medium betwixt the wild irregularity of the Arab, and the sophisticated vice of Paris'.[9] It was into this idyllic environment, this antipodean middle landscape, that the gold rush erupted.

Early in his *Land, Labour and Gold; Or, Two Years in Victoria*, William Howitt, the travelling English author, described a visit he had made to a house at the colonial Brighton, late in 1852. 'In the garden,' he wrote, 'you were surrounded by trees, and shrubs, and flowers, that would only grow in our conservatories . . . It was such a scene of luxuriance and beauty as you can scarcely imagine.'[10] Such places, Howitt observed, 'make one cease to wonder that intelligent men like to spend their lives in these distant colonies. There is a wild, fresh beauty about them that affects the imagination agreeably.'[11] The puzzle—why intelligent men like to spend their lives in distant colonies?—is answered by the very appearance of the garden. Victoria is the home of the picturesque, of an apparently wild yet cultivated beauty, that 'affects the imagination agreeably'.

Here, though, a discordant note intrudes into Howitt's description of the garden: 'the gold has disturbed the pleasant quiet and the prolific abundance of even these charming spots . . . "This used to be a pleasant quiet country", said the lady of the house, "but it is all over now!" ' Howitt's descriptions of his experiences in Victoria are mostly written in a tone of jocular detachment, as wry observations of the foibles of colonial life embodying all the sustained jollity of tone of middle-brow Victorian journalism. Yet occasionally, as in his evocations of Victorian gardens, something brings him to a more detailed and engaged treatment of his subject. In his travels through Victoria he takes particular note of the conditions of gardens, their abundance, their ability to reproduce the fruits of the old world; they seem to him to be a significant index of the possibilities of life in the new country.

When the gold discoveries occurred, and the exodus to the goldfields and the soaring cost of labour meant that both horticulture and agriculture in the colony were neglected, Howitt was particularly concerned to convey his sense of the abandonment involved. Noting the scarcity of labour, he moved rapidly to register the effect where it seemed to him most telling. 'The gardens and pleasure grounds of gentlemen, as well as the gardens of a humbler description, are regular wildernesses for the most part', he wrote:

> They have literally nobody to cultivate them; and I see arums, such as we cultivate in the house, now standing, putting up their white, marble-like, spathal flowers; with jonquils, splendid cacti, the native indigo, prickly pears, roses red and white, stocks as tall and large as shrubs, yellow jasmine, date trees, tobacco trees, India-rubber trees, and a host of strange shrubs and curious flowers . . . all these choked by a mass of weeds up to your waist. It is strange to drive up to a good house, with its English look, its English approach, and English fields all around, and on reaching its shrubbery, finding it looking as if the place were deserted. The walks all overgrown, and the most gorgeous flowers and tropical plants lost in a desert of weeds, whilst among them the cockatoos, parrots, and parroquets, flit about with strange voices . . .[12]

There is more here than simple middle-class concern for neglected property. The luxuriant yet deserted garden, with 'literally nobody' to cultivate it, overgrown, choking itself with its own spontaneous fertility, was a potent image of disorder, a standing indictment of a wilful human abandonment of the responsibilities of husbandry and stewardship of this especially endowed natural environment.

The gold discoveries were disturbing to contemporaries for many reasons. Disturbance implies a pre-existing state to be disrupted. Victoria was depicted as a cultivator's paradise, an extensive garden, and I argue that a great deal of contemporary response to gold constructed the gold rush primarily as a disruption of this vision of the possibilities of life in the new society. The literary term for the fantasy of a bountiful nature in which work was unnecessary is 'pastoral'. The practical distinction between pastoral and agricultural land use has been crucial in Australian history, and because it was most often *cultivation* of the soil that was strenuously and publicly advocated, I shall use the term 'agrarianism' here to denote the set of beliefs about the virtue of rural work that was so important a part of the response to gold in Victoria. The labour of gold mining was frequently contrasted unfavourably with the labour involved in agriculture in social criticism. This georgic theme was a staple of political comment in Victoria. The pastoral led a more fugitive existence, though it animated as fantasy much of the thought about the future of the colony. If we are to ask, then, how the gold rush was experienced in the context of the ideas of the 1850s, one of the first answers would have to be that it was experienced as a disruption to that agrarian ideology, with its physiocratic overtones, which held that real wealth came from the soil, that the destiny of the colony was agricultural, that there was an almost moral responsibility to cultivate the soil of so beneficent an environment, and that the small cultivator was liable to be among the most virtuous and useful of citizens. These ideas have often been influential in Australian history. Here their status as ideology is clearly marked by the fact that small farming scarcely existed in the colony; the agricultural society had to be *created*, not merely defended, in a colony founded in the wake of occupation by the squatters and their flocks of sheep.

There had been a sense of the enchantment of the Victorian landscape since its first European appropriation. 'The land is, in short, open and available in its present state, for all the purposes of civilised man', wrote Major Mitchell in his 1839 journal, praising the 'flowery plains and green hills, fanned by the breezes of early spring' of western Victoria. [13] Here was a landscape that could be constituted as a pastoral Arcadia positively inviting possession. So when settlement came, it was felt by many that it should enter the landscape, not merely transform it. Eugene von Guerard's homestead paintings often set the home and its improvements well back into the distance. The achievement being celebrated was not only the possession of property but the taking of a place in a landscape. The convention came from English country house painting, but as always there are questions to be asked about the colonial context and meaning of adopted metropolitan forms. Here, it seems, European romantic landscape conventions worked effectively to naturalise the recent pastoral invasion of the country, and to link this new possession of a landscape with the much older tenure of the English aristocracy.[14]

Importantly, though, agriculture was also to find effortlessly its place in the Australian landscape. Von Guerard's 1855 *Mr. Perry's Farm on the Yarra* depicted a neat vineyard on a hillside surrounded on all sides by uncultivated bush.[15] The *Argus* admired its 'spirit and beauty', but complained that 'the vineyard and other accessories are given with an accuracy rather incompatible with the picturesque effect'.[16] Perhaps, though, the painting was *about* the relationship between the precision of the diligent agriculturist and the sweep of 'untouched' nature—there need be, it argued, no tension. Indeed the myth of the enchantment of Australia Felix was one of a land which could absorb humanity and cultivation into its picturesque wildness without conflict, because labour was scarcely required to render it fruitful. The enchanted landscape was not a scene of labour but one of contentment; the task was not primarily to plough but to sit under one's vine and fig tree, amidst the eucalypts.

Of course not every one thought like this. One is dealing with the handful of people, mostly men, whose views found their way into print, and, even of these, some actively dissented from the agrarian idea. The Victorian Kooris, for whom the agriculture of the newcomers was almost as destructive as their mining, had nothing to do with these ways of seeing, except in their conspicuous absence from the landscapes evoked by the bluff and hearty proponents of the spread of British agriculture:

No, give us the lands that lie waste,
And our neat little homesteads shall rise
Then to labour we'll joyfully haste
While our merry songs ring to the skies.[17]

The language of agrarianism had its significant silences and absences. It was premised upon a construction of the land as empty or waste, a mere possibility of plenitude awaiting possession, and had nothing to say of its recent and sometimes violent appropriation.

With these qualifications, the pervasiveness of the agrarian response to gold remains striking. The pamphlet literature of the 1850s, written in either explicit or implicit response to the dislocation of gold, abounds with praise of agriculture and agriculturists. 'Husbandry may be justly considered the nurse of society, and the parent of every other art', wrote the secretary of the Victorian Philosophical Institute in 1853: 'the man who furnishes his fellow beings with the staff of life increases the *real wealth* and prosperity of his country'.[18] N.L. Kentish, senior Victorian public servant, wrote in 1855 in praise of the 'class of cultivators and producers', the 'enterprising Agriculturist, who proposes to reclaim the wild bush . . . by using his axe to clear primeval forests, and putting his spade and his plough into the virgin soil of Victoria' to produce 'potatoes and garden stuff, vines and fig trees, turnips and mangold-wurtzel, lucerne, and all other valuable productions'.[19] The sub-text of this fulsome praise of agriculture and its social role, in this time and place, was a criticism of gold mining and the society it was threatening to create. 'Whenever,' wrote T.T. a'Beckett, the Melbourne barrister, 'the pursuit of gold has caused a neglect of the cultivation of the soil, that neglected territory is doubly cursed.'[20] The vocabulary is a moral one, and it is clear that this was never simply an economic discussion. One Victorian radical wrote that:

> The tilling of the soil must be looked upon as the main business of our lives, to supply us with the necessaries of existence. Mining, is a business of secondary importance, to supply us with foreign luxuries and increase the wealth of the country. Agriculture will be the main stay of this as of other countries; compared with it all other pursuits will be fluctuating and uncertain.[21]

The distinctions here nicely articulate what seem to have been widely held and deeply rooted associations—the 'main business of our lives' against the pursuit of 'foreign luxuries'; certainty, stability and permanence against transience and unpredictability. 'All other labour, compared to this', H. Lill Lindsay, the civil engineer, wrote of agriculture, 'is as dross, "as chaff before the wind", as snow under the radiant heat of a summer's sun; all these pass away, to be forgotten, but that remains—a monument of vitality and worth, of glorious activity'.[22]

What lay behind this outpouring of agrarian sentiment? There were certain material circumstances which may have led people to talk in these ways. Mining *was* a depredatory rather than a renewable mode of wealth creation. The rewards were achieved once only, and the country was in a real sense impoverished, not improved, by the removal of its valuable minerals. Secondly, the gold discoveries did lead to a temporary large-scale abandonment of agriculture, as of all other occupations. The acreage under wheat in Victoria fell from 12 150 hectares in 1851, to 6885 in 1852, and only 3240 hectares in 1853—though by 1856, the area had increased to 32 400 hectares.[23] Some, Midas mindful, genuinely did fear food shortages. 'Gold would not feed them', Mr Hellicar dramatically told the Melbourne Chamber of Commerce in February 1855, 'They were at that moment almost entirely dependent upon importation; and if such a thing should happen—which heaven avert—that those importations were to cease, they would be left with their ships laden with gold, to die of starvation.'[24] In the medium and longer term, of course, the gold diggers created a local market for agricultural produce.[25] A third material circumstance was the domination of the Victorian land by the non-agricultural squatters: sheep grazing was seen as a less productive and less settled use of the soil; the

THE GOLD SEEKER

Eng.ᵈ by Thoˢ Ham

George Strafford, 'The Gold Seeker', and 'The Water Seeker'. Illustrated Australian Magazine vol.4 (January, 1851).

THE WATER SEEKER

political power of the squatters was resented. The squatters, leaders of the pastoral invasion of Victoria from the mid-1830s, had ever since been trying to turn their political influence and their occupancy of the land, into legal possession. So, the instrumentalist argument would go, agrarian ideology was simply a convenient rallying point for the anti-squatter forces, the elaborate praises of husbandry simply a coded way of saying, 'Unlock the lands', or 'Squatter go home'. 'Gold strengthened the urban bourgeoisie financially and politically, providing them with an immigrant constituency espousing petit-bourgeois agrarian ideals', Philip McMichael has argued. 'The urban bourgeoisie challenged the political pretensions of the squatters by mobilising the popular forces around the ideology of political rights to landed property.'[26]

Yet none of these material circumstances seems to go very far towards explaining the extent of the articulation of agrarianism. In most other respects, this society showed little concern about the consumption of non-renewable resources. The food shortage never eventuated, for the colony was quickly swamped with imports from the other Australian colonies, the United States and Britain. The argument about dependence upon the importation of food was a highly charged and highly ideological one, and immigrants from Britain, so soon after the repeal of the Corn Laws, were familiar with its provenance. Trusting to the free market for food, because other commodities could be produced more profitably at home, was a recent and controversial development in Britain, so when a similar-looking circumstance arose in colonial Victoria, the languages of response were pre-formed. The third material circumstance—the opposition to the social and political power of the squatters—provides no more convincing an explanation. If the wily urban bourgeoisie had really simply been about the business of mobilising popular forces against the squatters, they chose a rather elaborate and circuitous means of doing so by putting their energies into lengthy discursive pamphlets, few of which mentioned the squatting issue at all, and few of which, one suspects, were much read by the 'popular forces'. And the agrarianism, far from simply belonging to the petit bourgeoisie, ranged, with different inflections, across classes. As Dorothy Thompson has written of Britain, 'Land ownership, control and cultivation were involved in the politics of all political groups in the nineteenth century, and proposals for allotments, smallholdings, cooperative communities and emigration societies existed in every part of the political spectrum.'[27]

What was it about the gold rush that enabled it to be discussed in these ways? When the stability and certainty of agriculture were contrasted with the uncertain, fluctuating, transient nature of gold digging, several notes in a chord were being touched. The effects of the gold rush on the colonial economy were violent and dramatic—a rapid inflation set in, the price of labour and of consumer commodities rose to unheard of levels, then, within a year, as the miners began to return, the price of labour fell dramatically, and a small recession set in. The social costs of these fluctuations were high—unemployment, housing crises, reduced living standards for many. What the gold rush provided was a fore-shortened, exaggerated experience of life ruled by somewhat serendipitous market forces. Much of what it was about gold that placed it in such unfavourable comparison to agriculture in Victoria, was its perceived closer association with the instability of the capitalist economy, with the disruptive and careless play of market forces.

Related to this anxiety about the instability that gold would bring was a lingering unease about moneyed as against landed property, and the civic virtues likely to be fostered by each; one of the great themes of nineteenth-century British history. The product of gold mining was money: a moveable wealth. Agriculture was local—food for domestic consumption—while gold digging was an enterprise which only had meaning in the context of the international economy. The gold was loaded on to ships and sent to London. It was easier to conceive of fluctuations and uncertainty being associated with foreign markets than with local demands for food.[28] The portable profits of the gold finder, too, came to seem a peculiarly unstable basis for the building of a new society.

It cannot be argued that fear of food shortage and hostility to squatters had nothing to do with the agrarianisms of the 1850s; they form part of the context within which agrarian statements would have been received and interpreted, and a part of the intentions of the utterers. But they are not sufficient explanation. There was a *language* of agrarianism, by the mid-nineteenth century an old language, and it provided a mode of socio-political understanding which flourished in Victoria in the 1850s; but it was not made by the colonists, and it had a dynamic of its own beyond its local referents. It was not a language made for talking about gold rushes or about squatters, and yet, in complex ways, the fit was sufficient, the reference was achieved. The landscape was appropriated, for a time, by the discourse, and the gold rush was interpreted in its terms, as a disruption.

Conservatives contrasted gold digging unfavourably with agriculture because it did not attach population securely to the soil, because the labour involved seemed to be of a very anomalous kind, and because it threatened to remove a large body of the population from the influence of accustomed mechanisms of social control. In 1852, the Victorian Chief Justice, William a'Beckett, published a pamphlet with the comprehensive title, *Does the Discovery of Gold in Victoria, Viewed in Relation to its Moral and Social Effects, as Hitherto Developed, Deserve to be Considered a National Blessing or a National Curse?*. a'Beckett was troubled by the social effects of the gold discoveries, by their random and unplanned toyings with the proper rhythms of society, and he wanted government to intervene and regulate.

He suggested that gold digging be prohibited for certain periods of the year, 'in order that during that time corn may be reaped, sheep shorn, and . . . habitations built'; a desire, by legislation, to fit gold digging into traditional, agricultural, patterns of work.[29]

a'Beckett discussed the high wages that had to be paid to police to keep them from the attractions of the goldfields. 'The consequence,' he wrote, 'is that they are not *paid* but *bought*; not hired but outbid'.[30] Here the outrage is not just at the price to be paid, but at the blatant intrusion of market forces into social relations. The a'Beckett brothers were putting a last desperate conservative case, half recognising the futility of their project, for the retention of the control and authority of paternalistic, deference-based government, against the fickle and destructive sway of the market. The lament was for the loss of a world built on obligations and public responsibilities. Gold seemed to have destroyed the public sphere and replaced it with an orgy of private greed. 'Not only have public festivity and private hospitality been shorn of their fair proportions', wrote William a'Beckett, 'but we have seen public duties neglected, and public interests disregarded . . . ' The list of abandonments spoke for itself:

> Benevolent asylum meetings had to be adjourned, time after time—our only literary periodical . . . sunk to the ground—out of five cricket clubs, of which our city could boast, only one showed symptoms of vitality—the Town band disappeared from its usual place of meeting; the Temperance hall music meetings had to be discontinued—and, to crown the whole, not even a birthday ball could be got up in honor of the Sovereign whose rule we acknowledge, and whose name our colony bears.

What was threatening was no less than the 'ruin of the colony as a habitable place for all who value domestic comfort, or the growth of moral and intellectual civilisation'.[31]

Conservative critics objected to the labour of gold digging because it created the spectre of a society of masterless men, an anarchy of self-employment in which the 'great social bonds' no longer held. 'The labour employed in seeking for gold,' observed H. Lill Lindsay, 'is not of that legitimate character which enriches a new country.'[32] William a'Beckett's criticism was more pointed. 'I grant that the employment is one of toil,' he wrote, 'but it is toil deprived of all those associations which give to labour its true worth. It is labour cut off and isolated from its just relations to the body politic and social, of which the labourer forms a part.'[33] This was clearly a rather disturbing and unnatural kind of labour, and it stood in obvious and painful contrast in the conservative mind to those more orthodox forms of work which wedded the labourer to the social order. 'In directing his energies to that regular and steady industry which is required in the service of agriculture, trade, and commerce,' a'Beckett explained, 'the labourer establishes a tie between himself and his employers which

AN ENGLISH GOLD FIELD.

'An English Gold Field'. London Punch *vol.XXIII, 31 July 1852, pp.58–9.*

adds another link to the great social bond that unites the whole community.' Gold digging, in contrast, was an asocial and involuted activity, it turned in upon itself rather than leading outwards into the established forms of social relationships. The miners produced money, a medium of exchange. Conservatives saw this as a barren and unnatural kind of production, part of a self-enclosed but unproductive system, which only circulated and recirculated money. Thought along these lines led naturally to the questions: what was the nature of wealth? Could gold really be considered a form of wealth? Most conservatives went out of their way to argue that it could not.

Gold, it was argued, was not wealth but the mere representative of it. 'Wealth consists in the abundance of *things*', Thomas a'Beckett reminded his readers, 'and not in the accumulation of the signs by which they are represented'. In this case the penalty for the confusion of signifier and signified was high. Gold, a'Beckett wrote, 'brings moral and physical misery upon all who, delighting in it as a symbol, disregard that of which it is the sign'.[34] Conservatives stressed the merely symbolic status of money, and its illusory nature when compared to the real wealth that came from the

A GOLD FIELD IN THE "DIGGINS."

'A Goldfield in the "Diggins" '. London Punch vol.XXIII, 31 July 1852, pp. 58–9.

soil. Unease about gold as money was one manifestation of the agrarian framework of the response; gold was rejected as only the tawdry symbol of wealth, in itself worthless, for the worth of gold was constituted entirely in the relations of the market place.

Conservatives were also troubled by the restless, migratory character of the gold seeker. 'No one can deny,' wrote William a'Beckett, 'that the mode of life at the diggings is by far too great a contrast to that in the settled localities of civilised society, not to render a residence there, for any period of time, a hazardous experiment at the best.'[35] The subtext is again an implied contrast with the settled and civilised life of agriculture. A Church of England minister wrote from a Victorian country town in 1856 of his concern for his flock:

Beyond the acquisition of money or the enjoyment of pleasure, they appear to have little care or thought, and this recklessness is, I think, in no small measure connected with the consciousness that they are united to the locality, where for an uncertain period they are sojourning, by no ties of a permanent nature, no feeling of home, no vested interest in the soil . . . Hence the endearing, softening, humanising influences of a settled home are unknown to them.[36]

For conservatives wedded to the practices of old England, where the poor had for so long been effectively confined to their parishes, the weakness of local attachments and sanctions in the colony was disturbing. George Frederic Verdon wrote in 1858 of the anomalous development of government in Victoria. 'At present it would appear that Municipal Government is the result of central government, and that it therefore naturally follows it,' he observed, 'whereas the truth is, that central government is the last and finishing work which a new country has to effect.' Time, he was confident, would restore affairs to a more natural state, and eventually 'Municipal Government, instead of being the fruit, will appear as the root of the central'.[37]

The metaphors aptly express the conservatives' organic understanding—a vision of a society firmly rooted in the localities, growing out of them, stabilised by their fixity and age-old practices. This had clearly never been the case in colonial Australia, where the only fixity was at the centre, but gold heightened and strengthened apprehensions held about the interior of the country, which now seemed to be inhabited only by roaming, unattached burglars of the soil. 'The real difficulty,' Colin Campbell wrote in 1853 of education in Victoria, 'would arise from the unsettled character of the population, and the want of that localisation which exists in old countries.'[38] Charles Perry, Anglican Bishop of Melbourne, in a pamphlet addressed to the 'few zealous members' of his church in Victoria, wrote that, until the goldfields assumed a more 'settled character', they must 'in general, be first occupied as Missionary stations', their clergy supported from extraneous sources.[39] The goldfields were thus perceived to be beyond the pale of civilisation, and the index of their uncivilisedness was their unsettled character, the miners' lack of attachment to place and their inability to support the churches, schools and charities that were the indubitable responsibilities of settled and civilised communities. For conservatives, governmental action from the centre was anyway always a poor substitute for established local institutions and sanctions, and gold seemed to have brought into being a society largely ungovernable.

Conservatives brought to the critique of the effects of the gold discoveries the language of agrarianism—formed and shaped by British experience. In the face of the disruption of gold, they turned to the celebration of agriculture and the settled rural life. 'Towns,' R.L. Milne explained in 1853, 'though occasionally places of refuge in times of commotion, are merely resorts for business. Their improvements, therefore, interest only their mercantile owners; and are matters which do not in any way concern the general community.'[40] Conservatives argued eloquently for the opening up of the land to small farming settlement. 'Here', H. Lill Lindsay exclaimed:

is an inexhaustible source of Wealth! Here are Freedom; Happiness; Comfort . . . On his Farm, the labourer can retire to rest, well satisfied that . . . his incomings will all be so much gold, and how much more respectably made. He can sit under his own vine, and under his own fig tree, and exclaim with the poet Cowper:

'Oh! friendly to the best pursuits of man,
Friendly to thought, to virtue and to peace,
Domestic life in rural pleasure passed.'[41]

The gold discoveries raised certain fundamental questions for conservatives—questions to do with labour, wealth, government, authority and community. The implicit ideal animating their criticisms was a settled, agrarian, localised, hierarchical and deferential society, an idealised version of rural England—and in every key respect, gold-rush society was found dangerously wanting. Conservative prognoses for the future of Victoria were in general extremely pessimistic.

Turning to what remains of a *radical* response to the gold rush, one is struck by how much it shared the agrarian framework with the conservative reaction. Radicalism in Victoria in the 1850s was synonymous with the demand for land reform to 'Unlock the Lands'. 'It is the People who have a right to the land', wrote Frederick Coster in 1857.[42] Here again the answer to the grievances and unsettlednesses of the gold era was the creation of an agrarian society, though in radical discourse the stress on the independence of the yeoman farmer was much stronger, and the emphasis on the virtues of a society in which each knew their (fixed) place, much less. For radicals, more than any other group, land became a panacea for all social ills. 'Representative rights—good Government—a just system of taxation—security—independence—prosperity—comfort—happiness, all these would be ours', wrote 'Peter Papineau', 'if we had our rightful share of the LAND.'[43] On his own account the emergence of Peter Lalor, leader of the Eureka uprising, into political life, was prompted by a sudden recognition of the injustice of the miners being denied the chance of a farming life. 'I looked around me', he recalled:

I saw brave and honest men, who had come thousands of miles to labour for independence. I knew that hundreds were in great poverty, who would possess wealth and happiness if allowed to cultivate the wilderness which surrounded us. The grievances under which we had long suffered, and the brutal attack of that day, flashed across my mind; and with the burning feelings of an injured man, I mounted the stump and proclaimed 'Liberty!'[44]

Raffaello Carboni, too, set the radical grievances of the period in the context of the disruption of an agrarian ideal. He recorded his own spontaneous address to a monster meeting of miners at Ballarat, a lyrical evocation of the agrarian utopia that was not to be. 'I had a dream', he told them:

a happy dream. I dreamed that we had met here together to render thanks unto our Father in heaven for a plentiful harvest, such that for the first time in this, our adopted land, we had our own food for the year; and so each of us holding in our hands a tumbler of Victorian wine, you called on me for a song. My harp was tuned and in good order: I cheerfully struck up, 'O, let us be happy together'. Not so, Britons, not so! We must meet as in old Europe . . . for the redress of grievances inflicted on us, not by crowned heads, but by blockheads, aristocratical incapables, who never did a day's work in their life.[45]

The distinctive feature of *radical* agrarianism was its attribution of the denial of the land to the people, to the political system, or the corruption of it. Had labour, like capital, been properly represented in the colonial government, a meeting of the unemployed in Melbourne was told in 1854, 'the public lands of this fine province would long ere this have been thrown open to private enterprise, and many a happy home would have been now in existence, surrounded by agricultural prosperity, and affording abundant employment, with fair remuneration, to every working man in the colony'.[46] Conservative and radical agrarianisms were, though, close enough for confusion to be possible. N.L. Kentish began one of his pamphlets in 1855 with a long and anxious explanation of the differences between the Land League, of which he was a member, and the People's League, from which he wished to dissociate himself completely. He conceded that some members of the People's League were also members of the Land League, that both organisations met in Mooney's National Hotel and, of course, that both were concerned with land reform. But there, he insisted, the similarity ended. While the policy of the wholly admirable Land League was 'to confer wealth on the industrious and deserving cultivators of the soil—to give healthful employment to thousands—to create a substantial yeomanry, and honest and contented peasantry', the People's League, 'an association of the most objectionable kind', wished not only to open up the lands, but to snap asunder the attachment to the British throne; it was an organisation Kentish considered 'seditious, and of course, if so, illegal—viz., that of a knot of *brawlers*, consisting in no small degree, of ignorant demagogues, presuming to form a "*new* constitution" '.[47] There were clear political differences here, but some of the anxiety, I think, came from the similarity of aims of the two organisations. Left and Right agrarianisms shared, to a surprising extent, a common vocabulary.

The Chartist influence on both the form and content of the radical movements of the 1850s has been noted by all historians of the period, but there has generally been a feeling that the influence was limited, that there was something anomalous about the idea of a Chartism in Australia. 'Naturally, there was no chartist movement in Australia,' Gollan argues, 'for industrialisation was still a thing of the future.'[48] Here Gareth Stedman Jones' essay 'Rethinking Chartism' is extremely suggestive. Jones argues that Chartism makes no sense if interpreted simply as a response to the economic process we know as the industrial revolution.[49] The Chartists, he argues, saw industrial capitalism, not as later nineteenth-century socialism did, as an inevitable development accompanied inevitably by class conflict, but in the terms of eighteenth-century radicalism, as an aberration which would pass, a moral and political problem probably brought about by corruption and conspiracy in government. Their remedies were largely political too—manhood suffrage, payment of members, and so on—though Chartists also gave considerable attention to land reform, and Stedman Jones argues that during the 1840s, 'the end to the monopolisation of the land was in fact the main Chartist solution to the existence of industrial capitalism'.[50] Inadequate an analysis as that might seem, it flowed cogently from the eighteenth-century country ideology in terms of which the Chartists were still interpreting the changes occurring around them. Their critique was still directed towards an idle aristocracy, addicted to luxury, monopolising the lands, and living parasitically off the labour of the producing classes, rather than towards the greed of urban or industrial capitalists, or the inevitable consequences of an economic system. They still lived in the world of a moral economy and had not understood, let alone accepted, the industrial capitalist order and the rule of market forces. Only towards the end of the 1840s, Stedman Jones argues, did the alternative language of political economy creep into popular usage; only then was there 'greater acceptance of determination by market forces and increasing usage of the terms "labour" and "capital" without reference to the political system' in which, in the older radicalism, they had been 'inextricably inscribed'.[51]

Chartism is thus seen as the last late flowering of radicalism, rather than the first premature bud of socialism. The argument has consequences for the understanding of the Victorian radicals of the 1850s; it makes Gollan's conclusion seem less sure. What Stedman Jones points to is the *durability* of ideology. The meeting at Bakery Hill on 11 November 1854, outraged at the imposition of licence fees and the corruption of petty officials, voiced its protest, not only in the form of specific complaints about local conditions, but in the older language of Paine, Wilkes, and the American revolution. The meeting resolved that 'it is the inalienable right of every citizen to have a voice in making the laws he is called upon to obey. That taxation without representation is tyranny.' The five major social changes argued for by the Ballarat Reform League were: a full and fair representation, manhood suffrage, no property qualifications for members of the Legislative Council, payment of members, and short duration of parliaments—straight from the English Charter, a reflex response to the discovery of official corruption.[52] It did not matter that there was no industrialisation in Australia. The gold miners' grievances and the struggle to break the monopoly on the land fitted very nicely into the old radical paradigm; the idle squatter and the corrupt official could simply be interpolated into the position previously reserved for the idle aristocrat.

What argument there has been among Australian historians about the interpretation of the gold rushes has tended to focus on the radical movements and the radicalising influence of the diggers. The old Left, most importantly Russel Ward, sentimentalised and heroicised the gold digger, and ascribed to him a kind of proto-socialism. More recently Humphrey McQueen argued the opposing case, that is, far from producing a fraternal socialism, gold was socially individualising and diversionary; it wedded the working class more firmly to capitalism, 'sustained the belief that advancement was possible . . . that capitalism was not without its promise'.[53] The question posed is the extent to which a celebrated fraternalism and collectivism prevailed over the materialism and individualism apparently also inherent in gold seeking.

Yet gold-rush radicalism's own self-understanding seems pre-capitalist rather than anti-capitalist. Coral Lansbury in her *Arcady in Australia*, a study of English writings about Australia in the nineteenth century, has argued that in the 1840s and 1850s English writers were nostalgically seeking a pre-industrial past, and thought they had found it in Australia.[54] Lansbury is preoccupied with the distance of these English writings from Australian reality, their false and inappropriate qualities. She does not discuss Australian writings; yet, agrarian and even arcadian sentiments were just as plentiful in Australia, where they can be explained neither by unfamiliarity with the antipodean environment as it really was, nor by a distaste for an industrialisation that had not yet occurred. In Australia, gold was an event as transforming and disturbing as industrialisation in Britain, and the languages of radical response were remarkably similar—the reassertion of an older and agrarian mode of understanding whose diagnosis of the source of the social ills it recognised was always and curiously political. The attraction of Australia was thus not primarily that it contained no dark satanic mills, but that it was a new land which could be made free from the political corruption and aristocratic domination of the old. 'Chartism', Stedman Jones argues:

> was the last, most prominent and most desperate . . . version of a radical critique of society, which had enjoyed an almost continuous existence since the 1760s and 1770s. The vision . . . was of a more or less egalitarian society, populated exclusively by the industrious, and needing minimal government . . . In such a society, reward would be proportional to labour, dependence and clientage would be eliminated, there would be equal access to the land and the restoration of the balance between town and country.[55]

This seems just the programme which lay behind the radicalism of the 1850s in Victoria. It was not systematically opposed to capitalism, though it was profoundly unsympathetic towards it, because it did not yet recognise capitalism, with its attendant class competition, as the coming order.[56] The agrarian ideology, articulated by colonial radicals in response to the riot of market forces unleashed by the gold rushes, embodied a vision of a society restored to its natural state—one of non-competitive, independent agriculture. 'Every man able and willing to work', declared a pamphlet published in Melbourne in 1856,

> should have the opportunity of living with moderate comfort, and securing a retreat for his old age . . . To allow all the hope of attaining this reasonable object, and to prevent the growth of the unnatural state of society prevailing in old countries, we must endeavour to establish a rational and enduring union between land and labour. The earth was the gift of God to all, not a few.[57]

As a profound social disturbance, gold evoked the (re)affirmation of agrarian values that British contemporaries had brought to the disturbance of industrialisation. One irony was that, in the translation from one hemisphere to another, the language of agrarianism changed its context and hence its meaning. What was in Britain retrospective and nostalgic, became in Australia prospective, a widely endorsed programme for change, and, in Serle's phrase, a 'tragic delusion'.[58] Yet, such is the persistence of language, this colonial agrarianism retained its vocabulary of restoration and return. A novel situation does not always provoke a novel response, for culture is conventional and the skill of contemporary actors lies in seeing the local reference of more universalising metropolitan discourses, not in devising a set of isolating neologisms.

Laissez faire political economy was the alternative language most consistently used against the agrarians, and its chief proponents were the political *liberals*. Defenders of laissez faire among colonial liberals consciously rejected and repudiated agrarianism, and were less disturbed than conservatives or radicals by the wild fluctuations that gold brought. They did not engage in long discussions about the nature of real wealth, nor did the gold rush move them to posit the idea that some things were innately rather than relationally valuable. The political economist knew for certain what wealth was—as Nassau Senior told the students at Oxford in 1852, real wealth consisted of 'things limited in supply'.[59] If gold finding was more profitable than any other occupation then, the utilitarian liberals argued, the people should seek gold. There was no room here for any sentimental agrarianisms. The best interests of all were to be served by the maximising of the profits of each individual economic being.

It is striking, given what historians assure us was the growing strength of the urban bourgeoisie, how little of this kind of thinking there seems to have been in Victoria in the 1850s. Nassau Senior was, along with Adam Smith, on the Political Economy syllabus at the new and relatively modern University of Melbourne in 1855.[60] But the influence did not seem to have spread far. Even the Melbourne Chamber of Commerce appears to have

been strongly influenced by agrarian ideology. A report of a special committee of the Chamber in 1855 contained many of the common radical
agrarian demands. Land was to be sold at a low fixed price, on condition
that cultivation and improvement took place forthwith, and that a habitation was erected. In its attempt to enforce cultivation and habitation,
this was far removed from laissez faire. William Westgarth put in a
dissenting minority report to the Chamber. He argued that cultivation was
only one among many different modes of land use, and advocated sale of
land by auction—a free market in land.[61] What is surprising is not that
this view should exist in a Chamber of Commerce, but that so few there
should embrace it. When a Mr Goodman argued such a case to the
Chamber, he had all the defensiveness of a conscious heretic against a
dominant ideology: 'He maintained that no sensible man would use his
head or his hands for the purpose of turning up the soil unless he were to
get as much for doing so as he would by his labour elsewhere. That was
the common sense view of the question.' It presumably was the commonsense of the thousands who flocked to the diggings, but it did not seem to
make ideological sense to many at all. Goodman's argument was nakedly
to do with maximising profit:

> Labour employed in gold finding was so profitable, and gold, too, was so much
> more profitable than it had been, that a man could realise more money by it
> than from the culture of the soil; and so long as a man could in this way
> produce more money than he could produce out of the soil, it must be cheaper
> to the colony to import these breadstuffs than grow it themselves with
> enormously expensive labour. As a general rule, that most required for a small
> population was wealth and Sir Robert Peel's maxim applied in this case as it
> did all over the world, 'Buy in the cheapest, and sell in the dearest market.'[62]

This was the pure liberal response to the gold discoveries: unperturbed by
the market forces they unleashed, sanguine about progress, confident that
the market would provide. The dominance of the agrarian ideal was such
that these uncompromising friends of political economy and the self-regulating propensities of the market were always in a small minority. Very few
Victorians, it seems, were prepared to argue publicly that agriculture was
simply one among many modes of land use, to be judged only by its
profitability. Very few regarded land as just another commodity. Very few
embraced laissez faire without qualification. Governor Hotham, obviously
no radical, told the diggers at Forest Creek that 'land would be brought
into the market, and . . . the diggers must not bid one against another'.[63]

The squatters, who had de facto possession of much of the land of
Victoria, were among the few who did embrace laissez-faire arguments, for
state intervention in the Victorian economy would inevitably be directed
against them. Every country, argued Colin Campbell, 'should engage in
those branches of labour which it can carry on with greatest advantage',

just as 'every one in the country should be left in a natural way to do that which he can do, so as best to promote his own personal interest'. The state, he maintained, should only administer justice, and protect persons and property.[64] The squatters were thought of as the conservatives in Victoria, but among them were men like Campbell who embraced free-market liberalism rather than the more interventionist and morally based conservatism of urban conservatives.

What differences then did the language of agrarianism make, what traces did it leave? How are we to know that we are dealing here with a cultural phenomenon real in its effects, that this strain of Victorian pastoral had extra-linguistic entailments?

The dominant political issue in Victoria, after the excitement of gold subsided, was that of land. When the various land bills came before parliament there was remarkable consensus among all but the directly interested squatting representatives about the ends to be achieved—the establishment of an agrarian society, and the placing of the land above the capricious and destructive operations of the market. The state was to attempt to facilitate the establishment of a small-farming society. The liberal James Service told the Legislative Assembly that the object of the Nicholson Land Bill was that 'the land shall not be bought up for speculative purposes, but that persons desirous of having land shall use it for the purposes for which the country desires to part with it'.[65] T.H. Fellows, arch-conservative, told the Legislative Council that the main feature of the Bill was 'the privilege it gave to persons to obtain the land they desired without being subject to unnecessary competition, and that persons should not be allowed to purchase land except for the purposes of cultivation'.[66] But it was the workingman's representative, Charles Jardine Don, who provided the most elevated expression of this agrarian and anti-commercial doctrine. 'Every citizen', he told the Assembly, 'had a natural right to as much land as he required for the purpose of gaining a living, and any law which would prevent him from obtaining it was inimical to the interests of the country, and an infringement of a natural right'.[67] This was perhaps the logical resting place of agrarian thinking—the articulation of a natural right to the land, and a natural law prior to that dictated by an inherently unjust market place or made by venal legislatures.

Yet it was of course to the legislatures that the agrarians looked to protect them from the market. Mr Bennett, the squatter, was possibly correct in depicting the Land Bill as 'so complete a violation of every simple principle of political economy'. It sought, he argued, 'to give undue protection to one class, to create, as it were, farmers by act of parliament'.[68] To the few uncompromising friends of the market in Victoria, these were heresies. When the Western District squatter Niel Black ran for the Legislative Council in 1859, his slogan was 'What we want is free trade in land'.[69]

On the other side of politics, the Land Convention—elected at public meetings all over the colony to agitate on the land question, claiming to be more representative of the people than the parliament—was embracing protection for native industry and by 1861, Serle records, 'had been absorbed by the protectionist leagues'.[70] From the language of agrarianism to that of protection was no great step. Most recognised that in Victoria some state intervention would be necessary to establish an agricultural society, and perhaps to keep it functioning. If agriculture was to be established in Victoria, James Sim argued, 'some protection should be afforded . . . against the ruinous fluctuations of our markets, which render farming a perfectly hazardous operation'.[71] Victoria thus entered its long period of commercial prosperity and growth dominated by modes of socio-political understanding which constituted the market as a threat which needed to be curbed, a threat, above all, to a just and natural relationship to the land. This appears different from the rhetoric in New South Wales where, D.W.A. Baker has influentially argued, the ideas behind the land acts were not protectionist or even agrarian, but manifestations of 'liberal ideals of laissez-faire and equality of opportunity'.[72] The language of agrarianism may hold the key to some of the elusive differences in the development of the two colonies.

'It is a critical fact', Raymond Williams has observed of the long process of industrialisation and urbanisation in England, 'that in and through these transforming experiences, English attitudes to the country, and to ideas of rural life, persisted with extraordinary power, so that even after the society was predominantly urban its literature, for a generation, was still predominantly rural.'[73] Victoria in the 1850s experienced a late-flowering agrarianism, one already perhaps suffused with sentimentality. The puzzle for the historian of culture is that this Australian agrarianism comes from another country at another time, and that it now seems to have been often extraordinarily inappropriate.[74] There appears to be a contradiction between the dominance of agrarian ideology as a way of understanding, the consequent dominance in the written record of rejections of the whole idea of gold digging, and the facts that tens of thousands flocked to the goldfields, while few were eager to leave the cities to take up farming. If it had been only conservative elites who were agrarian, we could write off the whole business as an elaborate and unsuccessful attempt at social control. But how are we to explain the social diversity of the sources of agrarian thinking, and the apparent gap between these ways of talking and 'lived experience'?

'When discrepancies exist between ideology and social reality', asks the anthropologist Sally Falk Moore, 'what do people do?' The answer often appears to be: for a time, nothing.[75] Social life, Moore argues, is essentially indeterminate; rituals, laws, rules, customs, symbols, ideological models and so on, are attempts to fix social life, to keep it from slipping entirely into the sea of indeterminacy, but the fit is never exact. 'Established rules, customs, and symbolic frameworks exist, but they operate in the presence of areas of indeterminacy, of ambiguity, of uncertainty and manipulability. Order never fully takes over, nor could it.'[76] The gold rush provides a good example of a novel event—never, in a British society, had there been a gold rush before. The meaning of the event is not fixed, the models of interpretation not sanctioned by custom. Attempts are made to subsume the new event under pre-existing languages, with some success, but there is always slippage, always an area of indeterminacy. The pre-existing language, while reassuring in its familiarity, brings its own rigidities and blindnesses. Agrarianism gave many, on the Left and the Right, a moral, social and political vocabulary with which to discuss the disruption of gold—indeed, with which to constitute gold as disruption—but as time passed the appropriateness of the language was called into question, its constraints became more apparent.

Australian historians, very conscious of the gap between ideology and action, have been uneasy with all the rhetoric about the land and the virtues of agriculture in this period. Although the gold miners often raised the issue of land reform, writes Irving, 'it was more of a symbol of their hostility to the squatters than a serious demand'.[77] 'It is in the contradiction between a stated desire for land and a refusal to quit the cities,' argues McQueen, 'that the utopian face of land reform can be divined.'[78] Yet the language of agrarianism cannot be dismissed as merely symbolic, or utopian in the negative sense of having nothing to do with reality. Agrarian ideology, however inadequate it may now appear as an attempt to 'fix' the reality of mid-nineteenth century Australia, was a part of a set of perceptions of the country, which shaped the ways people thought about place, even if they did not always act, in any simple way, on their beliefs. When we read in the pamphlet, *Land and Labour in Victoria*, for example, the statement that 'Monopoly of the source of all wealth—the land—we should not tolerate on any account', we are in the presence of an expression of a political cosmology, a moral sociology, no less real or sincerely held for the fact that the author never (perhaps) attempted farming.[79]

We look back sceptically, with the knowledge of the general failure of the later attempts to establish small-farming settlement, and wonder that the agrarians of the 1850s did not realise that the land was unsuited to their vision. We look back knowing that the centre of the continent is a vast desert, and wonder that they foresaw the growth of a new seat of empire. We look back, steeped in an aesthetic of perception of the bush shaped in the 1890s, and have trouble understanding how the colonists of the 1850s could write so glowingly of the Australian forest, its verdant glades and grassy fields. Perhaps it is above all an aesthetic we are dealing with, a way of looking at the landscape that has been largely lost, so that we stand now in puzzlement before the still romantic landscapes of Chevalier, von Guerard and their contemporaries, and wonder that it took so long for the bush to be seen 'as it really was'. Yet Victoria actually was seen in those romantic terms. Recovering that vision is a necessary part of understanding not only the art and literature of colonial Australia, but its political and social theorising as well. The landscape was always political.

'To furnish the world with a few tons of yellow metal, which often turns out not a blessing but a curse to mankind,' wrote R.L. Milne in 1853, 'was not the object for which the Deity created the Southern continent. Its shading forests, its grassy plains, its beautiful skies, and its matchless climates, unmistakably indicate His design to make it the abode of generations to come.'[80] The landscape itself becomes an indictment of the rapacity of gold seeking. To the touring William Howitt, the whole Victorian countryside seemed like one vast and splendid gentleman's park. 'Indeed, we seem to be travelling all the way through such a park,' he wrote, 'so much so that one cannot, every now and then, help fancying that, on some height or slope amongst the trees, we shall catch sight of some gentleman's seat, or perceive a carriage . . . rolling downward to the road. But a moment's reflection reminds you that all is solitary wilderness . . .'[81] This extraordinary landscape, already park-like, apparently requiring only the insertion of white figures to reclaim it for civilisation, was materially threatened by the ecological devastation of gold mining. 'We have begun to destroy the beauty of this creek', Howitt wrote from Yackandandah. 'A little while, and its whole course will exhibit nothing but nakedness, and heaps of gravel and mud. We diggers are horribly destructive of the picturesque.'[82] 'The Digger is something like the Mole,' noted William Wilson Dobie, 'He does not improve the appearance of the country he passes through.'[83] To many observers the romantic and picturesque landscape was itself an argument for the colony having a future in store greater than mining. It seemed made for cultivation, for investment with English associations. 'They are English houses, English enclosures that you see,' Howitt crowed, 'English farms, English gardens, English cattle and horses, English fowls about the yards, English flowers and plants carefully cultivated.'[84]

The outward form of the landscape seemed to be a sign of its destiny. Why are we, the Reverend John Cooper asked his congregation at Geelong in 1856:

in the Providence of God, brought into this land of promise, of strange birth, of wonderful resources, and doubtless, to be of marvellous history, a land of milk and honey—a land born out of due season—a land brought among the nations in the most remarkable period of the world's history, in times of portentous greatness, in times of ominous commotions, in times of gigantic efforts, of rapid transit, of electric speed—a land of vast, varied and omnific resources, of pure atmosphere, of salubrious clime—the home of an energetic, enterprising, and rapidly increasing population—a region lying in the very bosom of the east, the cradle of the race, as if nourished and cherished in this vast hemisphere for deeds of great, and glorious, and blessed memory![85]

The language of agrarianism had always aesthetic as well as moral and political significances. It provided a way of seeing the newly taken land, of constituting the landscape as available for British appropriation, as always already full of British associations. Victoria seemed to possess a chosen landscape, which assured it of its place in history. 'It is a blessed land,' wrote Charles Gavan Duffy in old age, 'seamed with gold, fanned with healthy breezes, and bathed in a transparent atmosphere like the landscapes of Guido.'[86]

THE FATE OF THE PASTORAL IN NARRATIVES OF THE VICTORIAN GOLD RUSH

'If Life's a voyage, then let us travel' ran the motto inscribed on the title page of Dr John Shaw's 1858 *A Gallop to the Antipodes*. It was one of a large number of such books which appeared in the 1850s, mostly published in Britain and directed at an audience interested in 'our colonies'. The traveller's book was perhaps the major form of book publishing about Australia in the gold rush period. Dozens appeared during the 1850s, and some were extremely popular, running through several editions. All provided advice for those contemplating a visit or emigration to Australia, as well as a narrative of the author's own experiences. The line between the emigration manual and the travel book was not always clear, for as Dr Shaw observed in his *Gallop*: 'that emigration is one of the grand questions of the day cannot be doubted by any intelligent person.'[87]

Travellers' narratives from all periods form an almost irresistible source of commentary for cultural historians, and Australian historians have been drawing freely upon the observations of Twopeny, Trollope, Dilke and the others for decades, mining their works for comment on a great variety of topics. Russel Ward, constructing the definitive nationalist text of the recent period, found the comments of travellers among the most useful sources for defining the distinctive qualities of Australian life—indeed the key description of the itinerant bush workers as a 'nomad tribe', comes from Trollope. The Australian legend may be just a traveller's tale about travellers, but it has been an extraordinarily influential narrative in Australian cultural history.[88]

There are reasons for this dependence of historians on travellers. The projects of the traveller and of the traditional historian have certain similarities—the speaking position of each is that of the detached observer, able to delineate difference and oddity with the certainty born of just passing through. This relationship is heightened in both cases by the imperial relationship—the discourse of the historian/traveller names with metropolitan certainty the topography of colonial difference. The first stage of analysis of travellers' books should be a critical distancing from this (implicitly metropolitan) position. We need to treat the travellers' works as whole texts, rather than allowing them simply to be quarried for anecdote or information on particular topics, and we need to position their repetitive articulations of stories about the colonial. The initial analysis should thus be relatively formalist—what kinds of stories circulated in these books?

How would they have been read at the time? An historical account of reception must be largely speculative, but there are some things we can say. There was, for the young and immigrant population of post-gold-rush Australia, a horizon of interest and engagement around the travellers' books greater than that which surrounds the merely leisure-oriented travel pages of the newspapers today. 'For youth', as Kinahan Cornwallis pointed out in his *Panorama of the New World*, 'travel has many charms'.[89] But the audience for travel books was probably not limited to the young and adventurous. Nineteenth-century Australians were likely to have made at least one voyage. John Fitzgerald Leslie Foster, soon to be Victorian Colonial Secretary, observed in 1851 that:

> It is one of the characteristics of Australian society, that there are mingled through it men who have seen much of the world, and have also been more or less forced to use their minds. This gives an unusually diversified and manly tone to conversation . . . One may be heard to describe the delights of landing at Rio, on his outward-bound voyage, while another recommends his friends to proceed home via India and Egypt . . . No wonder that one is struck with the 'travelled aspect', if we may use the phrase, of Australian society.[90]

Emigrants were practical travellers and, ever after making their great choice, retained an interest in the qualities of countries and the life possibilities they held. The gold digger was seen as a particularly fickle and suggestible emigrant, but an emigrant none the less. 'Perhaps no bodies of people migrate so suddenly and in such numbers at a time as gold diggers . . . ', observed C. Rudston Read.[91] The relationship between travel experience and the textually created expectations of it is always an important theme in the study of travel literature, particularly where emigration was at stake. And so much was published about Australia after the gold discoveries that a Melbourne *Punch* satirist could strike a chord by expressing surprise at finding that Australia was 'not a mere literary fragment but solid and actual as the streets in London'.[92] The important point is that contemporary readers of these travel accounts had something at stake in their reading—in the century of emigration, travel talk was always at bottom about life possibilities.

The key rhetorical qualification for giving advice on emigration or gold-digging was the authenticity of one's own travel experience, and the titles and subtitles of the travel books advertised claims to this authenticity. Books such as William Hall's *Practical Experience at the Diggings of the Gold Fields of Victoria*, or Matheson's *Facts from the Australian Gold Diggings, with a few Practical Hints to Intending Emigrants by M. Matheson, just returned from the Colonies, and who was at the Mines in February last*, or Edward Saunders' *Our Australian Colonies: Notes of What I Saw, Heard or Thought, During a Visit to Australia, Van Diemen's Land and New Zealand, in the Years 1852–53* displayed little anxiety that the experience of the traveller might be significantly different from that of the settler—evidence perhaps of a residual sense in the mid-nineteenth century that journeying was a privileged mode of gaining knowledge. 'First impressions are not always to be relied upon for their correct judgement of men and things', observed Samuel Mossman and Thomas Banister in their *Australia Visited and Revisited*, 'still we are of opinion that, when faithfully related, they convey to others the general character of both, which subsequent experiences give in detail.'[93]

Rhetorical claims to authenticity were of course no guarantee that the author had been there, as the well-known case of John Sherer's *The Gold Finder of Australia* makes clear. Sherer's book, which went through three editions between 1853 and 1856, claimed to outline a series of adventures 'such as have absolutely been passed through'. Cited as a useful primary source by many eminent Australian historians, the book was republished as recently as 1973 with an introduction proclaiming it as 'the most colourful and realistic first hand report' of the gold rush. Sherer had though, as John Molony and T.J. McKenna demonstrated some years ago, clearly never been to Australia. *The Gold Finder* is a clever pastiche of existing travellers' accounts and interpolated fictional narratives, a pastiche which continually defers or hurries over the moment of speaking of its narrator's own experiences—'Without entering into all the trifling details of our departure from Forest Creek, much of which you can easily imagine, I must desire you to picture us already in the bush.' *The Gold Finder's* melodramatic narrative interludes are skilfully constructed around the S.T. Gill sketches which are pirated throughout the text. There are probably several other travellers' accounts of gold-rush Australia written by authors who had never left London; there is an air of generalising, of repetition of stock wisdom about many of them, which certainly makes one suspicious.[94] These are the accounts Samuel Mossman had in mind in 1853 when he warned British readers of 'those garbled compilations, plagiarisms, and romances, with wretched daubs of coloured prints, which piratical penny-a-liners and unscrupulous artists are at present pawning upon the British public for genuine sketches of life and scenery at the diggings'.[95]

But these textual pastiches are far from being valueless for historians. They are the purest distillations of the narratives once circulating in Britain and Australia about gold-rush Australia, unencumbered by the mere contingency of personal experience. Authors such as Sherer had at least done their research thoroughly, and were consciously reproducing the written, and probably spoken, folk wisdom of the day.[96] Sherer's text contains many of the characteristic arguments and tropes found in narratives written on the spot, but unburdened by specifics, and untroubled by the need to maintain a consistent authorial stance—for the pastiche is an open, inclusive, unhierarchised form.

Sherer wrote, as did all of the gold-rush travellers, dazzled by the temporarily high price of labour, of the inversion of the normal order of things in colonial society, and he assured the reader that 'anecdotes innumerable might be told of the singular transposition that had taken place in the circumstance of men'. These anecdotes must have been circulating in London—they appear in heightened form in *Punch* cartoons, and as the matter for serious discussion of permanent effects on the world economy in the quarterlies. The particular anecdote Sherer tells appears in variant forms in many, many books: 'One gentleman, a large sheep owner, went to a party of sheep-shearers who were at the diggings, and asked them to engage to clip his flocks.' They agree—if they can keep all the wool. The gentleman walks away in disgust, and the shearers call him back; they say they want a cook and will offer him fifteen shillings a day. Sherer concluded that episode with the observation that, in colonial society: 'It is not what you were, but what you are that is the criterion . . . by which you are judged.'

Undisturbed by particular and possibly contrary experiences, Sherer can produce in close to pure form the story of colonial inversion, and with it all the narrative pleasure of fantasy or carnival. 'The distinctions of class you find laid aside', he assured his readers, 'the highly-educated Oxonian is associated with the illiterate labourer from Wilts or Somerset; the descendant of those who sit in "lordly halls" has a mate in the reformed prisoner of Millbank or Pentonville . . . Everything is, in fact, the perfect realisation of a great republic.' Writing in this mode, Sherer celebrates the freedom and independence of Australian life, and in particular the 'openness and manliness of the character of the native-born population' —'drunkenness,' he adds, 'is almost unknown amongst them, and honesty is proverbial'. But elsewhere in his book, Sherer reproduces the other side of the argument, the common strictures on colonial licence, and the concern for social control. 'I must confess', he wrote, in an engaging rhetorical appeal to experience 'that in my estimation there is one great drawback on a digging life: and that is, whether successful or not, it seems generally to make men lose all relish afterwards for a steady, working life'.[97]

I call this important story, which was about the effects of gold, but more profoundly about colonial society in general, the colonial narrative. It told of a society characterised by inversion of the natural or metropolitan state of things, and could be used either to celebrate or to lament the consequences. The abundance of gold, in this story, made the poor rich, and the powerful powerless. The colonial narrative involved the delineation of a social world characterised by inversion and absurdity, the mockery of the authenticity of the social forms of the metropolis. It was a male story, and it had much to say about masculinity, for the colonial was depicted as both more manly and more unruly than the metropolitan. The narrative involved the depiction of the human relationship to the environment as one of struggle and conquest, a relationship which allowed scope for masculine heroism.

The other important story about gold-rush Australia, found in most of the travellers' books, is the pastoral narrative. Again, Sherer reproduces it in particularly pure form, setting his digging narrative in a luxuriant natural world:

> Long sweeps of rich verdure, here and there studded with clumps of trees; flowers of every hue springing up spontaneously through the velvety grass; birds of the rarest plumage hopping about from branch to branch; gentle noises amongst the foliage of the woods, and a clear stream running hard by, gave us the first taste of an evening in the country amidst the wilds of Australia. There was a luxury of feeling on looking at such a spot, weary though I was, which no pen can describe, whilst I felt myself so perfectly independent of, and unshackled by, the cares of this life, that I could have taken farewell for ever of the world, resigned myself to the groves, and relinquished the pursuit of gold, and the toils of ambition, without either a thought or a sigh.

Sherer rhetorically compares the 'attractions of the woods' to the limitations of the 'dirty streets' of town, and writes of the delightful atmosphere of Australia, where 'you respire with a freedom which astonishes yourself and makes you wonder at what can be the cause of your natural good spirits and cheerfulness'.[98]

The pastoral involved the evocation of a beneficent natural world, in which work was scarcely necessary, life easeful and consumption bountiful, and the pastoral and agricultural activities of humankind in harmony with, and a completion of, the work of nature.[99] The pastoral was also a masculine story, one about a landscape constructed as feminine. The pastoral interludes, nature reveries, which occur in the most masculine of digging narratives, represent flickers of bad conscience on the part of the tree-cutting gender about the whole colonial project, momentary toyings with another way of being which involved retreat from the 'world' into an idealised domesticity.

The colonial narrative was usually part of a comic and conservative story which looked forward implicitly to the restoration of metropolitan norms, the reintegration of the disruptive element into society. If a new society was to form around the digger, it would not be based entirely on a departure from the forms of the old. The colonial narrative was a story about the colonial as disruption, comic disruption, to be enjoyed for its transgressions, in the knowledge that it was a temporary state of affairs, quite incredible as a permanent condition—and all the stories about the foolish consumption of lucky diggers, the smoking of ten-pound notes, reinforced a belief in the self-correcting mechanisms built into society, in the eventual restoration of order, and a disbelief in the possibility of the maintenance of the carnival-like conditions. 'Such an anomalous state of affairs,' as Sherer commented prudently, 'amongst the subjects of Queen Victoria in the nineteenth century, would scarcely be credited if similar facts could not be corroborated by a thousand witnesses.'[100]

The pastoral narrative provided a language for naming the disruption of the colonial—it held out possibilities for colonial life which were quite at odds with the gold-mining present. Sherer understood this, and his 'luxury of feeling' on looking at the natural scene led him specifically and rhetorically to consider leaving the world behind, relinquishing the pursuit of gold—for gold, of all commodities, has meaning and value only in the world. The pastoral narrative also existed as a critique of the disruptions of the colonial in that it dwelt upon the way colonial society tore up the natural world—cut down the trees, burgled the soil—though rarely on how it murdered the original inhabitants. More often the pastoral, in its silences, functioned as a legitimating rhetoric for the appropriation of Aboriginal land, naturalising and idealising the possible relationship between the invaders and the land. But, with this crucial qualification, it remains true that in the discourses of the 1850s the colonial narrative was a story about a combative relationship between the human and natural worlds, while the pastoral narrative articulated a quest (a psychologising green history might say a yearning) for harmonious relations.

Both the colonial and the pastoral narratives structured understandings of the effects of the gold discoveries. They were the common discursive property which informed the questions that travellers brought with them to gold-rush Australia, questions which meant that the better of their books fulfilled Paul Fussell's prescriptive requirement for a travel book as 'a record of an inquiry and a report of the effect of the inquiry on the mind and imagination of the traveller'—though the gold-rush travellers' books were probably always too teleological to be considered classics of the genre, for it was not the journey itself, but the nugget or the home at its end which was the object of interest.[101]

The task of actual travellers was to reconcile personal narratives with the articulation or rebuttal of these dominating stories, to replace, as they invariably put it, false report with true knowledge. But intention to tell the truth was not a way out of the obligation to tell a story. Mossman and Banister in *Australia Visited and Revisited* typically promised that their account would be characterised by 'truthfulness and fidelity': 'the reader will find in these pages nothing more than a simple narrative of facts observed during a journey . . . presenting an unvarnished picture of the country and its inhabitants as they exist'.[102] Yet even these would-be empiricists end up articulating variants of the dominant narratives, discussing the 'manliness of deportment' of colonial bushmen, lamenting the 'desolation' of the deforestation of the diggings.

While the pastoral and colonial narratives obviously derived from metropolitan discourses and perceptions, as Sherer's articulation of both from London makes clear, later historians and critics have often derided the pastoral as foreign to Australian reality, an unthinking imposition on unsuitable material, or an interested invention of the proponents of emigration, while retaining a sense of the importance of the colonial narrative, or the refutation of the colonial narrative, to Australian self-understanding. The pastoral embodies a dead argument—we know they were wrong about that—while the colonial narrative, with its attendant debates about the workingman's paradise, the emergence of a distinctive Australian type different or opposite to the metropolitan, the character of Australian manhood, has provided the content of Australian nationalism and the subject matter of Australian history for much of this century.

CALIFORNIA

How happy is the miner's lot,
If he but thinks it so;
In many a sweet sequestered spot,
His life in peace may flow.

When birds are singing on the hills,
And skies are bright above,
A joy intense his bosom thrills,
If nature's scenes he loves.

W.H.D., 'The Gold Miner', 1857

Where, then is Eden! Ah! why should I tell
What every eye and bosom know so well?
Why name the land, all other lands have blest,
And traced for ages to the distant West?
Why seek in vain throughout th' historic page
For Eden's Garden and the Golden Age?
HERE! BROTHERS, HERE! NO FURTHER LET US ROAM
HERE IS THE GARDEN! EDEN IS OUR HOME!

W.H.Rhodes, 'Lost and Found', 1859

Californians thought of the land in some remarkably similar ways to their Victorian contemporaries. Many of them shared with Victorians a strong inherited belief in the rural virtues, and in the centrality of agriculture to a moral civilisation. 'The most important of all pursuits is that of agriculture', Tod Robinson told the California State Agricultural Society in September 1859, ' . . . we could strike from society the merchant, lawyer, doctor, manufacturer and mechanic, and still the human family could be sustained and supported in the enjoyment of life . . . but strike from society the farmer's calling . . . and society would not alone be shaken to its base, but its very foundations would be swept away so utterly as to leave not a wreck behind.'[103] These were the basic beliefs of agrarian thought, as strongly articulated in California as ever in Victoria. In the first issue of the *California Farmer*, the editor praised the love of truth inherent in farming people: 'The mind that is developed under the auspices of Agriculture, becomes too strongly wedded to the realities of life, and to the consecrated truthfulness of nature, to turn with a vigorous relish, to the fictions and follies of an artificial, and not unfrequently fantastic state of society.'[104]

The argument that it was in the countryside that the real future of California lay was commonly made in the publications of the 1850s and later. 'Her harvest will in the end be of more value than her mines,' argued the Reverend Charles Wadsworth.[105] 'The concurrent testimony of all ages,' Hinton Helper warned, 'proves that those nations who obtain their wealth by the indirect methods of agriculture, manufactures and commerce, are more happy and more prosperous than those who dig their treasures directly from the earth.'[106]

In California, then, we find a strain of agrarian thought which deprecated gold mining and praised the agricultural life. This way of thinking came from the east, and was not invented in California. It was an analysis known in advance, applied before the fact. The *Democratic Review* printed a poem, written in Albany, New York in 1849, which succinctly put the agrarian position on California gold:

Thus to California's vallies, gold, with its phantom glare,
Lures thousands but to show what their real treasures are.

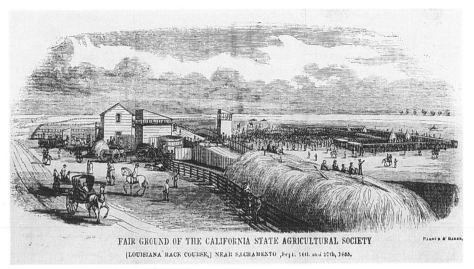

FAIR GROUND OF THE CALIFORNIA STATE AGRICULTURAL SOCIETY
[LOUISIANA RACE COURSE,] NEAR SACRAMENTO ,Sept. 26th and 27th, 1858.

Fairground of the California State Agricultural Society, Courtesy Bancroft Library.

The soil, the streams and harbors, whose wealth remains untold,
Together with the climate, will eclipse the yellow gold.[107]

Godey's Magazine dwelt upon the agrarian paradise that might have been but for the gold:

The fertility of the soil, the purity of the atmosphere and the evenness of the temperature justified their choice of home, and the prospect seemed to be that a rich and judicious cultivation would soon alter the whole face of the country, and that it would be populated by a race of Saxon land-holders. The gold discovery has wrought a sudden alteration . . .[108]

But this kind of thinking about gold was also articulated in California itself. 'Gold is not wealth', Samuel B. Bell told the California State Agricultural Society in 1858, ' . . . Agriculture is the prolific mother of wealth'.[109] Eliza Farnham's *California: Indoors and Out* was an extended agrarian tract. Farnham announced early in the text that she would not be discussing mining at any length, but rather Californian agriculture, an interest 'which is far more delightful to those who cultivate it, and which must be a chief instrumentality in her salvation, if any such fate await her'.[110] The Committee on Agriculture and Mines of the Colored Citizens Convention of 1855 argued from a very different position that 'agriculture, as a pursuit, is the road to wealth, honor and independence; the time has come when we must become owners and cultivators of the land'.[111] 'It is a well known fact', asserted a writer in the *California Farmer* in 1854, 'that agriculture is the main feature in the success of every civilized country'.

Even the 'richest mineral country in the world' must look responsibly to agriculture for its future:

> When the people of this State think less of the sudden accumulation of fortunes, and in connection with it, their own personal pleasures, turning their attention to the encouragement of agricultural pursuits, and the sustenance of agricultural interests, then, and not till then, will California exhibit to all nations a success hitherto unapproached and thereafter unapproachable.[112]

As in Victoria, this way of thinking was part of the stock wisdom of the age, part of an obvious truth for thinkers throughout the political spectrum. Agrarian thought gave Californians a way of comprehending and criticising the gold-mining present, a language with which to name the disruption of gold. The *San Francisco Whig* praised the California farmer at the expense of the gold miner: 'Theirs has not been the sudden acquisition of wealth, realized in a day, and when obtained carried away from the country; but rather the result of patient industry. Under their thrifty hands, the wilderness has been made to bloom, and the barren places made fruitful.'[113] When the *Democratic Review* spoke of California, it too was usually careful to remind its readers that the real wealth of the state would come from agriculture and commerce: 'The talisman that has wrought this wonderful change has been a few grains of gold, but it will prove but a symbol emblematic of the real wealth which human industry will create upon the soil, and extract from the shores of Asia.'[114]

The mention of Asia alerts us to the imperial dimension of agrarian thought in California. As in Victoria, but with a more restless and expansionary inflection, Californian agrarian thinking was a way of taking possession of the land, and of writing of its destined future in a way that removed from view the original inhabitants and owners. James Carson recorded a pastoral fantasy which ran through his mind as he looked over the Tulare valley:

> As we look on this—the garden of California—the pride of an American heart makes our mind to people it with the hardy farmers of this country. We can imagine their neat cottages peeping out from amidst fields of flowing grain. We can see the neat village with its church spires, marking the march of civilization—and hear the lowing herds that browse on the luxuriant grass around.

This relatively conventional fantasy was interrupted, however, by a significant observation:

> But those fancy pencillings of the mind are put to flight, as our eyes fall on the scene at our feet. Here, at the foot of the mound on which we have been viewing the scene, the grass has been trampled down—the smoke of an immense fire has scarce died away; the scene tells you that a large encampment has just left.[115]

Here we see the power of the pastoral perception in legitimating the appropriation of Indian land. In a neat reversal, the invaded become the invaders in this scene; they are recast as the disruptive intruders upon a scene of potential peace and harmony, neatness and prosperity. In California, with the evidence and the fear of Indian warfare all around, such persistence of the trope of the empty wilderness awaiting the hand of man is particularly striking. Franklin Langworthy, recording his arrival overland into California, wrote repeatedly *both* of the danger he faced from the Indians *and* of the beauty of the scenery he encountered. 'I had surveyed Nature's grandest works', he reflected from the safety of Sacramento, 'and had contemplated scenery where, undisturbed by man, earth still reposes in all her primitive loveliness and grandeur'.[116] California too was read as a land positively inviting occupation and 'improvement'.

The California pastoral thus often contained, barely submerged within it, an imperial or possessive strategy—a more strident tone than usually found in Victorian fantasies. The writers of a memorial to Congress asking for the endowment of an agricultural college in California saw fit to embellish their request with an energetic description of the onward march of an agriculture-led imperial progression:

> there is many a broad and fertile valley, that in coming years shall gladden us by fields of waving grain, and orchards of luscious fruits—many a bright hill side that soon shall be covered by the vine and fig tree—many a towering mountain, upon whose lofty summit now stand, in all their pride and glory, those giants of the forests, that . . . man will no longer spare, these too must give place to that onward march of the Anglo-Saxon race . . . marking its progress onward along the Pacific, by civilization, cultivation, and Christianization, even till it reaches and penetrates China, Japan, and the entire Asiatic region, and wending its way back again through the mother country, to our fatherland 'New England'.[117]

This was not the quiet contentment of the 'middle landscape', but an agriculture which was restless, invasive, and imperial. James Carson's version was equally imperial, but his was a laissez-faire pastoral. Spreading agriculture and then commerce was for him the natural state of things, if only government and Indian Commissioners would keep out of the way:

> Will this valley ever be settled? Will the bare places be made green with fruitful fields, through which the diverted crystal waters will be seen winding their fertilizing course? . . . Will the hum of the flouring mill and the factory's roar, ever waken from the sleep of ages the stillness that has ever reigned along her mighty rivers? . . . The answer is yes! and that, too, at no distant day . . . The thousands of the young and hearty sons of toil whom we see around us that have come to make this their home, tell us in thunder tones that with the blessings of God, that here nothing is impossible—that here, under the blessings of our glorious, free and republican government, there has been a

new era commenced in the world's history, so great that the civilized world looks on in wonder. Let not the wheels of government become foul and fall in our way, or obstruct the paths in which we are now treading, or 'the wilderness shall blossom as the rose', our mighty mountains tunnelled, our thousand rivers confined to their beds, and California become the seat of commerce, wealth and art.[118]

This was a developmentalist agrarianism, and one which conceived of expansion and change as the natural result of the energy of the population. Eliza Farnham also participated in this imperial agrarian imaginary, which fantasised the settled rural future of the newly appropriated land. On a journey from Santa Cruz to San Francisco, she recorded, she came upon a view from a hill, and began to imagine the future transformation:

Cover the bay with sails and steamers, variegate the uniform green of the fertile plain with grain-fields, orchards, gardens, farm yards, and houses; dot the sunny slopes with vineyards, and let the church-spires be seen pointing heavenward from among occasional groups of dwellings, and I know not what would be wanting to complete the picture, and make it one on which the heart and eye could dwell with equal delight.[119]

There was also often a sense expressed that California was an especially favoured environment, a chosen landscape. 'There are but few lands that possess more of the beautiful and picturesque than California', declared *Hutchings' California Magazine*, one of the earliest proponents of the arcadian account of the new state.[120] Its proprietor and chief author, James Mason Hutchings, wrote for the rest of his life of the natural wonders of California, and in particular of the Yosemite Valley.[121] 'In the valley, placidly glides the transparent stream; now impinging the mountain's base; now winding its serpent-like course up the fertile valley; its margin fringed with willow and flowers, that are ever blossoming, and grass that is ever green.'[122] This was clearly a promised land. What distinguished Californian pastoral from its Victorian equivalent was the greater investment of the landscape with religious significance. In 1851, the *Alta California* recommended the mountains as well as church on a Sunday: 'All nature is full of this magic power, which links the heart of man with Deity.'[123] This was also an individuating pastoral, which sought individual fulfilment in landscape; Wyatt argues that the 'literature of California everywhere explores the ways we express identity in terms of topography'.[124]

Nature in California seemed to many especially bountiful. Eliza Farnham thought that there might not be another state on earth 'in which agriculture can be so successfully pursued'.[125] Bayard Taylor propagated arcadian myths in his *Eldorado*, writing of the San Jose valley that: 'Vegetables thrive luxuriantly, and many species, such as melons, pumpkins, squashes, beans, potatos, etc., require no further care than the planting.[126] Eri Hulpert, in

New York on his way to California, met a friend from Chicago just returning:

> He tells the largest kinds of stories about the agricultural products of that country, equal to any thing you have seen in print. To wit that melon vines will bear three crops one after the other, cabbage stumps after cutting off the head on top will still live . . . and bear any quantity of the largest kinds of heads . . . Beets that will weigh sixty pounds. Onions four to six pounds. Potatoes of the largest and best kind he ever eat . . .[127]

There was, this early in the state's history, a prevalent sense of California as a place especially blessed for an agricultural future. It could become a land where work, as it was normally understood, might be unnecessary. This was a theme with deep resonances in the European imagination and, as generations of American scholars have demonstrated, also in the American imagination.[128] California, on the periphery of the American world, became for a time the privileged site of these imaginings.

To immigrants from the eastern American cities, an argument from the Californian landscape to the possibilities of life there seemed to come quite naturally. 'California is the New World of the Nineteenth Century,' proclaimed a writer in the *California Christian Advocate*, 'and her influence will be lasting as her majestic mountains, beautiful as her flower-starred valleys, wide as her white-winged commerce, and more precious than the gold of her . . . placers.'[129] Horace Bushnell maintained that arguments from nature to society were indeed too prevalent in California. 'Sometimes', he complained, 'a degree of discouragement has been derived from the analogical or symbolical fact, that there is not a stick of smart, hard timber in all California', but it was only superstition which allowed from this observation the conclusion that 'the future men of California' would also be brittle. 'Why any more a token than the giant pines, and redwoods, and cedars are a token of prodigiously tall men, a race at least twelve or fifteen feet high? Why any more than the often naked hills and plains are a token of no men at all?'[130] Bushnell's sarcasm emphasises the prevalence of the arguments he is disputing. In California the landscape was scrutinised for signs of human destiny within it.

At times, as in Victoria, the pastoral version of California seemed to be in great tension with the El Dorado promised by the gold mines. 'Previous to the gold-emigration', the writer Eliza Farnham explained, 'California was the home of peace and rest. Where was ever a people so steeped in contentment? . . . How they luxuriated in the ease of their abundance!' But gold intervened: 'now, how are all these aspects of their life changed!'[131] For Farnham, Arcadia and El Dorado were clearly different places. In California, the tension between mining and farming was accentuated by the miners' use of flooding techniques which were in direct competition with agricultural uses of water and land. Robert Kelley has analysed the way the 'complete freedom accorded the entrepreneur in California' had allowed the growth of a mining industry in the mountains which released mud and gravel into the river canyons of the Sierra, which then caused disastrous spring flooding in the Sacramento valley.[132] Hydraulic mining, developed from 1852, involved washing away banks of mud with powerful jets of diverted water. As early as 1856, farmers were expressing concern about the effects on their water supplies, and the conflict would grow over the next three decades.[133] This conflict was part of the material basis for the ideological conflict between mining and agriculture in California. In other accounts, though, the pastoral and mining versions of California were quite compatible, both of them routes to the ideal social existence in which labour would be more or less unnecessary. These blended arguments show the compromises of the pastoral ideal which Leo Marx documents in his *The Machine in the Garden*, the wedding of the quiet of pastoral to a source of energy or prosperity which disrupts but does not ultimately destroy it.

California, like Victoria, was dependent upon imported food after the influx of gold seekers. 'The thousands of immigrants were nearly all looking for gold to dig rather than a patch of ground to plow, and for a time agriculture was all but abandoned.'[134] As in Victoria, this perceived lack was a cause of some anxious public discussion. Lotchin argues, though, that any greater agricultural development would have throttled the development of San Francisco as commercial metropolis.[135]

In Victoria, the rhetoric of a democratic right to the land was used against the squatters, who had rapidly settled the area which would become the colony of Victoria with their hundreds of thousands of sheep from the mid-1830s. The Australian squatters had no title to their land, but used their wealth and substantial political representation against the popular agrarian movements, which sought (and obtained from the late 1850s) government measures intended to redistribute the lands of the colony. In California, the same rhetoric was used by the new gold settlers, but was also, more troublingly, used by a class of American squatters on land which was actually owned by the earlier inhabitants of California under Mexican land grants. Squatters around Sacramento in 1850 agitated to have the Mexican grants negated. Josiah Royce characterised their protest: 'Is this not a free land? Is it not our land? Is not the public domain free to all American citizens?' The movement culminated in a riot on 14 August— three men were killed as landowners and the squatters fought in the streets of Sacramento. The squatters after this followed more respectable political routes to their goals, organising as the Settlers' Party for the overthrow of the Mexican titles, against the older Hispanic settlers and landowners. This is a further context in which agrarian rhetoric in California had a distinctly imperial aspect—the ostensibly democratic and radical rhetoric about the right of all to the land having the specific local purpose of dislodging the earlier inhabitants and legalising the American appropriation of the land at the individual as well as the collective level.

The Victorian agrarians used the rhetoric of aristocratic dominance of the land against the wealthy and conservative squatters they wished to displace. The Californian agrarians were less likely to use this trope against the older Californians, and much more likely to develop the other radical democratic theme—that of a natural right to the land. John Sharp moved a resolution at the Californian Miners and Settlers Convention in 1852 which argued that 'usurpation of powers' had 'tied up large portions of the earth in the hands of a few, to the great injury of the many, and the positive misery of multitudes'. The United States, he argued, should be the first in promoting 'the right of man to free access to the elements so intimately connected with his happiness'. Lamenting the 'spirit of speculation' which gold mining encouraged, it was clear that Sharp thought of agriculture as the career most conducive to happiness.[136]

There were many in California who progressed beyond agrarianism to a pastoral thought which admired the picturesque country, and argued from the beneficence of nature to a position which sought a limitation on the development of unfettered commercial liberalism. This argument from wilderness was a more important strain of thought in California than in Victoria. The private and public writings of the period are full of signs of a strong reaction to the Californian landscape by the immigrants of the 1850s. 'There is something in its very atmosphere that seems to call up the most passionate practical feelings of our nature, something that makes more acute our sense of the beautiful and we unconsciously imbibe a love of grandeur and extravagance unknown to us before.'[137] This kind of reaction always had social and political meanings. J. Bayard Taylor sent back, early in his stay in California, a poem to *Godey's Magazine* which exulted in the California landscape:

O Deep, exulting freedom of the hills!
O summits vast, that to the climbing view
In naked glory stand against the blue!
O cold and buoyant air, whose crystal fills
Heaven's amethystine bowl! O speeding streams,
That foam and thunder from the cliffs below!
O slippery brinks, and solitudes of snow,
And granite bleaknesses, where the vulture screams!
O stormy pines, that wrestle with the breath
Of the young tempest; sharp and icy horns
And hoary glaciers, sparkling in the morns,
And broad, dim wonders of the world beneath!
I summon ye; and 'mid the glare which fills
The noisy mart, my spirit walks the hills![138]

The poem is in many respects a standard pastoral, finding in the wild, newly-occupied countryside spiritual qualities lacking in the life of the city. But in gold-rush society, the pastoral becomes social criticism, for most men had not come to California to experience the 'deep, exulting freedom of the hills'. They had made, rather, as Franklin Langworthy described his own passage to California, a 'long and hazardous pilgrimage to Mammon's temple'.[139]

As in Victoria, responses to the California landscape in the surviving record often articulated a male fantasy about retreat from the world into a contained and quiet rural space. John Ballou's novel *The Lady of the West* contained a loving description of the Carson valley with its 'vast green meadow' and snow-capped mountains all around: 'Here, excluded from the whole busy world, and protected by the strongest walls on earth, the emigrant knows no language that can express his admiration of so beautiful a garden among the wild mountains, for even its solitude is surpassed by its richness and grandeur.'[140]

The walled garden/valley, protected and isolated, is obviously here too a site of considerable emotional investment for emigrating men. Stephen Chapin Davis, born in Dunstable, Massachusetts, left New York city for San Francisco in July 1850, when he was seventeen years old. He ran a store for two years in Coulterville, California. In 1852 he took a trip down to Mariposa to visit some 'boys' he knew from Nashua, New Hampshire. On his way he encountered a valley:

> surrounded by towering hills, while a clear limpid brook, gurgled along through the park-like grounds by the house and was soon lost in the forest beyond— while surveying this scene and drinking in the loveliness of the landscape with my wondering eyes, I thought it a 'Paradise on earth', as the very place my imagination had pictured to me in younger days, as the realization of all the airy castles I had built in my romantic spells, where I would live and die, away from the selfish, wicked world in some retiring spot, 'some lovely dell', where nature has lavished all her charms, where the air is filled with the perfume of a thousand flowers, and where the sweet warbling of multitudes of beautiful feathered songsters combine to make it a residence more suitable for angels than for men.[141]

This is the working of what might here, as in Victoria, be termed the masculine pastoral imaginary. It involved the projection of a desired happy domestic scene onto an idyllic landscape, away from the 'selfish, wicked world', the discovery of a place which could be imagined as a happy and isolated (happy because isolated) home. E. Gould Buffum recorded a similar experience as he came across yet another idyllic valley:

> A tall growth of grass and wild oats, interspersed with beautiful blue and yellow autumnal flowers, covered the plain, and meandering through it, with a thousand windings, was a silvery stream, clear as a crystal . . . It was a beautiful

scene. The sun was just sinking behind the hills on the western side, and threw a golden stream of light on the opposite slope. Birds of gaudy plumage were carolling their thousand varied notes on the tree branches, and I thought if gold and its allurements could be banished from my thoughts, I could come here and live in this little earthly paradise for ever.[142]

In both Victoria and California, the landscape provided an obvious resource for those who wanted to comment upon the futility of the pursuit of gold. The worldliness of gold is here implicitly contrasted to the home and its quiet values, the possibilities of retreat and asylum.

In California, response to nature often had a religious meaning. James Carson offered a lyrical account of the relationship of the resident of the mountains to the landscape:

go to the homes and haunts of the mountaineer, in the lone forest, where the grandeur of Heaven's architecture surrounds you; where the music comes from babbling brooks, and songs of sportive birds, where the air you breathe is laden with the sweet perfumes from the flower-clad hills and vales around, which arise as a befitting incense for adoration; where the cloud-capped peaks of the mountains ever point into the azure vault above, and tell the heart there is a God.[143]

Californian ministers were more likely than Victorian ones to see divine purpose in the picturesque landscape. The Reverend R.B. Cutler, in his 1856 Thanksgiving sermon in San Francisco, offered a particularly striking example of this kind of argument from the landscape:

Why these picturesque landscapes, these winding streams, these mountains and vales intermingled with these waving forests and pounding oceans? Might not all the rivers have run to the sea in straight lines and sharp-cut channels and banks unadorned with fringing foliage? Might not all the arms of the trees have stood out at right angles from the supporting stem—and every twig at the erectness and stiffness of the porcupine's quill, and each leaf been squared as if by the carpenter's rule?[144]

The Divine hand had made the picturesque landscape for the gratification of all; it was a visible sign of his goodness.

Californian responses differ from Victorian ones in part because of the Transcendentalist stream in American thought. There was a kind of pantheism which was a particular feature of the response to California by the gold-rush immigrants. In California, David Wyatt has argued, the energies which in the north had gone into covenant theology or in the south into the rationalisation of southern history, were displaced into the encounter with the landscape. In California, he maintains, the 'experience of landscape is understood to control, or validate, human life'.[145] Even in the churches this had a hold, and Sandra Sizer Frankiel argues that 'even the most conservative churchmen sometimes translated the beauties of

California into religious terms'.[146] Samuel D. Simonds was a Methodist minister who, riding up the mountains from Shasta, experienced a 'rapture of beauty' contemplating them: 'yes, I will say it, what a great, all-feeling thing the mountain appears! . . . I sink into nothing and feel awe-struck before the all-encompassing, infinite Jehovah, whose presence penetrates with life these wilds of solitude and grandeur.'[147]

The most well known of these pantheist responses was that of Thomas Starr King, the influential Unitarian minister who arrived in California in 1860, and soon began offering it what Kevin Starr has described as a 'flatteringly high level of public discourse'.[148] As his biographer noted in 1865, Starr King found in California that 'the surpassing natural beauty and wonders of this region . . . ministered to his religious genius'.[149] Early on in his residence there he began to write of the mountains of California. 'Yesterday I devoted to the study of Mt Shasta', he told an audience at the Agricultural Fair in Stockton in 1860, 'I had it in view for ten hours. It is glorious beyond expression . . . The whole region is sublime.'[150] King's letters describing a vacation in the Sierras and Yosemite were published in the *Boston Evening Transcript* in 1860. Later sermons drew upon the experience. King's 1863 sermon, 'Lessons from the Sierra Nevada', linked the appreciation of the natural world in California to the nationalism he was also developing as the Union was threatened with dissolution: 'There can be no abounding and ardent patriotism where sacred attachment to the scenery of our civil home is wanting; and there can be no abiding and inspiring religious joy in the heart that recognises no presence and touch of God in the permanent surroundings of our earthly abode.'[151] The pantheism was quite explicit: 'I meet you tonight that we may together bow reverently before the mountains that guard the eastern frontier of our State . . .' Perhaps this attachment to the spiritual qualities of place was one of the reasons King rejected all suggestions of a political career—'I would swim to Australia before taking a political post' he is reported to have said.[152]

King was also too detached from and critical of the materialism of the age, the treating of nature as a mere resource to be exploited, to have expected much political success. He found an alternative to materialism in the natural world. He observed that:

> The great bane of modern life is materialism,—the divorce of spirit from power, order, bounty, and beauty in our thought of the world. We look upon nature as a machine, a play of forces that run of necessity and of course. We do not bow before it with wonder and awe, as the manifestation of a present all-animating will and art.[153]

King identified the Sierra Nevada as a source of value and inspiration ('lift up thine eyes unto the hills', he advised his listeners, 'from whence cometh thy help'). He brought an almost apocalyptic tone to their contemplation:

'And when we see it sixty miles off, under clouds that mimic its pinnacles and swells, it shows like a vision from another world, like the street and wall of the New Jerusalem.'[154]

The gold rushes, in California as in Victoria, involved much ecological devastation—more perhaps in California because of the greater use of hydraulic mining, which poured thousands of tons of mud and silt into the rivers. This devastation was sometimes celebrated by observers, who stood in awe of the transformative power of man. Alonzo Delano wrote of the 'mighty power' of man bringing his 'active busy life' to the high Sierras:

> Amid those sombre hills, beneath those waving pines, at the base of those huge castelled rocks, in those dark and almost inaccessible canyons, along the banks and on the bars of those rolling streams or mountain torrents . . . you will find a band of hardy freemen who are tearing up the soil, displacing immense boulders that have lain undisturbed for ages, and who are not only developing the rich resources of that mountain region for the use of the world, but are making the desolation, which reigned six years ago, the theatre of active busy life, the site of noble towns, and its forbidding deserts now smiling with happy homes.[155]

There is an interesting shift in this passage, from the opening with its admiration of the sublimity of the natural scene, to the conclusion, with its celebration of the intruders who are 'tearing up the soil' in the cause of civilisation.

In other cases, though, the natural world in which the gold was found provided a framework of critical response to the gold rush as a human event. The lessons from the Sierra Nevada were not only religious, though it was often within a religious framework that the natural world was harnessed to the criticism of the values of gold-rush society. For those who had reservations about the 'active, busy life' which Delano celebrated, the transformation of the natural world involved was less obviously a good thing. 'The whole mining region is finally to become a desolation . . . ,' lamented Horace Bushnell, 'Indeed there seems to be a kind of prior necessity, which nature must needs recognize, that gold and desolation go together.' Bushnell's observations on California, first published in the *New Englander*, were highly critical of the human impact on the region. As regards the scenery in California, he argued, 'everything here is inverted which we commonly assume in respect to the effects of culture'. Culture in California improved nothing; civilisation 'cuts down the oaks for firewood', converts the plains into a 'weedy desolation', and the whole scene into a 'most horrid desolation'. The destruction of the natural world only mirrored the moral effects of gold in the world, 'only represents too faithfully what holds good historically in the moral desolations of plunder, fraud, and avarice, instigated by this treasure of the mountains'.[156]

The strength of agrarian and pastoral sentiment in California was sufficient for it to be necessary for explicit anti-agrarian arguments to be mounted. W.A. Scott was the defender of urban and commercial life, who turned on agrarianism, labelling it an urban indulgence: 'The habit and capability of enjoying the romance and seclusion and repose of the country, is usually derived from the busy scenes of life.'[157] His defence of urban sophistication was pointed:

> If all the world were farmers they might have bread and beef enough, but the mass of mankind would be idle, untaught and narrow-minded. For it is the excitement of trade, the conflicts of a generous rivalry, and the enlargement of ideas consequent upon the exchange of the products of one country for those of another, that call forth the powers of the mind and the heart, that gathering wealth and social comforts expand into civilization.[158]

Scott's free-trade liberalism was but one of the strands making up the fabric of public argument in gold-rush California, though a more important one than it was in Victoria.

Agrarian and pastoral thought became languages of social criticism in California and Victoria. The resources were largely held in common, though the differences were also significant. British Chartism gave a specific inflection to Victorian agrarianism, just as American imperialism and Transcendentalism gave particular shape to Californian pastoral. But in the end, it seems that the commonalities in the content of the thought are more significant than the differences, though the constituency of agrarian thought in Victoria was larger and more influential. In California, as in Victoria, there were those who saw in the landscape the possibility of a return to the Garden, and used this utopian wish as a form of social criticism of the disorder of their societies. 'California will thus become an earthly paradise', wrote Franklin Langworthy, a Universalist minister from Illinois, 'rivalling in beauty Eden's primitive garden. Green fields will stretch over the broad plains, and through the countless fertile valleys among the mountains, and herdsmen tend their flocks upon a "thousand hills". Imagination can scarcely mount up to the future prosperity and greatness of this favoured land.'[159] Agrarian and pastoral thought were modes of extending a response to the natural environment into an alternate and oppositional vision of the possibilities of the new societies.

CHAPTER 5

DOMESTICITY

A poor new chum, well educated and at home well
connected. He is violently mad with a taste for theatricals.
He now indulges himself with ranting most Prodigious. In a
solitary cell with a straight waistcoat confining his limbs, he
dolefully proclaims 'that Britons never will be slaves'...
John Buckly Castieau (gaoler, Melbourne Gaol),
18 January 1855

One of the things men seemed to like about the life of gold seeking was
the 'independence' it offered. This independence had a public-political
meaning—it referred to independence from the constraints and hierarchies
of a deferential society still largely structured around the master–servant
relationship. But it also had a gendered meaning. Single men celebrated
their freedom from domestic constraints and responsibilities. The chorus
of contemporary observations is striking. 'The wild free and independent
life appears the great charm', James Bonwick wrote of gold digging, 'They
have no masters. They go where they please and work when they will.'[1]
'It is not everyone that likes a digger's life', wrote Jim Atlee to his sister
in England, 'as for myself I like it above all things, it is a roving free
independent life for a single man'. 'No life can be more independent and
free than that of the Australian digger', wrote George Henry Wathen in
1854. 'It is this free out-of-door life, and the buoyancy of spirit that goes
with it, this exemption from all restraint, which often allures men back to
the diggings after some months' artificial life in the towns.' 'The life of
the digger is very free and independent', observed Kinahan Cornwallis.
'The perfect freedom and thorough independence of a gold-digger's life
must be truly enchanting to the youth of energy, adventure, and courage',
wrote another chronicler. Diggers' earnings were not greater than in the
ordinary pursuits of the colony, Charles Gavan Duffy commented, 'but the

employment had the unspeakable charm of not being a servile one'.[2] Men in the 1850s who had read almost any of the published accounts of gold-rush Victoria knew what was attractive about the digging life. But there developed a contest in gold-rush society over masculinity, and there were some who explicitly challenged this valorisation of independence. James Daniel was one. He wrote repeatedly from Victoria to his brother, dissatisfiedly at work as a clerk in the East India office in London, to dissuade him from emigrating in pursuit of independence. 'There is no such thing as independence in this world', he maintained.[3]

This masculine independent freedom had its costs. Men left their families behind, in Britain or in the Australian cities, and were sometimes reluctant to rejoin them. Janet Kincaid wrote from Scotland to her husband in the Victorian gold town of Maryborough, with possibly representative anger. A substantial section of the letter is quoted here, as such material is understandably rare in the surviving record. The letter is dated 'Greenock, Sept. 19':

My *Dear* Husband,

I got your address from your *Father* you sent him a letter, to let him know that you was quite well, and that you left the ship to better your Family, you don't need to write that any more we have had enough of that talk, you had better do something for *them* you left the ship to better your *self* and to get your own *money* to your *self* you never cared much for your Family, far less for your *Wife*. You sent five *Pounds* two years and a half ago, did five Pounds keep you since you left the ship, you mention in a letter to *me* that you made more money at the *digging* than ever you made at *home* you might have sent us the half of what you made you are a hard hearted *Father* when you could sit down and eat up your *Childrens* meat your self. I was a poor unfortunate *Wretch* little did I think when I was young, what I had to come *through*, without your *conduct* we might have been the *happiest couple* in Greenock you got a good *Wife* and many a good *job* at home if you had been inclined to do well but folks that can't do well at home is not to be trusted *Abroad*. You complain of me not writing *you*, I wish I had all the sixpences and *shillings* I paid for letters it would get some *meat* for the *Boys Breakfast*. I answered all your *letters* by return of *post*, you ought to have sent me a *proper* address at the *first* where to write and keep by the one place where you could send and get *them* every letter I sent was to a different *place* + before it reached you were of to another place you ought to have sent a letter every month at least and money every three months . . . let me know what you intend to do for the *Boys* we are still in the same *House 15 West Stewart street where you left us*.

I was asking the *Boys* if they had any word to send to their *Father*. *Henry* says he hopes you are *well* + all your *friends* are well, Bob says you *owe* him a sixpence he sent you to go to *Port Glasgow*, Johny wants a pair of new *Boots* if you can spare as much, James is content with a *cocker nut*, poor Duncan does not know what sort of a thing a *Father* is he thinks it is something for *eating*, if you wish to correspond *with us* find out a proper place where I will send my *letters* no more at present from your *deserted Wife,*

Janet Kincaid[4]

It was stories such as this which outraged contemporary defenders of family life. The gold rush seemed to have licensed forms of masculine behaviour against which they had been campaigning for decades. Men were abandoning their economic and emotional responsibilities to their families, in order to pursue wealth. 'I am glad to hear that Emily is well and growing', William Sasse wrote somewhat defensively to the guardian of his daughter in 1858, 'but cannot understand how she can exhibit at any time signs of ignorance of the existence of a father for altho' I am away from her, I should have thought that her memory and your motherly office would have brought me often to her present thoughts'.[5]

It is in the letters that women wrote to their departed and gold-seeking men that we perceive most clearly the terms of the domestic critique of the disruptions of gold. Such letters also provide evidence of the popular diffusion of ideas which were circulating in the magazines and sermons of the period. The letter Chandler Harris received in Victoria from his friend Ellen back in the United States thus used the language of domesticity to reproach him for his folly. 'Oh Chandler did we not pass many happy hours together', she wrote, 'I thought what a pleasant home you had and kind parents with everything else any one could wish to make you happy and yet you left them all for *gold*. Oh Chandler I hope you may be blessed with good health and get enough to pay you for the sacrifice you made in going.'[6] The ideology of domesticity not only provided a language with which to criticise the effects of gold. It also meant that the response to gold was often clearly gendered in this way—women, such as Ellen, speaking from the position which argued that it would take a lot of gold to compensate for the loss of domestic happiness in a known community; men, such as Chandler, by their actions arguing that greater happiness might be gained from movement and speculation. It was expected in the 1850s that men and women would respond to gold in different ways.

Reformers such as Caroline Chisholm set out to publicise the costs of such independent wealth-seeking behaviour on the part of men. She ran a personal family reunion programme: 'I have promised parents to go in search of their children—I have promised wives to make enquiry for their husbands—I have promised sisters to seek their brothers, and friends to look for friends.'[7] Reformers such as Chisholm were also concerned to proselytise on behalf of the pleasures and comforts of domesticity. Chisholm understood that gold-rush society often made a hostile and threatening environment for the women within it. Contemporary male observers, and later historians, sometimes argued from the sex ratio to a privileged status for women. 'If there is any girl over sixteen years of age unmarried in Australia,' opined the Reverend David Mackenzie, 'it is her own fault, for she must have had several offers.'[8] But most contemporary comment recognised that domesticity was under threat in Victoria, that destitution and abandonment were the lot of too many colonial women. This view became a strain of critical response to gold—one of the most important, both in Victoria and California.

In contemporary sentimental songs, men would offer to forswear the pursuit of gold for true love, or family life. Some announced in verse that gold could not buy the charms of home:

But there is a spell that binds us to the land
Where in our childhood we have played with shells upon the strand;
And memory thro' the mist of years, still wistfully looks back,
And we long to tread, before we die, the old familiar track.

Let pleasure have its votaries—let the miner hoard his gold
'Till every spark of feeling is shrivelled up and cold,
Dearer to me than gold or song, the deep heart-thrilling sound,
The heaving of the anchor, when the ship's homeward bound.[9]

The problem, in the eyes of the proponents of domesticity, was that in real life few men seemed to have these values—few seemed prepared, that is, to place home before fortune. Some men, so accustomed to life in a market society, took the next logical step and advertised for a wife in the newspaper: 'Wanted a Wife. She must be of good figure, and have a fair share of personal beauty.'[10] Gold-rush society was simply not conducive to settled domestic peace, nor to tranquilly conducted romance. 'It is not difficult to get a wife here,' wrote George Reid in a letter, 'but the trouble is to keep her, when got. What with the diggers running away with them, and they with the diggers, it is no easy matter I assure you.'[11]

DOMESTICITY AND ITS DISRUPTION

The cultivation of the domestic affections is one of our most obvious duties. Is there not a fear in the hot pursuit of gold that the sweetest character of life will be forgotten?

Letter to **Geelong Advertiser** 1851[12]

To emigrate is no holiday pastime. The ship in which men abandon their fatherland for ever does not put to sea like the trim vessel of the summer tourist—'Hope at the helm, and pleasure at the prow'; but freighted with aching hearts, with mournful retrospects, and with dark forebodings.

Sir James Stephen, 'On Colonisation as a Branch of Social Economy'[13]

The gold diggers were mostly men. They were men, further, who had left their homes in pursuit of material wealth. Those facts were prominently in the minds of many of those who were disturbed by the sort of society that seemed to be in creation in Victoria in the 1850s. Of course there were many women on the goldfields, and they were engaged in a great diversity of occupations. Official figures estimated the total Victorian goldfields population in 1853 as 46 550 men, 10 740 women, and 11 590 children. But the imbalance was great. The perception of reformers was that gold-rush society was an unusually masculine society, and that that fact explained much about it.[14] When Governor Hotham visited the diggers at Forest Creek he 'urged them to settle in the country with their wives and children, and intimated that education would follow, and its attendants, law and order'.

The fear of many elite groups in Victoria was that the taste of masculine independence would be so attractive to the male population that it would never settle down, never find a new home. Optimistic observers of the gold rush stressed the evidence of homesickness they found, the longing for a more settled life or a place they had abandoned. P. Just recorded that, walking round Melbourne's extensive Canvas Town, a peep into a tent would 'sometimes reveal such articles of higher civilisation as a piano, from the melancholy strains of which brought forth by delicate fingers, would occasionally be heard "Sweet Home", or to the ear of the North Briton the beautiful air of "O why left I my hame?" '[15] Pessimistic observers, on the other hand, stressed the dangers of possibly permanent dislocation, of a society of men imbued with a lasting love of wandering.

An advice literature appeared, which saw in settled family life the solution to almost all of the problems which confronted the colony. These writers were in possession of a theory of the characteristics of the two sexes which was well stated by James Bonwick in the *Australian Gold Diggers' Monthly Magazine* in 1853: 'A nation of females might degenerate into a society of coarse and scratching vultures, like the Amazons of story. A community of men is a herd of selfishness and brutality. The association of the sexes elevates and refines both.'[16] Bonwick was the most insistent Victorian spokesman for this doctrine of the beneficial social effects of women, of the power of domestic life to soften and ameliorate the harshnesses of gold-rush society. 'Without woman', another article in the same magazine observed, 'man would be rude, unpolished, solitary; he would be a stranger to grace, which is no other than the smiles of life, like the honeysuckles of the forest which adorn the stately oak with their perfumed garlands'.[17]

The colonial writers did not invent this way of thinking. What historians have called the doctrine of separate spheres had been prevalent in British and North American society for decades. But the new colonial situation in Victoria, the threat of the creation, at least temporarily, of a society of men without women, brought forth vigorous reminders of the chief tenets of the doctrine, dire warnings as to the likely contours of the society coming into being on the fields, and in the cities and towns of the colony. When the Reverend H. Berkeley Jones, MA, previously curate of Belgravia chapel, visited Australia from 1852 to 1853, it was clear to him that 'the mind, not well fortified by religious sentiments, is apt, in the absence of the softening influences of domestic life, to be degraded step by step into paths which it never contemplated before without horror and dismay'.[18]

Men were associated with work, production, and the accumulation of money. Gold digging was thus, in terms of pre-existing thought, a paradigmatic masculine activity, more purely selfish and acquisitive than the industrial or commercial activities to which, in the old world, the ideology of domesticity had responded. Even the Melbourne Chamber of Commerce regarded the separation from domestic influence first among the undesirable features of gold digging. 'The vocation of gold-digging, under its present aspects, has many social disadvantages to weigh against its dazzling results in other respects,' argued one of its reports, 'The separation from home and domestic ties, the exposed and laborious mode of life, the semi-gambling character of the results, are all circumstances of a character adverse to social progress and welfare.'[19]

Women were associated with the home, consumption, reproduction—a set of domestic virtues which stood in opposition to, though necessarily complementarity with, the more grasping, avaricious and unrestrained world outside. 'We know of nothing', remarked the *Journal of Australasia* in 1856, 'that tends so much to keep alive the best feelings of our nature, and to prevent a man from sinking into a mere machine, working and eating and sleeping, without one thought beyond the present, one aspiration beyond the acquisition of wealth, than when woman appears to tend and soothe in distress, and share, as a wife alone can do, in the joys of success'.[20] Domesticity was what prevented life from being totally absorbed by the utilitarian ethic of the market place. The word 'humanising' was frequently used; the domestic hearth, and the woman who tended it, were what prevented men from succumbing to the outside pressures to become like machines, existing only to work, and inert when idle. For this reason, the radical press embraced the ideology of domesticity as eagerly as did the organs of the reforming middle classes. 'The emigrant sought these shores', one radical paper reminded its readers, 'to put the breadth of the world in every sense as well as a geographical one, between him and the machine existence'.[21] It was the home which would banish the machine existence. An idealised state of rural and domestic happiness in an idyllic landscape dominated the radical imagination of the period.

The 'separate spheres' argument was premissed upon a belief that men and women had separate and opposed, though complementary, natures.

'How great is the relief to a man wearied by constant drudgery', wrote the author of one pamphlet:

> when he turns to woman's society, and finds in her a nature refreshingly opposed to his own; her trivial occupations, unpractical ideas, careless expressions, and personal elegances, contrast delightfully with his own peculiarities . . . she preserves him from becoming sordid, coarse, and unsociable . . . it would be impossible for society to attain or preserve a high degree of civilization unaided by woman's refining influence.

The author goes on to suggest, however, that a class of *men* could perform some of the same functions, providing they had no work to do, and could devote themselves entirely to leisure and consumption: 'a class of men, idle in the ordinary sense of the word, attending to their pleasures while others attend to their business, and constantly come into contact with them'.[22]

The proponents of these views were mostly men. But there were also prominent women who expounded the separate spheres doctrine in the 1850s. The most famous of them was Caroline Chisholm.[23] Speaking to an audience in Castlemaine, she stressed the social importance of ensuring a population of domesticated men: 'what a cheer would the diggers give if the homes they go to at night were something better than the blankets under which they have to creep like dogs. Give them good homes, and if the Russians came tomorrow, the diggers would all turn out and fight in their defense like men (Applause)'. She looked forward to the time when the new immigrants and gold seekers would be 'really at home, with their wives and families—when they live in peace and quietness'.[24] Chisholm approved of gold digging, but only as a way of acquiring the means of purchasing land and commencing farming.

The first issue of the *Australian Home Companion and Illustrated Weekly Magazine* began with a poem which eloquently stated the arguments of the domestic ideology:

> Land of abundance, fruitful, rich and fair,
> No gaunt-eyed penury need wander there;
> Yet still, though nature's gifts are freely spread,
> Ripe to the hand of those thy soil who tread;
> Though brightest promise all newcomers greet,
> And Fortune showers her favours at their feet,
> There is a want—there is a longing, still
> A void, that wealth and rank may fail to fill:
> Where are home comforts? where that social band,
> Domestic pleasures of our Fatherland?
> Man is not born a miser life to lead,
> Fast fettered in the slavery of greed,
> With one idea seething in his brain,
> The blind, besotting, selfish strife for gain

No, let us soar above this vile control,
And spurn such wretched serfdom of the soul;
And mid the world's contention, crowd and noise,
Seek home's solicitudes and peaceful joys,
And find reward of toil, repose from strife,
In fireside pleasures of domestic life,
Where woman in her fairest phase we view,
So good, so gentle, trustful, fond and true.

Separate spheres thought, then, provided one of the dominant frames of response to the disruption of gold. It accentuated the extent to which thinking about gold proceeded in gendered terms. Gold seeking, it was implicitly or explicitly argued, was an activity which would exaggerate and aggravate certain inherent male behaviour traits, among them an excessive devotion to worldly and commercial activities which, without the softening influence of a domestic hearth and the relations around it, would lead to a coarsening and brutalising of the population.

The social vision which accompanied this concern was a fear of an atomised society, devoted entirely to individual wealth seeking. It was single gold-seeking men who seemed most likely to create such a society. In the efforts of colonial reformers of the time, we can see a conscious attempt to reform colonial manhood, to attach the male wealth seekers more firmly to domesticity, and the imagined quietness and tranquillity of the family hearth. These reform attempts had widespread support in Victoria, across the political spectrum. A conservative author in 1857, who objected to all other forms of public assistance for immigration, was quite satisfied that it was properly the business of government to promote and assist female immigration, for such immigration had 'for its object the advancement of morality by the equalisation of the sexes'.[25]

A Victorian writer recalled in 1852 a visit to a well-watered valley, some years before. It was uncultivated, he wrote, and 'I regretted that this lovely pass should be waste, where corn, and vines, and all things necessary for man in their richest profusion would grow, were it but a peopled spot'. The language ('this lovely pass') alerts us to something: there is emotion invested here. This is not the cold analysis of physiocratic economic thought. We are in the presence of a language of desire, of the evocation of an imagined, wished-for landscape:

Even now—and many things tend to render the Bush an undesirable home since the Gold discovery—even now, I feel that I could desire no happier destiny than to have this 'Pass' my own, where locked in at one extremity for at least half each year, by rocks on either side, and a narrow gorge at the south-western end, a man might spend the days allotted him on earth, improving his family, and live in happy oblivion of all the wild tumult of the world without.

OUR ADDRESS.

'Our Address', from **The Australian Home Companion and Illustrated Weekly Magazine** *30 January 1857, p.1.*

The writer concludes wistfully that he still remembers the 'summer perfection' of 'that unspoiled scene' and 'I wonder now, if I shall ever look upon its like again'.[26] This fragment from a Melbourne magazine in 1852, the year of keenest response to the disruption of gold, was entitled 'Gold'. It was a Victorian idyll; it sought to evoke that desirable state of affairs which had been and might have been, if the gold had not been found. It embodied a fantasy (a male fantasy, for the voice that speaks in the fragment is a male voice) of retreat from the world, into a rural and domestic space, one that could be owned and controlled. It was a statement of a deeply felt wish.

The happy valley was specifically the site of a *domestic* bliss, a place a man might spend his life 'improving his family' (they are not individuated; they are there to complete the domestic wish-scene, as proud possessions). Domestic, too, is the projected state of 'happy oblivion of all the wild tumult of the world without'. The valley is the extrapolation and exaggeration of the desirable home; the 'world' is seen as tortured and frenzied, the home as a retreat. Yet the isolation imagined here is far greater than

that of the suburban cottage. Cut off for half the year, there is here a real
abandonment of society and its projects, a fantasy of retreat into a private
world, removed from the competition outside. It is this imagined isolation
too, which may mark this as a masculine projection.[27] The family home
was a temporary retreat; the seat of a set of values opposed to those of the
world, but not a wholly realised alternative to it.[28] The home, through its
male breadwinner, was in practice, as in ideology, crucially tied to the
world outside. The agrarian fantasy, the yeoman farmer ideal, was the
closest this society could come to imagining a rejection of the world—for
the yeoman farmer, in his vaunted independence, could turn his back on
the market relations of the surrounding world. The figure of the yeoman
represented, as Marilyn Lake has argued, an attempt to imagine a non-
exploitative capitalism, a mode of production which did not involve
degradation or dependence. The home, like the yeoman's farm, was a key
site of alternate values.[29] And when the gold rush seemed to pose the
threat of a society entirely preoccupied with the paradigmatic masculine
activity of wealth seeking in a selfish and individualist mode, the two key
languages of response were those of agrarianism and domesticity.

The language of agrarianism and the language of domesticity operated at
the highest levels of colonial society; they provided ways of understanding
the disturbing events of the gold rushes, of formulating policies and responses
to them. They were thus, in colonial Victoria, a key part of what the French
social theorists Lefort and Castoriadis have called the 'social imaginary'. It
is in their sense of reference to another world, a 'perhaps possible' world,
that the term 'social imaginary' is used here—to express something of the
psychology, some would say pathology, of longing, of desire for another social
state.[30] The isolated pass, cut off from the world for half the year, is an
expression of this longing—'I could desire no happier destiny'.

In their private writings too, colonial men depicted ideal colonial land-
scapes, and indulged in fantasies of settlement and domestic retreat. Robert
Shortreid Anderson recorded in his diary his impressions of a trip to
Geelong in 1852:

> We came to the River Barwon, backed by boundless forests which met the
> horizon, a road we could see meandered its way through the wilderness over
> steep hills down valleys and beautiful slopes till it was lost in the distance,
> the scene was so novel and romantic we were loath to leave the spot . . . the
> day being as fine a one as we have experienced since our arrival in this
> romantic country: we sat down, lingering on the scene, the silence of the
> sabbath, and our own position made altogether an impression on me never to
> be forgot.[31]

Anderson was also confiding to his diary his desire for a wife:

> Finlayson agreed with me that for a young man in my circumstances in the
> Colony, marriage and a settled life was to be recommended. I had longed for

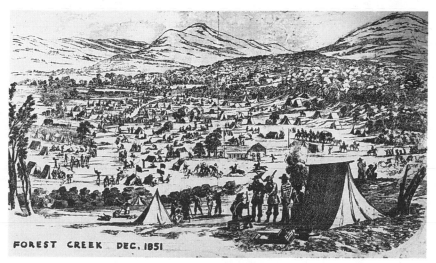

FOREST CREEK DEC. 1851

Robert Shortreid Anderson (1833–1874). 'Mount Alexander Gold Diggings Australia', lithograph, 1852. La Trobe Collection, State Library of Victoria.

a home I could call my own, a quiet retreat from the bustle of the town unmixed with the cares of the world and strangers . . . In conclusion I resolved to get married by hook or crook some day and at as early a period as possible.[32]

There is a close connection between the landscape reverie, and this desire for a domestic retreat from the world. To a respectable young man like Anderson, the attractions of the colony were bound up with its romantic landscape and its domestic possibilities, for both allowed fantasies of a retreat from a workaday world that seemed continually unfulfilling.

Daniel Pettman wrote to his parents in 1854 from Geelong, where he was sharing a house with a fellow tradesman. They were renting 'a nice little house' two miles from town with 'a fine view of Corio Bay and the surrounding picturesque and romantic scenery', and had purchased a small piece of land 'in the vicinity of My Employers House and I sincerely hope we shall shortly be able to build a House of our own . . . there is nothing better in this Country than for a Man to live in his own house . . .' But Pettman too was looking for a wife: 'We are both batchelors each wanting a good Wife for partners through life . . . the women that know us about here say it is a sin for such fine steady and industrious young Men to be living alone like this . . .' Victoria was to be the romantic and picturesque site of domestic retreat.

In January 1853 the newly arrived John Pettit wrote to his mother and father in England of a night spent on the edge of the Keilor Plains:

We pitched our tent on the edge of a steep declivity of about 150 ft. in depth which came round nearly forming a circle at the base enclosing a little level plot of about 100 acres, on which was a pretty little homestead, the greater portion of this island being cultivated—our road to the right laid thro' a low valley, rising a steep hill on the other side—mountains in the distance—this view was one of the prettiest I have seen in the colony, the low ground being very fertile . . .'[33]

The 'pretty' homestead, marooned on an 'island' of fertile ground, surrounded by mountains—Pettit's writing is restrained, but there is clearly here an expression of desire for a life in such a rural and idyllic location.

The settled tranquillity of the valley, though, stands in John Pettit's letters as a kind of implicit counterpoint to the other sort of possibility the colony offered—the unfettered masculine freedom of the bush.

If we want wood for firing or any other purpose we range up into the woods or the hills with an axe, and cut down whatever the country produces—it seemed strange to me at first, when chopping a fine lofty tree—I could hardly help turning my head round to see if I was observed—almost questioning within myself the right I had to do so—fancy cutting down a large tree to get a small piece from the top . . .[34]

Note the smothered self-censorship, the guilt, which is not just to do with the squandering of resources, but with the absence of control and obligations; the control which came with settlement on the one hand, and the obligations of domesticity on the other. Just as the dense bush was the landscape of uncontrolled masculinity, so there was a landscape of domesticity, epitomised by the happy, secluded, fertile valley, with its cleared land and pretty little homestead. In the imagination of the time, one was the direct opposite of the other.

Each had a political existence.[35] 'Good government means liberty,' Edward Wilson argued in his pamphlet on the *Principles of Representation*, 'It means thriving and contented homesteads, agreeable domestic relations, comfort and competency for ourselves, and a brilliant prospect for our children.'[36] There was a geography of domesticity to be evoked, and it stood in opposition to the actual appearance of the times. When the Quaker William Howitt visited the Reid's Creek diggings, he seemed to be struck by the connection between the character of the human population there and the landscape it had created: 'A more rowdy and uninviting scene I never saw. There was an indescribable air of blackguardism about it. All the trees were cut down.'[37] Although agriculture obviously also required a clearing of the land, a different set of metaphors could be used, and the discussions were of a bringing to fruition rather than of a laying waste. It was domesticity that made the difference—the barren violence of masculine gold seeking could be contrasted to the settled and productive landscape with the home at its heart. A letter to the editor of the *Argus* in 1852 confidently expressed the hope that one would voluntarily be exchanged for the other: 'The diggers will, when journeying to and from the Gold Field, see a beautiful country uninhabited, and they will never rest till they occupy it; friends will like to be beside friends, and in this way villages will be formed in this country.'[38] Domesticity was incidentally to involve a quietening and ruralising of the population. At a meeting in 1854 in Melbourne, called to raise a testimonial to Caroline Chisholm, Mr Chapman described her system of colonisation succinctly as one of 'binding the people to the soil by means of transplanting to Australia the ties of family affection'.[39] The project, Chisholm argued, was urgent: 'There are thousands and tens of thousands now at the diggings who have no earthly tie near them. They are fast losing all the associations of humanity. They are as isolated beings, caring for no one around them.'[40]

There were then two competing geographies in the gold period. One was the ravaged landscape of the goldfields themselves: pot-holed, denuded of vegetation—caught, for example, in the photographs of the French photographer Antoine Fauchery and his associate Richard Daintree, who took some goldfields scenes between 1857 and 1859.[41] The other was the settled and domesticated landscape of the small farms, nestling in a picturesque landscape, captured in some of the landscape art of the period. One was exclusively masculine, the other was founded on the domestic hearth, with its idealised relations between men and women.

In fragments of women's writings from the gold-rush period, we get glimpses of an outsider's view of the masculine landscape that was threatening to overtake Victoria, a view so alienated from the dominant ethos that it amounts to a critique of it. The comments of middle-class women observers point to their sense of the absurdity of the masculine, 'wealth at any cost', rapacity that they saw around them. Historians of Australian mateship have applauded the qualities of goldfields life. The digging life, Geoffrey Serle argued, 'drew men together, as in army life'.[42] Contemporary women observers too were sent searching for analogies with other all-male institutions. Frances Perry, wife of the Anglican Bishop of Melbourne, wrote in her journal on a trip through the goldfields that:

> Life in the camp is most amusing, and was quite a novelty to me. There is a large mess-tent, where the commissioners, military officers, superintendent of police, etc. etc., take all their meals, the Chief Commissioner presiding. Here we also messed, and I could not help being reminded of college rooms, though certainly there was no similarity, excepting that the party consisted only of gentlemen. I could not deliver myself of the idea that I was on board ship . . .[43]

Elizabeth Ramsay-Laye also viewed the digging enterprise from a considerable distance. When she travelled to the goldfields, far from being impressed by the industry and activity, a disturbing analogy sprang to her mind: 'On entering the diggings, the country has the appearance of one vast cemetery with fresh made graves.' 'Money absorbs every thought, every heart,' she noted, 'in this strange camp.'[44]

At times, then, the colony could seem like a society of and for men, its landscape rendered sterile and uninhabitable. There were clearly ways in which the whole colony was seen to be dominated by an adventurist and masculinist ethos that some women found unsympathetic; the demographic imbalance also made it difficult for them to reproduce the friendships of home.[45] Eliza Chomley recalled that her mother, on arriving in Melbourne in the early 1850s, as the wife of the barrister T.T. a'Beckett, found the colony a dispiriting place. Her mother, she wrote, was 'always kind and gentle, but I fancy in those days too much depressed by the strangeness, loneliness and uncertainty of her new life, and the recent parting from her friends, to be very happy'.[46] More strikingly, Jane Prendergast wrote to her father-in-law in 1853, complaining of her husband that:

> on one point certainly we shall never agree, he likes this country and I do not; I can understand a gentleman liking it, their life is so very free and independent, so much the reverse of the restraint that society imposes upon them in England, but no ladies like it: the fortunes of their families and a wish to get some gold out of the land of gold, has brought them here, and necessity obliges them to remain . . .[47]

At other times, a particular geography of gender was articulated, which suggested that women did find places in the colony to inhabit, and did find ways to use ideologies of domesticity to offer a critique, however privately, of the fortune-seeking ways of the colonial world. In Catherine Helen Spence's 1854 gold-rush novel, *Clara Morison*, Annie Elliott writes to her friend Minnie of the invasion of her domestic space by the preparations of the men leaving for the diggings. The tone is ironic, but there is here a sharp description of the invasion of one sphere by another, with all the offended sense of place and position that that involved:

> I wish, Minnie you were here to see how our parlour is confused with the purchases they make; it is now a lot of Guernsey shirts, then a collection of pannikins, that are displayed and commented on. The cradle stands in one corner, for they will not allow it to be turned into the kitchen; and George actually put their pick axes and shovels, and crowbars, and fossicking knives under the piano, till Grace remonstrated with him on the impropriety.[48]

In the private writings of men of the period, one gets a sense of the masculine world which gold had enlarged and prolonged. There had obviously always been masculine cultures, in the colonial cities as elsewhere; but gold meant that there were many more men without women, and this demographic imbalance meant that men were unlikely to settle quickly into domestic retreat. They were left occupying public spaces, ostentatiously displaying their masculine 'freedom and independence'. George Henry Wathen, who visited Victoria in 1854, noted Melbourne's 'large floating population of unlettered men, with plenty of money, low vicious tastes, and wholly debarred from the attractions of domestic comfort'.[49] Mark Daniel went to a promenade concert at Melbourne's Salle de Valentino in 1853 to hear the band of the regiment stationed in Melbourne. 'There was some singing,' he noted, 'nearly all the audience were men, and nearly all smoking furiously.'[50]

John Castieau also frequented the Salle de Valentino, as well as most of the other sites of Melbourne masculine low-life. 'After the Circus we went to the Salle de Valentino', he recorded of one not untypical night, 'from there to the Concert Hall, and from that to houses more known than esteemed, though much frequented. We drank and laughed.' He returned home at 4 am.[51] On another night, 'we went to Black's Concert Room, it was very hot and to me rather slow. Fooled about, had a nobbler or two, and left. Mr. Read inclined to be jolly, played two or three practical jokes.'[52] Castieau worked as a gaoler at the Melbourne Gaol, a secure position of considerable responsibility. He kept a diary through 1855, which was a record both of his strong desire to find a wife and a quieter domestic life, and of his bachelor existence in Melbourne, spent with other young men in a constant whirl of dissipation and subsequent regret. The self-criticism which followed the excesses, confided to his diary even as plans were being made for the next night on the town, seems intensely felt: 'My Life is proceeding most unsatisfactorily, each day more wearisome than the preceding. Each day commenced with the lassitude caused by the last night's debauch. Each day fresh resolutions of reformation made, each day such resolutions broken.' Castieau, as a subject of the domestic ideology of the day, is clear, at least in theory, as to the solution to his problems:

> I am not a Drunkard, I hate Blackguard Society, I long for genial friendship, and to find one woman that I could love and respect. Wanting these, and also not having strength of mind to study, nor a refuge in my own thoughts. After the day's confinement I am open to the calls of the first Idler, lounge about, drink, look at the whores, fool away my money at their homes, by paying for drink . . .[53]

He sees the cause of his problems, not in his own shortcomings, but in the purely masculine society in which he is obliged to spend his leisure time.[54] 'Feel very lonely, unsettled and dissatisfied with myself. Hardly know how it will end. I have no companions or friends but young men, and if I go with them I must drink and rattle.'[55] Respectable female company, or matrimony, are the only means of self-improvement he can imagine: 'I wish I had a wife or some girl that I could love and who would countenance my visits. This would be my salvation.'[56] Yet the lures of the masculine culture of dissipation at times seem irresistible:

> Mr Mather called and invited me to go out and dine with him. I foolishly consented. Drank some sparkling Hock, made a bet of 5 pounds, lost and paid

S.T. Gill, 'Diggers of Low Degree'. La Trobe Collection, State Library of Victoria.

it. Went with him to Black's concert, treated all the Detectives and everybody else there I met with whose face I was at all acquainted. Went into a Brothel, but by that time I was sober so I did nothing that I can reproach myself with . . . Got home, smoked a cigar, and went to bed. Thought of cutting my throat, and then of matrimony . . .[57]

This masculine culture had its own pleasures, and its own set of values. Castieau records celebrating the victory at Inkerman at Black's Concert Room. Two nights later he and his friends were still in patriotic spirit, 'we all joined in roaring lustily Patriotic Songs such as the Englishman, Rule Brittannia, +c'.[58] But in the end, his assessment of this period of his life was cast in regretful terms. Significantly, the solutions he prescribed for himself came directly from contemporary ideologies of domesticity. Castieau saw his own unhappinesses and shortcomings as evidence of what must be expected in a community of men without women, a community critically out of balance. It was constant and unmitigated male companionship which he felt to be the cause of his aimless existence. 'Feel very much the want of elevating company,' he lamented, 'Knowing numbers of young men, but I can do no more than join in Nobblers and smoke or bawdry, and these become tiresome.'[59]

The private writings of men of the gold period are full of such complaints about the consequences of demographic imbalance and sometimes reveal a grim world. Successive daily entries in James Muir's diary for March 1855 suggest some of the bleakness goldfields residence must have represented for many diggers:

Dick drunk—I working.
Dick fuddled—fell down hole.
(Sunday). Rather lonely.
Working in lieu of Dick.[60]

Men consequently turned to unaccustomed activities in search of sociability. When the Reverend George Goodman arrived in Victoria in the early 1850s, he was pleased by the large congregations he found at colonial services—'the large attendance of *men* is a healthy sign', he reported in the *Church of England Messenger*, 'and one that strikes an English observer'.[61] But men sometimes went to church for other than devotional reasons. 'I have heard of people being ashamed of not attending a Place of Worship,' John Castieau confided to his diary, 'but I too might feel ashamed of going . . . I felt myself a hypocrite, for I knew it was not religion brought me, but desire to see and be seen.'[62]

There was in gold-rush Victoria, then, a flourishing masculine culture, with its own institutions and beliefs. The hotels and theatres of Melbourne, the boarding houses and canvas towns in which many of the newly-arrived men lived, and of course the goldfields themselves, were predominantly

Eugene von Guerard, detail from 'Black Hill 21 February 1854'. Pencil and wash. La Trobe Collection, State Library of Victoria.

masculine environments, in which men probably necessarily developed distinctive modes of behaviour and attitudes. But the example of John Castieau suggests something of the dominance of domestic ideologies even amongst those apparently most outside their prescriptions. For every public celebrant of the masculine freedoms the colony offered, there were probably two public proponents of a more settled and domesticated version of masculinity. For the real outcomes of the contest over masculinity in the colony we would need to turn to the social history of family life, to the history of crime and of destitution and abandonment—topics which still largely await their historian.[63]

Male reformers began to concern themselves with the behaviour and attitudes of their sex. Manhood itself became contested territory. The ideological effort was necessary because of what were seen as the regrettable effects of the gold discoveries on the men of the colony. While radicals spoke approvingly of the possibilities the colonies offered for achieving *independence*, to the proponents of domesticity, independence was exactly the problem of colonial life. Lieutenant Governor La Trobe was troubled in 1853 by what he saw as 'a growing sense of independence' among colonial men—they were inclined, he thought, to 'undervalue the necessity of attachment to forms and institutions which might interpose restrictions, real or supposed, to their growing freedom of action'.[64] The Reverend Edwin Day wrote from Castlemaine in 1854 to the Church Missionary Society of his concern that 'persons coming hither . . . acquire an independence of thought and action which is not usual in England and which, as you will imagine, leads many into excesses'.[65] The concern was partly, both maintained, that the 'means of subsistence' could be earned in the colony with less exertion than in Britain—La Trobe spoke of the 'prosperity and comparative ease' of colonial life. But there was also a concern, often implicit, with the potential of widespread undomesticated masculinity. 'Isolated from the world, apart from the influence of domestic associations, with no local attachments', the liberal *Age* wrote of the diggers, 'and engaged in a temporary, precarious and exciting pursuit, they are a class eminently difficult to govern'.[66] Domesticity was to be an agent of social control; domestic associations were widely understood to be one of those forces which quietened a population, made it governable. And domesticity required crucial modifications to the prevalent notion of the attractive independence of colonial life.

Catherine Helen Spence in *Clara Morison* provided a critical portrait of the man of impulse and irresponsibility, the man whose influence the reformers feared was spreading. Mr Beaufort has decided to head for the diggings, and is asked about his wife:

'Mrs. Beaufort be hanged!,' said the gentleman. 'I am on my way to the diggings, and want one night's fling to put me in my mind of merry bachelor days.' 'Then you, too, are going to the Mount!,' said Harris. 'So am I. I start the day after to-morrow; but I leave nothing behind me, except a few small debts, not worth mentioning; while you leave a young wife, a fine farm, and a lot of sheep and cattle to look after themselves.'

'The fact is, Harris, that I am sick of the place,' answered Beaufort. 'I am tired of seeing nothing new, and hearing my wife talk of nothing but the comforts of domestic life; so I am going to try a little change.'[67]

Through the later 1850s in particular, the Victorian clergy and other proponents of domesticity seemed to be engaged in a concerted project of offering alternative views of masculine achievement, of describing other modes of masculine fulfilment. Their task was to describe a manhood that rested, not on independence, but on dependence and interdependence, a manhood that took its very centre and definition from the family hearth. They were combatting what they perceived to be the market-oriented, wealth-seeking, individualised inclinations of so many colonial men.

The discourses of these reformers were not invented in the colony. They came from contemporary Britain, where the evangelically influenced middle-class culture described by Davidoff and Hall had only recently become firmly established.[68] Davidoff and Hall argue for an evangelical consensus in Britain on gender roles:

Anglicans, Congregationalists, Quakers and Unitarians could all agree that the home must be the basis for a proper moral order in the amoral world of the market . . . that men could operate in that amoral world only if they could be rescued by women's moral vigilance at home. Such beliefs informed the creation of a network of institutions which formed the basis for a distinctive middle-class culture.[69]

In this new culture 'a man's ability to support and order his family lay at the heart of masculinity' just as 'a woman's femininity was best expressed in her dependence'. The important point is the newness of these developments still at the middle of the century, and their consequent fragility—'Far from carrying the blustering certainty of the late Victorian paterfamilias, early nineteenth-century masculine identity was fragile, still in the process of being forged and always measured against the background of condescension from the gentry as well as the long tradition of artisan pride'.[70]

Two elements of this story become particularly important in examining gold-rush Victoria. One is the inherited fragility of the new roles, and the anxious response of that fragility to an aberrant new society in which the sought-for balance and harmony between the sexes and their social roles were completely upset by massive demographic imbalance and a relatively primitive economy. In Victoria, the separate spheres had to be delineated and built up all over again—the publicists had much work to do. The second is the centrality of the middle-class institutions discussed by Davidoff and Hall. Victorian colonial life began at the point when these institutions were struggling for control in the English cities. They could begin in Victoria at the centre rather than the margins of public life—that is the other side of the often made argument that it was the middle classes who patronised the new mechanics institutes and schools of arts in Australian cities and towns.[71]

What has also often been overlooked is that these early Victorian institutions had a gender as well as a class project in mind. They were out, in league with respectable evangelical religion, to reform colonial understandings of masculinity. If the target was the behaviour of young men, the failure of mechanics institutes to reach the working-class constituency their name invoked, a failure which has troubled historians ever since, becomes explicable.[72] The strength of domestic ideology at the time meant that reformers were in possession of a gender as well as a class definition of the problems they faced in establishing and maintaining social order. Lending libraries for men, of any class, were thus an important achievement: the rhetoric of improvement which counterposed the library to the hotel was not merely class-specific. Temperance reformers, among others, hoped that in this new world, new forms of masculinity would achieve dominance:

Here in this beauteous land of gold
Shall wandering nations see
A race of sober men uphold
The standard of the free.[73]

Temperance reformers were at work in Melbourne and on the goldfields. William Drummond's goldfields diary, for example, contains plans for a large Tea Meeting, one hundred tickets to be sold at two shillings each.[74]

The reformers' fear was that the colony was an environment hostile to the type of masculinity they wished to see prevail; and certainly some men found it so. Robert Anderson, admirer of the 'novel and romantic' scenery outside Geelong, longing for 'a quiet retreat from the bustle of the town unmixed with the cares of the world and strangers', was a comprehensively respectable young man. He spent his evenings practising the flutina, reading, writing letters and his diary, taking walks with a fellow clerk from the post office, and even 'frequent real evenings of enjoyment at the Thursday weekly concerts at the Mechanics' Institution'. He was a reformer's dream come true; one senses also that he was often unhappy in Victoria.[75]

Arthur Shum, too, was a reformed man. He began keeping a diary in England in March 1852, to make for himself a record of his determination to change his ways. 'O what a mad part I have been acting! Who could have supposed that the winning yet deceitful smiles of an artful girl could have entailed so much misery?' He decided 'at once to abandon my present evil habits—to determine never to enter an Hotel or drinking house of any kind but to spend the time I have lately squandered in this way in endeavouring to improve my mind by reading, or in the cultivation of music, or in pursuing my favourite but long neglected study of ornithology'.

In late November, he stepped ashore at Melbourne. After three weeks he headed for the Bendigo goldfields. His first Sunday there he found his way to a Wesleyan chapel—'It was very full and strange to say the subject of the discourse was the prodigal son, the same that Mr. D preached from just before I left Bath.'[76] In a letter to a friend back in England, Shum reflected on the transformation he had wrought in his own life. 'How few there are who have plunged so deeply into dissipation as you and I that ever extricate themselves . . .' He reflected bitterly on the life of pleasure he and his companions had once led: 'these are what the world calls "Jolly Fellows" but can we hide from ourselves the majority of them are the destroyers of domestic happiness, the breakers of innocent hearts—the cause too often of their own ruin in this life and of their souls in the life to come?'[77] His reformed perspective led him to take an extremely critical view of the lives of the colonial men he saw around him: 'To give a just idea of the state of society is almost impossible—amongst the lower orders vice + brutality is rampant—ignorance + extortion with the grossest incivility equally characterises the trading classes whilst the merchants + those who assume more respectability prove by their actions that it extends no farther than assumptions + pretence.'[78]

Shum decided that the gold discoveries had been a 'great curse' to the colony, in part because the 'lower orders have become suddenly enriched. They have been raised above their level and the opportunity for the indulgence of every base passion has been afforded to those whom sheer ignorance has prevented the knowledge of any other enjoyment.' In keeping with his perception of the dismal possibilities the colony offered, Shum found the Victorian landscape profoundly disappointing: 'The almost entire absence of rivers giving the country a very barren + desolate appearance. The very trees even appear deformed + stunted in their growth as though labouring under some malevolent disease.'[79] Nevertheless, he worked hard. He ran two stores at Bendigo, often working, he said, until midnight. He sent back five pounds for the chapel in King Street Bristol, commenting: 'This is indeed a most heathenish land, and if missionaries are wanted anywhere it is surely here.'[80]

Shum was the reformed new man of the 1850s. As with Robert Anderson, his views led him to find the colony an uninviting place. He differed from Anderson though, in that he could not even indulge in fantasy about domestic retreat from the unsavoury aspects of the world around him. One or two cases cannot amount to any kind of substantive argument about what the colony was 'really' like. The dissatisfactions of Anderson and Shum do, however, reflect the issues that the male reformers were confronting. It was in the image of men like Anderson and Shum that they wished to remake the colony. But for more detailed articulations of this project, we have to turn to the reformers themselves.

The death of an early Melbourne industrialist provides a good opportunity to examine some of the concerns of the reformers of masculinity. In 1863, Henry Langlands, the patriarch of Langlands' foundry, died. One of Melbourne's largest industrial enterprises, Langlands was noted for the concern of its owner for his workers, displayed in the dinners he held for them on occasions of public celebration, and in the public banquets they held for him 'in attestation of their esteem'. At the funeral, the Reverend Isaac New of the Albert Street Baptist Church in East Melbourne delivered a 'Funeral Address and Discourse'.[81] The praise of Henry Langlands—as a man defined almost entirely by his relations with others, as a man whose keenly developed feelings and sympathies led him constantly out into the world—was symptomatic of the reforming discourses on masculinity by that time becoming familiar to colonists. 'Husband, Father, Brother, Friend, Servant of Christ, well done! Enjoy thy repose!' New declared:[82]

'Rectitude and goodness', appeared beautifully blended in symmetrical proportion in his character . . . Look at him as a husband, and ask his sorrowing widow, and she will tell you he was one of the kindest, most affectionate, considerate and devoted of husbands. Look at him as a father, and ask his sons, perhaps they would tell you that at times he was too stern and severe with them. Of course young men may think so, but yet his heart yearned over them with a fond, a tender, a generous love. Look at him as a brother, and ask the surviving sister, and she would tell you of his constant, uniform and invariable devotedness to her happiness, and of the intense affection of her heart which he had won. Look at him as a son, and we have been informed that his regard for his parents was most reverential, most delicate, most affectionate, unwearied and assiduous in promoting in every way their comfort . . . Look at him as a man, the law of kindness was on his lips; urbanity and courtesy were revealed in all his intercourse; sympathy the most acute and profound was in his heart with all the forms of human suffering. The sight of calamity, wretchedness and want never failed to excite his compassion. He felt for all the objects of human sorrow. He felt for the heathen, he felt for the aborigines of this colony; he felt for the hopeless victims of slavery, he felt for the afflicted poor, and was ever ready to relieve; he felt for poor drunkards . . . He felt for the unfortunates of our city, whose licentious life is hurrying them to ruin . . . His hospitality, springing from the same principle of benev- olence, was proverbial. His house was ever cordially open to his friends, who would partake of his bounty . . . There was never any coldness or awkwardness . . . Hence his benevolence did not consist in mere feeling and sentiment, but it revealed itself in the varied forms of an active beneficence, and generous effort.[83]

We have here, firstly, a family man, a man defined and assessed primarily by his relations with kin; he is presented as a model of the father, brother and son. But then we are given Langlands the man of feeling. His manliness is seen to be not incompatible with keenly developed sympathies, sensibil- ities and feelings. Finally, his empathetic benevolence allows him to overcome the selfish tenor of the times—he gave to others in numerous ways, and enjoyed doing so. The funeral address, published later as a pamphlet, was, in this time and place, polemical. New explicitly saw Langlands' life as full of an urgent significance for his colonial contempo- raries. 'Could our beloved friend speak to us today,' New exclaimed, 'methinks it would be with an agony of appeal, to convince us of our madness. Well, though dead, he *is* speaking to us those words of empathic meaning, "For what is a man profited if he gain the whole world and lose his own soul?" '[84] So much of cultural history is concerned with judgements about context and meaning. In this case New's sermon deals with themes which could obviously be found right through the history of Christian discourse. Yet we can also detect the special inflections and emphases that time and place lend to universal themes. New's 'agony of appeal' alerts us to the urgency of the evangelical project of articulating new forms of masculinity in this period.

An issue then, in the discussions of gold and its impact, was the nature of manhood. There was a vocabulary available to discuss the disruption of the domestic ideal brought about by gold. It came partly from those discourses of evangelicalism which had been, since the 1780s, engaged in a long and ultimately successful attempt to elevate domesticity in importance, and to reform understandings of what was entailed in being a man. The attempt in Victoria in the 1850s was to outline a version of masculinity which was socially rather than individually oriented. The emphasis was on responsibilities, on sociability, and on the proper, home-centred uses of wealth, and on the responsibility to support and nurture a family.

Two key themes can be distinguished in the reformers' discourse. One emphasised masculine 'maturity'—qualities of reflection, thoughtfulness—all the traits which meant that a man did not act solely on unreflective impulse or passion. The charismatic Congregational Reverend Thomas Binney,[85] in a sermon delivered in 1858 on the text 'Be Men', made just this point:

> In telling the Corinthians not to be 'children' but 'men' in 'understanding', he refers to that mature condition of both mind and heart and general character, which distinguishes a person of thought, prudence, discretion, common sense—of solidity and wisdom, of manly and dignified aims and purposes.[86]

Maturity meant a distance from the passions and the instincts, the victory of the conscience. Men, Binney argued, should be 'sagacious, prudent, discreet, loving, humble, modest, patient, free from the levities and follies of youth, conquerors of the selfishness and the passions of the flesh, ambitious only of what belongs to character and goodness'.[87] In similar vein, the Reverend Isaac New exhorted men to be like the oak rather than the hot-house plant, to stand against impulse—'where there is strength of will, a stout resolve, a noble purpose, and an invincible perseverance, man, whatever may be his sphere, must be great'.[88] In another sermon New elaborated on the will that was required to subjugate the disruptive self-will, the selfish passion:

> As a condition of peace, our self-will must be subdued, our unruly passions must be curbed, the spirit of strife must be allayed, the disposition to contend about trifles must be in abeyance, that almost irrepressible desire in human nature, for each man to have his own way . . . ought to be regulated, controlled and attempered by a desire for peace.[89]

Subduing the passions, though, was only one half of the reformers' project. The other important theme in reform discourse was sociability. 'Man is not made to live to himself,' the Reverend New explained, 'He is a social being—one among many.'[90] The sermons of the 1850s are full of exhortations to men to enter into a fully social existence, with all the reciprocal duties and obligations that that entailed. Men had to be persuaded that masculinity and dependence were not incompatible notions, that interdependence was a legitimate, even a welcome consequence of social existence. 'As members of one corporate body,' Joseph Taylor argued, 'we are mutually dependent, one on the other . . . to whatever class of the community we belong, we have reciprocal duties and reciprocal claims.'[91] Independence could too easily become selfishness, a trait repeatedly condemned in sermons. 'The disease which infects our nature is selfishness', the Reverend Richard Fletcher argued in 1856, 'enmity to God, indifference to our fellow-creatures, a proneness . . . to gratify ourselves at their expense'.[92] The Reverend Thomas Binney too saw as an essential quality of 'full grown men' their ability to 'subdue and master themselves . . . to help each other—mutually to serve, to honor, to prefer'.[93] George Rusden told an audience in 1854 that 'what each person does in his own sphere without reference to his fellow creatures must perish with him'.[94] And when the Reverend Isaac New came to list the faults of the men of the day, he mentioned not only their 'gratifying unhallowed lusts and passions', but dwelt upon their 'selfish, sordid, grasping, avaricious' qualities, the 'injuring one another, taking advantage of one another to subserve their own ends'.[95] While the ministers undoubtedly often felt that all men suffered from the faults they described, their sermons in Victoria must have reflected some sense of those sins they thought most urgently needed correction in the colony. In this they were not alone. 'Men feel no common bond of interest', the new *Age* newspaper lamented in 1854, 'they are not yet acquainted with one another; and each is so fully occupied with his own concerns'.[96] The emphasis on interdependence, and on suppressing passionate or unthought behaviour, amounted to a concerted attempt to change colonial thinking about masculinity and the social role of men.

It is not in sermons alone that this project can be detected. Melbourne in the 1850s was a city of institutions of improvement—'peculiarly in this country do we need the aid of institutions which have for their object the improvement of our social condition; which tend to gather us together for good purposes', George Rusden explained.[97] 'It is not good for man to be alone', the Reverend Adam Cairns explained to the Melbourne Young Men's Association in 1858. This was particularly so in the colony where 'society grows loose and incoherent'.[98] Many of these institutions were directed specifically at young men, who were objects of concern for a number of reasons. One was that they were demographically the predominant element in the colony. Then, they were seen, in the typically anxious way in which colonial societies scrutinise themselves for signs of worth, to be harbingers of the future, texts upon which the future destiny of the colony might be read. 'Our young men are the sons of promise', Adam Cairns told his audience at the Victorian Early Closing Association in 1856, 'On them depends mainly our prospects of solid and enduring prosperity'.[99] By 1856, too, the eight-hours movement in Victoria was provoking concern about the use of the new leisure time, and there was serious debate about the evils of alcohol and the need for provision of the means of rational recreation. Cairns warned his audience of the dangers of taverns, saloons and theatres—'we have little hope of any good from the youth who gives his evening to the theatre. He may be hurried into profligacy, or he may sink into sentimentalism.'[100] Finally, gold digging itself was held to exacerbate dangerously the natural tendency of men to be preoccupied entirely with the pursuit of wealth, and much discussion ensued on the uses of riches.

At the centre of the cluster of reform concerns, as always through the nineteenth century, was temperance. 'In this favoured colony', observed Melbourne's *Temperance Times* in its first issue, 'the work to be done is great'. The paper's sponsor, the Temperance League of Victoria, began its work in April 1857, and that year held meetings at Melbourne, Ballarat, Geelong, Richmond, Castlemaine, and Bacchus Marsh. It joined the Total Abstinence and the Band of Hope Societies and Victorian Liquor Law League which were already in existence.[101] The fear held by all these groups, was that young men congregating together, with money to spend, away from responsibilities, would turn to excessive drinking. Richard Heales, coach builder and member of the Victorian Parliament, addressed a Castlemaine temperance meeting in 1857, arguing this case. He said that it was his belief that the gold had been provided by Providence to elevate the class of working men, but that 'it would have been better for many of that class if the gold of Victoria had never been discovered. The blessing had been turned into a curse.'[102] Drinking, Heales told another meeting, 'is the curse of this portion of Her Majesty's dominions'.[103] Alcohol also seemed to promote the unreflective behaviour that the reformers were concerned to discourage. It was seen as yet another stimulant in gold-rush society, leading men into an unhealthily excited life. The uncertainty of life on the goldfields themselves seemed to encourage drinking. Parliamentary enquiries into the goldfields questioned all witnesses about drinking. 'Is there a large consumption of spirits at the Diggings', E.N. Emmett was asked in 1853. 'There is,' he replied, 'an immense consumption.'[104] Samuel Lazarus noted in his goldfields diary:

> It shocks one even on the diggings, where the vice rages so fearfully, to hear of a young man scarcely twenty drinking himself to death. It is painful to contemplate the horrible havoc which drunkenness makes on the diggings— many a poor unfortunate fool destroys in a few weeks the chance of placing himself in easy and happy circumstances for life—even women, feeling themselves relieved from the salutary checks which society in civilized life lays on them, fall . . .[105]

Temperance groups promoted the drinking of water, in a climate which they described as 'begetting . . . a perpetual thirst'. In Melbourne they held

Antoine Fauchery, photograph: 'Washing Out a Good Prospect'. La Trobe Collection, State Library of Victoria.

a Grand Temperance Demonstration to coincide with the opening of the Yan Yean water works by the governor, Sir Henry Barkly.[106]

Temperance was to become increasingly a women's movement, emphasising the extent to which intemperance was defined by reformers as a problem having to do with men and the behaviour of men—men both within and without domestic relations. 'Many a family has been broken up by this arch demon', J.R. Edwards wrote of alcohol in 1859, evoking the figure of the mother who had had 'tears of bitter anguish wrung from her bleeding soul' by a drunken husband.[107] In 1853 a petition signed by 2097 women and presented to the Victorian Legislative Council made it plain that substantial numbers of Victorian women viewed the drink issue in clearly gendered terms. The petition argued from the 'misery which we, as a class, suffer by the temptations of the public houses on our husbands, fathers, brothers or sons', for the enactment in Victoria of prohibition laws on the model of those recently introduced in Maine and other New England states. 'From our position as "Keepers at Home" ', the petition continued:

> we are the greatest sufferers by drunkenness. We see around us husbands neglecting their wives and spending their time in public houses. We behold them day after day spending their money on alcoholic drinks destructive to health and morals, instead of allowing it to feed or clothe their children; and

we witness time after time men and women who by drink have lost caste and character.

The colonial lunatic asylums and Coroners Courts, they argued, proved daily and 'only too truly that liquor not only dethrones reason, but causes premature dissolution'.[108] Another Maine law petition, got up in 1853 by the doctor John Singleton, carried 1618 signatures, and drew attention to the 'increased and increasing amount of immorality, crime, destitution, and domestic wretchedness, induced by habits of intemperance'.[109] In 1854, a Select Committee of the Victorian Legislative Council was set up to investigate intemperance and the merits of the Maine law. Its report argued that, while the prohibition of the sale of fermented liquors would be neither 'desirable nor practical', prohibiting the sale of spirituous liquors would be 'fraught with benefit' to the community. The committee seemed to be concerned about the relationship between intemperance and domesticity. William Robertson, a temperance advocate, was complaining about the drunkenness of persons leaving the Cremorne pleasure gardens on Sundays:

> Many of those persons were married, were they not, and had their wives with them? Many had females with them; but of course I cannot say whether they were married or not.
>
> Amongst the number whom you say you saw were intoxicated were there any married persons? The persons who were intoxicated appeared to be principally young men; there were children also there.[110]

The question was an important one for reformers who believed that domesticity was an antidote to intemperance, just as intemperance was corrosive of domesticity. But all was not despair in the temperance camp. Temperance rhetoric was by its nature optimistic, even utopian—it needed to posit an ideal state of domestic harmony which could be achieved were it not for the alcohol. The women's petition of 1853 concluded that they wanted prohibition so that 'instead of suffering and privations we may become happy and contented'.[111]

Various reform organisations devoted to the welfare of the young men of the colony had in common a desire to stimulate interests other than the pursuit of wealth. While the goals of self-improvement were obviously linked to ambitions of upward social mobility, they exhibit beyond that a concern with non-utilitarian values and non-instrumental knowledge. The idea was that non-instrumental concerns in themselves were useful correctives to the excessively worldly and grasping tone of the times. The Victorian Society of Young Friends, an organisation open to 'all young men of respectability', held lectures, drawing and music classes, and excluded from its discussions only political and religious subjects. The Melbourne Young Men's Mutual Improvement Society, established in 1856, also held lectures and discussions, and encouraged the writing of essays. It was devoted to 'the mutual improvement of its members in religious, literary and scientific knowledge'.[112] The Beechworth Young Men's Association had 50 members in 1856. The Reverend John Symons, addressing the association in that year, lamented that the peculiarity of the times had not been conducive to projects aimed at 'intellectual or moral improvement': 'The exciting nature of men's engagements,—the insane speculation which has been so rife—the engrossing cares to which men have given themselves up', all conspired to prevent reflection or improvement.[113]

Other reform organisations existed although little is known about them. Henry Langlands, for example, was a subscriber to a group with broad concerns, the 'Evangelistic, Temperance, Economic, Educational and Model Farm Society for the Benefit of Soldiers, Seamen, Policemen, Immigrants, the Uneducated and the Unemployed'.[114] Langlands was also a vice-president of the Evangelical Alliance of Melbourne, which held firm to the 'utter Depravity of Human Nature, in consequence of the Fall'. Better known and on a larger scale, was the Melbourne Mechanics Institute, which by 1857 had a circulating library of thirteen thousand books and two thousand magazines. The Institute also held lectures and ran evening classes—in 1857 the evening class in Latin began with 22 pupils, who were apparently mostly regular in their attendance. Lectures in 1857 and 1858 covered such topics as electricity, Cardinal Richelieu, the legend of Dr Faustus, the age of the earth, and the fallacies of phrenology.[115] Electricity and phrenology were big topics on the mechanics institute circuit: 'I really wish I could hear some sensible account of the probable history of this country and not the stuff about electricity which is crammed down one's throat, and which I always treat with abhorrence, for they have gone clean crazy about electricity', one young man wrote to his mother.[116] When Professor Hearn from the new University of Melbourne gave a lecture on adult education at the Melbourne Mechanics Institute, he was quite frank about the pragmatic goal in mind: 'When the members of the Mechanics' begin to regard science as a matter of earnest study, and not as an occasional substitute for the hotel or casino,' he said, 'we would have a truer estimate of the influence of science.'[117] Others, too, made it clear that the institutes were aiming, in particular, at the young men of the colony: 'The Mechanics' Institute was so particularly beneficial in a country like this', a Legislative Councillor argued in 1855, 'where the young men had not the same wholesome influences exerted over them as at home'.[118] By the late 1850s mechanics institutes were operating in the major suburbs of Melbourne, as well as in the provincial towns.[119] The Melbourne Public Library opened in 1856 with 4000 volumes, and was soon well patronised—in 1858 it had 77 925 visitors, and was open from ten am to nine pm.[120] The volunteer fire brigades in Melbourne, begun in part by the efforts of American merchants, attracted young men in the 1850s to a useful social endeavour, but rivalries between the fire companies led to a resurgence of competitiveness that would not have been pleasing to reformers—'even fisticuffs might be resorted to', one historian of the brigades reports, as the companies competed for first access to water, and 'petty squabbling besmirched a brave endeavour'.[121] The Religious Tract Society of Victoria was established in 1856, and distributed tens of thousands of Christian tracts. These organisations, and others like them, had as their chief reform target the men of the colony. All sought to woo young men from the uninterrupted pursuit of wealth to more reflective and social activities.

The fundamental concern of the reformers, though, was probably economic support of family life, that men not leave the families they had begun in search of their own fortunes. 'Our work necessarily begins with ourselves,' the Reverend John Potter told his Ballarat congregation, 'but it does not end there, on the contrary it begins with ourselves that it may go on to others . . . A man's first duty to his family is to provide them with a *decent maintenance* and if possible to secure a provision for them, so that if he should be taken away suddenly by death, they may not be left destitute to the mercy of strangers.'[122] As with any ideology, there was to the ideology of domesticity both a large vision of remaking society, and a more particular and quite urgent concern—in this case, that men not abandon their wives and families to destitution. 'But there is a serious social evil which is too often lost sight of,' James Bonwick wrote:

the breaking up of families. How many a bitter tear, and how much domestic trouble have the Gold Fields occasioned. Wives separated from husbands, and children far away from the care of fathers. The object of love in a happy home has a stranger to close his eyes of death. Some there are of whom no tidings arrive. The depths of the forest alone can reveal the sad tale.[123]

CALIFORNIA

If Eden with its ambrosial fruits and guiltless joys was still sad till the voice of woman mingled with its melodies, California, with all her treasured hills and streams, must be cheerless till she feels the presence of the same enchantress. It is woman alone that can make a home for the human heart . . .

Walter Colton, *Three Years in California*

There is no manlier life than ours,
A life amid the mountains,
Where from the hill-sides, rich in gold,
Are welling sparkling fountains

J. Swett, 'Song of Labor: The Miner'

They are mostly *men*, and in the prime of energetic manhood . . . There is
no general bond of sympathy, but simply that of *manhood*, a bond less firmly
tied, and more easily severed, than the Gordian knot.

American Journal of the Medical Sciences on California, 1855

According to the census of 1850, the population of California was 92 per
cent male.[124] The congregation of men without women at the goldfields
provided one of the most common frameworks of response in California
too, as social critics there elaborated the tenets of the new ideologies of
domesticity which had already been influential in American life for a
couple of decades. Americans had a clear practical and ideological sense
of the means of transition from frontier to settled society. 'The great
desideratum here,' the *Alta California* noted, 'most desired and most wanting, has been what is properly termed home, that is, woman, without whom
there is no such thing as home.' The absence of women, the paper argued,
had more to do with 'assimilating men to bloodthirsty beasts' than any
other cause.[125] Horace Bushnell wrote from California that 'no one needs
to be informed that men, living separately from women, are sure to make
a large stride towards barbarism'.[126] As Ralph Mann has noted, the 'cult
of true womanhood' was strong enough in California that early town leaders
'expected the advent of families virtually to eliminate disorder'.[127] Men
were 'courageous and daring', as well as 'calm, cool and cautious', explained
a writer in the San Francisco *Pioneer*, while women were 'fanciful' and
'imaginative': 'In short, man is the active, woman the passive verb of life'.[128]
It was clear that in these terms, the congregation of men without women
at the goldfields was dangerous. Gold-rush town newspapers routinely
linked domesticity with stability, morality and, crucially, prosperity.[129] The
Californian argument from domesticity was very similar to the Victorian.
'Men, unblest by the refining and hallowing influences of female society,'
a Boston journal reporting on California reminded its readers, 'naturally
tend to become selfish, coarse and cruel—tend toward a condition of
barbarism.'[130] Hinton Helper blamed the 'scarcity of women' in California
for the 'wild excitement, degeneracy, dissipation and deplorable condition
of affairs' he found there. He allowed one benefit that he had received
from California, in his otherwise pessimistic account: 'Had I received no
other benefit from my trip to California than the knowledge I have gained
. . . of woman's many virtues and perfections, I should account myself well
repaid.'[131]

The Reverend William Scott undertook a tour of the northern mines in 1859, delivering a sermon he had prepared, entitled 'Woman in California', which argued that one of the main reasons for the prevalence of crime in the frontier districts was the absence of women: 'nothing is more imperatively needed in California than the softening, purifying and elevating influence of women'. Scott, always a trenchant moral observer of Californian life, was well acquainted with the arguments from domesticity—he warned of the inevitable connection between men outside families and crime. 'An aggregation of men without their wives, mothers and sisters,' he reminded his flock in 1856, 'become reckless and degraded. The laws of nature cannot be trifled with.'[132]

The expounders of the ideology of domesticity opposed the goldfields to the hearth and home, as masculine to feminine, and dramatised the moment of departure:

Farewell, dear heart, awhile farewell!
I go o'er land and sea;
For wealth I brave the billows' swell
Afar from love and thee.
The vessel waits—the gathered crew,
With hope and vigor bold,
Impatient long for regions new
That teem and burn with gold.[133]

Domesticity provided a positive value that could be asserted against the rampant wealth seeking of California. 'Home!', exclaimed a writer in the *Pioneer*, 'How does the very thought of it chasten and soften the heart!'[134] It was home that the gold hunters had abandoned, and their choice had to be dramatised by the proponents of domesticity. Magazine fiction took up this task, and a number of short stories treated the subject of men deciding to leave their families in pursuit of California gold:

'You remember Holman?,' asked George, a few months after. 'Well, he started for California about two years since, and came back yesterday worth sixty thousand dollars. I begin to be tired of this stay-at-home life; business gets dull, and there is nothing to interest one.'

'*Nothing to interest one!*' Susan felt a choking sensation in her throat as she glanced from the children to her husband in silence.[135]

The fact that so many appeared to have made the wrong choice, and so swiftly, heightened already existing fears about domestic institutions in America. 'We have been forcibly reminded of De Tocqueville's declaration', H.T. Tuckerman wrote in 1849 'that the ties of home and kindred are essentially loose in a mercantile republic, while observing the extraordinary facility with which men have left accustomed pursuits, local obligations and family altars, to engage in this distant and hazardous enterprise'.[136]

The magazines were also concerned to dramatise the probable costs in health and happiness of going to California. 'I was returning from California rich in gold, but a poor, miserable, rheumatic invalid', the hero of one story introduces himself; it is only marriage to a beautiful young woman which can return him to society and happiness.[137] *Godey's Magazine* was quick to describe a role for women in the gold seeking. While arguing that the 'gathering of this gold is man's work', the magazine allocated to women the task of diffusing 'the wisdom that is more valuable than the fine gold', of spreading 'moral rectitude and social refinement'.[138]

Stuart McClean has noted the prevalence of what he terms the 'sentimental' framework in understanding the gold rush in the women's magazines of the east.[139] But the domestic ideologies were just as prevalent in California as they were in the east. Western journeys did not erode the stock of ideas that Americans took with them. 'What California wants is woman', argued Mrs S.A. Towner in the San Francisco *Pioneer*, 'Woman in her highest and holiest nature . . . woman as she should stand in this nineteenth century.'[140] As 'mothers of the nation', women, it was argued, needed to be well educated and of high status. 'An inane, a cringing, and ignorant, or an immoral brace of women', argued a letter to the editor of a Californian Methodist magazine, 'cannot be the mothers of a sage, noble, and enlightened, and pure race of men'.[141] The ideology of domesticity had life not merely in the magazines, though. Men travelling to California brought the terms of this way of thinking, and used them to explain their new situation to themselves, as well as to explore the consequences of their decisions to leave their homes. 'Oh how little do we really understand the value of the luxuries and comforts and blessings of home and friends', Albert Lyman wrote in his journal, 'and the endearing ties of father, mother, brothers and sisters, until we are thus deprived of their enjoyment.'[142]

The ideology of domesticity as articulated by men, in California as in Victoria, was only incidentally about the status of actual women. The future of the nation was often the underlying concern. 'A lack of family discipline operates upon the body politic,' argued the Reverend Orange Clark, 'not much unlike drunkenness and licentiousness upon the domestic welfare.'[143] Californian publications described the moral work which lay in front of the few women in California, work which has sometimes been thought, at the time and since, to have given them enhanced status. There may have been some advantages which accrued to Californian women as a result of their scarcity, but these can easily be overstated. One historian, for example, has recently argued that the 'opportunities for upward mobility among professional prostitutes were remarkably similar to those that the men enjoyed in other professions'.[144]

As at other times and places, though, the strength of this ideology of domesticity in California did give support to ways of thinking about society which emphasised the ascribed differences of men and women. In a demographically imbalanced society, the roles of the sexes would always be a topic of concern and interest, and, as many historians have shown, it was out of separate spheres thinking that first-wave feminism in America grew. Although Lotchin has claimed (on the basis of hostile comments in male journalism) that San Francisco feminism was 'weak', there was at least one Californian feminist in the development of whose thinking the experience of gold-rush society played a significant part.[145]

Eliza Farnham's 1856 *California: Indoors and Out* is a significant Californian articulation of the domestic ideology. Farnham was at the centre of the reform concerns of the day—she had been active in prison reform at Sing Sing Prison in New York State, and her interests included magnetism and mesmerism, dress reform, phrenology, hydropathy and women's rights. Her companion in California was Georgiana Bruce, a former resident of Brook Farm.[146] When her husband died in San Francisco in September 1848, Eliza Farnham decided to travel to California to attend to his business affairs, and attempted to organise a party of women to accompany her and to settle in California. As she explained in a circular issued in New York in February 1849, she was concerned that the men flocking to California would suffer from the 'absence of woman, with all her kindly cares and powers, so peculiarly conservative to man under such circumstances'.[147] Two hundred women contacted her, but only three actually made the journey west. Farnham looked forward to a time 'in a few years', when California would be the 'garden of the Union': 'There is no prosperity to which she cannot attain, with true manhood to control, and true womanhood to preserve.'[148] The Californian experience had demonstrated to Farnham the essential correctness of separate spheres doctrine, and the reforming role it assigned to women:

> In all that one sees of this phase of life, in this multifaced land, how clearly is evidenced the superior moral position of woman! In her home, and fitted by virtue, intelligence, and energy, for its presiding spirit, woman has a power far surpassing any which man possesses, and which he cannot divide with her.[149]

There were defects in the moral life of California, she was happy to concede, but nothing that Woman, 'this true missionary of love and purity', the 'efficient remedy for these great evils', could not put right. Happily, the Americans were distinguished by the high regard they held for women. This was fortunate, for:

> There is no country in the world where the highest attributes of the female character are more indispensable to the social weal than in California; for nowhere else have the indomitable energies, the quick desires, and the wide-reaching purposes of the Saxon nature been submitted to so severe a test of their self-regulating power.[150]

When Eliza Farnham came in the 1860s to write her philosophical work, *Woman and Her Era*, she made much of the contrast between men's innate love of power and gain, and women's gentler love of influence—'if she had wealth, she would not keep it to multiply idly in her hands, but make it subservient to charitable and helpful uses'. The text invites a reading as commentary on California.[151] Farnham posited a morally autonomous feminine world, one working to influence and change the masculine. 'In herself, Woman could not respect the aims which fill, and, *as aims*, satisfy, the great body of masculine life.' The love of gain in men, and in the 'masculine system', represented for Farnham but one stage of civilisation, and that not a high one—'the masculine, unbalanced by the harmonious action of the feminine . . . tends, of itself, to excess'.[152] This was a feminism, I suggest, animated in part by a reading of the avaricious excesses of gold-rush society.

As in Victoria, the objection to the absence of women was that life would be entirely preoccupied with the pursuit of wealth, and with work, rather than with the civilising and humanising practices of consumption. 'We are almost exclusively a nation of men,' Roger Baldwin wrote to his sister in 1851, 'Money is the god of our idolatry—our minds are sufficiently active—our hearts are as barren as the sun-burned hills.'[153] 'It can hardly be supposed that people come to California *to live*,' observed the Reverend Daniel Woods, 'since they are here only *preparing to live* . . . '[154] The Englishman Henry Veel Huntley described a condition in which the population was entirely fixated upon the pursuit of its particular goals, and that:

> when attainment is sated, or when means fail, a prostration takes place, and as the same avalanche which it resembled at its outset lies cold and motionless when it has terminated its sweeping career, so the American mind, prostrated for a time by its own heated impulse, succumbs beneath the impassioned exertion; but in this inaction it revives, and soon the community are seen chasing some other attraction, it matters not of what kind . . .[155]

What was missing from a life so constituted was rest, repose and quietness—the considered action that could only come, it was argued by critics, from domestic tranquillity. With a larger number of women and settled families, argued *Hutchings' California Magazine*, 'California would be, almost, a paradise of contentment; and, as the idea of making haste to be rich would then be abandoned, men would be content with a reasonable reward for their labor'.[156] Without women, F.P. Wierzbicki argued in San Francisco in 1849, the mass of human bodies in California 'have no souls; they are but a grand automaton, whose springs Mammon alone makes vibrate'.[157]

Californian men had their own cultural institutions—sanctuaries of undomesticated men, but also schools of reformed masculinity. As in other American cities, the fire companies provided men of some wealth with an institutional setting and a calendar of social and ceremonial events.[158] The companies had some welfare and nurturing functions; if any member of the St Francis Hook and Ladder Company, for example, notified the foreman that he was ill, 'it shall be his duty to appoint one or more members to visit him daily, and tender him such aid as his situation may require'.[159] In happier times there were plenty of convivial social events. The *Fireman's Journal and Military Gazette* recorded the visits of one company to another, and the elaborate entertainments provided:

> Confidence Engine Co. No.1, of Sacramento have accepted an invitation of 'Knickerbocker 5' of this city, to become their guests on the occasion of their visit on 3rd July. From the well known reputation of the 'fives' for courtesy and liberality, the Confidence Company, we are assured, will be elegantly entertained.[160]

Henry Veel Huntley commented on a parade of firemen in San Francisco— 'they dress in helmets, red woollen frocks, and black trowsers'—but asked in some puzzlement 'what strange enthusiasm makes them drag their engines, with all the appurtenances, about with them?'[161] If the rituals of the fire companies seemed to provide an alternative to domesticity, they were also, in their formality, to some extent an alternative to unregulated individualism. 'A set of men', the *Fireman's Journal* described them, 'banded together . . . for an object in which self-interest is lost sight of'.[162] Mrs Julia Dean Hayne read a poem at the benefit for San Francisco's St Francis Hook and Ladder Company in 1857, which elaborated the idea of the selflessness of the firemen:

> The Firemen also, dare each shape of death
> Yet not for fortune's gold, or glory's wreath
> No selfish throb, within their breast is known,
> No hope of praise or profit cheers them on.
> They ask no fame—no praise, and only seek
> To shield the suffering, and protect the weak.[163]

There was competition between fire companies, though not initially, Lotchin argues, the 'rowdyism' that attended eastern cities' fire departments—the Philadelphia companies studied by Bruce Laurie for example. Laurie found in Philadelphia a working-class 'traditionalist' culture in the fire companies, centred on drinking, cameraderie, and belligerent competition with other companies.[164] It was not until the 1860s that Californian fire companies became competitive to a degree that impeded their firefighting capacity—Haggerty refers to firemen 'fighting the Civil War among themselves'.[165] Fire companies in California had always, though, kept alive sectional and ethnic loyalties and hostilities. There are reports from 1854 of fire companies dousing Chinese houses.[166] In California the fire companies certainly represented—importantly in post-gold-rush

San Francisco photograph, 'Eureka fire company'. Courtesy Bancroft Library.

society—an alternative to individualism, though hardly in the manner that reformers would have wished. The San Francisco *Fireman's Journal and Military Gazette* expressed this communalism when it argued the case for a special firemen's cemetery: 'United as we are on earth, so should we be in death'.[167]

The volunteer militia companies of California performed a similar function. Many of them were the offspring of fire companies, and the *Fireman's Journal and Military Gazette*, itself an expression of the commonality, argued against firemen joining the Fourth of July parade in 1855 on the ground that: 'Nine tenths of those composing the military are also firemen, and should both parade, the ranks of the former would be very small'.[168] Membership fees, and the need to provide uniforms, as well as an extensive system of fines, meant that these companies too were the preserve of an elite. 'The expenses incident to these organizations are large and onerous', complained the Quarter-Master and Adjutant-General of the Militia of California in 1855.[169] As elsewhere in the United States, men in militia companies were 'liberated from domestic and commercial preoccupations', at least for the time they spent on parade or at dinner

185

together. Volunteer militia companies were fraternal as well as military organisations, and many had libraries and billiard saloons and organised balls, banquets, parades and receptions. The attachment of men to the forms and rituals of the militia companies is evident in the complaints frequently made about 'toy soldiers'. 'The militia system produces a swarm of Generals and Colonels and Majors every year', the *San Francisco Whig* complained, 'men who know as much of tactics or discipline as a cow does of a piano'. The journal felt that California was 'worse in this respect than any other place in the world'.[170] Militia companies were particularly popular in California. By 1853 the state had a militia establishment of 201 400, and a greater number of infantry than any other state reporting. There were 69 companies formed in California between 1849 and 1856, twenty of them in San Francisco.[171] Within the militia companies an alternative form of masculinity to that of the individualism and independence widely celebrated outside was articulated, as men experienced elaborate forms of fraternity and comradeship. In San Francisco the companies were perhaps more fraternal and ritually oriented. In the smaller towns they were more likely to be primarily for Indian fighting, violently preempting indigenous resistance to the invasion.[172]

Temperance groups in California, as in the rest of the United States, were in the early 1850s attempting to reform masculine behaviour. Like the fire companies, American temperance leagues offered men a rich ceremonial and symbolic life outside the home. While part of a national movement, Ralph Mann argues, the Sons of Temperance 'expressed perfectly' the perceived moral needs of the gold-rush towns.[173] Other groups active in California included the Independent Order of Good Templars, and the California State Temperance Society, begun in 1856, which aimed to 'create a popular sentiment in favor of temperance'.[174] Temperance leaders were expected to be charismatic—they needed to win men to another version of masculinity. Timothy Dwight Hunt recorded in his diary his disappointment at hearing a dull Sons of Temperance lecture in his own church. There was, he wrote: 'Too much parade, too stiff, + formal, too heartless. No enthusiasm. Speaker tame.'[175]

The Young Men's Christian Association also began its reforming work in gold-rush California. The first annual report of the San Francisco Association recorded 193 active members, thirteen meetings at which 'large audiences' heard essays read on such topics as 'Man as a Social Being', 'Home, Its Associations and Influences', 'Responsibility of Young Men for their Influence on Society', and 'Obstacles of the Present Age to Mental Culture'. The Association reported that there was a 'great work to be done here'.[176] In its second year, the Association heard an address from the Reverend W.A. Scott, who stressed the interdependence of men, and the influences they exerted upon each other. 'From our actions, and words, and example, there is continually going out a stream of influences. Society is so complicated, that no man can be a good man without doing good to others.'[177] As in Victoria, the main aim of the reformers was to persuade men to a new, more interdependent sense of masculinity. It was the habitual linking of masculinity and independence that had to be severed, the link made in the kind of celebratory rhetoric which *Hutchings' California Magazine* used in 1857 to describe 'The Miner': 'With an independence of action in keeping with the perfect freedom of his volition, under no control or restraint that his better judgement does not prompt him to exercise, he speaks his mind when, where, and how he will, and holds himself personally responsible for its utterance.'[178] This way of thinking about masculinity, in California as in Victoria, was the chief target of reform activity.

CHAPTER 6

EXCITEMENT

. . . if we can believe the newspaper accounts, the spirit
which has been awakened in the United States by the
intelligence of the great mineral wealth of this country, is
even more frightful and epidemic in its effects than it was in
California. We were prepared for a large emigration, but we
were not prepared for such a sweeping wave of *desire* as
seems to have rolled over the length and breadth of the
Union—we had calculated upon an excitement, but we had
thought that the Mexican war and the presidential election
would have exhausted for a time the mercurial portion of our
national character . . . the thirst for gold has rode the
public mind like a gorgon or a nightmare.
Alta California, **24 April 1849**

There is a natural taste in the human mind for powerful
stimulants.
Reverend Adam Cairns, **Melbourne, 1856**

Such is life: a vapour, a shadow, a flower—things transient
and hastening to change. And alas! there are those who from
the shortness of life, draw an argument to justify their
criminal indulgence of sensual desires!
Bishop John Bede Polding, **1852**

I know that there is a very
large number of quiet men here.
*Mr Thomas Budden, to the Victorian
Gold Fields Commission of Enquiry.*

The importance of studying key words in a cultural lexicon has been stressed by several cultural historians, most notably Raymond Williams.[1] This chapter is an attempt to explore some of the nuances of the repeated contemporary use of one particular word in and about gold-rush California and Victoria. Gold, it was said again and again in both places, caused excitement.

Dr Johnson recognised as the meaning of excitement only 'the motive by which one is stirred up, animated, or put in action'.[2] The *Oxford English Dictionary*, however, records a more recent usage, the 'condition of being mentally excited, whether by pleasurable or painful emotion', giving examples from the 1860s—there were now excited persons. The corresponding use of the verb, to excite, as meaning 'to move to strong emotion, stir to passion; to stir up eager, tumultuous feeling, whether pleasurable or painful', is first noted in the 1820s. It was this relatively new sense of the word, then, referring to a mental and emotional state, that observers and participants in the 1850s drew upon. More than any other word, it seemed to them to sum up what was both disturbing and exhilarating about the events around them, and what they did to people.

VICTORIA

In 1854 the *Mount Alexander Mail* published a poem dedicated to the 'First Rose of Muckleford, Reared by Mr. Hitchcock'. The poem took the first bloom of the first English rose in Muckleford (near Castlemaine on the Victorian goldfields) as a text for its meditation on the possibilities of transplanted life in the colony, using the language of asylum and retreat:

'To the First Rose of Muckleford, Reared by Mr. Hitchcock'

Hail! emblem of my native land,
Welcome to Muckleford's calm vale,
Where, by the southern breezes fanned,
Thy ruddy offspring ne'er shall pale,
What though thy head did droop awhile,
And tears bedewed thy wave-worn eye
Yet soon there dawned a flowing smile—
A rainbow midst the flowing sky.
Thy lovely cheek, thy sweet perfume,
Are lovelier, sweeter, than of erst;
Thus may our hearts transplanted bloom,
And into buds of happiness burst!
Sweet vale! my mind's prophetic sight
Beholds thy plains by Ceres drest,
Beholds the pearly harvest bright
Spangle thine undulating breast.
My fancy's ear drinks in the sound
Of Sabbath chimes, that seem to say—

'Here, weary traveller, Peace is found;
Here, only here, her tranquil ray.'
Here shall the world-sick heart repair,
Here shall he smooth his faded brow,
Here shall he cry, 'Sweet Peace, I dare
Gaze on thee, calm-eyed Goddess, now!'
CFA[3]

The language of asylum evoked by 'CFA', part of the very idea of the New World, had powerful resonance in the nineteenth century. The image of Victoria as a land of 'Sweet Peace', as a refuge from a world of trouble, was presumably one which played its part in enticing emigrants to it. This argument about home was, of course, part of a fantasy, a wish—Victorian life could also be represented as being as riven with conflict as life elsewhere—but it was an enormously important fantasy. It was not only in poetry that Victorians expressed such fantastic hopes for peace. A letter to the editor of the *Ballarat Times* in 1858 expressed the view that the people had hoped that 'in fleeing from the corruptions and seething sorrows of the old country, they would have found rest for their weary minds and breasts in the new'.[4] The British love of home and quiet was an important part of the ideology of this society. 'Now, of all nations, none are more truly attached to their own country than the English', argued the Reverend George Goodman, 'Home is their watchword'. The need for emigration had, he maintained, only temporarily upset the usual antipathy to change of residence among British people.[5] 'Society begins anew', promised Sidney Smith of the Australian colonies, 'amidst the profoundest tranquillity'. His language was rhetorical—its insistence, though, alerts us to the perceived appeal of the theme in England:

> The tempestuous sea of human life, and political passion, rages thousands of miles off, while they repose upon the great emerald of the South, becalmed in the profoundest repose of the placid Pacific.[6]

There seemed little concern here that calm, quiet and repose could descend into torpor or any other kind of pejorative inactivity. It was gold that endangered the ideal of asylum, threatened to reintroduce passions and unpredictabilities into colonial life. Optimistic visitors might argue, as Lord Robert Cecil did, that quietness would easily be maintained at the gold-field—Cecil noted the 'orderly quiet' of the Mount Alexander Sunday, and wrote that there was there 'less noise' than in his home village of Hat-field—but they were in the minority.[7] More commonly, gold was seen as an end to tranquillity. 'All the bad passions evoked at the gambling table are becoming rampant among us', lamented the *Melbourne Morning Herald* in 1851.[8]

Gold made it more likely that immigrants would be adventurers, restless fortune seekers rather than weary pilgrims seeking asylum and retreat. This was a problem that William Howitt, a Quaker deeply committed to the idea of peace, took up in his Victorian gold-rush novel, *Tallengetta*. One of the characters, Parson Docker, is describing to the assembled company the passionate and excited nature of most emigrants:

> There may be here and there an isolated man who is weary of the struggle and restless career of European life; who longs for repose, and dreams of a still, poetic, Arcadian existence in new regions, amid woods and far-off mountains, but such men are few. The bulk is of such as are impatient to plunge into new speculations and rivalries; who are calculating on fresh activities, on a new and impetuous race for great prizes, and who bring with them all the agitated passions and fierce competition of crowded Europe. The scene is but changed, the spirit and the impulses of life are the same.

The problem, the parson explained, was that these men could not leave behind the Old World habits of avarice and ambition, the 'graspings and contrivings and forestallings' which prevented the achievement of true happiness. The role of the minister was to point the way to a higher peace, 'a peace which even the serenest wilderness of earth does not yield'.[9]

In Victoria, as in California, the condition of the polity was discussed in metaphors of quietness and excitement. Indeed, English political thought was often and popularly constructed in these terms. Tennyson's 1852 'Ode on the Death of the Duke of Wellington' spoke of the 'seed of freedom' sown:

> Betwixt a people and their ancient throne,
> That sober freedom out of which there springs
> Our loyal passion for our temperate kings![10]

This was not only a conservative language. The talk of 'sober' freedom and 'temperate' rule was as likely to be used by liberals extolling the maturity of British institutions and the capacity of the people, with all their various interests, to govern themselves and maintain themselves within accustomed bounds, as it was to be spoken by conservative celebrants of settled deference. Radicals, too, posited an ideal and quiet existence which might await the people once they were released from subjugation to aristocratic elites. The Sydney radical John Dunmore Lang told New South Wales miners of his hope that in Australia gold mining itself would be pursued 'as quietly and peacefully as was any other form of honest industry'.[11] Charles Harpur, the radical New South Wales poet, in one of the best known poems written in colonial Australia, celebrated the quietness of 'A Mid-Summer Noon in the Australian Forest':

> O 'tis easeful here to lie
> Hidden from Moon's scorching eye,
> In this grassy cool recess
> Musing thus of Quietness.[12]

Texts such as these give a sense of the imagined colonial community so many seem to have longed for—a social world which would remain quiet, away from the strife of the world. 'Victoria is not to be a place unfit for the residence of the moral and refined', the *Australian Gold Diggers' Monthly Magazine* similarly observed, 'It will be a quiet resting place for ourselves, and a happy home for our children.'[13] Some satisfied emigrants seemed to agree. 'A New Comer' wrote to the *Illustrated Australian Magazine* to argue that what recommended the colony of Victoria was its quietness:

> It is equally clear that if there is less here to excite, there is far less to disturb, and that they who are willing to limit their gratifications . . . may find in this new world a happiness, such as is the lot of few, who are whirled about in the excitement of a mob of money-strugglers, or engrossed incessantly in carrying out schemes of worldly ambition and aggrandisement.[14]

Victorian commentators made it clear that they regarded excitement as the inevitable concomitant of gold seeking. It was quite natural to imagine, James Bonwick wrote, that:

> among a community of men, out of the pale of civilized life, removed from restraint, surrounded by degrading and deteriorating influences, and constantly excited by the very character of their occupation, there would be found much that is repulsive and much that is condemnable.[15]

The Reverend John Potter explained more particularly that it was the haste and uncertainty typically associated with rushing for gold which created excitement:

> Men make all the mistakes which haste invariably engenders. And then comes uncertainty about the results . . . This uncertainty produces excitement, that subdued but intense excitement which acts so powerfully on body and mind and unfits a man for taking a cool and dispassionate view of his position . . . intense anxiety and constant excitement . . . will in due time undermine the best constitution and bring the strongest to his grave.[16]

It was only the privileged who could escape this damaging spiral of excitement. Mary Stawell remembered of her husband that 'at the time of the gold fever Mr. Stawell often rode out to Woodlands late in the evening, and throwing himself on the lawn, would say, "Oh! this is peace!" '[17]

It was not only the actual employment of gold seeking that was held to promote excitement, however. The wealth that might follow could also be used in ways that multiplied excitement. As the Presbyterian Reverend Adam Cairns explained:

> the tendency here is to a life of ease and indulgence. The theatre, the casino, the ball-room, offer attractions which comparatively few resist, and multitudes of the young and the gay crowd these scenes of pleasurable excitement, and

acquire habits of thought which enfeeble their moral sense, and stimulate their vicious desires.[18]

The explanations given for the excitement which gold caused are very similar to analyses often produced of what turned men to drink—the search for stimulation which became a craving and an obsession—and one can see gold, in many of the arguments made about it, being constructed as something like a functional equivalent of alcohol. Thus the Reverend G.M. Drummond speculated about the causes of colonial drunkenness in terms that could have come from any discussion of gold-inspired excitement:

> Whether it be the severance of home ties or the removal of certain restraints that may have controlled our worst passions under a more settled system of things at home—or whether it be the recklessness consequent upon a fluctuating and unsettled state of things, or whether it be the stimulating and exhausting nature of the climate, or the sudden changes whereby the poor man becomes a rich man and the comparatively rich man becomes a poor man . . . the fact is beyond all question that the prevalence of this vice in this colony is most appalling . . .[19]

But it was the gold itself which was ultimately held responsible for the excitement. 'Within the last six or eight months', asked Chief Justice William a'Beckett, 'will any one deny that all classes have been more or less kept by it in a constant state of excitement?'[20] His brother described the condition more pointedly, as a 'universal and most pernicious excitement'.[21] Bishop Perry wrote gloomily in October 1852 of the 'great pressure of business' which made it: 'difficult for men to secure leisure for retirement and quiet reflection, and keeps them in a state of perpetual bustle and excitement'.[22]

The argument about excitement, then, involved extrapolation from a psychological state to a social one. The excited society was a more dangerous and terrible thing than the sum of the individual excited lives, for within an excited society, no individual quietness was possible. As the Reverend John Cooper explained it to his congregation, excitement filtered up from the individual, and all were responsible: 'the community cannot be in a state of prosperity and repose while its members are restless and conflicting; the body of man cannot be quiet and still while the mind is perplexed and agitated; the mind cannot be calm and serene while the spirit is disquieted'.[23] It is articulations such as this that show the contrast with California most clearly—for what Californian minister would have posited as the goal of his people 'prosperity and repose', the calm and serenity of social quietness?

The Victorian authorities, then, understood the gold rush as an eruption of excitement, and their social analysis was that quietness had to be restored. The best society that Lieutenant Governor Charles Joseph La Trobe and others like him could imagine was settled and hierarchical, ruled by a benevolent and enlightened government, which alone had a sense of the good of the whole—a society whose success would be measured by its peace, contentment and quietness. Gold was a troubling event for La Trobe because it excited the population. His famous despatch of 10 October 1851 warned the British government of the effect that the discoveries would have on 'our excitable population', the creation of an excitement so great that he was already referring to it as a 'mania'.[24] By December, the excitement had grown even greater, with the discovery of the Mount Alexander diggings. La Trobe wrote that the excitement had become 'general and unreflecting' in character, and 'now pervades the community'. He was concerned that members of the governing classes were defecting to the frenzied pursuit of gold, but his greatest anxiety was obviously about those outside this circle, about the excitement caused by the 'acquisition of wealth by the lower classes', as he bluntly put it in December 1851.[25] The problem was the 'intoxicating influence which the sudden and unexpected acquisition of great wealth in its most dazzling form exercises upon the minds of the multitude'.[26] At stake was the idea of Victoria as a place which offered 'a suitable home and place of refuge, not only to the poor, indigent, or restless, but for the sober and enlightened middle classes', for 'really respectable persons', defined here as those for whom 'good order' and 'respect for the laws' were considerations as important as the 'natural advantages' of the colony.[27] La Trobe also, significantly, saw excitement as a symptom of an individualising tendency in society, a 'growing sense of importance and independence arising from unexampled prosperity, emancipation from old ties and obligations, and powers of self-support, and self-government'.[28] He lacked the new, liberal imagination which could understand how the government of such an autonomous and diverse population was possible.

What were the effects of this concern about excitement in Victoria, and what was entailed in these judgements? And why was it a matter of such concern? One answer lay in the climate, always an important topic in nineteenth-century assessments of the worth of a 'new' country.[29] The most contradictory views could be held of the influence of climate, but few disputed that it exercised the profoundest influence on social and individual life.

Climatic metaphors entered into most discussions of excitement, for behind them was a racial theory which held that the races from warm climates were more emotional and excitable than those from cooler places. Hence, the argument went, the Mediterranean peoples produced art while the Germans produced philosophy, and the Tahitians lay indolently about their island paradise. The associations ran deep in western racism, and in London, Philadelphia and New York there was concern about southern settlements for these reasons—what if the Anglo-Saxon stock softened in the sun? When the Reverend Isaac New urged Victorian men to model themselves on the oak tree rather than on the hot-house flower, he had something like this theory in mind. His concern was that in Victoria, life might be luxuriant but brief. The hot-house plant, while it 'may diffuse its perfume in fragrant loveliness', would perish without the special care of the hot house. The oak tree, in contrast, 'planted on the mountain top, exposed to wind and rain, to cold, and snow, nursed amid storms and shaken by every blast, strikes its roots the deeper, and rises slowly and gradually, till it presents an aspect of majestic and venerable grandeur, perpetuating its existence for centuries'.[30] This was not only an argument about climate and about race, but also an important argument about masculinity—the oak had the fixity and dependability which the transitory men of Victoria so conspicuously lacked. The concern about excitement was an anxiety about men. Gold-rush women might suffer from the over-stimulation of the emotions, they might be described as melancholy, homesick or disappointed, but they were less often condemned for being too excited.

It was widely believed that the climate of Victoria was an exciting one, which made life more intense but possibly briefer. William Westgarth expounded this view at some length in his *Victoria: Late Australia Felix*, arguing that, while the Australian climate was 'not hostile to the development of high physical and mental exertion', it would not favour longevity. If existence in Australia would be less enduring, he wrote 'it may deserve to be called more joyous':

> There appears ever a vivid sense or enjoyment of physical existence. To be or not to be are, in their emphatic extremes, the sanitary text of the Australian.[31]

It was thus often held that the climate encouraged brief and ardent exertions, but made sustained labour difficult. The Anglican Dean of Melbourne, Hussey Burgh Macartney, wrote in 1854 of the problem faced by the newly arrived clergyman in Victoria, of how 'an exciting climate now stimulates him to exertion above his strength' and to consequent exhaustion.[32] This was one of the key arguments mobilised by the proponents of the eight-hour working day in the mid-1850s.[33]

A counterview did, it is true, hold that the Victorian climate was a relaxing one, and the argument for abridged hours of labour could also be made from this position. So J.A. Aldwell was awarded a prize by the Melbourne University for his 1856 essay written for a Melbourne Labor League competition on the 'Eight Hours and Early Closing Questions', in which he maintained that colonial experience had persuaded the working classes that:

> the period of labor under the relaxing influence of Australian climate, cannot extend to the length of daily toil ruling in the mother country, without sacrificing health, and shortening the duration of human life . . .[34]

William Howitt, too, thought the climate a depressing or relaxing one, but blamed it on the 'immense quantity of vegetable matter rotting on the surface of the earth'.[35]

Much more commonly, though, the heat of the Victorian climate and its changeable nature were thought to excite the body. In this the climate merely assisted the work of society, for 'colonial life generally has the effect of sharpening the faculties'.[36] Here the most optimistic case to be put was that the climate would stimulate the colonists to unusual achievement. Ferdinand von Mueller, the Victorian botanist, looked forward to a new classical age, observing that:

> In countries stretching through a climatic zone almost alike to ours, arose the genius of poetry, of arts, and of philosophy.[37]

The Mediterranean analogy had great appeal to those attempting to call into being the cultural development of the colony. The *Age* in 1857 argued that with its warmer climate, Victoria might produce more painters than poets. 'Our future Victorian artists, like the natives of all warm climates, should be good colorists', and might rival the achievements of artists from Spain and Italy.[38] Such optimism about the exciting climate, though, was more than balanced by pessimistic accounts which held that the stimulus would be excessive and the achievements unsustainable.

It was the fluctuation, as well as the comparative heat of the Victorian climate, that was feared to be overstimulating. J. William Mackenna, a surgeon, wrote in 1858 of the 'sudden rises and falls of temperature' in Victoria—greater, he thought, 'than in almost any other country'. He blamed the heat of the summer for the high rate of infant mortality. In Victoria, he wrote, spring and summer, far from being seasons of 'the renewal of health', had become seasons of 'grief, mourning, and desolation'.[39] The exciting effects of heat and change were thought to be often too much for infants to withstand. Even young adults, it was feared, would be overstimulated, and deleteriously affected. *Eliza Cook's Journal*, commenting from London in 1853, offered these theories on the Victorian climate:

> English men and women who emigrate in the heyday of life may expect to die about ten years sooner than in England; but those who have passed the meridian of life may expect to add ten or twenty years to their existence by the same cause. The climate usually cures dyspepsia; increases nervous debility, and develops the latent seeds of insanity.[40]

If the climate was understood as a stimulant, how much greater were the fears about alcohol, the most notorious of nineteenth-century stimulants? James Bonwick worried that 'this beautiful land—this scene of Arcadian happiness—this golden realm' would be 'desecrated by an increasing number of drunkards.'[41] The Reverend George Goodman warned in 1854 about the drinking of alcohol in relation to the exciting climate, but decided that in the end intoxication would not be prevalent in the colony:

> The consumption of spirits is simply suicidal, and will speedily consign its unhappy votaries to the horrors of *delirium tremens*, and the darkness of the grave. In this climate, the spirit-drinker burns the flame of life in an atmosphere of oxygen, and rapidly does he burn out. But . . . the air itself is a sufficient stimulant, stamping upon the community a universal cheerfulness . . .[42]

The high consumption of meat in the colony was also thought to be a part of the problem of overexcitement. Medical men, one proponent of agriculture reported, attributed diseases to the great quantity of animal food consumed in the colony 'without admixture of a due proportion of fruit and vegetables'.[43] Henry Brown agreed that the problem was that much of the Victorian population consisted of people who would rarely have been able to afford 'exciting foods' such as meat and alcohol at home in Britain, but who in the colony overindulged.[44]

The ultimate end of excitement in Victoria was madness, for the insane person was held to have an overstimulated mind and body, to have worn out his or her constitution too early. As the barrister representing Dr Robert Bowie, the Superintendent of Melbourne's Yarra Bend Lunatic Asylum, argued at an 1862 libel trial, when Bowie had arrived in Melbourne, 'owing to the gold mania, people were in a considerable state of excitement; society had not settled down', and he 'found a vast number of persons, who from various causes, were labouring under mental disease'.[45] There were persistent fears—articulated, for example, by Dr Godfrey Howitt to the 1858 parliamentary inquiry into the Yarra Bend asylum—that colonial rates of insanity were even higher than those already seen as troubling, through the early 1850s, in Britain.[46] Dr James Kilgour calculated in 1855 that one in every 1389 of the Victorian population was resident in its Lunatic Asylum—and, as he rightly commented, many more insane persons were sure to be at home or in the gaols: 'that the ratio is extremely high no doubt can be entertained.'[47] John Singleton recollected of his medical practice in the early 1850s that he saw great numbers of immigrant young men who, 'between the heat of the climate and strong drink, were deprived of reason and were sent to the lunatic asylum'.[48] There was also concern expressed in the Victorian press at the high rates of insanity—'this malady is frightfully on the increase', the *Argus* commented in November 1852, blaming 'the excessive use of ardent spirits, and the excitement of sudden wealth acquired at the goldfields'.[49] From the goldfields themselves came reports of insanity. 'There are a great number of insane persons wandering about the District,' the Benalla Crown Lands Commissioner wrote to the Colonial Secretary in 1852, 'to the great alarm and annoyance of the

Inhabitants . . . with the facility of making money (by procuring Gold) and purchasing intoxicating liquors therewith, the evil is on the increase.'[50]

This colonial discussion of insanity was another of the ways in which established analyses of industrialising Britain provided a framework for the interpretation of gold-rush Victoria. Historians interested in the social construction of mental illness have pointed to the connections between the social dislocation of industrialisation and nineteenth-century lunacy. 'Large cities whose growth was fuelled by long-distance migration, and whose inhabitants lacked the solidarity which soon arose from shared work experiences . . . were generous providers of lunatics for the new custodial institutions'.[51] It is my argument that gold provided a similarly dislocated social setting in a society of immigrants in Victoria. Gold provided a concentrated experience of life in a market-governed society. Here the argument of Andrew T. Scull, that the rise of the asylum is linked to 'the commercialisation of social existence and the advent of a full-blown capitalist market economy', becomes relevant.[52] Contemporary comment was not about capitalism, but about excitement—among other things a description of the effect on individuals of the unmitigated pursuit of wealth in a society which placed no constraints upon that pursuit. It was only liberal theory which provided an answer to the question of how the excited, individualised, self-seeking society might be governable.

Gold and alcohol, climate and madness, excitement—the connections were clear in contemporary thought.[53] The 1858 Victorian Parliamentary Select Committee of Inquiry into the Yarra Bend Lunatic Asylum took evidence from a number of expert witnesses, many of whom saw links between the climate, intemperance, excitement and insanity—'a climate with such hot windy days is exceedingly exciting', the proprietor of Melbourne's private lunatic asylum explained.[54] Dr John Maund told the same inquiry that lunatics were 'less able to contend' with a very hot climate than the sane. The authorities at the Yarra Bend asylum estimated that a third of their male inmates in 1853 were there because of drinking, while sunstroke accounted for one in fifteen. When these physical stimulants were added to the mental overstimulation of gold-rush society—the factor of 'disappointment' which put one in fifteen of the male patients into Yarra Bend, or the 'melancholy' which had driven one in five of the women inmates mad—the contemporary diagnosis of a prevalence of an excessive emotional life becomes clear.[55] The Victorian asylum was located just on the edge of Melbourne, at a bend in the Yarra river, its tranquil, semi-rural location meant to win its inmates away from their apparent determination to lead brief and passion-governed lives.

The Yarra Bend Case Book, official medical register of the lunatic asylum, ascribed causation in ways that clearly follow from these understandings. Intemperance, disappointment, insolation (exposure to the sun), and

THE YARRA BEND LUNATIC ASYLUM, STUDLEY PARK.—SEE PAGE 41.

'The Yarra Bend Lunatic Asylum', from Illustrated Melbourne Post *25 June 1862, p.41.*

irregularity of life are frequently mentioned causes. William M., admitted 21 May 1853, was driven insane by 'a family quarrel and disappointment in love'. Richard W., admitted 17 June 1853, a 55-year-old weaver from Ireland, went mad from 'Drinking and beating by bushrangers'. Louisa H., 33 and married, suffered from 'disappointed hopes'. Eliza A., had to be committed when 'jealousy' drove her to chronic melancholia. James S., a 24-year-old draper from Scotland who had only two months since migrated to Collingwood, signalled his insanity by expressing 'Exalted ideas of his own prosperity'. The cause of Margaret B.'s moral insanity was given as 'irregularity of life'. John P., a 40-year-old unmarried labourer originally from Ireland, was brought in from 'The Diggings' (his previous address being given as 'The Bush'), insane simply from 'Drink'. Mary G., who had left Ireland for 'The Diggings', had the causes of her madness described as 'Drinking and Disappointment'. The unfortunate William M., a 22-year-old miller residing in 'The Bush', had to be put away because of 'Excitement and overjoy at the expectation of returning to England'. Richard P.'s acute mania arose from 'several exciting causes, among them long walks, exposure to the Sun, and drinking to excess'. Of Alexander A., the asylum doctor wrote that his discharge was given only 'on the understanding that he would return to England, there being every reason to believe that unless he went to a cooler climate and got among his relatives who are wealthy and respectable, he would soon again become Insane'.[56]

There were differences in the sorts of causes of insanity ascribed to men and women. Women often had insanity diagnosed after childbirth and in connection with the emotions of grief, disappointment and melancholy. Women in 1852 and 1853 had the following causes listed: Disappointed Hopes; Grief; Dissolute Habits (Intemperate and Very Bad); Sedentary Life; Grief for the Loss of Her Mother; Grief upon hearing of the supposed death of her husband at The Diggings; Reverses of Fortune; Exposure to Heat of the Sun; Desertion of her husband; Death of husband; Jealousy; Fright with domestic grief; Intemperance lately; Fright; Excessive use of spirits; Fear and anxiety; Fright at sea; After Labour; Disappointed hopes. These were emotions of depression rather than excitement. These diagnoses make clearer the point that excitement was a condition ascribed to men. There was much ideology in the ascription of causes, but the symptoms of the madness were real enough. William Tomlinson described in his diary the madness of Mrs Cramp, the wife of a gold digger who had died a week before:

> She had been there 2 or 3 days, very grieved in her mind. But however, we were startled out of our beds last night about 11 o'clock by her shouting and screaming . . . I found her standing on a box in the corner of the house in a state of the wildest madness . . . She was the most frightful creature I ever saw. She tried to bite me, and gnashing her teeth and making the most horrible noises that we ever heard, and making use of the most awful language . . . I shall never forget that night as long as I live.[57]

Men seem to have been affected much more by drink, drugs and violent accidents. Some of their ascribed causes of madness for the same period were: Intemperance; Dissolute Habits; Fall from Horse; The effects of a violent thunderstorm; Something given in his drink; Religious delusion; Excessive drinking and irregular habits; Opium; Disappointed in Love; Long while in the Gaol; Insolation; Religion and excesses in opium; Syphilis; Typhoid fever; Irregularity of life; Distressed circumstances; Repeated Losses; Anxiety of Mind in being about to commence business.[58] While the women patients displayed the symptoms of melancholia and disappointment, the men had been often violently excited.

More detailed descriptions of individual cases are hard to find in this period. Some glimpses of the circumstances of the apprehension of the insane can be gained from a small number of letters that have survived from 1855. Written by the gaoler of the Eastern Gaol in Melbourne to Dr Bowie at Yarra Bend, they accompanied lunatics who were being transferred from one institution to the other. James G., the gaoler reported in October, had been a stock driver on a station near Sydney. He had been in Melbourne about a month:

during which time he has been very mad. He used to rush about the streets cracking a heavy whip and inviting people to go with him and get money he would give them. He was arrested at the theatre, having got from the Upper Boxes on the Stage in the midst of the performances.

The theatre was obviously full of delusional potential. The boy Francis E. was arrested as a dangerous lunatic in September, and his father stated then that 'he believed his son had become wrong in his mind from brooding over Plays and fancying he had a talent for Stage Impersonations'. Francis had been 'in a situation as Waiter in Dining Rooms, he ran away from it about three days before his arrest, and when found was eating cabbages in a garden'. But if skills of theatrical impersonation were dangerous, money and ideas on its distribution were more so. William C., arrested in December, was described as 'very quiet and harmless', and had in his possession only one pound one shilling and sixpence, and a ring. But, the gaoler warned, 'he will no doubt explain to you a grand scheme of distributing the lands of the colony'. Another lunatic had in his possession a nugget of gold.[59] James Thomas Harcourt, who ran for some years a private lunatic asylum in Victoria, stated in the course of a trial in the Victorian Supreme Court in 1862 that it was a 'common feature' with Victorian lunatics to secrete their own excrement in their pockets and say it was gold:

The Attorney General: Is that confined to the mining population?

Witness: Not by any means.[60]

Gold was, not surprisingly, part of the content of the delusional life of Victorian lunatics.

In contemporary diagnoses of the causes of insanity, we can see dramatised prevailing beliefs about the dangers of excitement. By the 1850s, most observers were prepared to look for social explanations for insanity. 'Insanity,' the Catholic Bishop of Hobart reminded Victorians, '. . . is not a crime, and in itself no disgrace, no more than blindness or loss of speech.'[61] In an 1857 plan for new and more scientific classification of patients in a new asylum, the categories chosen reflect a belief that quietness was preferable to excitement. At the difficult end of the spectrum we have the convict lunatics, 'the Loquacious and Troublesome, and the Noisy, Refractory and Dirty, while at the other end we have the Tranquil and Melancholy, and the Clean and Industrious'.[62] These categories, of course, come from the transnational discourses of contemporary medical science, but they articulate very well a local sense of the socially desirable. In 1853 a young man admitted himself to the asylum by swimming across the Yarra river and clambering up the 'precipitous bank' and over the fence into one of the men's yards:

It was immediately discovered that he was in a state of mental derangement and greatly excited. He had in his hand an open Bible and acquainted us that the Lord had appointed to meet him there that morning.

Dr Bowie's comment, though, was that 'he is a respectable looking young man, and I am in hopes a day or two of quietness will set him to rights'.[63] The 'moral treatment' that the Victorian asylum at Yarra Bend was offering in the 1850s involved the restoration of quietness in a more ordered environment than the excited world outside.[64] This project it shared with the Californian asylum at Stockton, but their relationship to the ethos of the societies outside their walls differed significantly. The Victorian asylum shared a project with dominant groups in the society—the construction of a quieter world—while the Californian asylum stood as an embattled island of quiet in a culture which increasingly sanctioned excitement as a social state.

The analytic connections between gold, excitement and madness serve to give great pointedness to contemporary critiques of the excitement caused by gold, for at stake were the welfare and sanity of the people. William a'Beckett criticised gold seeking because 'the pursuit is carried out in a constant state of excitement . . . and carried on under the influence of one solitary overwhelming idea—the acquisition of Gold'.[65] He toyed with the idea of a whole nation becoming insane:

> Sudden changes in an individual's fortune have often been found to turn his head, and to render other care necessary for his protection, than he has been able to afford for himself. Why is a nation, in the first heyday of similar excitement, to stand on steadier ground?[66]

William's brother T.T. a'Beckett agreed that gold caused an excitement so intense as to drive men insane. By late 1851 he had issued a pamphlet condemning the 'universal and most pernicious excitement' which the gold had created, lamenting that 'we are . . . little better than a community of madmen'.[67] The depiction of a nation entirely surrendered to destructive emotion was the logical culmination of the Victorian discussions of excitement. Excitement destroyed reason just as surely as it destroyed order and quiet. And it was ultimately the gold which was responsible.

In April 1852, a letter was published in the Melbourne *Argus* from one who offered 'a few observations on the question of lunacy in reference to the present mania upon gold finding'. Claiming to have made 'careful observation' on the subject, the author warned that Victoria could expect a considerable increase in madness as a consequence of the 'unfortunate discovery of gold'. He told of a trip to Geelong on the steamer, on which was a party of four men who had been at the diggings only five weeks, and who had made 1100 pounds each. One of the men had been 'quite demented' by his good fortune:

I made the remark at the time, 'that the gold had turned this man's head', and certainly from the state of excitement he was in, it can be scarcely hoped that he will ever settle down again into the calmness he previously enjoyed; others, I have known, whose minds have been quite upset, so that strange delusions of unbounded wealth and night dreams of Eldorados have completely disqualified them for the sober duties of every day life.[68]

Victorian social critics during the gold period looked forward to the time when excitement would have subsided and quiet was restored. After time out at the goldfields, the *Illustrated Australian Magazine* confidently predicted:

The citizens, on whom reliance must be placed to maintain the progress of business and labour, and the farmers, will have pretty well sown their wild oats by the excursion, and will return with more content to the quietude of their ordinary engagements . . . the framework of our society will be undisturbed . . .[69]

William Bakewell, writing the 1854 preface to Catherine Helen Spence's *Clara Morison*, wrote lyrically of the quietness of the city of women which Adelaide became after the men had departed for the goldfields. 'An unwonted silence prevailed', he observed:

a state of society unsung by poets, and such as was never seen before, existed, in which gentleness, and courtesy, and loving kindness reigned, and which will never be forgotten by those whom a supposed hard fortune compelled to remain behind.[70]

In the Victorian 'social imaginary' then, quietness was a virtue—not uncontestedly and not everywhere of course—but routinely, commonly and unthinkingly.

CALIFORNIA

For who can anticipate events, or prescribe a policy consistent with their consequences, in an age when they cast no shadows before them . . . This remarkable feature of the times has produced a restless and feverish condition of the community, embracing all classes, and extending throughout our common country; but in no part has its influence been felt so much, perhaps, as in the West . . . This excited condition, occasioned chiefly by the recent discoveries of gold in California, has already produced the most extraordinary movement that has occurred since the days of the crusades.

Western Journal, April 1850

It is almost inconceivable what an excitement was produced upon nations and individuals by the discovery, less than four years since, of gold among the mountains of Upper California. Tides of human life soon set in toward this one point; currents here met, whirling and contending with increasing force; and, where all was silent and calm before, was heard the roar, and seen the violence and agitation of the maelstrom.

Daniel B. Woods, **Sixteen Months at the Gold Diggings**

Gold, it was said at the time of the Californian rushes, excited men. As in Victoria, we need to ask what meanings this metaphor of excitement carried, what arguments it enabled. Too much of the history of California gold unquestioningly uses the same terms as contemporaries did. 'The excitement which accompanied the rush,' Ralph Bieber wrote in 1948, 'was more intense and more widespread than any other peacetime excitement in the nation's history.'[71]

Contemporary responses to this perceived 'excitement' varied. There was a debate in California over the appropriate level of excitement in society. As anywhere, there was conflict. But one can, looking back, begin to offer argument as to where the centre of the spectrum of debate lay. To critics of the effects of gold, excitement posed serious problems for the maintenance of an ordered society, for it unfitted men for a quiet and routine existence. 'The stranger in San Francisco at this time is at once impressed with the feverish state of excitement that pervades the whole population,' wrote Frank Marryat, 'there is no attention paid to dress, and every one is hurried and incoherent in manner.'[72] To such critics, the fevered excitement produced by gold was hardly conducive to the existence of a rational public life. But many others in California argued that excitement was not necessarily a bad thing. Even Eliza Farnham, a severe critic of excitement, wrote favourably of change and movement, arguing 'that advancement is not standing still, that development is the opposite of stagnation, and no more comes of it than grapes of thorns, or figs of thistles'.[73] Her spiritualism led her to the belief that 'spiritual growth makes the human career a perpetual revolution!'[74] The optimists argued that excitement was but an exaggeration, an intense form, of the admirable energy which had spread the American empire from ocean to ocean. Quietness was not the solution to social disturbance in California that it was in Victoria. David E. Shi has argued that in America the virtues associated with simplicity were 'clearly on the defensive after 1820', and the same might be argued for quietness.[75]

Hidden not too deeply in these discussions were attitudes to the desirable condition of society. The theme of excitement brought together all the other key responses to gold. Were energy, expansion, growth, the continual flux of the market and the ever-changing face of the city, the marks of American greatness? Or did the true America still reside in the countryside, in the quietness of rural life, and in Jeffersonian values? Or perhaps in the wilderness, high in the stillness of the Sierras? Was excitement or serenity the better state?

CRITICAL VOICES

'To say that it was a period of intense excitement does not describe it', one of the pioneers recalled of the atmosphere of 1849. 'It was a raging, seething, red hot pandemonia, in which men struggled to accomplish their purpose in the shortest possible time.'[76] The gold itself promoted excitement. 'There is an excitement connected with the pursuit of gold which renders one restless and uneasy,' observed the Reverend Daniel Woods, 'ever hoping to do something better.'[77] Samuel Willey described the commercial origins of the excitement he vividly recalled:

> The possibility, the chance of speedy and large gains, and perhaps of sudden wealth, excited the whole community. The miner was excited about his claim; the speculator about his lands, and the merchant about his profits of trade.[78]

Hinton Helper also wrote of the 'excitability' of the Californians:

> The least thing of unusual occurrence fires their fancy and sets them in motion. If a terrier catches a rat, or if a big turnip is brought to market, the people cluster together and scramble for a sight with as much eagerness and impetuosity as a party of children would scramble after a handful of sweetmeats.[79]

Californian poets took this apparently peculiar level of activity and change as a theme for social comment:

> Restless! Restless Man! God does pity thee.[80]

And Californian social critics confirmed the diagnosis:

> In the struggle for gold, Californians are in a state of moral intoxication. In comparison with the calm, plodding pace of those we have left behind, we are reeling and staggering in excitement.[81]

It is little wonder then that easterners arriving in California commented first of all on the excitement. Mrs D.B. Bates described her arrival in San Francisco: 'Such a hurry, such a bustle, so much excitement!'[82] 'Ralph Raven' was less sympathetic:

> After several hours thus spent in wandering from one centre of attraction to another, we returned to the ship, weary of excitement, and hoping to find there at least one place free from the general infection.[83]

Bayard Taylor, whose *Eldorado* remains one of the most widely read of the contemporary accounts of gold-rush California, offers a lurid picture of the prevailing excitement:

> men dart hither and thither, as if possessed with a never-resting spirit . . . It is impossible to witness this excess and dissipation of business without feeling something of its influence. The very air is pregnant with the magnetism of bold, spirited, unwearied action, and he who but ventures into the outer circle of the whirlpool is spinning ere he has time for thought, in its dizzy vortex.[84]

Taylor portrayed San Francisco as an altogether bewildering place, a place in which previous habits of perception were of no use at all:

> The mind, however it may be prepared for an astonishing condition of affairs, cannot immediately push aside its old instincts of value and ideas of business, letting all past experiences go for naught . . . Never have I had so much difficulty in establishing, satisfactorily to my own senses, the reality of what I saw and heard.[85]

This talk of excitement referred in part to the simple freedom from restraint that frontier society in general, and California in particular, seemed to offer. The former principal of a Providence, Rhode Island grammar school, described the behaviour of his party in California:

> . . . the spirit of merriment was rife among us, and our pranks and capers resembled very much those of a group of children just let loose from school. Each apparently endeavoured to outvie his fellows in leaping over stumps, logs, clumps of bushes, ditches, etc.[86]

But contemporaries also used the term 'excitement' to refer to economic and wealth-seeking activity, and it is clear that there was a frenzied quality to economic life in gold-rush California. Part of the concern of the agrarians was that farming simply could not compete as an activity for the enthusiasm of the people, once they had been excited. Henry Veel Huntley recorded that, in 1852, he had spoken with many of the farmers along the Feather River, and 'every one would sell, wanting to go to the diggings; the farm does not produce fast enough; and though the diggings may not, yet there is the daily excitement so much desired by the American'.[87]

Excitement was understood as a concentration of energies on one object, usually frantic wealth seeking, and it was thought by many to have deleterious psychological as well as social effects. The concentration on one all-absorbing activity, in which much (perhaps everything) was at stake, was often further said to produce effects analogous to those produced on men by gambling. In California as in Victoria, this analogy better than most captured contemporaries' sense of the hypnotic but ultimately irrational behaviour associated with gold seeking. Excitement also referred to restlessness and mobility—and social historians have established that, even in the context of a nation characterised by very great geographical mobility, Californians were an extremely mobile people—three out of four employed males in San Francisco in 1852 had departed the city by 1860.[88]

Excitement was also political. The issue most frequently debated about the vigilance episodes in Californian political history was whether they were the excited work of mobs or the calm and calculated activities of responsible citizens. The *Alta*, for example had little doubt that the 1849 'hounds' terrorising the camps of Chilean immigrants were a turbulent force:

> One of those whirlwinds of excitement which may now be said to have become periodical in San Francisco, was witnessed on Monday July 16 1849.[89]

In contrast, it was the silence and calm of the 1851 and 1856 vigilantes which were always stressed by their defenders. Eliza Farnham found comfort in the vigilance episodes, proof that 'the excitement in which men daily lived, gave them calmness and cool self-control in those emergencies, when people, whose everyday life is quiet, lose them'.[90]

To critics, social turbulence and excitement were dangerous things. Timothy Dwight Hunt, in a sermon in San Francisco in 1851, condemned what he called 'fast living', a kind of 'rapid and wasteful life' which he found to be everywhere visible. Like many others, Hunt ascribed the fastness to the conditions of life in California:

> The natural energy of this people is great; but the extraordinary facilities for gain have afforded an unusual stimulus to that energy. It has been, and is, taxed to its utmost . . . to keep pace with a racing competition, unusual exertion has been required. men have grown old rapidly . . .

Excitement was seen as a kind of drug which enabled these extraordinary exertions:

> More hours in the day, and harder every hour, they have labored, than ever before. The excitement of the times has sustained them under this extraordinary pressure of cares and burdens. But excitement is a prop that must fail . . .[91]

Some feared that after experiencing such excitement, there would be a permanent craving for excessive stimulation. E.L. Cleaveland wrote censoriously of the 'intense excitement produced by recent discoveries of mineral wealth', a 'most unhealthy excitement' and a 'mental and moral fever'.[92] He worried that the turmoil might never be thrown off:

> Suppose you survive the dangers . . . will you return as you went? Will you be disposed to settle down in a quiet, unostentatious, useful mode of life? Will you not bring back with you a restless, morbid desire for change, excitement, and wild adventure?[93]

Outsiders often thought the excitement an American rather than a Californian trait. 'Excitement there must be,' wrote Henry Veel Huntley, 'it is the food of the American mind; with it the American acknowledges no restraint—without it, his exertions scarcely supply his wants; he is either impetuously bounding forward, or idly depending upon others.'[94] Timothy Dwight Hunt described on another occasion the emotional state in which men were driven to California in search of gold, emphasising the loss of rational control over their actions which they suffered as they heard of the treasure to the west:

> The effect was electric. The news . . . seemed like successive shocks of a powerful battery, by which the hands of men in business, all over the world, were paralized at their work . . . They came as famished men rush to the fountain. Like the hungry eagle, they alighted on the mountains. Like the devouring locust, they swarmed the banks of our rivers. Like birds of prey they settled down upon the coast. Starting hither under a sudden and powerful impulse, they here continued under the excitement of an irresistible passion.[95]

How, his audience must have wondered, could such unreflective action possibly be consonant with civilized progress? How could such a population be governed? If the expectation of great wealth could effect this disturbing transformation, it was patently not a rational and ordering force in human affairs. The effects attributed to the gold were not unlike those usually attributed to alcohol. Excessive stimulation of body and mind was held to be both a cause of men turning to alcohol and a product of it. The Englishman J.D. Borthwick claimed that Americans generally 'live more in a given time than other people, and naturally have recourse to constant stimulants to make up for the want of intervals of abandon and repose'. But in California he found the 'ordinary rate of existence' was even faster than that in the Atlantic states, and drinking to excess was common.[96] Stimulating drinks, turned to by those already in a state of excitement, only further excited. Hinton Helper gloomily described the pattern: 'driven to desperation by bitter and repeated calamities, they betake themselves to the bottle for solace, become insane from extreme anxiety or over-activity of mind'.[97] The critique of a life lived at unnatural speed took many forms in the writings about gold-rush California. At one extreme, nature itself in California could seem faster and less sound than elsewhere. 'Vegetables attain an unusual size in California . . .' observed Frank Marryat, 'but I have observed an insipidity in every thing that has thus rapidly matured, and size is attained at the expense of loss of flavour.'[98]

Reformers hoped to stem the tide of excitement with the example of other and quieter modes of being. Lorena Hays in 1855 looked to the mountains as a source of a set of values opposed to excitement:

> Within sight of all of us are situated most beautiful cool and delicious places (our country is well) where one might hide away from the bustle, toil, heat and excitement of life . . . but alas the Californian has no time—He swelters, tugs and toils on in his struggle for gold until excitement disappointed hopes

and unsatisfied ambition or a reckless life leads him to dissipation, the insane asylum or a premature grave.[99]

When the Reverend H. Bellows gave an address at the dedication of San Francisco's Bush Street Grammar School, he placed the need for such a school in the context of combating excitement with discipline:

> And do you know, that just in proportion to the amount of motion, activity, and excitement that stimulates the mind and heart of man, is the necessity of that drill and training which can reduce these powerful instincts of human passion, human desire, human aspirations, and interests, to something like a well-regulated control? The human heart is liable to burst out here in California in strong passion, power, and vitality . . . and it is the duty of schools and churches to harness those tremendous powers . . .[100]

Schools and churches, in Bellows' reform project, stand out against the excitement of the times, attempting to harness its energy for orderly purposes. It was quietness that the critics had to oppose to the excitement of gold, the quietness of a more stable economy, and less fickle patterns of production and consumption.

In George Washington Peck's pseudonymous 1849 novel, *Aurifodina, or, Adventures in the Gold Region*, the narrator, returning from finding gold in California, loses his way and stumbles across a mountain kingdom where gold was a common substance. The superior inhabitants of Aurifodina are described as a 'quiet, orderly people, robust and cheerful, but not given to popular commotions and epidemics'.[101] The prince of Aurifodina is very critical of what he hears of American life. The American people, he decides, value power over beauty, and will spend their lives in labour to gain it, thus denying themselves the repose necessary to enjoy beauty:

> The appetite for power is so absorbing that it consumes all others, and keeps you in a perpetual fever. You will not preserve yourselves in quietness; your constitution is such that none of you can enjoy inward peace until he is lording it over his neighbour. There is the beautiful world lying around you—the same sun that shines here, you tell me, the same air, trees, flowers—there also is within, the inexhaustible delights that spring from the affections, friendship, love, all the sweet charities of life—and in the midst of all this, which with moderate labor you might enjoy, you think only of acquiring new territories and building new cities.[102]

The gold rush merely heightened tendencies already present in American life—the cure, for critics like Peck, was a dose of quietness and repose.

Gold created excitement, which lessened rational control over action. Release of the passions was here an important theme. There was within this discussion a submerged theory of an economy of the passions, which assumed that passionate energies could be spent and exhausted, and that an excessive indulgence of them would debilitate a man, and eventually deprive him of his reason. Excitement, in California too, was thought to drive men mad. 'Life is so fast or intense among us', wrote Thomas Starr King of the Californian insane asylum at Stockton, 'that candidates for its wards multiply at a rate which is not pleasant to contemplate; and the saying that a man is "on the way to Stockton", means that he is spending his nervous capital at a rate that will soon dissolve the co-partnership of Reason and Will'.[103] Gold-rush society itself contributed to this melancholy cycle. The high expectations with which men came to California were seen to give rise to a cycle of destructive emotional excess. Eliza Farnham described this effect:

> One of the most painful results of this excitement, is a frightful amount of insanity, and of desperation, so closely bordering upon it . . . The incessant strain upon the mental powers; the constant torture of the affections . . . the disappointment of hopes; the prostration of plans . . . the absence of repose, and of those restoring influences of home and society, which elsewhere soothe the irritability, and mitigate the weariness, of the commercial and speculating life; all these influences . . . must inevitably result in the frequent dethrone-ment of reason. Only the benignity of nature; only the miraculous climate . . . could save such a country, inhabited by such a people, from becoming a vast mad-house.[104]

As in Victoria, there was speculation in California that the climate was too exciting, and thus conducive to madness. William Scott defended the Californian climate against these claims, arguing that the 'Creator has not made these radiant shores, bright skies and graceful landscapes, to deprive men of their reason'. He had no doubt that the causes of insanity lay rather in 'gambling, novel reading, and the society of abandoned women'.[105]

In California, as in Victoria, there was concern that the rate of insanity was abnormally high. The view persisted through the nineteenth century. Richard Fox reports that, in California, not only were the climate and the prevailing social conditions seen as disturbing, but there was also the 'particularly unsettling shock of rapidly acquiring and losing wealth' to be contended with.[106] Dr Praslow recalled that 'mental diseases' were common among immigrants 'who hoped to be millionaires . . . in a few weeks and were disappointed'.[107] When *Hutchings' California Magazine* visited the Stockton Lunatic Asylum in 1856, it met an inmate who had become enriched at the goldfields, and who, hoping to purchase the island of Madagascar, was writing the laws by which to govern it: a Californian lunatic, preoccupied with the nexus between individual wealth and social order.[108] 'In proportion to the population', opined Bishop Kip: 'insanity is perhaps five times more frequent in California than in any other country. Adventurers come here from every corner of the globe, with extravagant hopes of speedy fortune. When these fail, the restless undisciplined brain is easily upset.' Kip recalled a visit one morning from a miner 'entirely deranged', whose topics of conversation were 'a mixture of religion and mining':

> He had met with something in Job, about 'the vein of gold and silver', and also about 'the island of the innocent', and he wished to find them again. He wanted an explanation of the book of Revelations . . . I said what I could to calm him—advising him to let the prophecies alone, and to confine his reading to the Gospels . . .[109]

Kip was not the only one to recognise in the combination of religion, and the experience or expectation of sudden changes in fortune, the danger of men losing their grip on reason. The reports of the Medical Superintendents of California's Stockton Lunatic Asylum reveal an urgent and critical analysis of the excitement of Californian society. The report presented for the year 1853 described a 'frightful increase' in the number of the insane, and placed the blame squarely upon the excited condition of society:

> It is fearful to contemplate the amount of mental excitement, the violent passions, the ungoverned tempers and continued turmoil prevailing throughout the entire population of the State. These are the agents, which, operating on the brain and its membranes, produce such an amount of mental alienation.

The superintendent listed among the 'moral' causes of insanity:

> long and continued intellectual labor . . . constant and powerful excitement of the mind in the struggle for distinction and honor, for wealth and power . . . the violence of the passions in ungoverned dispositions, when ambition, hope and pride are frustrated—when jealousy and envy, sorrow and despair are exalted or depressed.[110]

As David Rothman has pointed out, ante-bellum asylum superintendents in the United States were offering a comprehensive critique of American life. The lack of fixity and the social mobility which characterised American society seemed to these professionals 'wilfully designed to produce mental illness'.[111] The gloomy diagnosis which most lunacy professionals shared was that it was civilization itself which created insanity. American society could therefore be expected to pay the inevitable price of its progress.[112] Horace Bushnell attributed insanity to 'our American vice' of overdoing things. 'It is as if the man were all momentum and nothing else', he observed critically of the American.[113] In their asylums, the superintendents sought to effect cures by creating artificially a world which really was stable, quiet, and fixed. The California superintendents fit perfectly Rothman's model—warning of the effects of civilization on mental health, effects which California, with its mobility and excitement, seemed to possess to a dangerous degree. So the Stockton report for 1853 pointed out that 'the brightest intellects in the land, men of genius, persons of wealth and education, are more subject to the disease than the poor, the lowly and the ignorant'. The great number of the insane in California, it was made quite clear, arose from the peculiarly advanced and excited character of the population:

> No better evidence of the great mental activity of our people is necessary, for it is a well established physiological fact, that where the greatest degree of mental excitement prevails, there, also, is the greatest amount of insanity. In highly civilized and enlightened communities, in countries which have a great degree of political and religious liberty, there mental diseases are most common.[114]

The report for the next year restated the analysis:

> In the struggle, which is now continually maintained and absolutely necessary to acquire wealth, power or distinction, it requires an immense amount of mental energy, incessant application and the utmost tension of all the faculties. The brain is in perpetual excitement . . . Never since the world was made, has there ever been exhibited such an amount of mental energy, activity and determination. There is no cessation—no rest—no relaxation.[115]

In the tables they produced listing the supposed causes of insanity, Stockton superintendents also evinced their belief in the ability of excitement to create insanity. Between 1851 and 1855, 67 men and women (though the asylum population, like the general population, was overwhelmingly male) were put away because of 'mental excitement' and 22 from 'religious excitement' (spiritualism and Mormonism accounted for a further eighteen), 86 on account of 'pecuniary disappointment' and three from 'political disappointment', while 'intemperance in spirits', that other stimulant, was responsible for the madness of 159.[116]

In 1856 a new Superintendent took over at Stockton, and he claimed in his first report that California had then a rate of insanity less than that of other states. It was true, he admitted, that:

> at first, in the over-strained exercise of daily business and constant exertion— in the fatigue, the loss of sleep, the over-anxiety to become rich, and the anticipations of suddenly accumulating wealth . . . the physical system and nervous energies were expended, and if not exciting, rendering us peculiarly susceptible to diseases of the mind . . .

Those days had passed, he assured the legislature, 'the golden dream is over', strenuous mental exertion was now diminishing in California, and 'may we not hope', he wrote, 'that insanity would also decline'.[117] His hope was perhaps a forlorn one, for there were many in Californian society who were celebrating the very qualities which he had found to be the effective causes of insanity.

In California, then, there was a critical tradition which held that excitement could go too far, that a quiet, agrarian or domestic life held better possibilities for fulfilment. It produced impassioned criticisms of the kind of society gold seemed to be hastening into being. 'Are we not progressing to the end?', wondered Lorena Hays in 1856. 'Will not such rapid development soon bring about a new dispensation—will not the millennial day dawn with its Sabbath peace after this rushing turmoil and strife and active life?'[118]

The critical tradition, though, never achieved dominance. Commentators on gold-rush California were inclined to qualify their criticism, and were much more likely than their Victorian counterparts to argue that a measure of excitement was a necessary constituent of a vigorous national life.

COMING TO TERMS WITH EXCITEMENT

Nathaniel Frothingham, addressing his congregation in the First Church in Boston on the Sunday before Christmas in 1848, took as his theme the subject of 'Gold'. He did so, he said, because of the 'excitement of important discoveries away to the West', then agitating the community. His sermon was full of warnings. He invoked the story of Midas to warn the congregation of the perils of forsaking the 'culture of the earth and the industrious pursuits that are the foundation of all real wealth'. He railed against the individual who 'in the haste to be rich, deserts honest occupations for magical enterprises', and who would 'turn everything in life into mercenary gain'.[119] Wealth, he reminded them, was 'the fruit of human toil and intelligence', it did not consist merely of money—though even this was 'forgotten by the grasping'.[120] Yet there were limits to Frothingham's agrarian doctrines. Money, in its place and properly understood, he reassured his audience, was a legitimate commodity—he did not join in 'that slighting estimate of money, which no one in his sound senses nowadays can pretend without insincerity'. Even a modest accumulation was acceptable, for 'who doubts the privilege or the responsibility of having enough for convenient using, and something to spare?'[121] In condemning the unbridled pursuit of wealth in the individualist mode, even Transcendentalist-connected ministers like Frothingham did not wish to go too far.

Many sermons reflect a complex ambivalence towards wealth and wealth seeking. Their advice to young men headed for the California fields was often contorted and qualified. They warned about the excited and unreflective pursuit of wealth for its own sake, the neglect of all that was really important in life. They conceded that seeking wealth was not in itself a bad thing. When William Ingraham Kip took up his appointment as Episcopal Bishop of California, he was struck by the energetic demeanour of his congregation. 'Everything,' he wrote, 'betokened activity and energy of mind.'[122] This was a mild and approving form of a common description of Californian men. 'Excitement' over gold could be seen in California *both* as a kind of mania, a disruptive, obsessive, destructive pursuit of wealth which could only render it, once attained, almost worthless, *and* as a kind of admirable energy and determination, an example of the spirit which had allowed the United States to spread itself so providentially from ocean to ocean. The *San Francisco Whig* explained in 1852 that for Americans:

'progress' possesses an intensified meaning. In most of the narcotized old world, it is a word simply significant of the lapse of years, the slow and sickly bloating of despot-trammelled states, or their stages of decay. To the American, it is indicative of commonwealths wrested with magic celerity from the dominion of nature; of a commerce clouding with its canvass every sea, pouring its merchandise into every port . . . of liberty allied to rational subordination; of unprecedented intellectual activity and advance.[123]

It was this optimistic interpretation of the excited condition as a part of progress which became the dominant one.

Optimistic eastern observers often took for granted that 'excitement' was the best description of the state of society in California, and assumed like the pessimists that it was a natural American tendency which the gold in California had powerfully exaggerated. The *Democratic Review* linked the response to California gold to a perceived American character, observing in 1849 that: 'The course taken by the excitement is singularly illustrative of the American character . . . which attracts the attention, and awakens the admiration of foreign observers.'[124] Optimistic Californians writing of their society seemed convinced that it was more excited, faster and more intense, than any other society, and that those were positive qualities. 'We live faster than any other people', opined a writer in the San Francisco *Pioneer*: 'We think more promptly; a thousand times more freely than our fathers of the east and of Europe. Our passions are stronger; our intellects keener; our prejudices weaker . . . we give our passionate energies full scope in carrying out their impulses'.[125] The authors of the *Annals of San Francisco*, an 1856 city-boosting chronicle, wrote with similar enthusiasm of the energies of 'the ever plotting, restless and "wide awake" people of San Francisco'.[126]

Many Californian social critics found excitement to be socially beneficial. 'There is joy in action, in enterprise, in aggression, in minor achievement, in subduing nature, in self-conquest', wrote J.A. Benton in California. Benton took on and rejected the pastoral language of retreat and asylum, revealing though his familiarity with its characteristic premises:

It pains us to see a man of fine genius, noble talents, and vast knowledge, dwelling secluded in some wooded vale, passing his time in indolence, and letting his powers run to waste, because the rough atmosphere of active life chills him, and the noise and stir of the busy world jar his sensibilities, and toil and strife irk him. He is out of place. The world has need of him.[127]

California was not to be a refuge from the world, for an energetic Christian like Benton, but rather a new scene of struggle.

Excitement was often given a specifically commercial meaning, which those optimistic about the market could approve. When Mr Crosby was arguing to the California Senate in 1850 for the virtues of common over civil law, he contrasted the excited activity which the Anglo common law invoked to the lethargy which the civil code ensured:

> In the one, you perceive the activity, the throng, the tumult of business life—in the other, the stagnation of an inconsiderable and waning trade; in the one, the boldness, the impetuosity, the invention of advancing knowledge and civilization—in the other, feebleness of intellect, timidity of spirit, and the crouching subserviency of slaves; in the one, the strength and freshness of manhood—in the other, the weakness of incipient decay. The one possesses a progressive and reforming nature—the other partakes of quietude and repose . . .[128]

Here, as so often, the bustle and progress of American commerce was contrasted with the backward-looking quietness which was 'the spirit of the past'.

One of the symptoms of excitement was the 'spirit of speculation', which could be condemned as gambling, but was often praised as enterprise. The *Western Journal*, from Cincinnatti, thought that the first influx of gold into California markets would:

> doubtless incite a spirit of speculation; and we have more to apprehend from this than from any thing else connected with the discovery; but this is an evil that cures itself in time, and though much to be deprecated, is not altogether void of good; for a spirit of speculation frequently prompts men to undertake enterprises that might otherwise have slumbered for ages.[129]

In California it was not only commerce which was seen to flourish in an excited society. In 1859, the President of the California State Agricultural Society, defending the quickening pace of life which resulted from the progress of the world, argued in his annual address to the society that:

> Now, as formerly, the human mind needs excitement—a stimulus to incite and keep up an interest in any great work. We tire of the routine labor and the routine harvest. It is not enough to receive into our granaries and partake around our own board of the bountiful gifts of our mother-earth, however rich and tempting . . .[130]

This was heresy in terms of agrarian ideology. Agrarians posited quietness as the necessary context of human happiness—yet here was a spokesman for the agricultural interest advocating the stimulus of excitement. This defence of excitement marks one of the important lines of difference between Californian and Victorian ideologies.

Some Californian writers defended 'enthusiasm', as a productive form of excitement: 'Enthusiasm! There is magic in the word. It is the great moving cause of all that is great and noble in human actions. It is enthusiasm that leads men to great and heroic deeds; it is that which impels to great efforts and great sacrifices.'[131] Ministers of religion took up the open defence of excitement as a force in social life. 'Man is a creature of impulses', the Reverend J.H. Avery told a party in Ohio about to proceed to the Californian fields:

> He loves excitement, and it is proper he should have it. It is that by means of which all efforts, physical, intellectual and moral, are accomplished . . . It is the *elixir vitae* and it is a benevolent arrangement of Providence, that man should love that, and seek that which is the instrument of so much good.

Avery's address was a protracted defence of the exciting features of life, that the party of men before him might expect to meet in California. He asked them to imagine a life without excitement:

> Without stimulus, the mind falls back upon itself, and settles into a torpid, lifeless state, like stagnant pools, whose poisonous exhalations fill the atmosphere with death. Did you ever see a man who had no aim, no plan, no purpose of life, who floated upon the bosom of society as dead bodies upon the face of the waters? Did you discern upon his brow the glow of health, or in his eye the gleam of heartfelt joy, or in his buoyant step, the evidence of undying, indomitable energy of purpose? And why not? He acts under no excitement. No stimulating motives impel him to effort. He acts rather that he may enjoy the rest consequent thereon, than because he is filled with purposes of noble daring.[132]

Sylvester Woodbridge, preaching at the dedication of the First Presbyterian church at Benicia, California, praised what he called the 'restless spirit of the race': 'Where did it ever show itself stronger than in the multitudes that have swarmed, and will again speedily swarm, from the parent hive, and by mountain, plain, or ocean, find their way to this El Dorado.'[133]

One of the most concerted defences of excitement came in a series of lectures given by the Reverend William Anderson Scott to the San Francisco Mercantile Library Association in 1856. Scott embarked, before his undoubtedly sympathetic audience, upon a major defence of commerce and commercial excitement, and the urban environment in which both prospered. 'Mental efforts,' he argued, 'are usually put forth either by high excitement or for large rewards of money. Both of these are found in cities.'[134] Excitement presented few dangers in Scott's philosophy. His was the pure liberal belief in the inevitably beneficent outcome of unfettered market activity and social ferment:

> The restlessness of our time, and the fierceness of party strife—even the murmurings of one nation against another, is evidence of healthful activity.

Where there is no life, there will be no movement. The strugglings and overactings of some portions of modern society, is evidence of the depths of its breathings . . .[135]

Scott explicitly condemned quietness as a social goal:

It is only under a despotism that men can neither move nor mutter. It is under such a government that all public feeling and popular intelligence are smothered to death, and the people are left sitting, *quietly*, it may be, but it is the quietness of dejection, the sullenness of despair, and the lethargy of death.[136]

Motion and activity were signs of life in this way of thinking—excitement was almost always good. Scott's defence of excitement here was the more striking in that elsewhere he recognised the destructive possibilities of other kinds of excitement. The excitement aroused by gambling, he observed on another occasion, left men 'exhausted, nervous and unhappy'.[137] It was Edward Pillock writing in the San Francisco *Pioneer* who put the defence of excitement most eloquently. Perfection, he argued, was unattainable in human affairs—it was the pursuit of it which mattered: 'Perfection infers the subjugation of all passion, the removal of all necessity for exertion, of all motive to labor. It supposes an existence of quietude—of perfect rest. A state of such a nature would differ in nothing but name from annihilation.'[138] For this confident modern liberal, quietness signifies only death, not the highest ambition of social life. It is in relation to this question that the difference between California and Victoria seems sharpest.

The Reverend William Scott was always one of the most articulate defenders of the pursuit of wealth in California. 'In many respects,' he maintained, 'a man has more reasons to love money in this country than in any other.' 'Repeatedly has it been declared from this pulpit', he justly observed, 'that true religion is not a declaration of war against wealth, refinement or elegance of taste and manners. Repeatedly have we shown that riches are in themselves blessings. Money is a good thing. A man may be very rich, and yet be a saint.'[139] Scott condemned 'the complete devotion of the heart to money', but, as befitted one of his belief that 'modern civilization owes its extension to commercial enterprise', he argued that it was only the manner of wealth seeking that needed to be watched, for the activity itself was undoubtedly praiseworthy. Commerce he regarded as 'one of Heaven's . . . agencies for overcoming the barbarism of the savage, and for elevating the moral feelings of the civilized.' And wealth itself, once obtained, he argued, had 'a tendency to improve the general health and prolong the mean duration of human life'.

Some ministers engaged in explicit defences of the legitimacy of gold seeking as an activity. 'The seeking for gold is as legitimate and laudable an object as the seeking for any thing else', the Reverend Charles Farley assured his congregation. 'It is in fact the indispensable condition upon which . . . depends the civilization and Christianization of the world. All our social life, our commerce, education, religion, involves the necessity of seeking for money.'[140] The *Western Journal* also explicitly defended gold seeking:

> we are not prepared to admit that poverty and immorality are necessary consequences of mining for gold. The principle involved in the use of money may be regarded as essential to a state of civilisation; and it is difficult to conceive how man could have emerged from a state of barbarism, without its use . . .[141]

The *Democratic Review* offered a similar account of the motive force of history, arguing that: 'The lust of gold has been in all ages the chief incentive to daring enterprises, and the most magnificent of these was the attempt to discover a new world, supposed to abound in the desired object.'[142]

In California, then, while there was an important critical tradition which opposed itself to excitement in the name of the home, the landscape or the farm, there was also a vigorous strand of social thought, emanating often from the Protestant clergy, which offered qualified defences of excitement. Connections existed between endorsement of excitement, acceptance of the market as prime determinant of social life, and confidence that a population of ethically diverse wealth seekers could be governed. Acceptance of the place of excitement in society led to endorsement of the liberal, individualist, capitalist outlook that historians of nineteenth-century America now see to have been everywhere in battle for dominance with a receding republican tradition. The market had long been understood to be fickle—Adam Smith had acknowledged that, as had Thomas Jefferson when he wrote of the 'casualties and caprice of customers'.[143] Fickleness inevitably created excitement, for men could not count on the steady and predictable rewards of, for example, agricultural activity, but instead gambled on big profits and risked big losses. Gold mining, within these terms, was understood to be an extremely speculative and market-oriented activity. The rewards were uncertain, as in gambling, and the product useful not for itself, but only for exchange. In California, many were prepared to argue that these activities and emotions were a suitable basis for a social order that was progressive and dynamic.

The discussion of excitement in Victoria and California brings together many of the key themes of the response to the gold rushes. The metaphors of quietness and excitement enabled many nineteenth-century Victorians and Californians to discuss the kind of life they desired and the kind of society in which they wanted to live. They provide a small insight into the emotional history of modernity, and illustrate one of the ways in which some of the qualities of social change could be conceptualised and argued over. The gold rushes, with their riot of market forces, provided an occasion for such argument. Should gold-rush society be allowed to develop as it would? Or ought it be directed and controlled? Those proponents of laissez faire who argued that excitement should be left to take its course were the optimists about gold-rush society. They saw in excitement many enlivening and expansive possibilities, a bustling and purposeful future. Those opponents of laissez faire who argued that excitement had to be vigorously opposed, by various kinds of reform activity, were the pessimists about gold-rush society. They saw in excitement only dislocation and cruelty, a society characterised by an absence of the ties of dependence and love. They advocated quietness and a settled life as the best context for human happiness. We argue about these questions still, though in rather different languages. There were differences in the emphases of the answers found in California and Victoria, but here I have been stressing the shared questions, the shared vocabularies of social argument—the participation of these two societies in that larger British history, much of which still remains to be written.

CONCLUSION

When S. Mulliken proposed a toast at the American Fourth of July banquet in Melbourne in 1856, he expressed a hope that the future Australian nation would combine 'American tact, industry, and energy, with English prudence, sagacity and judgement'.[1] The stereotypes would be more or less recognisable today. Academic taking apart of the category of the nation has to come to terms with the real existence of national stereotyping and caricature which lives all around us. The issue is of course not whether the Italians are 'really' flamboyant and the Germans 'truly' diligent, but how these characterisations operate, how they are sustained, and what work they do. The differences discussed in this book were not the product of innate character differences between Australian and American peoples— such arguments are especially implausible in these recently constituted immigrant societies. Rather, the discursive strategies pursued become themselves constitutive of identity. That is why we need to pay careful attention to those moments when these national narratives were being constructed. We need to study their ingredients and their competitors, not merely repeat them. Approached in this way, the constitution of national difference will remain an intellectually respectable subject of historical inquiry—a subject too important to be left entirely to journalists and comedians.

To an Australian, the United States is a strange culture made from some very familiar ingredients. Different connections are made in arguments, novel conclusions drawn from familiar premises. To study differences between the societies need not be, though, to resurrect the categories of 'Americanness' and 'Australianness' as somehow explanatory of themselves. Homogeneous descriptions of nations have historically often been exclusivist, ways of defining out the challengers and the powerless as culturally marginal ('un-American'). Nations are sites of difference and conflict as much as they are of similitude and harmony. The comparativist is probably more likely than other historians to posit homogeneous national traditions, in struggling to say something about more than one society. Only so much difference can be accommodated within a conventional historical narrative—when contrasting apples and oranges we spend less time on differences between apples than we otherwise might. The close connection between the consensus historiography of the 1950s and the comparativist project has often been noted.[2] Social history since the 1960s has taken apart the large categories—'Americans', 'Australians'—and made us constantly aware of the ways in which race, class and gender intersect and fragment national categories.

By the 1980s, this fragmentation had been added to by some of the deconstructive currents of thought in intellectual and cultural history, and by the happy pluralism of postmodernism.[3] A slew of books on the nation described the ways in which it was a recent invention, a fiction which was imagined or invented by those with power.[4] Conservative alarm grew—where was the possibility in all this of a national history? And without a national history, whence would come the national virtues of pride and patriotism? Radicals too were often unhappy that the historian's final word should be the mere acknowledgment of diversity, for where was the possibility in this of larger explanation? The problem now is how the national can be recuperated as an historiographical category in a way which recognises difference at home but still allows space for discussion of transnational themes and international comparisons. My answer here has been to study the construction of national themes from transnational materials.

In looking at the cultural resources of these two societies facing similar disruptive events, both the commonalities and the distinctive mix of common ingredients are revealed. The gold seekers were harbingers of modernity, and one had to be rather modern in 1850 to be untroubled by the world they seemed to foreshadow, to be sure that a society dominated by self-interested, wealth-seeking men would be worth living in. That is what has since easily been forgotten. The critics of gold, turning older discourses to unfamiliar uses, were no less creative in their thought than the theorists of liberal modernity. When Victorians and Californians came to argue against the gold rush, they made selections from the cultural resources available to them. The selections were made in the context of specific debates and particular local needs, but the choices made had implications, and local traditions developed.

The dislocations of the gold rush were symptomatic because they resembled the dislocations of modernity. The astuteness of the critics I have discussed in this book lay in seeing that and in adapting some familiar arguments to this new event. Gold-rush society raised deep questions for those who observed it, about the nature of the good life. The chapters of this book have laid out these questions, and some of the answers that were ventured in 1850s Victoria and California. Were the liberal individualists right when they argued that out of all the individual wealth seeking would come a self-governed society? Or was there, as republican thought suggested, a social danger in the general spread of wealth? Were more government and more improving and surveying institutions the answer to a society characterised by great mobility and unsettledness, as prominent Victorians tended to argue? Or were they quite useless, as their Californian counterparts were likely to maintain, without a virtuous population? Was the steady improvement of the land in agriculture, and the settled life that went with it, the best panacea for a society characterised by haste and waste? Was a society in which men predominated likely to be always critically out of balance, distant from the values of the hearth and home? Did madness loom for those who followed the injunction of the age to seek their own fortunes before all else? Was it haste and wealth and excitement that made people happy, or was it rather peace and quiet and asylum from the troubles of the world? The very oppositions were constituted by the critical responses to capitalism, with their secularising of older oppositions between the world and something better.

These were profound discussions. We tend not to recognise them as such, because we miss the key terms of the debate, fail to *see* debate in the writings of the time. These questions, and the particular answers to them that were found in Victoria and California, have not been well remembered, have not formed a part of the popular or historical memory of gold. That was in part because they were arguments which came from the metropolises of the day—Britain and the eastern United States. It was also in part because these old-fashioned arguments receded further as the nineteenth century progressed. Arguments from agrarianism or domesticity would continue to be put against the development of a capitalist society, with its mobility and individual pursuit of wealth, but they would become less and less central, more clearly recognisable as fantasy. We tend to think of the cultural and intellectual life of these frontier societies as derivative because they cast up few major original social thinkers. But their skill lay in adaptation rather than innovation—or rather, there comes a point at which adaptation *is* innovation. Seeing the relevance of familiar metropolitan discourses to novel situations, turning the hopeful arguments of reformers at home to account in the New World—these were creative activities. Historians of Australia and the western United States used to write of adaptation as though it meant abandoning old ideas once they had been shown to be of no use against the brute realities of the frontier—they continually celebrated the triumph of pragmatic frontier informality over metropolitan decorum, the gradual adoption of clothing, housing, diet, even ways of painting and writing, more suitable to the new conditions. But the earlier settlers' attachment to modes of understanding they had brought with them was not mere stubbornness or stupidity, a refusal to see what was plainly in front of them. To debate the relationship of the morality of the population to the achievement of order, to understand the gold rush as interrupting an idyllic agrarian scene, to bring contemporary gender theory to the analysis of frontier society, to perceive the dangers that sustained excitement might pose to fervent hopes for a tranquil new world, to see in the outbreak of self-interest that was gold seeking a testing of the theories of the political economists and perhaps a glimpse of the future—these were collectively sustained acts of insight and interpretation that we should not retrospectively belittle, especially as so much of our own intellectual activity takes similar form—spotting the relevance of the latest metropolitan ideas to a local world we know so well yet desperately need to contextualise, to stand back from, in order to glimpse a larger picture.

ENDNOTES

INTRODUCTION

1 Rodman W. Paul, *California Gold—The Beginning of Mining in the Far West* (Cambridge, Mass., 1947), p.25; Carl J. Mayer and George A. Riley, *Public Domain, Private Dominion* (San Francisco: Sierra Club, 1985), p.56.

2 'That abrupt, tragic decrease was a consequence of the gold rush: disease, starvation, homicide, and a declining birthrate for native people took a heavy toll.' Albert Hurtado, *Indian Survival on the California Frontier* (New Haven: Yale University Press, 1988), pp.1, 213.

3 Geoffrey Serle, *The Golden Age: A History of the Colony of Victoria 1851–1861* (Melbourne: Melbourne University Press, 1963), pp.2–3; M.F. Christie, *Aborigines in Colonial Victoria 1835–86* (Sydney: Sydney University Press, 1979), p.78. Estimates of the pre-contact population in Victoria have ranged from 5000 to Butlin's estimates of between 50 000 and 100 000: see Diane E. Barwick, 'Changes in the Aboriginal Population of Victoria, 1863–1966', in D.J. Mulvaney and J. Golson, eds, *Aboriginal Man and Environment in Australia* (Canberra: Australian National University Press, 1971), pp.288–315; N.G. Butlin, *Our Original Aggression: Aboriginal Populations of Southeastern Australia 1788–1850* (Sydney: Allen & Unwin, 1983), p.144.

4 Centenary publications included *Historical Studies: Eureka Supplement* (Melbourne: Melbourne University Press, 1954), and E.A. Doyle, ed., *The Golden Years 1851–1951: Published by the Victorian Government to Celebrate the Centenary of the Discovery of Gold in Victoria* (Melbourne: Victorian Government, 1951).

5 But the reconstructed fields at Sovereign Hill are, as Davison observes, 'necessarily quieter, cleaner and more orderly' than the original: Graeme Davison, 'The Use and Abuse of Australian History', *Australian Historical Studies* 23, no.91, Oct. 1988: p.72. See also Michael Evans, 'Historical Interpretation at Sovereign Hill', in *Australian Historical Studies* 24, no.96, April 1991: pp.142–52.

6 *Dreams of a Golden Harvest: Gold Seekers in Victoria. An Exhibition in the Irving Benson Hall, La Trobe Library* (Melbourne: State Library of Victoria, 1982).

7 John Molony, *Eureka* (Ringwood, Vic.: Penguin, 1984), pp.9, 19.

8 C.M.H. Clark, *A History of Australia* vol.4 (Melbourne: Melbourne University Press, 1978), p.13.

9 P. Just, *Australia, or notes taken during a residence in the Colonies from the Gold Discovery in 1851 till 1857* (Dundee: Durham and Thomson, 1859), p.46.

10   E. Gould Buffum, *The Gold Rush: An Account of Six Months in the California Diggings* [1850] (London: Folio Society, 1959), p.125.

11   Chas. R. Thatcher, *Thatcher's Colonial Songster* (Melbourne: Charlwood, 1857), p.7.

12   Patricia Nelson Limerick, *The Legacy of Conquest: The Unbroken Past of the American West* (New York: Norton, 1987), p.239.

13   John R. Umbeck, *A Theory of Property Rights, with Application to the California Gold Rush* (Ames: Iowa State University Press, 1981), p.71, quoting the *California Civil Practice Act*, 1851, Section 621.

14   *The Fremont Decision. Decision of the Supreme Court of the State of California in the Case of Biddle Boggs vs Merced Mining Company* (San Francisco: Royal P. Locke, 1859), pp.25, 29.

15   Umbeck, *A Theory of Property Rights*, p.72.

16   Joseph Ellison, 'The Mineral Land Question in California, 1848–1866', in Vernon Carstensen, ed., *The Public Lands: Studies in the History of the Public Domain* (Madison: University of Wisconsin Press, 1963), pp.73–7, 87.

17   Geoffrey Blainey, 'The Gold Rushes: The Year of Decision', *Historical Studies* 10, no.38, May 1962, pp.136–7. cf. T.H. Irving and Carol Liston, 'State intervention and equality: administration in the New South Wales goldfields 1851–1853', in J.J. Eddy and J.R. Nethercote, eds, *From Colony to Coloniser: Studies in Australian Administrative History* (Sydney: Hale and Iremonger, 1987), p.108, who accept the erroneous advice given to the NSW government that a Californian licence system was in place in 1851.

18   'Report from the Select Committee of the Legislative Council on Gold Mining on Private Property', in Victoria Parliament, *Votes and Proceedings of the Victorian Legislative Council 1856/57* (Melbourne, 1856), p.4.

19   G. Blainey, *The Rush that Never Ended: A History of Australian Mining* 2nd edn (Melbourne: Melbourne University Press, 1969), p.42.

20   Victoria, after the Eureka rebellion in 1854, was to get miners' courts on the Californian model, in which panels of miners settled disputes. In California a formal legal system quickly developed, but it recognised the customs of the miners' courts as law: see Theodore Grivas, *Military Governments in California 1846–1850* (Glendale, Calif.: A.H. Clark Co., 1963), p.133.

21   Limerick, *The Legacy of Conquest*, p.66.

22   Letter, William Walker, Sacramento, 13/3/1853, in Eri S. Hulpert and William Walker, *Land of Gold: An Ill-Fated Journey to California*, Bancroft Library ms.

23   Daniel T. Rodgers, *The Work Ethic in Industrial America 1850–1920* (Chicago: University of Chicago Press, 1978), p.xi.

24   Edward Stone Parker, *The Aborigines of Australia: A Lecture Delivered in the Mechanics Hall Melbourne* (Melbourne: Hugh McColl, 1854), p.5.

25   *Argus*, 2 July 1851.

26   'The Aborigines', *Illustrated Australian Magazine* 3 (1851): p.50.

27   George M. Chalwill, *An Address Delivered Before Morning Star Temple of Honor* (San Francisco: Whitton, Towne, 1854), pp.6–7.

28   *Report of the Select Committee of the Legislative Council on the Aborigines* in

Victoria Parliament, *Votes and Proceedings of the Legislative Council 1858–59*, pp.44–5.

29 See Henry Reynolds, *Frontier: Aborigines, settlers and land* (Sydney: Allen & Unwin, 1987), ch.7 for a discussion of this theme.

30 *Argus*, 10 Aug 1857.

31 Henry David Thoreau, 'Life Without Principle', in *The Writings of Henry David Thoreau*, vol. iv, (Boston: Houghton, Mifflin, 1906), p.463.

32 *Church of England Messenger* 1 (1854): p.232.

33 Eliza Farnham, *California, Indoors and Out; or How we Farm, Mine, and Live Generally in the Golden State* (New York: Dix, Edwards, 1856), pp.368–9.

34 'The Gold Mania', *Illustrated Australian Magazine* 2, no.12, June 1851: p.374.

35 Pakington to La Trobe, 2 June 1852, Despatches from the Secretary of State, VPRS 1087, Victorian Public Record Office.

36 John Ruskin, 'Essays on Political Economy', *Fraser's Magazine* 65, no.390, June 1862: pp.788–90.

37 Karl Marx, *Capital* (Moscow, n.d.), p.133.

38 George Shephard and S.L. Caldwell, *Addresses of Rev. Professor George Shephard and Rev. S.L. Caldwell* (Bangor, Maine: Smith and Sayward, 1849), p.4.

39 J.G.A. Pocock, *The Machiavellian Moment: Florentine Political Thought and the Atlantic Republican Tradition* (Princeton: Princeton University Press, 1975), p.548.

40 Franklin Langworthy, *Scenery of the Plains, Mountains and Mines: Or, a Diary kept upon the Overland Route to California* (Ogdensburgh, Ohio: J. C. Sprague, 1855), p.199.

41 California's rush happened first, of course, and that was also sometimes important—Victorians always had the example of California before them.

42 Ray Billington, *The Far Western Frontier 1830–1860* (New York: Harper, 1956), p.235; Russel Ward, *The Australian Legend* (Melbourne: Oxford University Press, 1958). See also, H.C. Allen, *Bush and Backwoods: A Comparison of the Frontier in Australia and the United States* (East Lansing: Michigan State University Press, 1959) for arguments, influenced by Ward, about the differences between the Australian and American frontiers. Fred Alexander, *Moving Frontiers: An American Theme and its Application to Australian History* (Melbourne: Melbourne University Press, 1947) was an earlier exercise in this vein. The historiography on comparative frontiers is now substantial: see Dietrich Gerhard, 'The Frontier in Comparative View', *Comparative Studies in Society and History* 1 (1959): pp.205–29; Paul Sharp, 'Three Frontiers: Some Comparative Studies of Canadian, American and Australian Settlement', *Pacific Historical Review* 24. (1955): pp.369–77; W. Turrentine Jackson, 'A Brief Message for the Young and/or Ambitious: Comparative Frontiers as a Field for Investigation', *Western Historical Quarterly* 9, no.1, Jan. 1978: pp.5–18; Morris W. Wills, 'Sequential Frontiers: The Californian and Victorian Experience, 1850–1900', *Western Historical Quarterly* 9, no. 4, Oct. 1978: pp.483–94; David Harry Miller and Jerome O. Steffen, eds, *The Frontier: Comparative Studies* (Norman: University of Oklahoma Press, 1977); Jerome O. Steffen, ed., *The American West: New Perspectives, New Dimensions*

(Norman: University of Oklahoma Press, 1979); Jerome O. Steffen, *Comparative Frontiers: A Proposal for Studying the American West* (Norman: University of Oklahoma Press, 1980); Robin W. Winks, *The Myth of the American Frontier: Its Relevance to America, Canada and Australia* (Leicester, 1971); Howard Lamar and Leonard Thompson, eds, *The Frontier as History: North America and Southern Africa Compared* (New Haven: Yale University Press, 1981), with its important stress on the frontier as a meeting place of two societies.

43   Peter Decker, *Fortunes and Failures: White Collar Mobility in Nineteenth-Century San Francisco* (Cambridge, Mass.: Harvard University Press, 1978), p.256; Ralph Mann, *After the Gold Rush: Society in Grass Valley and Nevada City, California, 1849–1870* (Stanford: Stanford University Press, 1982), p.1; Graeme Davison, *The Rise and Fall of Marvellous Melbourne* (Melbourne: Melbourne University Press, 1978); Weston Bate, *Lucky City: Ballarat* (Melbourne: Melbourne University Press, 1978).

44   Donald Worster, 'Beyond the Agrarian Myth', in Patricia Nelson Limerick, Clyde A. Milner and Charles E. Rankin, eds, *Trails: Towards a New Western History* (Lawrence: University Press of Kansas, 1991), p.18.

45   Limerick, *The Legacy of Conquest*, pp. 269, 291; Steffen, *Comparative Frontiers*. See also Annette Kolodny, 'Letting Go of Our Magnificent Obsessions: Notes Toward a New Literary History of the American Frontiers', *American Literature* 64, no.1, March 1992, pp.1–18.

46   Bernard Bailyn, *The Peopling of British North America: An Introduction* (New York: Vintage Books, 1986), p.113.

47   *San Francisco Whig* 1, no.6, Sept. 1852: p.2.

48   *San Francisco Whig* 1, no.10, 1 Jan. 1853: p.1.

49   Speech at banquet for Chrystal Palace exhibition, reported in *Household Words* no.3, 13 April 1850, p.68.

50   *Warrnambool Examiner*, 28 May 1858.

51   Jay Monaghan, *Australians and the Gold Rush* (Berkeley: University of California Press, 1966), p.154.

52   Susan Townsend, letter, 12 June 1851. Bancroft Library ms.

53   *Household Narrative* (April 1850), in clippings collection, Bancroft Library.

54   Frances Perry, wife of the Anglican Archbishop of Melbourne, wrote in her diary in 1851 on the subject of gold, 'that hateful, fearful, baneful subject. All wise and good men look with great alarm on this new feature in our history, and California, with all its horrors, is held forth to our view; but I trust we shall mercifully be preserved from such a state of things as exists there.' A. de Q. Robin, ed., *Australian Sketches: The Journals and Letters of Frances Perry* (Melbourne: Queensberry Hill Press, 1984), p.155.

55   'Unfortunately, the body of work that qualifies as comparative history in the strict sense is characterised both by its relative sparseness and by its fragmentation' George M. Fredrickson, 'Comparative History', in Michael Kammen, ed., *The Past Before Us: Contemporary Historical Writing in the United States* (Ithaca: Cornell University Press, 1980), p.459.

56   Ibid., p.217.

57 C. Vann Woodward, ed., *The Comparative Approach to American History* (New York: Basic Books, 1968), p.xi.

58 Ian Tyrrell, 'American Exceptionalism in an Age of International History', *American Historical Review* 96, no.4, Oct. 1991, pp.1035–8.

59 David Thelen, 'Of Audiences, Borderlands, and Comparisons: Towards the Internationalization of American History', *Journal of American History* 79, no.2, Sept. 1992, p.436.

60 See e.g., Donald Denoon, *Settler Capitalism: The dynamics of dependent development in the Southern Hemisphere* (Oxford: Oxford University Press, 1983.

61 John Higham, 'Paleface and Redskin in American Historiography: A Comment', *Journal of Interdisciplinary History* 16, no.1, summer 1985: p.113.

62 See e.g. Jo Ann Levy, *They Saw The Elephant —Women in The California Gold Rush* (Norman: University of Oklahoma Press, 1992).

63 W.A. Scott, *A Lecture on the Influence of Great Cities* (San Francisco: Whitton, Towne and Co., 1854), p.12.

CHAPTER 1

1 Henry Mayer, ed., *Marx, Engels and Australia* (Melbourne: Cheshire, 1964), p.104; James Ward, *A History of Gold as a Commodity and as a Measure of Value. Its Fluctuations both in Ancient and Modern Times, with an Estimate of the Probable Supplies from California and Australia* (London: W.S. Orr, 1852), p.9; 'California', *The American Review: A Whig Journal*, April 1849: p.331; Eliza Farnham, *California Indoors and Out*, p.329; Thomas a'Beckett, 'The Gold Mania', *Illustrated Australian Magazine* 2, no.12, June 1851: p.380; *Times*, 7 July 1852, p.7; Prof. W. Beschke, *The Dreadful Suffering and Thrilling Adventures of an Overland Party of Emigrants to California: their terrible conflicts! with savage tribes of Indians!! and Mexican bands of robbers!!!* (St Louis, Mo., 1850).

2 Mayer and Riley, *Public Domain, Private Dominion*, p.56; Ralph Raven [George Payson], *Golden Dreams and Leaden Realities* (New York: G.P. Putnam, 1853), p.5.

3 See for Victoria, Tom Griffiths, 'Country Towns', in Graeme Davison and Chris McConville, eds, *A Heritage Handbook* (Sydney: Allen & Unwin, 1991), pp.142–60, and his *Beechworth: An Australian Country Town and its Past* (Melbourne: Greenhouse, 1987).

4 'Old Forty-Nine', *Hutchings' California Magazine* 1, no.4, Oct. 1856: p.170.

5 See Gunther Barth, *Instant Cities: Urbanisation and the Rise of San Francisco and Denver* (New York: Oxford University Press, 1975), pp.159–60.

6 John S. Hittell, *Marshall's Gold Discovery: A Lecture Delivered before the Society of California Pioneers* (San Francisco: B.F. Sterrett, 1893), p.4.

7 Earl Pomeroy, 'California's Legacies from the Pioneers', in George H. Knoles, ed., *Essays and Assays: California History Reappraised* (San Francisco: California Historical Society, 1973), p.81.

8 Henry Childs Merwin, *The Life of Bret Harte, with Some Account of the California Pioneers* (London: Chatto and Windus, 1912), p.55–6.

9   *Alta California*, 3 Jan. 1851; *Alta California*, 5 Jan. 1851; Mark Twain, *Roughing It* (Signet: New York, 1980), p.309.

10 Henry J. W. Dam, 'A Morning with Bret Harte', *McLure's Magazine* (Dec. 1894), in *Bret Harte: Gold Rush Storyteller* (Oakland, 1986), p.3. As a younger man Harte had been more sceptical about the self-promotion of the Pioneers—'the less said about the motives of some of our pioneers the better'. Garry Scharnhorst, ed., *Bret Harte's California: Letters to the Springfield Republican and Christian Register, 1866–67* (Albuquerque: University of New Mexico Press, 1990), p.88.

11 Kevin Starr, *Americans and the California Dream 1850–1945* (New York: Oxford University Press, 1973) p.156.

12 Merwin, *The Life of Bret Harte*, p.157.

13 Kim Newman, *Wild West Movies* (London: Bloomsbury, 1990), pp.18–19.

14 Robert W. Broomall, *California Kingdoms* (New York: Fawcett, 1992).

15 Charles Thatcher, 'Two Years Ago', sheet.

16 W.E. Adcock, *The Gold Rushes of the Fifties* (Melbourne: E.W. Cole, 1912), pp.7–9; On colonial 'period' films, see Susan Dermody and Elizabeth Jacka, *The Screening of Australia: Anatomy of a National Cinema Vol.2* (Sydney: Currency Press, 1988), pp.31–4.

17 Michael Wilding, ed., *Portable Australian Authors: Marcus Clarke* (St Lucia: University of Queensland Press, 1976), p.638; Colin Roderick, ed., *Henry Lawson: The Master Story Teller: Prose Writings* (Sydney: Angus and Robertson, 1984), p.733; Ibid., p.793; Henry Lawson, 'An Old Mate of Your Father's' (1893).

18 Edward Dyson, 'To the Men of the Mines', in *Rhymes from the Mines and Other Lines* (Sydney: Angus and Robertson, 1896), p. 7.

19 'Stop and See', in *Rhymes from the Mines*, p.64.

20 *The Australian National Dictionary* (Melbourne: Oxford University Press, 1988), p.390.

21 Mrs W. May Howell, *Reminiscences of Australia: The Diggings and the Bush* (London, 1869), p.8.

22 Rolf Boldrewood, *The Miner's Right: A Tale of the Australian Goldfields* (Sydney: Sydney University Press, 1973), pp.67–70.

23 Henry Handel Richardson, *The Fortunes of Richard Mahony* (Harmondsworth: Penguin, 1986), p.13.

24 See John Walton Caughey, *Gold is the Cornerstone* (Berkeley: University of California Press, 1947). The historiography of the California gold rush is extensive. There are many narrative accounts, beginning with the nineteenth-century works of H.H. Bancroft and Theodore Hittell, and including mid-twentieth-century works such as Paul, *California Gold*; Caughey, *Gold is the Cornerstone*; and William H. Ellison, *A Self-Governing Dominion: California, 1849–1860* (Berkeley: University of California Press, 1950). Recently, social historians have begun a more critical evaluation of the period, see e.g., Mann, *After the Gold Rush*; Decker, *Fortunes and Failures*; R.A. Burchell, *The San Francisco Irish, 1848–1880* (Berkeley: University of California Press, 1980). Starr, *Americans and the California Dream* is a rather descriptive cultural history; Roger Lotchin, *San Francisco, 1846–56: from Hamlet to City*

(New York: Oxford University Press, 1974) and Barth, *Instant Cities*, deal with San Francisco from an urban history perspective.

For the Victorian gold rush, there are nineteenth-century histories by G.W. Rusden, H.G. Turner, T. McCombie and others, and several treatments in the general histories of the early and mid-twentieth century. The outstanding work, though, is Serle, *The Golden Age*: still enormously impressive in its scope and surety. See also, Geoffrey Blainey, *The Rush that Never Ended* (Melbourne: Melbourne University Press, 1963), and Weston Bate, *Lucky City: The First Generation at Ballarat 1851–1901* (Melbourne: Melbourne University Press, 1978), and his survey, *The Victorian Gold Rushes* (Melbourne: McPhee Gribble, 1988) which emphasises the urban and town-building context.

25 Billington, *The Far Western Frontier*, p.218.

26 Serle, *The Golden Age*, p.369.

27 W.K. Hancock, *Australia* (London: 1930), pp.35–6.

28 G.V. Portus, 'The Gold Discoveries', in Ernest Scott, ed, *Australia* vol. VII, part I, *Cambridge History of the British Empire* (Cambridge: Cambridge University Press, 1933), pp.270–1; W.P. Morrell, *The Gold Rushes* (London: A. and L. Black, 1940), p.415; Serle, *The Golden Age*, p.47.

29 Russel Ward, *Australia since the coming of man* (Melbourne: Macmillan, 1987), p.117.

30 Serle, *The Golden Age*, pp.373–4; ibid. pp.92–3; Ward, *The Australian Legend*, p.117; Bate, *Victorian Gold Rushes*, p.40.

31 Starr, *Americans and the California Dream*, pp.65–6.

32 Mann, *After the Gold Rush*, p.1.

33 Lotchin, *San Francisco*, p.142; Ibid., p.297; Barth, *Instant Cities*, p.130; Ibid., pp.180–1.

34 Josiah Royce, *California, from the Conquest in 1846 to the Second Vigilance Committee in San Francisco* (Boston: Houghton Mifflin, 1896), p.313; Ibid., p.469. But for Royce, unlike some of the later historians, agency was also crucially involved. The significance of the period of disorder and of lynch law was that it awakened the consciences of the community—'They saw the fearful effects of their own irresponsible freedom.' (p.295)

35 *Pioneer*, 1, no.1, Jan. 1854: p.34.

36 James L. Tyson, *Diary of a Physician in California* (New York: Appleton, 1850), p.63.

37 California Legislature, *Journals of the Legislature of the State of California at its Second Session* (San Jose, 1851), pp.14–15.

38 *Alta California*, 24 May 1849; *Alta California*, 18 Jan. 1849; E. Gould Buffum, *Six Months in the Gold Mines. From a Journal of Three Years' Residence in Upper and Lower California* (Philadelphia, 1850), pp.100–1. For one description of a massacre, see S. Weston, *Four Months in the Mines of California; Or, Life in the Mountains* (Providence: B.T. Albro, 1854), pp.10–13.

39 *Alta California*, 24 Jan. 1851. On the Commissioners see Gerald Thompson, *Edward F. Beale and the American West* (Albuquerque: University of New Mexico Press, 1983), ch.4.

40 *Alta California*, 14 Jan. 1851.

41 Dello Grimmett Dayton, 'The California Militia 1850–1866', PhD Dissertation (University of California, Berkeley, 1951), p.218. Alonzo Delano, 'A Live Woman in the Mines', in Glenn Loney, ed., *California Gold Rush Plays* (New York: Performing Arts Journal Publications, 1983), p.95.

42 Hurtado, *Indian Survival on the California Frontier*, p.123.

43 Dayton, 'The California Militia 1850–1866', p.174.

44 California. 'Majority and Minority Reports of the Special Joint Committee on the Mendocino War' in *Journal of the California Senate*, appendix 11th session (Sacramento, 1860), p.6; James F. Downs, 'California', in Eleanor Burke Leacock and Nancy Oestreich Lurie, eds, *North American Indians in Historical Perspective* (New York: Random House, 1971), p.307; 'Indian Difficulties', *Alta California*, 1 Jan. 1851.

45 But see the frank reminiscences in Thomas Francis Bride, ed., *Letters from Victorian Pioneers* (Melbourne: Heinemann, 1969) [1898].

46 Note the publication of the writings of the white participants in the wars as unambiguously and unembarrassedly part of a Californian heritage, e.g., C. Gregory Crampton, ed., *The Mariposa Indian War 1850–1851* (Salt Lake City: University of Utah Press, 1957).

47 *Mount Alexander Mail*, 10 Nov. 1854.

48 *Victorian Christian Herald*, 5, no.3, March 1851: p.37.

49 *Argus*, 17 March 1856, cited in Christie, *Aborigines in Colonial Victoria*, p.152.

50 Aristides [R.L.Milne], *A Glance at the Forerunners of the Crisis; or, the Evils and the Remedies of the Present Modes of Tranportation, Emigration and Colonisation* (Melbourne: *Melbourne Morning Herald*, 1853), p.15; Ibid, appendix, p.14; Edward Stone Parker, *The Aborigines of Australia*, p.14; William Wills, letter to his mother February 1853, and letter to Charley n.d., La Trobe Library, ms 9504; Eugen von Guerard, *Barter*, oil on canvas, 1854, Geelong Art Gallery, Geelong, Victoria.

51 Victoria Parliament, 'Report of the Select Committee of the Legislative Council on the Aborigines' in Victoria, *Votes and Proceedings of the Legislative Council 1858–59* (Melbourne, 1859), p.iv.

52 Ibid., p.iii.

53 'Aborigines: Return to Address', in Victoria Parliament. *Votes and Proceedings, Victorian Legislative Council, 1853–54*, vol.3, pp.5–6.

54 Christie, *Aborigines in Colonial Australia*, p.68.

55 'Aborigines: Return to Address' in Victoria Parliament, *Votes and Proceedings, Legislative Council 1853–54*, vol.3, p.10; 'Report of the Select Committee of the Legislative Council on the Aborigines', p.35; Ibid., p.85.

56 Ibid., p.84.

57 Diane E. Barwick, 'Changes in the Aboriginal Population of Victoria, 1863–1966', in D.J. Mulvaney and J. Golson, eds, *Aboriginal Man and Environment in Australia*, p.303.

58 James J. Rawls, *Indians of California: The Changing Image* (Norman, Oklahoma: University of Oklahoma Press, 1984), ch.5.

59 Ibid., p.76.

60 Ibid., pp.86–7. Robert F. Heizer and Alan F. Almquist, *The Other Californians* (Berkeley: University of California Press, 1971), pp.40–4; ibid p.53.

61 Rawls, *Indians of California*, p.115; James H. Carson, *Recollections of the California Mines* [1852] (Oakland, 1950), p.59. See Hurtado, *Indian Survival*, p.165; Rawls, *Indians of California*, p.126.

62 'Report of the Select Committee of the Legislative Council on the Aborigines', p.22.

63 'Aborigines: Return to Address', in Victoria Parliament, *Votes and Proceedings, Victorian Legislative Council, 1853–54*, vol.3: pp.10, 28.

64 For discussion of this issue in Victoria, see Susanne Davies, 'Aborigines, murder and the criminal law in early Port Phillip, 1841–1851', in Susan Janson and Stuart Macintyre, eds, *Through White Eyes* (Sydney: Allen & Unwin, 1990), pp.104–5.

65 'Gold Fields' Commission of Enquiry: Report of the Commission Appointed to Enquire into the Condition of the Gold Fields of Victoria', in Victoria Parliament, *Votes and Proceedings, Victorian Legislative Council, 1854–55*, vol.2, p.51.

66 Ibid., p.ii, pp.55, 72.

67 Doyle, ed., *Golden Years*, p.95.

68 Serle, *The Golden Age*, p.320; Kathryn Cronin, *Colonial Casualties: Chinese in Early Victoria*, (Melbourne: Melbourne University Press, 1982), pp.46–58; 'Regulations for the Chinese on the Gold Fields', in Victoria Parliament, *Votes and Proceedings of the Legislative Assembly 1856–57*.

69 United Church of England and Ireland, *The Seventh Annual Report of the Church Missionary Society of the Diocese of Melbourne* (Melbourne, 1861), p.7.

70 *Christian Times*, 30 Oct. 1858, p.6.

71 Andrew Markus, *Fear and Hatred: Purifying Australia and California 1850–1901* (Sydney: Hale and Iremonger, 1979), p.16.

72 Stephen Williams, *The Chinese in the California Mines 1848–1860* (Stanford, 1930), p.70; Limerick, *Legacy of Conquest*, p.261.

73 Markus, *Fear and Hatred*, p.7.

74 Ping Chiu, *Chinese Labor in California, 1850–1880: An Economic Study* (Madison: Univ. Wisconsin History Dept, 1963), pp.1–19; Markus, *Fear and Hatred*, p.6.

75 California Legislature: Assembly, Committee on Mines and Mining Interests, *Report of Committee on Mines and Mining Interests* (1856), pp.3, 8.

76 California Legislature: Senate, *Minority Report of the Select Committee on Resolutions of Miner's Convention of Shasta County* (1855), p.4.

77 *Alta California* 20, 22 April 1854.

78 John Archibald, *On the Contact of Races: Considered Especially with Relation to the Chinese Question* (San Francisco: Towne and Bacon, 1860), p.8; Rev. William Speer, *Answer to Objections to Chinese Testimony and Appeal for their Protection by our Laws* (San Francisco: Chinese Mission House, 1856), p.1; Rev. William Speer, *China and California; Their Relations, Past and Present. A Lecture, in conclusion of a series in relation to the Chinese people, delivered in the Stockton Street Presbyterian Church, San Francisco* (San Francisco: Marvin and Hitchcock, 1853), pp.4, 15.

79 Hinton Helper, *The Land of Gold: Reality Versus Fiction*, p.37; Langworthy, *Scenery of the Plains, Mountains and Mines*, p.222; Kenneth Johnson, ed., *The*

Gold Rush Letters of J.D.B. Stillman (Palo Alto, 1967), p.38; Ward, *A History of Gold*, p.13.

80 *Alta California*, 25 Feb. 1850; C. Rudston Read, *What I heard, saw, and did at the Australian gold fields* (London: T. and W. Boone, 1853), p.211; Kinahan Cornwallis, *A Panorama of the New World* (London: T.C. Newby, 1859), pp.122–3. Rev. Daniel B. Woods, *Sixteen Months at the Gold Diggings* (New York: Harper, 1851), p.167; G.W. Rusden, *History of Australia* (London: Chapman and Hall, 1883), pp.747–8. The quoted passage is from Carlyle.

81 Beverley Kingston, *The Oxford History of Australia*, vol.3 (Melbourne: Oxford University Press, 1988), p.109.

82 Robert Haldane, *The People's Force: A History of the Victoria Police* (Melbourne: Melbourne University Press, 1986), p.60.

83 Andrew Wells, *Constructing Capitalism: An Economic History of Eastern Australia 1788–1901* (Sydney: Allen & Unwin, 1989), pp.26, 40.

84 Ian Tyrrell, *Sobering Up: From Temperance to Prohibition in Antebellum America 1800–1860* (Westport Ct.: Greenwood Press, 1979), p.125.

85 Mann, *After the Gold Rush*, p.33.

86 Ibid., p.35.

87 *Pioneer*, 4, no.3, Sept. 1855: p.132; John Ashworth, *'Agrarians' and 'Aristocrats': Party Political Ideology in the United States* (London: Royal Historical Society, 1983), pp.17–19; Ibid., pp.52–84.

88 W. Hearn, *A Lecture on the Proposed Formation of Adult Educational Classes* (Melbourne: Wilson, Mackinnon and Fairfax, 1856), p.8.

89 Just, *Australia*, p.46.

90 *Speech of Mr. Benton of Missouri, On the Adjudication of Land Titles, and Sale of Gold Mines in New Mexico and California* (Washington, 1849), p.10.

91 Edmund Randolph, *Address on the History of California, from the Discovery of the Country to the Year 1849* (San Francisco, 1860), p.70.

92 'California', *The American Review: A Whig Journal*, April 1849: p. 331.

93 'California Gold', *The US Magazine and Democratic Review* 24 Jan. 1849: p.3.

94 'California: Its Position and Prospects', *United States Magazine and Democratic Review* 24, May 1849: p.427.

95 C.E. Havens, 'America as it is, and as it will be', *Pioneer* 2, no.1, July 1854: p.20.

96 *Times*, 1 July 1852, p.4; *British Quarterly Review* 17, no.34, May 1853: p.546; W.R. Greg, 'Our Colonial Empire and our Colonial Policy', *North British Review* 19, no.38, Aug. 1853: p.368.

97 'The Gold', *Church of England Messenger* 3, Jan. 1852: p.6.

98 Charles Perry, 'The Ballarat Gold Fields', *Church of England Messenger* 2, Nov. 1851: p.329; A. de Q. Robin, ed., *Australian Sketches: The Journal and Letters of Frances Perry*, p.155; Ibid., p.6; Ibid., p.11.

99 T.A.B., 'The Gold Mania', *Illustrated Australian Magazine* 2, no.12, June 1851: p.381.

100 Reverend Charles A. Farley, 'Thanksgiving Sermon, 1850', *California Historical Society Quarterly* 19: p.305.

101 D.T. Coulton, 'Gold Discoveries', *Quarterly Review* 91, no.182, Sept. 1852: p.540.

102 Speer, *China and California*, pp.26–7.

103 *Journals of Ralph Waldo Emerson 1849–1855* (Boston: Riverside, 1912), p.7.

104 Archibald Alison, 'The Currency Extension Act of Nature', *Blackwood's Edinburgh Magazine* 69, no.423, Jan. 1851: p.7; *Addresses of Reverend Professor George Shephard and Reverend S.C. Caldwell*, p.5; John Bernard McGloin, *California's First Archbishop: The Life of Joseph Sadoc Alemany 1814–1888* (New York: Herder and Herder, 1966), p.126.

105 *Australian Gold Diggers Monthly Magazine* 1, no.3, Dec. 1852: p.78; 'The Hand of God in the Gold Region', *New Englander* 8, Feb. 1850: pp.84–5.

106 Thoreau, 'Life Without Principle', *Writings* vol. 4, p.464; 'But why go to California for a text?' Thoreau further asked, 'She is the child of New England, bred at her own school and church'. (p.468)

107 William Newmarch, 'On New Supplies of Gold', *Report of the Twenty Third Meeting of the British Association for the Advancement of Science* (London, 1854), p.111.

108 *Economist* 10, no.461, 26 June 1852: p.712.

109 'Increase in the Quantity of Gold: Its Effects', *Western Journal* 2, no.3, March 1849: p.148.

110 *Sydney Morning Herald*, 14 Feb 1853, quoted in T. Irving, 'The Development of Liberal Politics in New South Wales, 1843–1855', PhD thesis (University of Sydney, 1968), p.473.

111 'Effects of the New Discoveries of Gold', *British Quarterly Review* 17, May 1853: pp.561–2; Ibid., p.565.

112 John Chapman, 'Our Colonial Empire', *Westminster Review*, 2, Oct. 1852: p.404.; Ibid., p.402.

113 Some, for example, disputed that gold acted as a stimulus. Professor Cairnes, convinced that gold was not real wealth, told the 1857 meeting of the British Association for the Advancement of Science that 'the new gold had no direct tendency to stimulate industry or increase real wealth . . . The gold discoveries had not added to the fertility of natural agents, nor to the intelligence of capitalists, nor to the health or strength of labourers; nor, therefore . . . to the motives to exertion of the human race.' But even Cairnes saw benefit in the discoveries, for he expected the gold could be used in trade with India and China, where it could be traded for items of real wealth, to the cost of those nations: 'the transfer was in favour . . . of the Anglo-Saxon race at the expense of the rest of the world. The effect would be the same as if a tax were laid on the idle for the benefit of the industrious.' 'On Some of the Principal Effects of the New Gold', *Report of the Twenty-Seventh Meeting of the British Association for the Advancement of Science* (London, 1858), pp.157–8.

114 John Lalor, *Money and Morals: A Book for the Times* (London: Chapman, 1852), p.182; Ibid., p.272; Ibid., p.98.

115 For rejection of the theory that the value of gold would fall see e.g., Joshua Trimmer 'Gold Mines', *North British Review* 14, Feb. 1851: pp.452–85.

116 Ward, *History of Gold*, pp.55–6.

117 Richard Cobden, Preface, to Michel Chevalier, *On the Probable Fall in the*

Value of Gold: The commercial and social consequences which may ensue, and the measures which it invites (New York: Appleton, 1859): pp.7, 128.

118 'Chevalier on the Depreciation of Gold', *North American Review* no.159, April, 1853: p.509. The writer, though, was careful to dissociate himself from radicalism or socialism: 'The great inequality in the distribution of wealth is the most frightful social evil that civilized man has to contend with—an evil which is felt more keenly, because all the remedies which theorists have proposed for it, looking, as they always do, to some infraction of the right of property, would unquestionably tend to an aggravation of the disease.' It was fortunate then, that, in the guise of the gold, 'God's moral government of the world' was to supply a gentle solution (Ibid., p.510).

119 He estimated the fall in the value of gold at somewhere between 9 and 15 per cent: W. Stanley Jevons, 'A Serious Fall in the Value of Gold Ascertained, and its Social Effects Set Forth' [1863], in his *Investigations in Currency and Finance* (London: Macmillan, 1884), pp.16–17, 77.

120 Ibid., p.79.

121 Ibid., pp.81–5; Ibid., p.97.

122 *British Quarterly Review* 17, no.34, May 1853: p.558.

123 Archibald Alison, 'The Currency Extension Act of Nature', *Blackwood's Edinburgh Magazine* 69, no.423, Jan. 1851, pp.14–15; Ibid., p.17. See also Archibald Alison 'Political and Monetary Prospects', *Blackwood's Edinburgh Magazine* 71, no.435, Jan. 1852: p.18: 'That universal fall which our rulers, governed by the moneyed interest, have so long laboured with such success to effect, will be at first arrested, and then turned into a rise . . . Labour will be again adequately remunerated, because its produce, instead of constantly declining, will be constantly advancing in price.'

124 Serle, *The Golden Age*, p.61.

125 Sidney Fine, *Laissez Faire and the General Welfare State: A Study of Conflict in American Thought* (Ann Arbor: University of Michigan Press, 1956), p.23. More recent American historiography seems agreed that the direction of change in the United States was away from the economically interventionist government which had characterised the early national period, towards a more decentred system in which legislatures were losing economic power to the courts and to private corporations. See e.g., L. Ray Gunn, *The Decline of Authority: Public Economic Policy and Political Development in New York State, 1800–1860* (Ithaca: Cornell University Press, 1988), p.1: 'Beginning about 1840 . . . public involvement in the economy began to contract.' See also Harry N. Scheiber, 'Government and the Economy: Studies of the "Commonwealth" Policy in Nineteenth Century America', *Journal of Interdisciplinary History* 3, 1972: pp.135–51.

126 John Walton Caughey, *The California Gold Rush* (Berkeley: University of California Press, 1974), pp.259–62; Robert Kelley, *Battling the Inland Sea: American Political Culture, Public Policy, and the Sacramento Valley, 1850–1986* (Berkeley: University of California Press, 1989), p.18; Ibid., pp.36–7; Ibid., p.40.

127 David Alan Johnson, *Founding the Far West: California, Oregon and Nevada, 1840–1890* (Berkeley: University of California Press, 1992), p.256.

128 Brian Fitzpatrick, *The British Empire in Australia: An Economic History 1834–1939* (Melbourne: Macmillan, 1949), p.119.

129 In G.R. Quaife, ed., *Gold and Colonial Society 1851–1870* (Stanmore, NSW: Cassell, 1975), p.17; *Argus*, 4 June 1852; letter to the *Times*, 17 April 1852, quoted in Serle, *The Golden Age*, p.39. There was also a conservative version of this sentiment: 'The labouring classes should have been trained long ago', observed a writer in *Fraser's Magazine*, 'to regard the waste lands of the colonies as their birthright'. Emigration, he argued, was the 'safety valve of all old countries in which . . . poverty is pressing upon property, and leading men's thoughts to social changes'. 'Gold and Emigration', *Fraser's Magazine* 46, no.272, Aug. 1852: p.135.

130 An English Radical, 'Our Colonies', *Dublin University Magazine* 41, no.246, June 1853: p.762; Ibid., p.763.

131 Frederick Vines, *A Glorious Future for Australia; or, the Freeman's Guide Book* (Melbourne, 1856), p.11. See also An Old Colonist, *Land and Labour in Victoria*, p.13, for the argument that in England 'the restrictions imposed by the feudal system, but slightly modified, are in force to the present day'.

132 *Age*, 9 Nov. 1857.

133 Speech of C.J. Don at the 'West of England', 15 Oct 1864. Printed flyer, in J.J. Walsh papers, La Trobe Library, Melbourne.

134 *Argus*, 11 June 1851.

135 It could be argued that the working classes voted their approval of the gold rush by flocking to the diggings, but it seems reasonable to expect that some radical critique might have arisen of an event which, in the end, served mainly to enrich the merchants and shopkeepers of the colony—the gold rush, McMichael argues, 'consolidated the political and economic power of urban capital'. P. McMichael, *Settlers and the Agrarian Question: Foundations of Capitalism in Colonial Australia* (Cambridge: Cambridge University Press, 1984), p.210.

136 Asa Briggs, *Victorian People: A Reassessment of Persons and Themes 1851–67* (Chicago: University of Chicago Press, 1972), p.12.

137 *Melbourne Morning Herald*, 2 Dec. 1851.

138 Perhaps women especially—the story of the 'digger's wedding', whose point is the absurdity of an Irish servant girl being dressed in expensive clothes and conveyed to her wedding in a carriage by a lucky digger, was one of the most frequently recycled stories of gold-rush Victoria.

139 D.T. Coulton, 'Gold Discoveries', *The Quarterly Review* 91, no.182, Sept. 1852: p.518.

140 *Lecture Delivered by His Honor Mr. Justice a'Beckett Before the Members and Friends of the Melbourne Total Abstinence Society* (Melbourne: John Ferres, 1851), p.3. Education, he argued, would produce worth and virtue in the working classes which would make the gradations in society 'fewer and less wide': 'I say to you emphatically, Educate your Children.' (p.8)

141 Colonus [William a'Beckett], *Does the Discovery of Gold in Victoria, Viewed in Relation to its Moral and Social Effects, as Hitherto Developed, Deserve to be Considered a National Blessing or a National Curse?* (Melbourne: Benjamin Lucas, 1852), p.25.

142 T.T. a'Beckett, *The Gold and the Government* (Melbourne: Daniel Harrison, 1851), p.14.

143 Paul de Serville, *Pounds and Pedigrees: the Upper Class in Victoria 1850–80* (Melbourne: Oxford University Press, 1991), p.21.

144 Sally Graham, ed., *Pioneer Merchant: The Letters of James Graham 1839–54* (Melbourne: Hyland House, 1985): p.227.

145 Melbourne Chamber of Commerce, *Reports on the Condition and Progress of the Colony of Victoria since the Discovery of Goldfields* (Edinburgh: Oliver and Boyd, 1853), pp.70–1.

146 *British Quarterly Review* 17, no.34, May 1853: p.558.

147 'California Gold', *United States Magazine and Democratic Review* 24, no.127, Jan. 1849: p.7; Ibid., p.13.

148 'California', *American Review: A Whig Journal*, April 1849: p.335.

149 Rev. Laurens P. Hickock, *A Discourse on Behalf of the American Home Missionary Society* (New York, 1853), p.4; Scott, *The Wedge of Gold*, p.148.

150 Ashworth, *'Agrarians' and 'Aristocrats'*, p.58.

151 Rev. W.A. Scott, *Trade and Letters: Their Journeyings Around the World.* (New York: Robert Carter and Brothers, 1856), p.112; Starr, *Americans and the California Dream*, pp.74–5.

152 Rev. William Scott, *The Wedge of Gold, Or Achan in El Dorado* (San Francisco: Whitton, Towne, 1855), p.174.

153 David Matthew Watson, letter, 10 Feb. 1853. La Trobe Library, ms 8297.

154 Albert Lyman, *Journal of a Voyage to California and Life in the Gold Diggings* (Hartford: E.T. Pease, 1852), p.114.

CHAPTER 2

1 Russell Nye, *Society and Culture in America* (New York: Harper and Row, 1974), p.18.

2 Fred Somkin, *Unquiet Eagle: Memory and Desire in the Idea of American Freedom, 1815–1860* (Ithaca: Cornell University Press, 1967), p.33.

3 H.T. Tuckerman, 'The Gold Fever', *Godey's Magazine and Lady's Book* 38, Mar. 1849: p.205.

4 J. Swett, 'Love of the Beautiful', *Pioneer* 1, no.4, April 1854: p.210.

5 Rev. R.B. Cutler, *A Thanksgiving Sermon, Delivered in the First Unitarian Church* (San Francisco, 1856), p.5.

6 Farnham, *California: Indoors and Out*, p.250; Ibid., p.323.

7 *Sermon Preached by the Rev. Flavel S.Mines, on Sunday Jan. 25 1852, at the opening of the New Trinity Church in Pine Street, San Francisco* (San Francisco: F.A. Bonnard, 1852), p.10.

8 Thoreau, 'Life Without Principle', *Writings*, vol.iv, p.477; Ibid., pp.458, 460–1.

9 Cutler, *A Thanksgiving Sermon*, p.4.

10 Rev. J.H. Avery, *The Land of Ophir, Ideal and Real: A Discourse Delivered at Austinburg Ohio before a Company About Proceeding to California* (New York: E.O. Jenkins, 1853), p.13.

11 See e.g., James T. Kloppenberg, 'The Virtues of Liberalism: Christianity,

Republicanism, and Ethics in Early American Political Discourse', *Journal of American History* 74, no.1, June 1987; J.G.A. Pocock, *The Machiavellian Moment*.

12   Lance Banning, 'Quid Transit? Paradigms and Process in the Transformation of Republican Ideas', *Reviews in American History* 17, no.2, June 1989: p.200.

13   Johnson, *Founding the Far West*, p.7.

14   Scott, *The Wedge of Gold*, p.174.

15   See e.g., J.G.A. Pocock, 'The Machiavellian Moment Revisited: A Study in History and Ideology', *Journal of Modern History* 53, March 1981: p.70; Henry May, *The Enlightenment in America* (New York: Oxford University Press, 1976).

16   Rev. Laurens P. Hickok, *A Discourse in Behalf of the American Home Missionary Society, Preached in the Cities of New York and Brooklyn, May 1853* (New York, 1853), p.3; Ibid., p.6; Ibid., p.7; Ibid., p.8; Ibid. p.9.

17   Cf Sydney E. Ahlstrom, 'Religion, Revolution, and the Rise of Modern Nationalism', *Church History* 44, 1975: p.502. 'The nation which entered world history with the inauguration of George Washington was the product of two traditions: one, particularist, providential, supernaturalistic, Puritan and Judaic: the other universalist, rational, naturalistic and cosmopolitan.' Ahlstrom sees Enlightenment thought in America losing its vitality in the ante-bellum period in the face of the evangelical revival and the 'oppressive' strength of the Protestant mainstream. The rediscovery of republican thought enables a qualification to be made to this characterisation, for it now seems that the universalist republican strain could combine quite happily with the Puritan tradition—the language of virtue and inevitable corruption, and the language of the jeremiad were not, after all, so far from each other in intention—though it could be argued that the republican argument was more pessimistic, in that there was little talk of the possibility of revivals.

18   Colin Brummitt Goodykoontz, *Home Missions on the American Frontier—with Particular Reference to the American Home Missionary Society* (Caldwell, Idaho: Caxton Printers, 1939), p.282.

19   J.W. Douglas to Rev. Drs Badger and Hall, 29 June 1849, American Home Missionary Society: Incoming Correspondence, Reel no.2.

20   W.W. Brier, Marysville, 11 Jan. 1851, ibid.

21   Benton, *The California Pilgrim*, p.242.

22   Rev. Orange Clark, *A Discourse on Family Discipline* (San Francisco: R.P. Locke, 1860), p.14.

23   'California', *American Review: A Whig Journal*, April 1849: p.336. The Australian conservative knew that it was government that should intervene and restrain—the American Whig turned to somewhat vaguer 'better influences', a moral or envangelical force which would, it was hoped, exert social control and restraint.

24   Reynell Coates MD, 'The Golden Future', *Sartain's Magazine* 7, no.3, Sept. 1850: p.139.

25   C.E. Havens, 'America as it is, and as it will be', *Pioneer* 2, no.1, July 1854: p.20.

26 H.T. Tuckerman, 'The Gold Fever', *Godey's Magazine and Lady's Book* 38, Mar. 1849: pp. 207-8.

27 Rev. Charles A. Farley, 'Thanksgiving Sermon 1850', *California Historical Society Quarterly* 19: p.303.

28 Oliver Outcast, The Homely Man', *Pioneer* 4, no.5, Nov. 1855: p.291.

29 Samuel McNeil, *McNeil's Travels in 1849, To, Through, and From the Gold Regions in California* (Columbus: Scott and Bascom, 1849), p.5; Ibid., p.34.

30 Farnham, *California: Indoors and Out*, p.353.

31 *McNeil's Travels*, p.29.

32 See chapter 4 below.

33 James H. Carson, *Life in California, Together with a Description of the Great Tulare Valley* 2nd. ed. (Stockton: The San Joaquin Republican, 1852), p.40.

34 Alonzo Delano, 'A Live Woman in the Mines', in Loney, ed., *California Gold Rush Plays*.

35 J. Ross Browne, *Report of the Debates in the Convention of California on the Formation of the State Constitution* (Washington: J.T. Towers, 1850), p.114.

36 Ibid., p.117.

37 Johnson, *Founding the Far West*, p.125.

38 John Sharp, letter to the editor, in *California Christian Advocate*, 4 Feb. 1852.

39 Cf the earlier nineteenth century, at least in New South Wales—'During the brief neo-classical period in Australia, from 1788 to about 1840, the course of empire was a dominant theme of literature and the visual arts, providing the painter, the poet and the explorer with a rhetoric with which to announce the imperial destiny of a young nation . . .' Robert Dixon, *The Course of Empire: Neo-Classical Culture in New South Wales 1788–1860* (Melbourne: Oxford University Press, 1986), p.3.

40 Redmond Barry, *Inaugural Address Delivered Before the Members of the Victorian Institute* (Melbourne, 1854), p.7.

41 W. Shaw, *The Land of Promise; Or, My Impressions of Australia* (London: Simpkin, Marshall and Co., 1854), p.10. I suspect that Shaw's may be one of the books about Victoria written by someone who had never left London, but his rather formulaic social criticisms are no less valuable for that. They express baldly commonplaces about gold-rush society.

42 'The First Report of the Commissioners of National Education for the Colony of Victoria, for the year 1852' in Victoria Parliament *Votes and Proceedings, Legislative Council*, 1853–54, vol.1, p.6.

43 *The Eye of Faith: The Pastoral Letters of John Bede Polding* (Kilmore, Vic., 1978), p.6.

44 George M. Hardess, *Notes by the Wayside; or, Silent Thoughts for Quiet Hours* (Melbourne: H.T. Dwight, 1860), p.6.

45 John Thomas Smith, *Three Addresses by the Right Worshipful the Mayor of Melbourne* (Melbourne: Lucas Brothers, 1858), p.5.

46 Rev. A. Cairns, *New Year's Sermon; with remarks suggested by the decease of the late Governor, Sir Charles Hotham* (Melbourne: Wilson, Mackinnon and Fairfax, 1856), pp.10–11.

47 Rev. Robert Hamilton, *A Sermon and Biographical Sketch delivered on the*

Occasion of the Death of the Reverend James Ritchie Dalrymple (Melbourne: Wm. Goodhugh and Co., 1858), p.12.

48 'The Ballarat Gold Fields', *Church of England Messenger* 2, Nov. 1851: pp.321, 324; Ibid., p.323. Louisa Meredith records being told by 'my valued friend our excellent Bishop' a story about the origin of the gold. During the devastating bushfires of Black Thursday 1850, he told her, 'amidst bereavement, suffering, affliction and despair', the Devil was abroad in Victoria, walking to and fro upon the earth, sowing the gold. 'And when the flames abated, and the land cooled once more, and men went forth to their wonted labours—Lo! there it was!' Perhaps this was closer to the views of the Anglican hierarchy, in private, than all their public wrestlings with Providential plans. Louisa Meredith, *Over the Straits; A Visit to Victoria* (London, 1861). 'The Ballarat Gold Fields', *Church of England Messenger* 2 (Nov. 1851): p.325.

49 'Our Social Evils', *Church of England Messenger* 3, Oct. 1852: p.291.

50 Ibid., p.325.

51 Ibid., p.325; p.326; p.328.

52 Ibid., pp.327, 330.

53 Rev. Dr Cairns, *The Dangers and Duties of the Young Men of Victoria; or, Counsels Adapted to the Present Crisis* (Melbourne: Wilson, Mackinnon and Fairfax, 1856), p.5.

54 Ibid., p.16; p.20.

55 M. Mackay, *Sermon Preached Before the Synod of the Free Presbyterian Church Of Victoria* (Melbourne: G. Robertson, 1855), p.18.

56 Rev. F.G. Barton, *The Uses and Responsibilities of Affliction* (Kyneton: W. Fairfax and Co., 1858), p.7; Ibid., p.10.

57 George W. Rusden, *Gathering Together for the Good of Work and Learning: A Lecture on the Occasion of Opening the Exhibition Building in Melbourne, October 1854* (Melbourne: George Robertson, 1857), p.22.

58 T.A.B., 'The Gold Mania', *Illustrated Australian Magazine* 2, June 1851: p.377.

59 Melbourne Chamber of Commerce, *Reports on the Conditions and Progress of the Colony of Victoria*, p.47.

60 Rev. John C. Symons, *The History and Advantages of Young Men's Associations* (Melbourne: George Nicholls, 1856), p.2.

61 George Butler Earp, *What we did in Australia, being the practical experience of three clerks, in the stockyard and at the goldfields* (London: Routledge, 1853), p.144.

62 Dr John Shaw, *A Gallop to the Antipodes, Returning Overland through India* (London: J.F. Hope, 1858), p.96.

63 Henry Brown, *Victoria as I found it during five years of adventure* (London: T. Cautley Newby, 1853), p.40.

64 Earp, *What we did in Australia*, p.117.

65 E. Spencer Childers, ed., *The Life and Correspondence of the Rt. Hon. Hugh C.E. Childers* (London: J. Murray, 1901), vol.1, p.42.

66 Arbella Cooke to Samuel Cooke, 1 June 1852, Cooke correspondence, La Trobe Library.

67 *Argus*, 29 April 1852. The 'cooee' is a high-pitched shouted call, used

especially in the bush to communicate across distances—'sound used to attract attention, esp. at a distance', *The Australian Concise Oxford Dictionary* (Melbourne, 1987), p.224. Hence 'to be within cooee of'—to come close to. *The Australian National Dictionary* (Melbourne: Oxford University Press, 1988) p.166, records usage back to the 1790s, and argues that the expression was learnt from Aboriginal languages.

68 Mary Stawell, *My Recollections* (London: Richard Clay, 1911), p.97.

69 Spence, *Clara Morison*, Book 2 (London: Parker, 1854), p.127.

70 Ibid., p.244.

CHAPTER 3

1 Helper, *The Land of Gold*, p.243.

2 Royce, *California*, p.271.

3 See e.g., Rodman Paul, ' "Old Californians" in British Goldfields', *Huntington Library Quarterly*, 17, no.2, 1954: p.162. Paul notes the 'superior degree of law and order maintained in the gold fields of the British Empire as compared with those of the United States'. What is usually referred to is the contrast of the American (and Californian) history of vigilantism as compared to a perceived greater British respect for constituted legal forms and procedures—though it is not clear how much advance there has been on the nineteenth-century arguments about innate tendencies. Richard Maxwell Brown goes so far as to argue that 'the phenomenon of vigilantism appears to be native to America': Richard Maxwell Brown, *Strain of Violence: Historical Studies of American Violence and Vigilantism* (New York: Oxford University Press, 1975), p.22. There was vigilantism on a small scale in Victoria but it usually provoked an increased government presence and the rapid return to constituted forms: 'Again and again, governments only reinforced authority when frightened by the spectre of Judge Lynch, but despite the extent of vigilante activity, it is rather the moderation and continual regard for authority by the diggers which stand out', Serle, *The Golden Age*, p.218. There is now a very large historiography on California vigilantism. All studies of the California gold rush have something to say about vigilantism and the San Francisco Committees of Vigilance of 1851 and 1856 but see especially H.H. Bancroft, *Popular Tribunals* (San Francisco: The History Company, 1887); Josiah Royce, *California*; Mary F. Williams, *History of the San Francisco Committee of Vigilance of 1851* (Berkeley: University of California Press, 1921); Stanton Coblentz, *Villains and Vigilantes* (New York: Wilson-Erickson, 1936); Peter Decker, *Fortunes and Failures*; Robert M. Senkewicz, *Vigilantes in Gold Rush San Francisco* (Stanford: Stanford University Press, 1985). Most of the older works are sympathetic to the Vigilance Committees, most of the recent ones hostile to them. John Walton Caughey, *The California Gold Rush*, p.238, notes of vigilante justice, the 'tendency to continue it and prefer it after legal courts were available'. John Walton Caughey, *Their Majesties the Mob* (Chicago: University of Chicago Press, 1960) offers a general survey, and condemnation, of the American vigilante tradition.

4   *Household Words* 97, 31 Jan. 1852: p.437; *Household Words* 113, 22 May, 1852: p.217.

5   Ward, *A History of Gold*, p.15.

6   'History of the Australian Gold Diggings', *Australian Gold Diggers' Monthly Magazine* 1, no.2, Nov. 1852: p.45.

7   'The Homes of the South', *Dublin University Magazine* 52, no.209, Sept. 1858: p.298.

8   Ernest Scott, ed., *Lord Robert Cecil's Gold Fields Diary* (Melbourne: Melbourne University Press, 1935), p.24.

9   'Gold Fields Correspondence: Letter of Lieutenant Colonel Valiant' in Victoria Parliament, *Votes and Proceedings, Legislative Council, 1853–54*, vol.1, p.893.

10   'Homes of the South', *Dublin University Magazine* 52, no. 209: pp.298–9.

11   T.T. a'Beckett, *The Gold and the Government* (Melbourne, 1851), p.16.

12   William Howitt, *Two Years in Victoria* (London: Longman, 1855), p.22; Aspinall, *Three Years in Melbourne*, p.8. Sidney Smith in his emigrants' guide, *Whether to go and whither?*, warned his English readers that the Americans were 'essentially a vain, arrogant, conceited people . . . they live, feast, and gorge upon the praise and admiration of others', and that for this reason women in particular found the United States 'a miserable resting place' (pp.iv-v).

13   Scott, ed., *Lord Robert Cecil's Gold Fields' Diary*, p.35.

14   Henry Mundy, diaries vol.1, p.247. La Trobe Library, ms 10416.

15   Philip Prendergast, letter to his father from Melbourne, 21 September 1852. La Trobe Library, ms 5405, Box 31/2(a).

16   See E. Daniel and Annette Potts, *Young America and Australian Gold: Americans and the Gold Rush of the 1850s* (St Lucia: University of Queensland Press, 1974), passim.

17   Aristides [R.L. Milne], *A Glance at the Forerunners of the Crisis*, appendix, p.9.

18   L.G. Churchward, *Australia and America 1788–1972: An Alternative History* (Chippendale, NSW: Alternative Publishing, 1979), p.56.

19   *Melbourne Morning Herald*, 2 Dec. 1851.

20   *Mount Alexander Mail*, 24 Nov. 1854.

21   *Argus*, 26 Dec. 1854, quoted in E. Daniel and Annette Potts, 'American Republicanism and the Disturbances on the Goldfields', *Historical Studies* 13, no.50, April 1968: p.161.

22   E. Daniel and Annette Potts, *Young America and Australian Gold*, p.164.

23   Captain H. Butler Stoney, *Victoria: With a Description of its Principal Cities, Melbourne and Geelong, and Remarks on the Present State of the Colony* (London: Smith, Elder, 1856), p.153.

24   Serle, *The Golden Age*, p.95.

25   *Lord Robert Cecil's Gold Fields Diary*, p.34.

26   William Howitt, *Tallengetta, The Squatter's Home. A Story of Australian Life* (London: Longman, 1857), p.8.

27   *Lord Robert Cecil's Gold Fields Diary*, p.35.

28 'Regulations and Instructions for the Gold Fields' in Victoria Parliament, *Votes and Proceedings of the Legislative Council, Session 1853–54*, vol.2, p.10.

29 Ibid., p.10.

30 La Trobe to the Duke of Newcastle, Governor's Despatch Book, VPRS 1084, vol.2, no.139, 3 Aug. 1853, Victorian Public Record Office.

31 *Lecture Delivered by His Honor Mr. Justice a'Beckett Before the Members and Friends of the Melbourne Total Abstinence Society*, p.3.

32 *Mount Alexander Mail*, 9 Sept. 1854.

33 *Bendigo Advertiser*, 11 Nov. 1854.

34 *Bendigo Advertiser*, 21 Feb. 1855.

35 C.J. La Trobe, General Correspondence, Letter 511, Draft of Despatch to the Duke of Newcastle, 17 Sept. 1853, Victorian Public Record Office, 630/11.

36 Edward Wilson, ed., *An Enquiry into the Principles of Representation* (Melbourne, 1857), p.v.

37 Ibid., p.22.

38 Francis H. Nixon, *Population: Or, a Plea for Victoria* (Melbourne, 1862), pp.5, 13.

39 R. L. Milne, *A Glance at the Forerunners of the Crisis*, p.22.

40 Ibid., p.23.

41 VPRS 3219, Letter from Colonial Secretary Foster to Chief Commissioner of Police, 24/9/1853.

42 See Michel Foucault, 'On Governmentality', *Ideology and Consciousness*, 6, 1979: pp.5–22.

43 Haldane, *The People's Force*, pp.87–8.

44 Colonial Secretary's Correspondence, VPRS 1189, Box 145, 53/10442.

45 Haldane, *The People's Force*, p.42.

46 La Trobe to the Duke of Newcastle, Governor's Despatch Book, VPRS 1084, vol.2, no.139, 3 Aug. 1853; Serle, *Golden Age*, p.388.

47 Lotchin, *San Francisco*, pp.102, 202.

48 William Kerr, in 'Report from the Select Committee on Police', Victoria Parliament, *Votes and Proceedings, Victorian Legislative Council 1852–53* vol.2, p.34.

49 Letter from Superintendent of Police to Colonial Secretary 26/10/1852, Colonial Secretary's Correspondence, Victorian Public Record Office, VPRS 1189, Box 143, 52/74629.

50 Ibid. Only 100 of 170 men were reported to be in uniform at this time.

51 Colonial Secretary's Correspondence, VPRS 1189, Box 16, 52/2971.

52 'Report from the Select Committee on Police', Victoria Parliament, *Votes and Proceedings, Victorian Legislative Council 1852–53*, vol.2, p.15.

53 VPRS 1189, Box 143, 52/74629.

54 VPRS 1189, Box 145, D53/8629.

55 VPRS 937, Box 5.

56 Raffaello Carboni, *The Eureka Stockade* (Melbourne: Melbourne University Press, 1969) [1855], p.149.

57 Douglas Hay, in Douglas Hay et al., *Albion's Fatal Tree: crime and society in eighteenth-century England* (London: Alan Lane, 1975).

58 Barry's Supreme Court Letter Book, VPRS 830, Unit 1, 2/52.

59 Colonial Secretary: Outward Correspondence. Letter from G.W. Rusden to R. Barry, 13 May 1852, VPRS 3219, vol.13.

60 Lonsdale to Barry, 5 June 1852, VPRS 3219, vol.13.

61 Barry's Supreme Court Letter Book, 6/52.

62 *Argus*, 8 June 1852.

63 Redmond Barry, *Address of His Honor Mr. Justice Barry, One of the Judges of the Supreme Court of the Colony of Victoria, On the Opening of the Circuit Court at Portland, on June the 15th., 1852* (Melbourne, 1852), p.5.

64 Ibid., p.7.

65 Ibid., p.9.

66 Ibid., p.10.

67 Ibid., pp.12–13.

68 Colonial Secretary's Correspondence, VPRS 1189.

69 *Portland Guardian and Normanby General Advertiser*, 17 June 1852.

70 Barry, Portland *Address*, p.18.

71 Anxiety about jurors can be seen also in Lieutenant Governor La Trobe's despatch to the Colonial Secretary in London about the success of the new Circuit Court at Castlemaine, on the goldfields. La Trobe praised the 'regularity, order, and good feeling' which prevailed during the court's session, and commended the 'most intelligent and respectable jurors' who had been secured, United Kingdom Parliament, *Further Papers Relative to the Recent Discovery of Gold in Australia* (1853), p.61.

72 Barry, Portland *Address*, p.19.

73 Something of Barry's concern on the question of democratic reform can be judged from his ordering of the books for the Melbourne Public Library. When the Irish politician Charles Gavan Duffy visited, he found little on the English Commonwealth, or the American or French revolutions, not a single volume on Australian affairs or political economy, and no modern poets, novelists or philosophers. 'But the antiquities of Athens and Attica were abundantly represented. Three hundred volumes of Greek and Latin classics and the Book of Common Prayer in German, French, Italian, Greek, modern Greek, and Spanish.' C. Gavan Duffy, *My Life in Two Hemispheres* vol.2 (London: T. Fisher Unwin, 1898), p.134.

74 Barry, Portland *Address*, p.19.

75 Peter Ryan, 'Sir Redmond Barry', *Australian Dictionary of Biography*, pp.108–11.

76 Barry, Portland *Address*, p.17.

77 Redmond Barry, *Lectures and Addresses*, vol.2, La Trobe Library collection: newspaper clipping: 'Castlemaine Circuit Court, Thursday, Dec 9, 1852'.

78 Ibid.

79 Redmond Barry, *Lecture on the History of the Art of Agriculture* (Melbourne, 1854), p.36.

80 Victoria Parliament, 'University of Melbourne Report', *Votes and Proceedings, Victorian Legislative Council*, 1854, pp.8–9.

81 Microfilm of Airy papers, University of Melbourne archives.

82 See e.g., David Goodman, 'Fear of Circuses: founding the National Museum of Victoria', *Continuum*, 3, no.1 (1990): pp.18–34.

83 Lawson B. Patterson, *Twelve Years in the Mines of California* (Cambridge Mass., 1862), p.15.

84 Susan Townsend letter, 12 June 1851. Bancroft Library ms.

85 Edward Pillock, 'Thoughts toward a New Epic', *Pioneer* 2, no.2, Aug. 1854: pp.77–8.

86 California Legislature, *Journal of the Sixth Session of the Legislature of the State of California* (Sacramento, 1855), p.37.

87 John Ballou, *The Lady of the West, or, The Gold Seekers* (Cincinnati, 1855), p.110.

88 Rev. B. Brierly, *Thoughts for the Crisis: A Discourse Delivered in the Washington St. Baptist Church, San Francisco, California, On the Sabbath following the Assassination of James King of William by James P. Casey* (San Francisco, 1856), p.17; Ibid., p.9.

89 Scott, *The Wedge of Gold*, p.97.

90 Stanley Elkins, *Slavery: A Problem in American Institutional and Intellectual Life* 2nd ed. (Chicago: University of Chicago Press, 1968), pp.33, 142.

91 George M. Fredrickson, *The Inner Civil War: Northern Intellectuals and the Crisis of the Union* (New York: Harper and Row, 1968), p.22; Ibid., p.9.

92 Ralph Henry Gabriel, *The Course of American Democratic Thought: An Intellectual History Since 1815* (New York: Ronald Press, 1940), p.3.

93 John Patrick Diggins, *The Lost Soul of American Politics: Virtue, Self-Interest, and the Foundations of Liberalism* (New York: Basic Books, 1984), p.150.

94 *Pioneer* 1, no.4, April 1854: p.213.

95 Henry James, *Lectures and Miscellanies* (New York: Redfield, 1852), p.13.

96 Ibid., p.28; p. 47

97 J.A. Benton, *The California Pilgrim: A Series of Lectures* (Sacramento: S. Alter, 1853), p.66; p.241.

98 For testimony to Wadsworth's impact in California, see 'A Clergyman' [Rev. George Burrows], *Impressions of Dr. Wadsworth as a Preacher* (San Francisco: Towne and Bacon, 1863). 'None but a great orator could produce on such congregations, for years in succession, the effects so uniformly produced by Dr. Wadsworth', (p.19); his sermons were 'bold and original, brilliant and suggestive' (p.20).

99 Rev. Charles Wadsworth, *Thankfulness, A Sermon, and Character, A Sermon, Preached on Thanksgiving Day, November 20, 1856 in the Arch Street Church, Philadelphia* (Philadelphia: T.B. Peterson, 1856), p.36.

100 Ibid., p.43.

101 Ibid., p.44.

102 Ibid., p.45.

103 Ibid., p.67.

104 Ibid., p.68.

105 Ibid., p.71.

106 See ch.6 below for an extended discussion of 'excitement'.

107 Ibid., pp.67, 71.

108 Ibid., p.48.

109 'Up to the time of this visitation, we were fast becoming the most mercenary people on earth . . . Gold was fast becoming our national idol . . . we were fast sinking into the unleavened sordidness of avarice; and this insane greed of gain was working our ruin; for by an immutable law of life, wealth begets luxury, and luxury palsies the strength and digs the grave of nations.' The war would give Californian men 'a nobler style and type of manhood', instead of 'sordid selfishness' and 'impatience of restraint', they would develop self-denial and self-sacrifice, and a new patriotism would replace 'our ever growing idolatry of popular sovereignty'. Charles Wadsworth, *War a Discipline. A Sermon Preached in Calvary Church, San Francisco, on Thanksgiving Day, November 24, 1864* (San Francisco: H.H. Bancroft, 1864), pp.10–15.

110 David. A. Johnson, 'Vigilance and the Law: The Moral Authority of Popular Justice in the Far West', *American Quarterly* 33, no.5, winter 1981: p.564.

111 An exception was the Reverend W.A. Scott in 1856: see below; Royce's comment: Josiah Royce, *California*, p.461.

112 Jenkins was caught stealing a safe from a San Francisco shipping company office. Bancroft describes him: 'Rough, tall, powerful, of fine physique, with English dress and cast of feature . . . He was an Australian convict . . . ' H.H. Bancroft, *Popular Tribunals*, p.229.

113 Timothy Dwight Hunt, *Sermon Suggested by the Execution of Jenkins on the Plaza, by the 'People' of San Francisco, during the Night of the 10th of June 1851* (San Francisco: Marvin and Hitchcock, 1851), p.6.

114 Ibid., pp.8, 11, 13.

115 Brierly, *Thoughts for the Crisis*, p.7. The vigilantes, Brierly argued, were 'no more a mob than the Tea Party at Boston, or the stalwart, honest Saxons at Runymede' (p.19).

116 Provided they worked within a procedural framework, Nicholson argues, the people in the United States could displace the government; the procedures, that is, could be performed by anyone. In the British colonies on the other hand, she argues, procedures could only be carried out by the 'proper' people, those who could imbue them with the requisite dignity. The 'principle of legitimation' was thus different in the two kinds of societies. Jan Nicholson, 'Procedures and Perceptions of Authority: The Gold-Rush Camps of Australia, Canada and the United States', *Public Administration: The Journal of the Australian Regional Groups of the Royal Institute of Public Administration* 32, no.4, Dec. 1973: pp.392–403.

117 *Daily Alta California* account, reprinted in Frank Fargo *A True and Minute History of the Assassination of James King of William, and the Execution of Casey and Cora* (San Francisco: Whitton, Towne, 1856), p.13.

118 'Whoever wishes, for health's sake, or for any other reason, to change the sceneries or the objects and associations of his life, should set off, not for Europe, but for California.' Horace Bushnell, *California: Its Characteristics and Prospects* (San Francisco: Whitton, Towne, 1858), p.3.

119 Horace Bushnell, *Society and Religion: A Sermon for California, Delivered on Sabbath Evening, July 6, 1856, at the Installation of Rev. E.S.Lacey, as Pastor of the First Congregational Church, San Francisco* (San Francisco: Sterett and Co., 1856), p.5.

120 Ibid., pp.7, 16, 17, 19, 26.

121 See Fredrickson, *The Inner Civil War*, pp.25–6.

122 Scott, *A Discourse for the Times*, pp.2, 7, 8.

123 Clifford M. Drury, *William Anderson Scott, 'No Ordinary Man'* (Glendale: H. Clark and Co., 1967), p.193.

124 Stephen J. Field, *Personal Reminiscences of Early Days in California* (San Francisco, 1893), pp.17, 21.

125 *Statement of the Controversy Between Judge William R. Turner, of the Eighth Judicial District of California, and Members of the Marysville Bar, and their Reply to his Violent Attacks Upon Them* (Marysville, 1850), pp.3–6.

126 William R. Turner, *Documents in Relation to Charges Preferred by Stephen J. Field and Others* (San Francisco, 1853), p.7; *Statement of the Controversy* , p.6.

127 Ibid., p.9.

128 Ibid., pp.6–9.

129 Ibid., p.6.

130 Turner, *Documents*, pp.4, 8.

131 *Statement of the Controversy*, p.7.

132 Ibid., p.16.

133 Carl Brent Swisher, *Stephen J. Field, Craftsman of the Law* (Washington: Brookings Institution, 1930), p.47.

134 Turner, *Documents*, op. cit., p.5.

135 Swisher, *Stephen J. Field*, p.52.

136 Turner, *Documents*, p.8, pp.19–23.

137 The most famous duel of the period was that between California Supreme Court Judge David S. Terry and US Senator David C. Broderick in 1859, in which Broderick was killed. Duelling was not unknown among gentlemen in Victoria, though the historian of the practice comments: 'They seem to have been more ritual in nature, and one of the rare times blood was shed . . . resulted from an impetuous contestant shooting himself in the foot.' Paul de Serville, *Port Philip Gentlemen and Good Society in Melbourne Before the Gold Rushes* (Melbourne: Oxford University Press, 1980), p.107. Redmond Barry fought a duel during the 1840s; he arrived in a bell-topper hat, 'strap-trousered, swallow-tail-coated, white-vested, gloved, and cravatted to a nicety', but in the event merely fired into the air, Ibid., p.110.

138 *Pacific*, 7 Nov. 1851.

139 *Statement of the Controversy*, pp.15–18.

140 Turner, *Documents*, p.11.

141 *Statement of the Controversy*, pp.19–20, 33.

142 Turner, *Documents*, pp.17–18.

143 *Statement of the Controversy*, p.30.

144 Field carried a derringer pistol and a bowie knife: Swisher, op. cit., p.66. This was apparently not unusual: 'Even when the judges were honest, court procedure in early Stockton was rough. It was customary for attorneys, principals, and audience to attend court well armed.' A. Russell Buchanan, *David S. Terry of California: Dueling Judge* (San Marino, 1956), p.9. A witness, admittedly hostile to Judge Terry, described him as 'a rough fellow, and,

sitting on the Supreme Court Bench, he would take out his pistol and lay it on his desk, and sit with his heels as high as he knew': Ibid., p.81.

145 On the history of the duel, see V.G. Kiernan, *The Duel in European History: Honour and the Reign of the Aristocracy* (Oxford: Oxford University Press, 1988).

146 *Pacific*, 7 Nov. 1851.

147 Quoted in Buchanan, *David S. Terry*, p.12.

148 Oliver Macdonagh, 'The Nineteenth-Century Revolution in Government: A Reappraisal', in Peter Stansky, ed., *The Victorian Revolution: Government and Society in Victoria's Britain* (New York: New Viewpoints, 1973), p.12.

149 Stephen J. Field, 'Opinion of the United States Supreme Court in Tennison vs Kirk' (1878), in *Some Opinions and Papers of Stephen J. Field* (n.p., n.d.).

150 Victoria Parliament, *Debate in the Legislative Council of the Colony of Victoria on the Second Reading of the New Constitution Bill* (Melbourne, 1858), p.38.

CHAPTER 4

1 Samuel Sidney, *The Three Colonies of Australia*, (London: Ingram, Cooke, 1852.)

2 *Australian Gold Diggers Monthly Magazine* 1, 1853: p.126.

3 See Raymond Williams, *The Country and the City*, (Oxford: Oxford University Press, 1973).

4 Sidney Smith, *Whether to Go and Whither? Being a Practical View of the Whole Southern Field of Settlement* (London: John Kendrick, 1852), p.xi.

5 Editorial, *Mount Alexander Mail*, 15 Sept. 1854.

6 John Fitzgerald Leslie Foster, *The New Colony of Victoria, formerly Port Philip* (London: Trelawney Saunders, 1851), p.33.

7 William Howitt, *A Boy's Adventures in the Wilds of Australia* (London: Arthur Hall, Virtue and Co., n.d.), p.9.

8 James Daniel letter, 1/7/1852, in Daniel family papers, La Trobe Library, ms 10222.

9 Smith, *Whether to Go*, p.75.

10 Howitt, *Two Years in Victoria*, p.33.

11 Ibid., p.34.

12 Ibid., p.18.

13 Major T.L. Mitchell, *Three Expeditions Into the Interior of Eastern Australia; With Descriptions of the Recently Explored Region of Australia Felix* (London: T. and W. Boone, 1839), vol.2, p.333.

14 R. Paulson, *Literary Landscape: Turner and Constable*, (New Haven: Yale University Press, 1982), p.41.

15 Eugene von Guerard, *Mr. Perry's Farm on the Yarra*, 1855, private collection.

16 Candice Bruce, *Eugene von Guerard* (Canberra: Australian National Gallery, 1980), p.34.

17 Frederick Vines, *The Cue to Prosperity: or, Our Lands and How to Get at Them* (Melbourne: James Caple, 1856), p.51.

18 S. Wekey, *The Land, Importance of its Culture to the General Prosperity of Victoria* (Melbourne: James J. Blundell, 1854), p.9.

19   N.L. Kentish, *The Question of Questions* (Melbourne: J.J. Blundell, 1855), p.17.

20   T.T.a'Beckett, *The Gold and the Government*, p.13.

21   An Old Colonist, *Land and Labor in Victoria* (Melbourne: George Robertson, 1856), p.15.

22   H. Lill Lindsay, *The Industrial Resources of Victoria* (Melbourne: George Robertson, 1856), pp.24–5.

23   Lynnette J. Peel, *Rural Industry in the Port Phillip Region 1835–1880* (Melbourne: Melbourne University Press, 1974), p.59. Peel warns that the figures are unreliable but 'do indicate the general trend of events'.

24   *Proceedings of the Melbourne Chamber of Commerce and the Special Committee Appointed*, p.7.

25   Peel, *Rural Industry in the Port Phillip Region*, p.62.

26   McMichael, *Settlers and the Agrarian Question*, p.213.

27   Dorothy Thompson, *The Chartists: Popular Politics in the Industrial Revolution* (New York: Pantheon, 1984), p.302.

28   The associations went back to the beginnings of the analysis of capitalism. Adam Smith himself had warned that 'the capital . . . that is acquired to any country by commerce or manufactures, is all a very precarious and uncertain possession till some part of it has been secured and realised in the cultivation and improvement of its lands. A merchant, it has been said very properly, is not necessarily the citizen of any country. It is in a great measure indifferent to him from what place he carries on his trade . . . ' Adam Smith, *The Wealth of Nations* [1776] (Harmondsworth: Penguin, 1982), p.519.

29   Colonus [W. a'Beckett], *Does the Discovery of Gold*, p.38.

30   Ibid., p.37.

31   Ibid., p.8.

32   Lindsay, *The Industrial Resources of Victoria*, p.3.

33   Colonus, *Does the Discovery of Gold*, p.16.

34   T.T. a'Beckett, *The Gold and the Government*, p.7.

35   Colonus, *Does the Discovery of Gold*, p.19.

36   Appendix to T.T. a'Beckett, *A Defence of State Aid to Religion* (Melbourne: James J. Blundell, 1856), p.22.

37   G.F. Verdon, *The Present and Future of Municipal Government in Victoria* (Melbourne: W. Fairfax, 1858), p.13.

38   Colin Campbell, *Remarks on National Education* (Melbourne: Benjamin Lucas, 1853), p.58.

39   Charles Perry, *A Letter on the Financial Position of the Church, To the Few Zealous Members of the United Church of England and Ireland in Victoria* (Melbourne, n.d.), p.7.

40   Aristides [R.L. Milne], *A Glance at the Forerunners of the Crisis*, p.15.

41   Lindsay, *The Industrial Resources of Victoria*, pp.4–5.

42   F. Coster, *A Land System for Victoria* (Melbourne: James J. Blundell, 1857), p.18.

43   Peter Papineau, *Homesteads for the People* (Melbourne: S. Goode, 1855), p.8.

44   *Argus*, 10 April 1855.

45 R. Carboni, *The Eureka Stockade* [1855] (Melbourne: Melbourne University Press, 1975), p.53.

46 *Mount Alexander Mail*, 10 Nov. 1854.

47 N.L. Kentish, *The Question of Questions*, pp.iii–iv.

48 R.A. Gollan, *Radical and Working Class Politics: A Study of Eastern Australia 1850–1910* (Melbourne: Melbourne University Press, 1960), p.15.

49 G. Stedman Jones, 'Rethinking Chartism', in his *Languages of Class: Studies in English Working Class History 1832–1932* (Cambridge: Cambridge University Press, 1983), p.171.

50 Ibid., p.155.

51 Ibid., p.166.

52 In Frank Crowley, ed., *A Documentary History of Australia* vol.2, (Melbourne: Heinemann, 1980), p.287.

53 Humphrey McQueen, *A New Britannia*, (Ringwood, Vic.: Penguin, 1980), p.142.

54 Coral Lansbury, *Arcady in Australia: The Evocation of Australia in Nineteenth-Century English Literature*, (Melbourne: Melbourne University Press, 1970), chs. 3–5.

55 Stedman Jones, *Languages of Class*, p.168.

56 Ibid., p.122.

57 An Old Colonist, *Land and Labor in Victoria*, p.14.

58 Serle, *The Golden Age*, p.269.

59 Nassau Senior, *Four Introductory Lectures on Political Economy Delivered Before the University of Oxford* (London: Longman, 1852), p.74.

60 *Statutes and Regulations of the University of Melbourne* (Melbourne, 1855), p.17.

61 *Proceedings of the Melbourne Chamber of Commerce and of the Special Committee Appointed*, p.32.

62 Ibid., p.25.

63 Reported in *Mount Alexander Mail*, 9 Sept. 1854.

64 Colin Campbell, *The Squatting Question Considered, With A View to its Settlement* (Melbourne: Walker, May and Co., 1861), p.12.

65 Victoria Parliament, *Victorian Hansard: Debates and Proceedings of the Legislative Council and Assembly of the Colony of Victoria* vol.5 (1860), p.122.

66 Ibid., vol.6, p.1170.

67 Ibid., p.281.

68 Ibid., p.1170.

69 Quoted in Margaret Kiddle, *Men of Yesterday: A Social History of the Western District of Victoria 1834–1890* (Melbourne: Melbourne University Press, 1962), p.227.

70 Serle, *The Golden Age*, p.305.

71 A Colonist, *Protection Versus Free Trade. Gold not National Wealth. Victoria: As She Was, As She Is, As She Should Be* (Melbourne: Walker, May and Co., 1860), p.15.

72 D.W.A. Baker, 'The Origins of Robertson's Land Acts', *Historical Studies: Selected Articles, First Series* (Melbourne: Melbourne University Press, 1967), p.122.

73 Williams, *The Country and the City*, p.2.

74 For a geographer's analysis of this inappropriateness, see J.M. Powell, *Mirrors of the New World: Images and Image-Makers in the Settlement Process* (Canberra: Australian National University Press, 1978), ch.4 'The "Yeoman Farmer" and the Quest for Arcady'.

75 Sally Falk Moore, *Law as Process: An Anthropological Approach* (London, 1978), p.32.

76 Ibid., p.39.

77 Terry Irving, in Crowley, ed., *A New History of Australia*, p.141.

78 McQueen, *A New Britannia*, p.151.

79 An Old Colonist, *Land and Labor in Victoria*, p.15.

80 Aristides [R.L. Milne], *A Glance at the Forerunners of the Crisis*, appendix 10, p.12.

81 Howitt, *Two Years in Victoria*, pp.76–7.

82 Ibid., p.205.

83 William Wilson Dobie, *Recollections of a Visit to Port Phillip Australia, in 1852–55* (Glasgow: T. Murray and Son, 1856), p.51.

84 Howitt, *Two Years in Victoria*, p.57.

85 Rev. J. Cooper, *An Inquiry into the Relation of Christ to the World and of the Church to the State* (Geelong: Thomas Paterson, 1856), p.27.

86 Duffy, *My Life in Two Hemispheres*, p.157.

87 Shaw, *A Gallop to the Antipodes*, p.10.

88 Ward, *The Australian Legend*, p.9.

89 Kinahan Cornwallis, *A Panorama of the New World* (London, 1859), p.12.

90 Foster, *The New Colony of Victoria*, pp.74–5.

91 Read, *What I Heard, Saw and Did at the Australian Gold Fields*, p.145.

92 Melbourne *Punch* 1 (1855): p.4, cited in Macintyre, *A Colonial Liberalism*, p.18.

93 Samuel Mossman and Thomas Banister, *Australia, Visited and Revisited: A Narrative of Recent Travels and Old Experiences in Victoria and New South Wales* (London: Addey and Co., 1853), p.28.

94 Michael Cannon, ed., John Sherer, *The Gold Finder of Australia* (Ringwood: Penguin, 1973), p.ii; John Molony and T.J.McKenna 'All that Glisters', *Labour History* 32, May 1977: pp.33–45; *The Gold Finder*, p.237. California also had its fabricated first-person accounts: see 'Spurious Californiana', *California Historical Society Quarterly* 1, no.1, March 1932: pp.65–8, on J. Tyrwhitt Brooks', *Four Months Among the Gold Finders in Alta California*, which was also written from London.

95 Samuel Mossman, *Emigrants' Letters from Australia* (London: Addey and Co., 1853), p.3.

96 Mulvey makes a similar case for the armchair traveller: 'He would at least know that his judgement was suspect and that his generalisations were at a dangerous remove from reality.' In contrast, the actual traveller often showed little awareness that 'speech, just like writing, came between consciousness and reality to deter and defer meaning': Christopher Mulvey, 'Anglo-American Fictions: National Characteristics in Nineteenth-Century Travel

Literature' in Ian F. Bell and D.K. Adams, eds, *American Literary Landscapes: The Fiction and the Fact* (London: Vision, 1988), p.75.

97 Sherer, *The Gold Finder*, pp.9, 249, 319, 195.

98 Ibid. pp.16, 19.

99 Paul Fussell, thinking of the ease and luxury enjoyed by the elite traveller rather than the implied possibility of a future society, regards travel books as a form of displaced pastoral romance. Here, though, the imperial context of the metropolitan traveller to the colonies is crucial; the p⁓ ⁓al fantasy is now an imperial fantasy: Paul Fussell, *Abroad: British Literary Travelling Between the Wars* (New York: Oxford University Press, 1980), pp. 209–11.

100 For an argument about the 'elective affinities' between comic emplotment and conservative ideological implication, see Hayden White, *Metahistory: The Historical Imagination in Nineteenth-Century Europe* (Baltimore: Johns Hopkins University Press, 1973), p.29; Sherer, *The Gold Finder*, p.230.

101 Fussell, *Abroad*, p.39.

102 Mossman and Banister, *Australia, Visited and Revisited*, p.iii.

103 Tod Robinson, 'Agricultural Address', in *Transactions of the California State Agricultural Society During the Year 1859* in *Journal of the California Senate*, appendix, 11th session (Sacramento, 1860), p.441.

104 *California Farmer and Journal of Useful Sciences* 1, no.1, Jan. 1854.

105 Charles Wadsworth, *War a Discipline. A Sermon Preached in Calvary Church, San Francisco, on Thanksgiving Day, November 24, 1864* (San Francisco: H.H. Bancroft, 1864), p.7.

106 Helper, *Land of Gold*, p.106.

107 'California Gold: A Song for the Occasion', *United States Magazine and Democratic Review*, Oct. 1849: p.368.

108 H.T. Tuckerman, 'The Gold Fever', *Godey's Magazine and Lady's Book* 38, Mar. 1849: p.206.

109 'Transactions of the California State Agricultural Society, 1858', in appendix to the *Journals of the California Senate*, 10th session (Sacramento, 1859), p.57. Lotchin claims that the California Agricultural Society was 'almost entirely an urban project', with very few actual farmers involved: Lotchin, *San Francisco*, p.80.

110 Farnham, *California: Indoors and Out*, p.30.

111 Quoted in Lotchin, *San Francisco*, p.133.

112 'Agriculture: The Future', *California Farmer and Journal of Useful Sciences* 1, no.1, 5 Jan. 1854: p.2.

113 'Agriculture in California', *San Francisco Whig* 1, no.10, 1 Jan. 1853: p.1.

114 'California: Its Position and Prospects', *United States Magazine and Democratic Review*, May 1849: p.412.

115 Carson, *Life in California*, p.51.

116 Franklin Langworthy, *Scenery of the Plains, Mountains and Mines*, p.155.

117 *California Farmer and Journal of Useful Sciences* 1, no.1, 5 Jan. 1854.

118 Carson, *Life in California*, p.64.

119 Farnham, *California: Indoors and Out*, p.75.

120 'The Yo-ham-ite Valley', *Hutchings' California Magazine* 1, no.1, July 1856: p.2.

121 On Hutchings see Starr, *Americans and the California Dream*, p.181; Tanis Thorne, 'The Almanacs of the San Francisco Bay Region, 1850–1861', *Journal of the West* 17, no.2, April 1978: pp.37–45.

122 'The Yo-ham-ite Valley', *Hutchings' California Magazine* 1, no.1, July 1856: pp.2–3.

123 *Alta California*, 9 Feb. 1851.

124 David Wyatt, *The Fall into Eden: Landscape and Imagination in California* (Cambridge: Cambridge University Press, 1987), p.18.

125 Farnham, *California Indoors and Out*, p.30.

126 Bayard Taylor, *Eldorado* (New York, 1949), p.96.

127 Eri S. Hulpert letter, 28 April 1852, in Eri S. Hulpert and William W. Walker, *Land of Gold: An Ill Fated Journey to California via Nicaragua* (1852): Bancroft Library, ms. Langworthy, *Scenery of the Plains, Mountains and Mines*, p.166, records reports of cabbages 66 inches in circumference.

128 See Leo Marx, *The Machine in the Garden* (New York: Oxford University Press, 1964).

129 'The Hot Mineral Springs and Steam Fountains of California', *The California Christian Advocate: A Methodist Episcopal Newspaper*, 10 Oct. 1851: p.1.

130 Bushnell, *California: Its Characteristics and Prospects*, pp.28–9.

131 Farnham, *California: Indoors and Out*, pp.323–5.

132 Robert Kelley, *Gold vs Grain: The Hydraulic Mining Controversy in California's Sacramento Valley. A Chapter in the Decline of the Concept of Laissez Faire* (Glendale, Calif.: A.H. Clarke and Co., 1959), p.14.

133 Ibid., p.57.

134 Lotchin, *San Francisco*, pp.10, 49.

135 Ibid., p.14.

136 Royce, *California*, p. 370. *Californian Christian Advocate*, 4 Feb. 1852.

137 Watson, ed., *To the Land of Gold and Wickedness*, p.243.

138 J.Bayard Taylor, 'The Mountains', *Godey's Magazine and Lady's Book* 39, Sept. 1849: p.199.

139 Langworthy, *Scenery of the Plains, Mountains and Mines*, p.155.

140 Ballou, *The Lady of the West*, p.91.

141 Benjamin Richards, ed., *California Gold Rush Merchant: The Journal of Stephen Chapin Davis* (San Marino: Huntington Library, 1956), p.73.

142 Buffum, *Six Months in the Gold Mines*, pp.26–7.

143 Carson, *Life in California*, p.39.

144 Rev. R.B. Cutler, *A Thanksgiving Sermon*, p.10.

145 Wyatt, *The Fall into Eden*, p.xvi.

146 Sandra Sizer Frankiel, *California's Spiritual Frontiers: Religious Alternatives to Anglo-Protestantism, 1850–1910* (Berkeley: University of California Press, 1988), p.15.

147 Samuel D. Simonds, 'Itinerancy and Scenes in California', *Ladies' Repository* (May, 1860), p.296.

148 Starr, *Americans and the California Dream*, p.100.

149 Richard Frothingham, *A Tribute to Thomas Starr King* (Boston, 1865), p.176.

150 Charles W. Wendte, *Thomas Starr King: Patriot and Preacher* (Boston, 1921), p.115.

151 In Edwin P. Whipple, *Christianity and Humanity: A Series of Sermons by Thomas Starr King* (Boston, 1880), p.286.

152 William Day Simonds, *Starr King in California* (San Francisco: Elder and Co., 1917), p.82.

153 Whipple, *Christianity and Humanity* p.286.

154 Ibid., p.293.

155 Alonzo Delano, *Old Block's Sketch Book* (Santa Ana, 1947), pp.ii–iii.

156 Bushnell, *California*, p.15.

157 Scott, *Trade and Letters*, p.35.

158 Ibid., p.41.

159 Langworthy, *Scenery of the Plains, Mountains and Mines*, p.195.

CHAPTER 5

1 James Bonwick, *Notes of a Gold Digger and Gold Diggers' Guide* (Melbourne: R. Connebee, 1852) [1942] p.25.

2 Jim Atlee, 1859 letter, La Trobe Library, ms 9873/76; George Henry Wathen, *The Golden Colony: or, Victoria in 1854* (London: Longman, 1855), pp.52–3; Cornwallis, *A Panorama of the New World*, p.136; A Melbourne Merchant, *The Gold Era of Victoria: being the present and future of the colony* (London and Melbourne, 1855), p.101; Duffy, *My Life in Two Hemispheres*, vol.2, p.156.

3 James Daniel to Austin Daniel, 15 May 1853, La Trobe Library, ms 10222.

4 Miscellaneous letters written to Maryborough, 1850s, La Trobe Library, Melbourne, ms 10943.

5 William Sasse to Mrs Wignall, 28 Aug. 1858, La Trobe Library, ms B538.

6 Letter dated 11 Aug. 1852, La Trobe Library, ms 10943.

7 *Mount Alexander Mail*, 10 Nov. 1854.

8 Rev. David Mackenzie, *The Gold Digger: A Visit to the Gold Fields of Australia in February 1852* (London: W.S. Orr, 1852), p.83.

9 S. Lemaitre, 'Homeward Bound' in *Songs of the Gold Fields* (Sandhurst, n.d.), p.24.

10 *Argus*, 21 June 1852.

11 George Ross Reid, letter, 1853, La Trobe Library ms 12430.

12 Letter to *Geelong Advertiser*, in *Argus*, 4 Oct. 1851, in G. Quaife, ed., *Gold and Colonial Society*, p.17.

13 Sir James Stephen, 'On Colonisation as a Branch of Social Economy', *Transactions of the National Association for the Promotion of Social Science* (London, 1859), p.103.

14 United Kingdom Parliament, *Further Papers Relative to the Recent Discovery of Gold in Australia*, (London, 1853), p.186.

15 Just, *Australia*, p.114.

16 'A Diggings' Home', *Australian Gold Diggers' Monthly Magazine* 1, Jan. 1853: p.129.

17 'A Father's Advice', *Australian Gold Diggers' Monthly Magazine* 1, Nov. 1852: p.57.

18 Rev. H. Berkeley Jones, *Adventures in Australia in 1852 and 1853* (London: Richard Bentley, 1853), p.295.

19 Melbourne Chamber of Commerce, *Reports on the Condition and Progress of the Colony of Victoria*, p.71.

20 'Shadows of the Golden Land', *Journal of Australasia* 1, 1856: p.132.

21 'The Rights of Labor', *The Convention and True Coloniser* 4, 19 Mar. 1859: p.6.

22 *Protection to Native Idleness, Socially, and not Politically Considered* (Melbourne, n.d.), p.7.

23 On Chisholm see Margaret Kiddle, *Caroline Chisholm* (Melbourne: Melbourne University Press, 1950), and Mary Hoban, *Fifty One Pieces of Wedding Cake: A Biography of Caroline Chisholm* (Kilmore, 1973).

24 *Mount Alexander Mail*, 10 Nov. 1854.

25 Conservative, *The Settlement of the Country, An Inquiry* (Melbourne, 1857), p.4.

26 Y.B.A., 'Gold', *Illustrated Australian Magazine* 4, 1852: p.102.

27 See Kolodny, *The Land Before Her*, p.203: 'If, as R.W.B. Lewis argues, American fiction written by men often concerns itself with "an Adamic person . . . at home only in the presence of nature and God", the fiction composed by nineteenth-century American women stubbornly returned that figure to the human community.' While mid-nineteenth century Australian men seem to have imagined both wild bush landscapes that could function as arenas for conquest, and the domesticated landscapes of settled agriculture, it could be argued that both were marked by a solitary, almost abstract character. They offered not new communities but an escape from humanity. Alan Atkinson has recently offered an extremely suggestive reading of the poetry of the native-born New South Wales writers of the 1830s and 1840s, which reaches a similar conclusion about the colonial Australian masculine landscape, though his contrast is Australia and Britain rather than men and women: 'Native-born sensibility and idealism had an airy thinness, a self-indulgence, a lack of energy which made a special virtue of simply being still, recording one's sensations within an unchanging landscape.' Alan Atkinson, 'Time, Place and Paternalism: Early Conservative Thinking in New South Wales', *Australian Historical Studies* 23, April 1988: p.13.

28 On the opposition of home and world in early nineteenth-century Britain, see Leonore Davidoff and Catherine Hall, *Family Fortunes: Men and Women of the English Middle Class 1780–1850* (London: Hutchinson, 1987). Davidoff and Hall place particular emphasis on the role of evangelical religion in shaping and promoting the distinction: 'A key aspect of Evangelical thinking was its refusal of the "world" and consequent turn to domesticity' (p.112). For an argument about the alternate values of the domestic sphere, their opposition to the world of the cash nexus in early nineteenth-century America, see Nancy Cott, *The Bonds of Womanhood. 'Woman's Sphere' in New England 1780–1835* (New Haven: Yale University Press, 1977), passim but especially pp.58–74.

29 Marilyn Lake, *The Limits of Hope* (Melbourne: Oxford University Press, 1987).

30 John B. Thompson, Editor's Introduction, Claude Lefort, *The Political Forms of Modern Society: Bureaucracy, Democracy, Totalitarianism* (Cambridge: Polity Press, 1986), p.16; Cornelius Castoriadis, 'The Imaginary Institution of Society', in John Fekete, ed., *The Structural Allegory: Reconstructive Encounters with the New French Thought* (Minneapolis: University of Minnesota Press, 1984), p.10.

31 Robert Shortreid Anderson, diary, La Trobe Library, p.155.

32 Ibid., p.166.

33 John Pettit to father and mother, Forest Creek, 20 Jan. 1853. Mitchell Library ms.

34 Ibid.

35 Though it was not until late in the century that the masculine freedom of the bush was to become a political doctrine at the hands of the *Bulletin*. See Marilyn Lake, 'The politics of respectability: Identifying the masculinist context', *Historical Studies*, 22, April 1986: pp.116–31.

36 Wilson, ed., *An Enquiry into the Principles of Representation*, p.i.

37 Howitt, *Two Years in Victoria*, p.181.

38 *Argus*, 4 June 1852.

39 *Age*, 17 Oct. 1854.

40 *Argus*, 16 June 1855.

41 Dianne Reilly and Jennifer Carew, eds, *Sun Pictures of Victoria* (Melbourne, 1983). See especially 'Deserted Diggings, Spring Creek', 'Doctor's Gully, Jim Crow', and 'Great Eastern Tunnel, Jim Crow'.

42 Serle, *Golden Age*, p.94.

43 Robin, ed., *Australian Sketches: The Journal and Letters of Frances Perry*, p.161.

44 E. Ramsay-Laye, *Social Life and Manners in Australia* (London: Longman, 1861), pp.14, 18.

45 Cf A. Kolodny, *The Land Before Her*; what most women objected to in the move to the American west was 'the irrevocable separation from friends and family'.(p.93) Interestingly, she finds in mid-nineteenth-century women's writing about the west a recurring 'fantasy of a landscape that might figuratively reconstitute some prior domestic landscape'(p.98), a simulation of an extended family.

46 Eliza Chomley, *Memoirs*, typescript (1920), La Trobe Library, Melbourne.

47 Jane Prendergast, letter, 28 Jan. 1853, La Trobe Library, ms 5405.

48 Spence, *Clara Morison*, p.221.

49 Wathen, *The Golden Colony*, p.43.

50 Mark Daniel, letter, 9 Aug. 1853. La Trobe Library, ms 10222. He was only 15 years old.

51 J. Castieau, diary, National Library, Canberra, microfilm. Entry for 15 May 1855.

52 Ibid., entry for 29 Jan. 1855.

53 Ibid., entry for 30 Jan. 1855.

54 It is the lack of 'respectable' women he is lamenting, for prostitutes make frequent (though usually coyly or obliquely recorded) appearances in the pages of the diary. The semi-visibility of prostitutes in the diary replicates Castieau's sense of their place in the world. While he frequented brothels at

night, he had a firm idea that prostitutes had no place in respectable, day-time, public Melbourne. This comes out most clearly in the diary entry for 28 May 1855, which records Castieau's attendance at the funeral of Sir Robert Nickle, the commander of the military forces in the colony: 'It was a very pompous affair. The whole of the Military, Principal Government officers, and Town Council were present . . . The affair made quite a holiday in the town and folks seemed very jolly. 3 notorious prostitutes dressed in the most glaring finery with brazen impudence were seated in an open carriage drawn up at the side of the road by which the procession marched. I should have liked to have seen them well pelted with mud, the shameless Jezabels.' The funeral of the military man was an occasion for public and respectable Melbourne, and the vehemence of Castieau's response to the transgression of the boundary suggests the depth of conviction on this subject. The point here is not just the double standard evinced by the frequenter of brothels who wants to stone the prostitutes who 'brazenly' show their faces in public, but the line being marked between public and private, legitimate and illegitimate, day and night.

55   Castieau diary, 19 Feb 1855.

56   Ibid.

57   Ibid., entry for 17 Feb. 1855.

58   Ibid., entry for 10 Feb. 1855.

59   Ibid., entry for 18 Jan. 1855.

60   James Muir diary, La Trobe Library ms. Entries for 16 to 19 March 1855. Gold of course only reinforced an existing demographic imbalance; the other great colonial industry, wool, had also created economic conditions which favoured the development of a society of men without women. The isolation of the worker in the pastoral industry was more extreme than that faced by the gold digger. 'It will be necessary to put two singular articles on the estimates this season, viz. a ready made Coffin + a Straight Jacket, as I am likely to die right out or go mad this season . . . ', A.C. Cameron of the Clyde Company run wrote to his supervisor, 'Why the very loneliness of this quarter now is frightful . . . '. A.C. Cameron to W. Lewis, 24 Sept 1852, in P.L. Brown, ed., *Clyde Company Papers* (London: Oxford University Press) vol.5, p.342.

61   'Thoughts of a New Colonist', *Church of England Messenger* 1, 1854: p.40.

62   Castieau diary, entry for 21 Jan. 1855.

63   Though see Jane Beer, Charles Fahey, Patricia Grimshaw and Melanie Raymond. *Colonial Frontiers and Family Fortunes*, Melbourne: 1989, and Christina Twomey, University of Melbourne PhD in progress, 'The Government of Abandonment.'

64   La Trobe to Pakington, General Correspondence 630/11, Letter 501, 1 June 1853, Victorian Public Record Office.

65   Rev. Edwin Day, letter, La Trobe Library, ms 5711.

66   *Age*, 30 Oct. 1854, editorial.

67   Spence, *Clara Morison*, p.66.

68   Davidoff and Hall, *Family Fortunes*. Similar arguments were taking place in the United States, see E. Anthony Rotundo, 'Learning about manhood:

gender ideals and the middle-class family in nineteenth-century America', in J.A. Mangin and James Walvin, eds, *Manliness and Morality: Middle-class masculinity in Britain and America 1800–1940* (Manchester: Manchester University Press, 1987), p.36, which outlines three competing modes of masculinity: the Masculine Achiever, the Christian Gentleman, and the Masculine Primitive. Christian Gentlemen were 'rejecting the greed, selfishness and dishonesty of the market place'. (p.38).

69 Davidoff and Hall, *Family Fortunes*, p.74.

70 Ibid., pp.114, 229.

71 cf Bate, *Victorian Gold Rushes*, p.62: 'In broad cultural terms the goldfields seem to have generated in Victoria an institutional approach to society and the arts that had no parallel in New South Wales.'

72 See George Nadel, *Australia's Colonial Culture: Ideas, Men and Institutions in Mid-Nineteenth Century Eastern Australia* (Melbourne: Melbourne University Press, 1957), pp.111–60. See the further discussion of mechanics institutes below.

73 W. Stitt Jenkins, 'The Land of Gold', *Temperance Times*, 14 Aug. 1858, p.97.

74 William Drummond, notebook, La Trobe Library, ms 11575.

75 Robert Anderson, diary, pp.160, 166. It may have been a series of unhappy love affairs which left Anderson melancholy (though he does eventually marry), or a slightly peevish temperament, but it seems also that the colony did not provide a sympathetic environment for him. 'I had good reason for leaving Melbourne', the diary concludes, 'having been most unjustly treated'.

76 Arthur Shum, diary, La Trobe Library, ms H15588, entry for 12 Dec. 1852.

77 Arthur Shum, letter book, La Trobe Library, letter to James Mowat, n.d.

78 Shum, letter book, letter 'My very dear Sir', n.d.

79 Ibid.

80 Shum, letter book, letter to James Mowat, n.d.

81 Langlands had left the Presbyterian church for the Baptist in 1833.

82 Rev. Isaac New, *A Memorial of Christian Excellence: The Funeral Address and Discourse Delivered at the Albert Street Baptist Church on the Death of Henry Langlands Esq. by the Rev. Isaac New*, (Melbourne: W.B. Stephens, 1863), pp.6, 12.

83 Ibid., pp.29–30.

84 Ibid., p.13.

85 'Not less than 1000 persons' assembled in the Oxford Street chapel in Collingwood to hear Thomas Binney on 21 Nov. 1858. *Christian Times*, 27 November 1858.

86 Rev. Thomas Binney, *Be Men: A Sermon Preached in the St. Kilda Congregational Church on Sunday Morning 11 April 1858* (Melbourne: W. Fairfax and Co., 1858), p.3.

87 Ibid., p.8.

88 Rev. Isaac New, *The Greatness of Man: A Lecture* (Melbourne: W. Fairfax and Co., 1858), p.10.

89 Rev. Isaac New, *A Christian Church* (Melbourne: W. Fairfax and Co., 1858), p.10.

90 New, *The Greatness of Man*, p.7.

91 Joseph Taylor, *The Church, the State, and the World* (Melbourne: Wilson Mackinnon and Fairfax, 1856), p.18.

92 Rev. Richard Fletcher, *Truth and Love* (Melbourne: Wilson, Mackinnon and Fairfax, 1856), p.6.

93 Binney, *Be Men*, p.8.

94 Rusden, *Gathering Together for the Good of Work and Learning*, p.20.

95 Rev. Isaac New, *Religion: All Profit and No Loss*, (Melbourne, 1860), p.3.

96 *Age*, 18 Oct. 1854.

97 Rusden, *Gathering Together for the Good of Work and Learning*, p.22.

98 *Christian Times*, 16 Oct. 1858.

99 Cairns, *The Dangers and Duties of the Young Men of Victoria*, p.7.

100 Ibid., p.13.

101 *Temperance Times*, 1, 2 Nov. 1857.

102 *Temperance Times*, 1, 28 Nov. 1857.

103 *Christian Times*, 23 Oct. 1858.

104 *Report of the Select Committee of the Legislative Council on the Gold Fields* (Melbourne, 1853), p.4.

105 Samuel Lazarus, diary, 15 Nov. 1853. LaTrobe Library, ms 11484.

106 *Temperance Times*, 1, 24 Dec. 1857; *Temperance Times*, 1, 7 April 1858.

107 J.R. Edwards, *Essay on Drunkenness* (Melbourne: Wilson, Mackinnon and Fairfax, 1859), p.3.

108 Victoria Parliament, *Legislative Council, Votes and Proceedings*, vol.3, 1853–4; Petition, ordered by the Council to be printed, 18 Oct. 1853; another petition presented to the Council, in November 1854, was signed by 6500 women.

109 Ibid., ordered to be printed 14 Oct. 1853.

110 Ibid., *report from the Select Committee of the Legislative Council on Intemperance* (Melbourne, 1854) p.15.

111 Petition, 18 Oct. 1853, op.cit.

112 *Melbourne Young Men's Mutual Improvement Association, First Annual Report* (Melbourne, 1857).

113 Symons, *The History and Advantages of Young Men's Associations*, pp. 11–12.

114 See John Milton, *The Evangelistic, Temperance, Economic, Educational and Model Farm Society, for the Benefit of Soldiers, Policemen, Immigrants, the Uneducated and the Unemployed* (Melbourne, 1855).

115 *Report of the Committee of Management of the Melbourne Mechanics' Institution and School of Arts for 1857* and ditto for 1858 (Melbourne, 1858 and 1859).

116 David Watson, letter to his mother, 26 March 1853, La Trobe Library, ms 8297.

117 Hearn, *Lecture on the Proposed Formation of Adult Educational Classes*, p.5.

118 Quoted in A. Wesson, 'Mechanics' Institutes in Victoria', *Victorian Historical Magazine* 42, Aug. 1971: p.612.

119 Some dates of mechanics institute foundation through the gold period: 1852: Benalla; 1853: Warrnambool, Williamstown; 1854: Bendigo, South Melbourne, Kerang, Kilmore, Maldon, Kyneton, Prahran; 1855: Beechworth, Castlemaine, Cheltenham, Eldorado; 1856: Footscray, North Melbourne, Belfast, St Kilda; 1857: Gisborne, Mount Moriac, South Yarra; 1858: Ceres,

Dunolly, Kew, Mitta Mitta, Newtown, Sale; 1859: Ararat, Ballarat, Brighton, Hamilton, Maryborough, Moorabool, Queenscliff, Richmond, Tarraville, Wedderburn; 1860: Amherst, Baringhup, Clunes, Daylesford, Kingston, Stawell. Source: A.Wesson, 'Mechanics' Institutes in Victoria', p.613.

120 *Address of the Trustees of the Melbourne Public Library* (Melbourne, 1859); Serle, *Golden Age*, p.354.

121 Alan Gross, 'The History of Melbourne Fire Fighting', *Victorian Historical Magazine*, Aug. 1960, pp.52–3. On American merchants and Melbourne fire companies see E. Daniel and Annette Potts, eds, *A Yankee Merchant in Goldrush Australia: The Letters of George Francis Train 1853–55* (Melbourne: Heinemann, 1970), pp.81–2, 92–3.

122 Rev. John Potter, *The Days are Evil: A Sermon* (Ballarat, n.d.), p.7.

123 Bonwick, *Notes of a Gold Digger*, p.33.

124 Paul, *California Gold*, p.82.

125 *Alta California*, 22 Mar. 1851, editorial.

126 Bushnell, *California*, p.23.

127 Mann, *After the Gold Rush*, p.4.

128 *Pioneer* 1, no.2, Feb. 1854: p.86.

129 Mann, *After the Gold Rush*, pp.42–5.

130 *Littell's Living Age* 24, 1850: p.464.

131 Helper, *Land of Gold*, pp.39, 114.

132 Drury, *William Anderson Scott*, 'No Ordinary Man', pp.159–60; Scott, *A Discourse for the Times*, p.6.

133 Park Benjamin, 'The California Gold Seeker to his Mistress', *Godey's Magazine and Lady's Book* 38, Apr. 1849: p.265.

134 *Pioneer* 1, no.4, Apr. 1854: p.215.

135 Ella Rodman, 'Going to California', *Peterson's Magazine of Art, Literature and Fashion* 25, 1849: p.170.

136 H.T. Tuckerman, 'The Gold Fever', *Godey's Magazine and Lady's Book* 38, Mar. 1849: p.207.

137 A.L. Otis, 'My Return From California', *Peterson's Ladies National Magazine* 21, 1852: p.275.

138 'Editors' Table', *Godey's Magazine* 38, Apr. 1849: p.294.

139 Stuart A. McLean, 'Opposition to the California Gold Rush: The Sentimental Argument: 1849–1853', in *American Renaissance and American West* (Laramie: University of Wyoming Press, 1982), pp.87–94.

140 *Pioneer* 2, no.2, Aug. 1854: p.80.

141 *California Christian Advocate*, 10 Oct. 1851.

142 Lyman, *Journal of a Voyage to California*, p.114.

143 Rev. Orange Clark, *A Discourse on Family Discipline* (San Francisco: R.P. Locke, 1860), p.30.

144 Jacqueline Baker Barnard, *The Fair But Frail: Prostitution in San Francisco 1849–1900* (Reno: University of Nevada Press, 1986), p.16.

145 Lotchin, *San Francisco*, p.306.

146 See Georgiana Bruce Kirby, *Years of Experience: An Autobiographical Narrative* (New York: G.P. Putnam's Sons, 1887).

147 Circular, 'California Association of American Women', in Eliza Farnham, *California: Indoors and Out*, reprint ed. (Nieuwkoop, 1972), p.xv.

148 Farnham, *California: Indoors and Out*, p.507.

149 Ibid., p.255.

150 Ibid., pp.295, 294.

151 Eliza Farnham, *Woman and Her Era* (New York: A.J. Davis, 1864), vol.2, p.44.

152 Ibid., pp.45, 67.

153 Quoted in Senkewicz, *Vigilantes in Gold Rush San Francisco*, p.129.

154 Rev. Daniel B. Woods, *Sixteen Months at the Gold Diggings* (New York: Harper, 1851), p.73.

155 Henry Veel Huntley, *California: Its Gold and Its Inhabitants* (London: T.C. Newby, 1856), p.220.

156 *Hutchings' California Magazine* 2, no.2, Aug. 1857: p.91.

157 F.P. Wierzbicki, *California as it is and as it may be*, (New York, 1970) [San Francisco, 1849], p.65.

158 Peter Decker has estimated that a little less than half of the members of the fire companies were merchants. Decker, *Fortunes and Failures*, p.109.

159 *Constitution and By-Laws of St. Francis Hook and Ladder Company* (San Francisco, 1857), p.17. The provision was a common one.

160 *Fireman's Journal and Military Gazette*, 16 June 1855.

161 Huntley, *California: Its Gold and Its Inhabitants*, p.2.

162 *Fireman's Journal and Military Gazette*, 23 June 1855.

163 *Hutchings' California Magazine* 2, no.2, Aug. 1857: p.90.

164 Lotchin, *San Francisco*, p.180. Further investigation would be needed to discover whether San Francisco's fire companies underwent the process of proletarianisation which Laurie describes for Philadelphia: Bruce Laurie, *Working People of Philadelphia, 1800–1850* (Philadelphia: Temple University Press, 1980), pp.58–61; Bruce Laurie, 'Fire Companies and Gangs in Southwark: the 1840s', in Allen F. Davis and Mark H. Haller, eds, *The Peoples of Philadelphia: A History of Ethnic Groups and Lower-Class Life* (Philadelphia: Temple University Press, 1973), pp.71–87.

165 Timothy J. Haggerty, 'The San Francisco Gentleman', *California History* 65, no.2, June 1986: p.101.

166 *Alta California*, 22 Aug. 1854; 23 Sept. 1854.

167 *Fireman's Journal and Military Gazette*, 14 April 1855.

168 *Fireman's Journal and Military Gazette*, 2 June 1855.

169 'Communication from Quarter-Master-General', in appendix to California, *Journals of the California Assembly* 6th session (Sacramento, 1855).

170 *San Francisco Whig* 1, no. 6, 1 Sept. 1852: p.1.

171 Dayton, The California Militia, pp. 24, 72. Dayton, though, warns that the figures on membership are unreliable.

172 Marcus Cunliffe, *Soldiers and Civilians: The Martial Spirit in America 1775–1865* (New York: Free Press, 1973), p.230; Dayton, The California Militia, p.103.

173 Mann, *After the Gold Rush*, p.57.

174 *California State Temperance Society* (Sacramento, 1856), p.4.

175 Timothy Dwight Hunt, diary 1853–54, microfilm C-B 835, Bancroft Library.
176 *First Annual Report of the Young Men's Christian Association of San Francisco, California* (San Francisco, 1854), pp.8–12.
177 *Second Annual Report of the Young Men's Christian Association* (San Francisco, 1855), p.34.
178 'The Miner', *Hutchings' California Magazine* 1, no.7, Feb. 1857: p.340.

CHAPTER 6

1 Raymond Williams, *Keywords* (London: Fontana, 1983). Michael Kammen has called for an American equivalent of Williams' seminal English work, which would make clear for the US 'the role that language has played as both symptom and determinant of thought and behaviour', Michael Kammen, *Selvages and Biases: The Fabric of History in American Culture* (Ithaca: Cornell University Press, 1987), p.133. A work which takes up this challenge, with regard to American political thought, is Daniel T. Rodgers, *Contested Truths: Keywords in American Politics Since Independence* (New York: Basic Books, 1987).

2 Samuel Johnson, *A Dictionary of the English Language* [1755] (New York, 1979).

3 *Mount Alexander Mail*, 8 Dec. 1854. Hitchcock was a local farmer and auctioneer.

4 *Ballarat Times*, 1 June 1858.

5 *Church of England Messenger* 1, 1854: p.36.

6 Smith, *Whether to go and Whither?*, p.vii.

7 Scott, ed., *Lord Robert Cecil's Gold Fields Diary*, p.26.

8 *Melbourne Morning Herald*, 9 Dec. 1851.

9 Howitt, *Tallangetta, The Squatter's Home*, vol.2, pp.250–1.

10 Tennyson, the Poet Laureate, apparently wanted to sail to Victoria in 1852 to seek for gold with his friends, and would have done so 'but for Mrs. Tennyson': Serle, *The Golden Age*, p.50.

11 D.W.A. Baker, *Days of Wrath: A Life of John Dunmore Lang* (Melbourne: Melbourne University Press, 1985), p.342.

12 Elizabeth Perkins, ed., *The Poetical Works of Charles Harpur* (Sydney: Angus and Robertson, 1984), p.200.

13 'The New Year', *Australian Gold Diggers' Monthly Magazine* 1, Jan. 1853: p.119.

14 'First Impressions of Australia', *Illustrated Australian Magazine* 2, 1851: p.306.

15 Bonwick, *Notes of a Gold-Digger*, p.28. While admitting the naturalness of the connection, Bonwick goes on to argue that in fact crime had not been rampant.

16 Rev. John Potter, *The Days are Evil*, pp.9–10.

17 Stawell, *My Recollections*, p.97.

18 Rev. Dr Cairns, Introduction, to Rev. J. Cumming, *A Lecture on Labor, Rest, and Recreation* (Melbourne: Wilson, Mackinnon and Fairfax, 1856), p.6.

19 G.M. Drummond, *Three Valedictory Sermons* (Melbourne, 1854), p.15. Drummond stressed the need for sobriety and seriousness of mind, 'calmness,

reflection . . . in a word, a frame of mind the very reverse of that feverish, excited, tumultuous state that every where prevails here where everyone is hurrying to be rich, and calm reflection is lost in the vortex of pressing and overwhelming worldly concerns'.

20 Colonus, *Does the Discovery of Gold*, p.8.

21 T.T. a'Beckett, *The Gold and the Government*, p.iv.

22 *Church of England Messenger* 3, Oct. 1852: p.293.

23 Cooper, *An Inquiry into the Relation of Christ to the World*, p.7.

24 *Further Papers Relative to the Recent Discovery of Gold in Australia* (London, 1852), p.45.

25 Ibid., pp.51, 53.

26 Ibid., p.68.

27 Ibid., p.53.

28 C.J. La Trobe, General Correspondence, La Trobe Library, ms 630/11, Letter 501.

29 William Howitt wrote that 'people are very subject to cramp in this country. Cramp and paralysis are very prevalent; the dogs especially are extraordinarily affected with paralysis . . . As soon as I arrived I was extremely pestered with it; a thing quite new to me. The Doctor said, "Oh! this is a terrible crampy country".' William Howitt, *Two Years in Victoria*, p.151.

30 New, *The Greatness of Man*, p.10. The oak as symbol of British virtue in Australia was the subject of some minor verse, see e.g., Howard Simcox, *Rustic Rambles in Rhyme, Collected in Various Parts of Victoria* (Ballarat, 1866), p.44, 'On Gathering Acorns':

> Recollections you recall,
> Of the land which gave us birth;
> England far surpassing all
> Other nations of the earth.

31 William Westgarth, *Victoria; Late Australia Felix, or Port Philip district of New South Wales* (Edinburgh: Oliver and Boyd, 1853), pp.19, 31.

32 HBM, 'Hindrances and Encouragements to the Ministry in Australia', *Church of England Messenger* ns, 1, 1854: p.66.

33 See K.S. Inglis, *The Australian Colonists* (Melbourne: Melbourne University Press, 1974), p.118.

34 J.A. Aldwell, *The Prize Essay of the Melbourne Labor League on the Eight Hours and Early Closing Questions* (Melbourne: Wilson, Mackinnon and Fairfax, 1856), p.6.

35 Howitt, *Two Years in Victoria*, p.231.

36 Just, *Australia*, p.53.

37 Ferdinand Mueller, *Address of the President, Delivered to the Members of the Philosophical Institute* (Melbourne: Mason and Firth, 1860), p.6.

38 *Age*, 31 October 1857.

39 J. William Mackenna, *Mortality of Children in Victoria* (Melbourne: W. Fairfax and Co., 1858), pp.7, 5.

40 *Eliza Cook's Journal* no.199, 19 Feb. 1853: p.271.

41 *Australian Gold Diggers' Monthly Magazine* 1, no.8, May 1853: p.283.

42   GG, 'Thoughts of a New Colonist', *Church of England Messenger* n.s. 1, 1854: p.39.

43   Wekey, *The Land, Importance of its Cultivation*, p.36.

44   Brown, *Victoria as I Found It*, p.168.

45   *A Report of the Inquiry into the Management of the Yarra Bend Lunatic Asylum, as detailed in the Nine Days' Trial of the Action for Libel, Bowie v. Wilson* (Melbourne, 1862), p.1.

46   'Report of Select Committee on Yarra Bend Lunatic Asylum', in Victoria Parliament, *Victorian Legislative Assembly, Votes and Proceedings, Session 1857–58*, vol.1, p.26. The Yarra Bend asylum suffered through the 1850s from alleged mismanagement, and feuds between staff. On British rates see *Lancet*, 29 August 1857, p.234.

47   James Kilgour, *Effect of the Climate of Australia Upon the European Constitution in Health and Disease* (Geelong: William Vale, 1855), p.29.

48   John Singleton MD, *A Narrative of Incidents in the Eventful Life of a Physician* (Melbourne: Hutchinson, 1891), p.117.

49   *Argus*, 17 Nov. 1852.

50   Benalla Crown Lands Commissioner to Colonial Secretary, 21 June 1852, Victorian Public Record Office, Colonial Secretary's Inward Correspondence, VPRS 1189, Box 21, 52/2420.

51   John K. Walton, 'Lunacy in the Industrial Revolution: A Study of Asylum Admissions in Lancashire, 1848-50', *Journal of Social History* 13, no.1 (1979): p.18.

52   Andrew T. Scull, 'Madness and Segregative Control: The Rise of the Insane Asylum', *Social Problems* 24, no.3, 1977: p.349.

53   'Many cases called "lunatics" in Police Courts are only cases of temporary derangement arising principally from habits of intemperance and other irregularities in the mode of life pursued by persons of weak mind and shattered constitutions.' *Argus*, 31 May 1854.

54   'Report of Select Committee on Yarra Bend Lunatic Asylum', p.45.

55   Robert Bowie, Superintendent of the Yarra Bend asylum since 1852, told the 1858 inquiry that young women were often admitted to the asylum soon after their arrival in the colony—they arrived maniacal, he said, and, rejecting the suggestion that the problem was uterine in origin, he argued that it was disappointment which created the mania (ibid., p.11). The unsympathetic parliamentary questioner described the problem as 'a mere disease arising from separation from their friends'.

56   Yarra Bend Case Book, 1848–54, and Yarra Bend Letter Book, 1854–1856, Victorian Mental Health Authority archives.

57   William Tomlinson, diary, 4 December 1852. La Trobe Library, ms 12183.

58   Yarra Bend Case Book.

59   Letters from gaoler, Eastern Gaol, to Dr Bowie—esp. letters of 13 Sept. 1855, 30 Oct. 1855, and 14 Dec. 1855: Mental Health Authority archives. For an essentially negative view of the possibility of using the content of psychotic delusions as historical evidence, see John C. Burnham, 'Psychotic Delusions as a Key to Historical Cultures: Tasmania, 1830–1940', *Journal of Social History* 13, no.3 (spring, 1980), pp.368–83.

60 *A Report of the Inquiry into the Management of the Yarra Bend Lunatic Asylum*, as detailed in the Nine Day's Trial of the Action for Libel, Bowie v. Wilson, p.34.

61 Rt. Rev. R.W. Willson, *A Few Observations Relative to the Yarra Bend Lunatic Asylum* (Melbourne: Wm. Goodhugh and Co., 1859), p.7.

62 'Plan for a New Asylum', MHA archives.

63 Letter, Bowie to Colonial Secretary, 7 October 1853, Victorian Public Record Office, VPRS 1189, Box 132, 53/10094.

64 On moral treatment in Victoria, see Keith M. Benn, 'The Moral Versus Medical Controversy: An Early Struggle in Colonial Victorian Psychiatry', *The Medical Journal of Australia* 1, no.5, Feb. 1957, p. 125.

65 Colonus, *Does the Discovery of Gold*, p.16.

66 Ibid., p.10.

67 T.T. a'Beckett, *The Gold and the Government*, p.iv, p.3.

68 *Argus*, 17 April 1852.

69 *Illustrated Australian Magazine* 3, 1851: p.266.

70 William Bakewell, Preface, to Spence, *Clara Morison*, p.xi.

71 Ralph Bieber, 'California Gold Mania', *Mississippi Valley Historical Review* 35, no.1, June 1948: p.3.

72 Frank Marryat, *Mountains and Molehills: Or Recollections of a Burnt Journal* (New York, 1855), p.35.

73 E.W. Farnham, *A Lecture on the Philosophy of Spiritual Growth* (San Francisco: Valentine and Co., 1862), p.7.

74 Ibid., p.16.

75 David E. Shi, *The Simple Life: Plain Living and High Thinking in American Culture* (New York: Oxford University Press, 1985), p.100.

76 C.R. Street, 'Crossing the Plains in '49', *Associated Pioneers of the Territorial Days, Sixteenth Annual Meeting, 1891*, p.24, cited in Mary Floyd Williams, *History of the San Francisco Committee of Vigilance of 1851*, p.432.

77 Woods, *Sixteen Months at the Gold Diggings*, p.181.

78 Samuel H. Willey, *Decade Sermons. Two Historical Discourses, Occasioned by the Close of the First Ten Years Ministry in California, Preached in the Howard Street Presbyterian Church, San Francisco* (San Francisco: Towne and Bacon, 1859), p.33.

79 Helper, *The Land of Gold*, p.179.

80 HJM, 'Street Thoughts', in *California Visions and Realities; A Series of Poems* (San Francisco, 1855), p.6.

81 Thren, 'The Poetry of California', *Pioneer* 1, no.1, January 1854: p.20.

82 Mrs D.B. Bates, *Incidents on Land and Water, Or, Four Years on the Pacific Coast* (Boston, 1860), p.99.

83 Ralph Raven [George Payson], *Golden Dreams and Leaden Realities*, p.77.

84 Taylor, *Eldorado*, p.87.

85 Ibid., p.44.

86 Weston, *Four Months in the Mines of California*, p.4.

87 Huntley, *California: Its Gold and Its Inhabitants*, p.83.

88 Decker, *Fortunes and Failures*, p.74.

89 *Alta California*, 2 August 1849.

90 Farnham, *California: Indoors and Out*, p.316.

91 Timothy Dwight Hunt, 'Fast Living', *Pacific*, 14 Nov. 1851.

92 E.L. Cleaveland, *Hasting to be Rich. A Sermon Occasioned by the Present Excitement Respecting the Gold of California, Preached in the Cities of Bridgeport and New Haven* (New Haven, 1849), pp.8–9.

93 Ibid., p.17.

94 Huntley, *California: Its Gold and Its Inhabitants*, p.222.

95 Timothy Dwight Hunt, 'Haste to be Rich', *Pacific*, 1 August 1851.

96 Borthwick, *The Gold Hunters*, p.78.

97 Helper, *The Land of Gold*, p.99

98 Marryat, *Mountains and Molehills: Or Recollections of a Burnt Journal*, p.195.

99 Watson, ed., *To the Land of Gold and Wickedness*, p.259.

100 *The California Teacher* 2, no.5, November 1864: p.114.

101 Cantell A. Bigly [George Washington Peck], *Aurifodina, or, Adventures in the Gold Region* (New York: Baker and Scribner, 1849), p.49.

102 Ibid., p.61.

103 Thomas Starr King, *A Vacation Among the Sierras: Yosemite in 1860* [1860] (San Francisco, 1962), p.6.

104 Farnham, *California: Indoors and Out*, p.367.

105 Rev. W.A. Scott, *Our Young Men*, pp.26–7.

106 Richard W. Fox, *So Far Disordered in Mind: Insanity in California, 1870–1930* (Berkeley: University of California Press, 1978), p.21.

107 Dr J. Praslow, *The State of California: A Medico-Geographical Account* (San Francisco, 1939) [Gottingen, 1857], p.84.

108 'Musings in a Madhouse', *Hutchings' California Magazine* 1, no.2, August 1856: p.88.

109 Rt Rev. William Ingraham Kip, *The Early Days of My Episcopate* (New York, 1892), p.121.

110 'Annual Report of the Resident Physician of the Asylum for the Insane of the State of California', in California, *Journal of California Senate, 5th Session, 1854*, appendix, p.23.

111 David J. Rothman, *The Discovery of the Asylum, Social Order and Disorder in the New Republic* (Boston: Little, Brown, 1971), p.114.

112 'Before the Civil War, practically no one in the United States protested the simple connection between insanity and civilization.' Ibid., p.113.

113 Horace Bushnell, *Moral Uses of Dark Things* (New York: Scribner, 1903), pp. 252–3.

114 'Annual Report of the Resident Physician', 1853, p.24.

115 'Annual Report of the Resident Physician of the Asylum for the Insane of the State of California, 1854', in California, *Journal of California Senate, 6th Session, 1855*, appendix, p.20.

116 'Annual Report of the Resident Physician of the Asylum for the Insane of the State of California', in California, *Journal of the California Assembly, 7th Session, 1856*, p.14.

117 'Annual Report of the Resident Physician of the Asylum for the Insane', in California, *Journal of the California Assembly, 8th Session, 1857*, appendix, p.16.

118 Watson, ed., *To the Land of Gold and Wickedness*, p.272.

119   N.L. Frothingham, *Gold: A Sermon Preached to the First Church on Sunday Dec. 17 1848* (Boston, 1849), pp.8, 4.

120   Ibid., p.6.

121   Ibid., pp.11–12.

122   Kip, *The Early Days of My Episcopate*, p.90.

123   *San Francisco Whig* 1, no.6, 1 September 1852: p.1.

124   'California Gold', *US Magazine and Democratic Review*, January 1849: p.4.

125   C.D.H., 'Our Divorce Law', *Pioneer* 1, no.4, April 1854: p.213.

126   Frank Soule, John H. Gihon and James Nisbet, *The Annals of San Francisco* (New York, 1854), p. 256.

127   Benton, *The California Pilgrim*, p.92.

128   'Report of Mr. Crosby on Civil and Common Law', appendix O, California, *Journal of the Senate of the State of California at their First Session* (San Jose, 1850), pp.471–2.

129   'Increase in the Quantity of Gold: Its Effects', *Western Journal* 2, no.3: p.147.

130   *Transactions of the California State Agricultural Society During the Year 1859* (Sacramento, 1860), p.384.

131   Oliver Outcast, 'Rest', *Pioneer* 3, no.2., Feb. 1855: p.88.

132   Avery, *The Land of Ophir, Ideal and Real*, p.5.

133   Woodbridge, *Sermon Preached at the Dedication of the First Presbyterian Church, Benicia*, p.9.

134   Scott, *Trade and Letters*, p.48.

135   Ibid., p.22.

136   Rev. Dr Scott, *A Lecture on the Influence of Great Cities* (San Francisco: Whitton, Towne and Co., 1854), p.12.

137   Scott, *The Wedge of Gold*, p.73.

138   Edward Pillock, 'Thoughts Toward a New Epic', *Pioneer* 2, no.2, Aug. 1854: p.76.

139   Scott, *The Wedge of Gold*, p.170.

140   Rev. Charles A. Farley, 'Thanksgiving Sermon of 1850', in *California Historical Society Quarterly* 19: p.301.

141   'Increase in the Quantity of Gold', *Western Journal* 2, no.3: p.145.

142   'California Gold', *United States Magazine and Democratic Review* ns, 24, no.127, Jan. 1849: p.3.

143   Thomas Jefferson, 'Notes on the State of Virginia', in Merril D. Peterson, ed., *The Portable Thomas Jefferson* (New York: Penguin, 1975), p.217.

CONCLUSION

1   *Celebration of the Eightieth Anniversary of the Independence of the United States, by the American Citizens Resident in Melbourne, Australia* (Melbourne, 1856), p.36.

2   John Higham, 'Changing Paradigms: The Collapse of Consensus History', *Journal of American History* 76, 1989: p.465; Ian Tyrrell, 'Comparing Comparative Histories: Australian and American Modes of Comparative Analysis', *Australasian Journal of American Studies* 9, no.2, Dec. 1990: p.2.

3   See David Goodman: 'Postmodernism and History', *American Studies International* 31, no.2, October 1993: pp.17–23.

4   See e.g. Benedict Anderson, *Imagined Communities: Reflections on the Origin and Spread of Nationalism* (London: Verso, 1983); Eric Hobsbawm and T. Ranger, eds, *The Invention of Traditions* (Cambridge: Cambridge University Press, 1983); Richard White, *Inventing Australia* (Sydney: Allen & Unwin, 1981).

Bibliography

Manuscript Sources

LA TROBE LIBRARY, MELBOURNE
a'Beckett, T.T. Diary. Ms 9035.
Adeney, Henry. Diary. Ms 9110.
Allan, George L. Papers. Ms 7720.
Anderson, Robert. Diary. Ms 8492.
Atkinson, David. Letters. Ms M436.
Atlee, Jim. 1859 Letter. Ms 9873/76.
Austin, Anna. Letter. Ms 10514.
Baker, George. Diary. Ms 11374.
Barker, Alfred. Letters. Ms 1162.
Birchall, Lucy. Letter. Ms 9328.
Booth, Mr and Mrs A. Journal. Ms 9715.
Brensley, Henry. Letters. Box 91.
Bristow, Mary. Journal. Ms 5716.
Brooks, Thomas. Letter. Ms 8906.
Castieau, John Buckly. Diary. National Library of Australia. Microfilm.
Chapple, John. Diary. Ms 11792.
Chomley, Eliza. Memoirs. Typescript (1920). Ms 9034.
Clark, Seth. Diary. Ms 10436.
Clow, James. Letters and papers. Ms 9570/74.
Cooke, Arbella. Correspondence. Ms 10840.
Cooper, Rev. John. Newspaper clipping book. Ms 12061
Corbett, Richard and John. Letters. Ms 6748.
Daniel, Mark. Letter, and Daniel family papers. Ms 10222.
Day, Rev. Edwin. Letter. Ms 5711.
Dexter, Caroline. Correspondence. Ms 11630.
Dick, Alexander. Diaries. Ms 11241
Drummond, William. Notebook. Ms 11575.
Drysdale, Anne. Diary. Ms 9249.
Embling, Thomas. Diary. Ms 11106.
Fedden, Olcher. Letters. Ms 8379.
Gibson, Aleck. Letters. Ms 8420.
Hadfield, John. Letter. Ms 8172.
Haig, Robert. Diary. Ms 7626.
Howitt, Alfred. Papers. Ms 9356.
Kincaid, Janet. Letter. Ms 10943.
La Trobe, Charles Joseph. General correspondence. Ms 630/11.

Lazarus, Samuel. Diary. Ms 11484.

Lucas, Eliza. Diary and reminiscences. Ms 12104.

Lyall, William. Letters. Ms 10014.

McGregor, William. Diary. Ms 8563.

Macknight, Charles. Diaries. Ms 8999.

Mair, William. Journal. Ms H5547.

Miscellaneous letters written to Maryborough, 1850s. Ms 10943.

Muir, James. Diary. Ms 10056.

Mundy, Henry. Diaries. Ms 10416.

Newton, William. Diary. Ms 10251.

Palmer, Nimrod. Letter. Box 332/7E

Peristtet, Charlotte. Letter. Ms 10251.

Pettman, Daniel. Letter to his parents. Ms 10926.

Pohlman, Robert. Diaries. Ms 10303.

Prendergast, Jane. Letter, 28 Jan. 1853. Ms 5405.

Prendergast, Michael. Letters. Ms 5405.

Prendergast, Philip. Letter to his father, 21 Sept. 1852. Ms 5405, Box 31/2(a).

Ramsay, Andrew Mitchell. Diary. Ms 11021.

Ramsay, Robert. Poetry ms. Ms 11021.

Rayment, William. Diary. Ms 4471.

Reid, George Ross. Letter. Ms 12430.

Sasse, William. Letters. Ms B538.

Shum, Arthur. Diary and letter book. Ms H15588.

Sparks, George. Papers. Ms 9335.

Tomlinson, William. Diary. Ms 12183.

Tucker, Gordon. Journal. Ms 10649.

Walsh, J.J. Papers. Ms 7763.

Watson, David Matthew. Letters. Ms 8297.

Wills, W.J. Letters. Ms 9504.

Wilson, James. Letters. Ms 12416.

VICTORIAN PUBLIC RECORD OFFICE, LAVERTON

Colonial Secretary's Correspondence file. VPRS 1189.

Confidential Despatches from the Secretary of State. VPRS 1090.

Governor's Despatch Book. VPRS 1084.

Supreme Court Letter Book. VPRS 830.

OTHER MELBOURNE ARCHIVES

Airy papers. University of Melbourne Archives.

Letters from gaoler, Eastern Gaol, to Dr Bowie—esp. letters of 13 Sept. 1855, 30 Oct. 1855, and 14 Dec. 1855. Victorian Mental Health Authority archives, Melbourne.

Yarra Bend Case Book, 1848–1854, and Yarra Bend Letter Book 1854–1856. Victorian Mental Health Authority archives, Melbourne.

Bishop's Letter Book, Church of England archives. St Paul's Cathedral, Melbourne.

Macartney, H.B. Memoirs. Church of England archives. St Paul's Cathedral, Melbourne.

MITCHELL LIBRARY, SYDNEY
Pettit, John. Letters.

BANCROFT LIBRARY, BERKELEY
Hall, Milton. Letters.
Hulpert, Eri S. and William W. Walker. *Land of Gold: An Ill Fated Journey to California via Nicaragua* (1852).
Hunt, Timothy Dwight. Diary, 1853–1854. Microfilm C–B 835.
Prevaux, Rev. Francis E. Letters.
Shaw, G. Diary.
Townsend, Susan. Letters.

MICROFILM
American Home Missionary Society. Incoming correspondence. Microfilm.
American Heritage microfilm series.

GOVERNMENT PAPERS, VICTORIA

Victorian Hansard: Debates and Proceedings of the Legislative Council and Assembly of the Colony of Victoria. 1856–
Votes and Proceedings of the Legislative Council. 1851–
Victoria: Gold Regulations. 1854.
'Report of the Select Committee of the Legislative Council on the Aborigines'. In *Votes and Proceedings of the Legislative Council*. 1858–59
'Report from the Select Committee on Police'. In *Votes and Proceedings, Victorian Legislative Council*. 1852–53 vol.2.
Report of the Select Committee of the Legislative Council on the Gold Fields. 1853.
'Report from the Select Committee of the Legislative Council on Intemperance'. 1854.
University of Melbourne Report, in *Votes and Proceedings, Victorian Legislative Council*. 1854.
'Report of the Board Appointed to Enquire into Circumstances Connected with the Late Disturbance at Ballarat'. In *Votes and Proceedings of the Victorian Legislative Council*. 1854.
Debate in the Legislative Council of the Colony of Victoria on the Second Reading of the New Constitution Bill. 1858.
'Report of Select Committee on Yarra Bend Lunatic Asylum'. In *Victorian Legislative Assembly, Votes and Proceedings*. Session 1857–8, vol.1.

PARLIAMENTARY PAPERS, BRITAIN

Correspondence Relative to the Recent Discovery of Gold in Australia. 1852
Further Papers Relative to the Recent Discovery of Gold in Australia. 1853
Further Papers Relative to the Alterations in the Constitutions of the Australian Colonies. 1852

GOVERNMENT PAPERS, CALIFORNIA

'Annual Report of the Resident Physician of the Asylum for the Insane of the

State of California'. In *Journal of California Senate*. 5th session. 1854. Appendix.

'Annual Report of the Resident Physician of the Asylum for the Insane of the State of California, 1854'. In *Journal of California Senate*, 6th session. 1855. Appendix.

'Annual Report of the Resident Physician of the Asylum for the Insane of the State of California'. *Journal of the California Assembly*. 7th session. 1856.

'Annual Report of the Resident Physician of the Asylum for the Insane'. *Journal of the California Assembly*. 8th session. 1857. Appendix.

Journal of the Senate of the State of California at their First Session. San Jose: 1850.

Journals of the Legislature of the State of California at its Second Session. San Jose: 1851.

'Transactions of the California State Agricultural Society, 1858'. In *Journals of the California Senate*. 10th session. 1859. Appendix.

'Transactions of the California State Agricultural Society During the Year 1859. Appendix. In *Journal of the California Senate*. 11th session. 1860. Appendix.

PERIODICALS AND NEWSPAPERS, NORTH AMERICAN

Alta California.
American Review: A Whig Journal.
Californian Christian Advocate.
California Farmer and Journal of Useful Sciences.
Fireman's Journal and Military Gazette.
Godey's Magazine and Lady's Book.
Harper's New Monthly Magazine.
Hutchings' California Magazine.
Knickerbocker.
New Englander.
North American Review.
Peterson's Magazine of Art, Literature and Fashion.
Pioneer.
San Francisco Whig.
Sartain's Magazine.
United States Magazine and Democratic Review.
Western Journal.

BRITISH PERIODICALS AND NEWSPAPERS

Blackwood's Edinburgh Magazine.
British Quarterly Review.
Chambers's Edinburgh Journal.
Dublin University Magazine.
Economist.
Edinburgh Review.
Eliza Cook's Journal.
Fraser's Magazine.

Household Words.
North British Review.
Punch.
Quarterly Review.
Times.
Westminster Review.

VICTORIAN PERIODICALS AND NEWSPAPERS

Age.
Argus.
Australian Gold Diggers Monthly Magazine.
Australian Home Companion and Illustrated Weekly Magazine.
Ballarat Times.
Bendigo Advertiser.
Convention and True Coloniser.
Freeholder and Convention Expositor.
Freesoil Papers for the People.
Illustrated Australian Magazine.
Journal of Australasia.
Ladies Almanack, The Southern Cross or Australian Album and New Year's Gift.
Melbourne Church of England Messenger.
Melbourne Morning Herald.
Melbourne Punch.
Mount Alexander Mail.
My Note Book.
Portland Guardian and Normanby General Advertiser.
Rural Magazine.
Temperance Times.
Victorian Christian Herald.
Victorian Monthly Magazine.
Warrnambool Examiner.
Wesleyan Chronicle.

BRITISH REACTIONS

British Association for the Advancement of Science. *Report of the Twenty-Third Meeting of the British Association for the Advancement of Science.* London: 1854.
——.*Report of the Twenty-Seventh Meeting of the British Association for the Advancement of Science.* London: 1858.
Cairnes, J. E. 'Mr. Ruskin on the Gold Question'. *Macmillan's Magazine* 9, Nov. 1863: pp.67–69.
Chevalier, Michel. *On the Probable Fall in the Value of Gold: The commercial and social consequences which may ensue, and the measures which it invites.* New York: D. Appleton and Co. 1859.
Jevons, W. Stanley. 'A Serious Fall in the Value of Gold Ascertained, and its Social

Effects Set Forth' [1863]. In his *Investigations in Currency and Finance*. London: Macmillan, 1884.

Lalor, John. *Money and Morals: A Book for the Times*. London: Chapman 1852.

National Association for the Promotion of Science. *Transactions of the National Association for the Promotion of Social Science 1855–61*.

Ruskin, John. 'Essays on Political Economy'. *Fraser's Magazine* 65 (1862), pp.788–90.

Senior, Nassau. *Four Introductory Lectures on Political Economy Delivered Before the University of Oxford*. London: Longman, Brown, Green, and Longmans 1852.

Ward, James. *A History of Gold as a Commodity and as a Measure of Value. Its Fluctuations both in Ancient and Modern Times, with an Estimate of the Probable Supplies from California and Australia*. London: W.S. Orr 1852.

CONTEMPORARY WRITINGS, CALIFORNIA

Address of the State Executive Committee to the Colored People of the State of California. Sacramento: 1859.

Anderson, Rev. W.C. *The Substance of Four Discourses on the Bible in Common Schools*. San Francisco: Towne & Bacon 1859.

Anon. (HJM.) *California Visions and Realities; A Series of Poems*. San Francisco: C.M Chase and Co. 1855.

Anon. *The Gold Key Court or the Corruptions of a Majority of it*. San Francisco: 1855.

Archibald, John. *On the Contact of Races: Considered Especially with Relation to the Chinese Question*. San Francisco: Towne & Bacon 1860.

Audubon, John Woodhouse. *Audubon's Western Journal 1849–1850*. Tucson: Univ. of Arizona Press 1984.

Avery, Rev. J.H. *The Land of Ophir, Ideal and Real: A Discourse Delivered at Austinburg Ohio before a Company About Proceeding to California*. New York: E.O. Jenkins 1853.

Bacon, Rev. Leonard. *A Discourse in Behalf of the American Home Missionary Society, Preached in the Cities of New York and Brooklyn, May 1852*. New York: Baker, Goodwin 1852.

Baer, Warren. *The Duke of Sacramento*. San Francisco: Franklin Press 1856.

Ballou, John. *The Lady of the West, or, The Gold Seekers*. Cincinnati: Ballou, 1855.

Ballou, Mary. *'I hear the hogs in my kitchen': A woman's view of the gold rush*. New Haven: F.W. Beinecke 1962.

Barker, Charles Albro, ed. *Memoirs of Elisha Crosby: Reminiscences of California and Guatemala from 1849 to 1864*. San Marino: 1945.

Bates, Mrs D.B. *Incidents on Land and Water, Or, Four Years on the Pacific Coast* 10th ed. Boston: 'For the Author' 1860.

Bellows, Henry W. *In Memory of Thomas Starr King: A Discourse Given to his Flock in San Francisco*. San Francisco: F. Eastman 1864.

Benton, J.A. *The California Pilgrim: A Series of Lectures*. Sacramento: S. Alter 1853.

Benton, Thomas Hart. *Speech of Mr. Benton of Missouri, On the Adjudication of Land Titles, and Sale of Gold Mines in New Mexico and California*. Washington: 1849.

Bidlack, Russell E. *Letters Home: The Story of Ann Arbor's Forty Niners*. Ann Arbor: Ann Arbor Publishers 1960.

Bigly, Cantell A. [George Washington Peck]. *Aurifodina, or, Adventures in the Gold Region.* New York: Baker and Scribner 1849.

Black, Eleanora and Sydney Robertson, eds. *The Gold Rush Song Book.* San Francisco: The Colt Press 1940.

Booth, Edmund. *Edmund Booth, Forty-Niner.* San Joaquin: San Joaquin Historical Society 1953.

Borthwick, J.D. *The Gold Hunters.* Oyster Bay: New York, 1917.

Brier, Rev. William Wallace. *The Opening Sermon Before the Synod of Alta California.* San Francisco: Towne and Bacon, 1860.

Brierly, Rev. B. *Thoughts for the Crisis: a Discourse Delivered in the Washington St. Baptist Church, San Francisco.* 2nd ed. San Francisco: Eureka Book and Job Office 1856.

Browne, J. Ross. *Report of the Debates in the Convention of California on the Formation of the State Constitution.* Washington: J.T. Towers 1850.

Buffum, E. Gould. *Six Months in the Gold Mines: From a Journal of Three Years' Residence in Upper and Lower California.* Philadelphia: Lea and Blanchard 1850.

Burgess, Rt Rev. George. *Bishop Burgess' Sermon at the Consecration of the Missionary Bishop of California.* Albany: 1853.

[Rev. George Burrows] A Clergyman. *Impressions of Dr. Wadsworth as a Preacher.* San Francisco: Towne and Bacon 1863.

Bushnell, Horace. *California: Its Characteristics and Prospects.* San Francisco: Whitton, Towne and Co. 1858.

——.*Moral Uses of Dark Things.* New York: Scribner 1903.

——.*Society and Religion: A Sermon for California, Delivered on Sabbath Evening, July 6, 1856, at the Installation of Rev. E.S. Lacey, as Pastor of the First Congregational Church, San Francisco.* San Francisco: Sterett and Co. 1856.

Bynum, Lindley, ed. *Muleback to the Convention: Letters of J. Ross Browne.* San Francisco: Book Club of California 1950.

Canfield, Chauncey L., ed. *The Diary of a Forty-Niner.* San Francisco: M. Shepard and Co. 1906.

Carson, James H. *Life in California, Together with a Description of the Great Tulare Valley.* 2nd ed. Stockton: The San Joaquin Republican 1852.

Chalwill, George M. *An Address Delivered Before Morning Star Temple of Honor.* San Francisco: Whitton, Towne, 1854.

Chauviteau, J.J. *The Plaza (Portsmouth Square), San Francisco, As It Should Be and May Be, According to the Plan Proposed by J.J. Chauviteau.* San Francisco: 1854.

Clark, Rev. Orange. *A Discourse on Family Discipline.* San Francisco: R.P. Locke 1860.

Cleaveland, E.L. *Hasting to be Rich. A Sermon Occasioned by the Present Excitement Respecting the Gold of California, Preached in the Cities of Bridgeport and New Haven.* New Haven: J.H. Benham 1849.

Colton, Walter. *Three Years in California.* New York: S.A. Rollo 1860.

Crampton, C. Gregory, ed. *The Mariposa Indian War 1850–1851.* Salt Lake City: University of Utah Press 1957.

Cutler, Rev. R.B. *A Thanksgiving Sermon: Delivered in the First Unitarian Church.* San Francisco: Commercial Book and Job Steam Printing Establishment 1856.

Delano, Alonzo. 'A Live Woman in the Mines'. In Glenn Loney, ed., *California Gold Rush Plays*. New York: Performing Arts Journal Publications, 1983.

——.*Old Block's Sketch Book*. Santa Ana: Fine Arts Press 1947.

Dickens, Charles. *American Notes and Pictures from Italy*. London: Oxford University Press 1957.

Emerson, Ralph Waldo and Waldo Emerson Forbes, eds. *Journals of Ralph Waldo Emerson 1849–1855*. Boston: Riverside 1912.

Ewing, W.A.D. *The Little Book of Moral Philosophy*. San Francisco: 1857.

Fargo, Frank. *A True and Minute History of the Assassination of James King of William and the Execution of Casey and Cora*. San Francisco: Whitton, Towne 1856.

Farnham, Eliza. *California: Indoors and Out; or How we Farm, Mine, and Live Generally in the Golden State*. New York: Dix, Edwards 1856.

——.*A Lecture on the Philosophy of Spiritual Growth*. San Francisco: Valentine and Co. 1862.

——.*Woman and her Era*. New York: A.J. Davis 1864.

Field, Stephen J. 'Opinion of the United States Supreme Court in Tennison vs Kirk'. In *Some Opinions and Papers of Stephen J. Field*. n.p.: n.d.

——.*Personal Reminiscences of Early Days in California*. San Francisco: 1893.

Fremont, Jessie Benton. *Mother Lode Narratives*, ed. Shirley Sargent. Ashland, Calif.: L. Osborne 1970.

The Fremont Decision. Decision of the Supreme Court of the State of California in the Case of Biddle Boggs vs Merced Mining Company. San Francisco: Royal P. Locke 1859.

Frothingham, N.L. *Gold: A Sermon Preached to the First Church on Sunday Dec. 17, 1848*. Boston: J. Wilson 1849.

Frothingham, Richard. *A Tribute to Thomas Starr King*. Boston: Ticknor and Fields 1865.

Giffen, Helen, ed. *The Diaries of Peter Decker: Overland to California in 1849 and Life in the Mines, 1850–51*. Georgetown. Calif.: Talisman Press 1966.

Gordon, Mary McDougall, ed. *Overland to California with the Pioneer Line: The Gold Rush Diary of Bernard J. Reid*. Urbana: Univ. of Illinois Press 1987.

Helper, Hinton R. *The Land of Gold. Reality Versus Fiction*. Baltimore: H. Taylor 1855.

Hickok, Rev. Laurens P. *A Discourse in Behalf of the American Home Missionary Society, Preached in the Cities of New York and Brooklyn, May 1853*. New York: American Home Mission Society 1853.

Hines, Rev. J.W. *Address Delivered at Vallejo, on Thanksgiving Day*. Vallejo, Calif.: B.F. Sterett 1863.

Holliday, J.S. *The World Rushed In: The California Gold Rush Experience, An Eyewitness Account*. New York: Simon and Schuster 1981.

Hunt, Timothy Dwight. *Address Delivered Before the New England Society of San Francisco*. San Francisco: Cooke, Kenny and Co. 1853.

——.*Sermon Suggested by the Execution of Jenkins on the Plaza, by the 'People' of San Francisco, during the Night of the 10th of June 1851*. San Francisco: Marvin and Hitchcock 1851.

Huntley, Henry Veel. *California: Its Gold and Its Inhabitants*. London: T.C. Newby 1856.

Independent Order of Good Templars. *Address to the Grand and Subordinate Lodges of the Independent Order of Good Templars of the State of California.* Nevada: E.G. Waite 1860.

James, Henry. *Lectures and Miscellanies.* New York: Redfield 1852.

Johnson, Kenneth, ed. *The Gold Rush Letters of J.D.B. Stillman.* Palo Alto: L. Osborne 1967.

Kelly, William. *A Stroll Through the Diggings of California.* London: Simms and McIntyre 1852.

Kewen, E.J.C. *Idealina and other Poems.* San Francisco: Cooke, Kenny and Co. 1853.

King, Thomas Butler. *California: The Wonder of the Age.* New York: W. Gowans 1850.

King, Thomas Starr. *A Discourse in Memory of Frederick William Macondray.* San Francisco: Towne and Bacon 1862.

——.*Fourth of July Oration. Delivered at the Celebration of the Fourth of July, 1861, at Sacramento.* San Francisco: J. G. Coggins 1862.

——.*Patriotism and Other Papers.* Boston: Tompkins and Co. 1864.

——.'Peace: What it would cost us'. Address delivered in Platt's Music Hall, San Francisco. San Francisco: Francis Valentine, 1861

——.*A Vacation Among the Sierras: Yosemite in 1860.* San Francisco: Book Club of California 1962 [1860].

Kip, Rt Rev. William Ingraham. *The Early Days of My Episcopate.* New York: T. Whittlaker 1892.

Kirby, Georgiana Bruce. *Years of Experience: An Autobiographical Narrative.* New York: G.P. Putnam's Sons 1887.

Langworthy, Franklin. *Scenery of the Plains, Mountains and Mines: Or, a Diary kept upon the Overland Route to California.* Ogdensburgh, Ohio: J.C. Sprague 1855.

Loughead, Flora Haines, ed. *Life and Diaries of Oscar Lovell Shafter.* San Francisco: Blair-Murdock Co. 1915.

Lyman, Albert. *Journal of a Voyage to California and Life in the Gold Diggings.* Hartford: E.T. Pease 1852.

McKee, Irving, ed. *Alonzo Delano's California Correspondence.* Sacramento: Sacramento Book Collectors Club 1952.

McNeil, Samuel. *McNeil's Travels in 1849, To, Through, and From the Gold Regions in California.* Columbus, Ohio: Scott and Bascom 1850.

Marryat, Frank. *Mountains and Molehills: Or Recollections of a Burnt Journal.* New York: Harper and Brothers 1855.

Mines, Rev. Flavel S. *Sermon Preached by the Reverend Flavel S.Mines, on Sunday January 25th, 1852, at the Opening of the New Trinity Church in Pine Street, San Francisco.* San Francisco: F.A. Bonnard 1852.

Muller, J. *California, Land of Gold; or, Stay at Home and Work Hard.* San Francisco: Book Club of California 1971

Nunis, Doyce B., ed. *A Medical Journey in California by Dr. Pierre Garnier.* Los Angeles: Zeitlin and Ver Brugge 1967.

Patterson, Lawson B. *Twelve Years in the Mines of California.* Cambridge, Mass.: Miles and Dilligham 1862.

Pfeiffer, Ida. *A Lady's Visit to California, 1853.* Oakland, Calif.: Biobooks 1950.

Pollock, Edward. *Opening Address Delivered at the Inauguration of the Fair of the*

Mechanics Institute of San Francisco. San Francisco: Whitton, Towne and Co. 1857.

Praslow, J., trans. Frederick Cordes. *The State of California: A Medico-Geographical Account*. San Francisco: J.J. Newbegin 1939 [Gottingen: 1857].

Put's Original California Songster. San Francisco: D.E. Appleton 1868 [1854].

Randolph, Edmund. *Address on the History of California, from the Discovery of the Country to the Year 1849. Delivered before the Society of Californian Pioneers, at their Celebration of the Tenth Anniversary of the Admission of the State of California into the Union*. San Francisco: 1860.

Raven, Ralph. [George Payson]. *Golden Dreams and Leaden Realities*. New York: G.P Putnam and Co. 1853.

Richards, Benjamin, ed. *California Gold Rush Merchant: The Journal of Stephen Chapin Davis*. San Marino: Huntington Library 1956.

Root, Riley. *Journal of Travels from St Josephs to Oregon*. Galesburg, Ill.: Gazeteer and Intelligencer 1850.

Shaw, Pringle. *Ramblings in California*. Toronto: J. Bain 1857.

Scott, Rev. W.A. *The Bible and Politics*. San Francisco, H.H. Bancroft 1859.

——.*A Discourse for the Times, Delivered in Calvary Church, Sunday July 27, 1856*. San Francisco: 1856.

——.*A Lecture on the Influence of Great Cities*. San Francisco: Whitton, Towne and Co. 1854.

——.*Our Young Men: Who Are to Care for Them?* Philadelphia: Presbyterian Board of Publication 1858.

——.*Trade and Letters: Their Journeyings Around the World*. New York: Robert Carter and Brothers 1856.

——.*Two Worlds United. The Atlantic Submarine Telegraph*. San Francisco: O'Meara and Painter 1858.

——.*The Wedge of Gold, Or Achan in El Dorado*. San Francisco: Whitton, Towne and Co. 1855.

Shephard, George and S.L. Caldwell. *Addresses of Rev. Professor George Shephard and Rev. S.L. Caldwell*. Bangor, Maine: Smith and Sayward 1849.

Society of California Pioneers. *Inaugural Ceremonies at the Opening of the New 'Pioneer Hall'*. San Francisco: Alta California Book and Job Office 1863.

Soule, Frank, John H. Gihon and James Nisbet. *The Annals of San Francisco*. New York: D. Appleton and Co. 1854.

Statement of the Controversy Between Judge William R. Turner, of the Eighth Judicial District of California, and Members of the Marysville Bar, and their Reply to his Violent Attacks Upon Them. Marysville, Calif.: 1850.

Speer, William. *Answer to Objections to Chinese Testimony and Appeal for their Protection by our Laws*. San Francisco: Chinese Mission House, 1856.

——.*China and California: Their Relations, Past and Present*. San Francisco: Marvin and Hitchcock 1853.

Stillman, J.D.B. *Observations on the Medical Topography and Diseases of the Sacramento Valley, California, in the Years 1849–50*. New York: J.F. Trow 1851.

Street, Franklin. *California in 1850*. Cincinnati: R.E. Edwards and Co. 1851.

Taylor, Bayard. *Eldorado*. New York: A.A. Knopf 1949.

Taylor, Mart. *The Gold Digger's Song Book: Containing the Most Popular Humorous and Sentimental Songs and Sung by his Original Company with Unbounded Applause throughout California.* Marysville, Calif.: Marysville Daily Herald Print 1856.

Taylor, William. *The Model Preacher: comprised in a series of letters illustrating the best mode of preaching the gospel.* Cincinnati: Swormstedt and Poe 1860.

Thoreau, Henry David. 'Life Without Principle', in *The Writings of Henry David Thoreau;* vol. iv. Boston: Houghton, Mifflin 1906.

Turner, William R. *Documents in Relation to Charges Preferred by Stephen J. Field and Others.* San Francisco: Franklin Book and Job Office 1853.

Twain, Mark. *Roughing It.* New York, Signet: 1980.

Tyson, James L. *Diary of a Physician in California.* New York: D. Appleton and Co. 1850.

Vail, R.W.G., ed. 'California Letters of the Gold Rush Period: The Correspondence of John Ingalls, 1849–1851'. *Proceedings of the American Antiquarian Society;* 47, part 1 (1937): pp.145–82.

Wadsworth, Rev. Charles. *A Mother's Sorrow. A Sermon Preached Before the Young Men's Christian Association, San Francisco, in Calvary Church, Sabbath Evening, September 25, 1864.* San Francisco: YMCA 1864.

——.*Thankfulness, A Sermon, and Character, A Sermon, Preached on Thanksgiving Day, November 20, 1856 in the Arch Street Church, Philadelphia.* Philadelphia: T.B. Peterson 1856.

——. *War a Discipline. A Sermon Preached in Calvary Church, San Francisco, on Thanksgiving Day, November 24, 1864.* San Francisco: H.H. Bancroft 1864.

——. *America's Mission. A Sermon Preached in the Arch Street Presbyterian Church, Philadelphia, on Thanksgiving Day, 22 November 1855.* Philadelphia: McLaughlin Brothers 1855.

Watson, Jeanne Hamilton, ed. *To the Land of Gold and Wickedness: The 1848–59 Diary of Lorena L. Hays.* St Louis: Patrice Press 1988.

Weston, Silas. *Four Months in the Mines of California; Or, Life in the Mountains.* Providence, R.I.: B.T. Albro 1854.

Whipple, Edwin P., ed. *Christianity and Humanity: A Series of Sermons by Thomas Starr King.* Boston: Houghton, Osgood and Co. 1880.

Wierzbicki, F.P. *California as it is and as it may be.* New York: 1970 [San Francisco: W. Bartlett 1849].

Willey, Samuel H. *Decade Sermons. Two Historical Discourses, Occasioned by the Close of the First Ten Years Ministry in California, Preached in the Howard Street Presbyterian Church, San Francisco.* San Francisco: Towne and Bacon 1859.

Williams, Rev. Albert. *Farewell Discourse.* San Francisco: B.F. Sterett 1854.

Winslow, C.F. *The Nazarite's Vow: An Address Delivered Before The Sons of Temperance in San Francisco.* Boston: Crosby 1855.

Woodbridge, Reverend Sylvester. *Sermon Preached at the Dedication of the First Presbyterian Church, Benicia, California, 9 March 1851.* Benicia, Calif.: St Clair, Pinkham and Co. 1851.

Woods, Rev. Daniel B. *Sixteen Months at the Gold Diggings.* New York: Harper and Brothers 1851.

Woods, Rev. James. *Recollections of Pioneer Work in California.* San Francisco: J. Winterburn 1878.

YMCA. *First Annual Report of the Young Men's Christian Association of San Francisco, California*. San Francisco: 1854.

YMCA. *Second Annual Report of the Young Men's Christian Association*. San Francisco: 1855.

CONTEMPORARY WRITINGS, VICTORIA

Aldwell, J.A. *The Prize Essay of the Melbourne Labor League on the Eight Hours and Early Closing Questions*. Melbourne: Wilson, Mackinnon and Fairfax 1856.

Anon. (A Colonist.) *Protection Versus Free Trade. Gold not National Wealth. Victoria: As She Was, As She Is, As She Should Be*. Melbourne: Walker, May and Co. 1860.

Anon. (A Gold Digger.) *Laughing a Crime, or Twenty Pounds No Comedy, A Poem*. Melbourne: Hunter 1853.

Anon. (A Melbourne Merchant.) *The Gold Era of Victoria: being the present and future of the colony*. London and Melbourne: 1855.

Anon. (An Old Colonist.) *Land and Labor in Victoria*. Melbourne: 1856.

Anon. (Conservative.) *The Settlement of the Country, An Inquiry*. Melbourne: Walker, May and Co. 1857.

Anon. *Letters from the Diggings: A True Picture of Australia and the Goldfields*. London: n.d.

Anon. *Protection to Native Idleness, Socially, and not Politically Considered*. Melbourne: James Caple n.d.

Anon. *The Present and Future of Victoria as She Is and As She May Be*. Melbourne: 1853.

Archer, W.H. *Noctes Catholicae: Lecture on Catholic Education and Civilisation*. Melbourne: Michael T. Gason 1856.

Aristides [R.L.Milne]. *A Glance at the Forerunners of the Crisis; or the Evils and the Remedies of the Present Modes of Transportation, Emigration and Colonisation*. Melbourne: Melbourne Morning Herald 1853.

——. *To The Right Honourable the Secretary of State for the Colonies*. Melbourne: Melbourne Morning Herald 1852.

Aspinall, Clara. *Three Years in Melbourne*. London: L. Booth 1862.

Barry, Redmond. *Lecture on the History of the Art of Agriculture*. Melbourne: Lucas Brothers 1854.

——. *Address of His Honor Mr. Justice Barry, One of the Judges of the Supreme Court of the Colony of Victoria, On the Opening of the Circuit Court at Portland, on June the 15th., 1852*. Melbourne: B. Lucas 1852.

——. *Inaugural Address Delivered Before the Members of the Victorian Institute*. Melbourne: 1854.

Barton, Rev. F.G. *The Uses and Responsibilities of Affliction*. Melbourne: W Fairfax and Co. 1858.

Beaton, James. *Life Among the Anglo-Saxons, Showing the Necessity of the Extension of the Franchise Among the British People*. Edinburgh: 1858.

a'Beckett, T.T. *The Gold and the Government*. Melbourne: Daniel Harrison 1851.

——. *A Defence of State Aid to Religion*. Melbourne: James J. Blundell and Co. 1856.

a'Beckett, William. *The Earl's Choice and Other Poems*. London: Smith, Elder and Co. 1863.

——. *Lecture Delivered by His Honor Mr. Justice a'Beckett Before the Members and Friends of the Melbourne Total Abstinence Society*. Melbourne: John Ferres 1851.

Binney, Rev. Thomas. *Be Men. A Sermon Preached in the St. Kilda Congregational Church on Sunday Morning 11 April 1858*. Melbourne: W. Fairfax and Co. 1858.

Collison Black, R. D., ed. *Papers and Correspondence of W.S. Jevons*. London: Macmillan 1973.

Blake, Les, ed. *A Gold Digger's Diaries, by Ned Peters*. Geelong: Neptune Press, 1981.

Bonwick, James. *Notes of a Gold Digger and Gold Diggers' Guide*. Melbourne: R. Connebee 1852.

Brown, Henry. *Victoria as I found it during five years of adventure*. London: T. Cautley Newby 1862.

Brown, P.L., ed. *Clyde Company Papers*, vol.5. London: Oxford University Press 1963.

Cairns, Rev. Dr A. *The Dangers and Duties of the Young Men of Victoria; Or, Counsels Adapted to the Present Crisis*. Melbourne: Wilson, Mackinnon and Fairfax 1856.

——. *The Inauguration of the Political Independence of Victoria*. Melbourne: Wilson, Mackinnon and Fairfax 1856.

——. *New Year's Sermon; with remarks suggested by the decease of the late Governor, Sir Charles Hotham*. Melbourne: Wilson, Mackinnon and Fairfax 1856.

Campbell, Colin. *The Land Question*. Ararat, Victoria: Banfield and Merfield 1861.

——. *Remarks on National Education*. Melbourne: Benjamin Lucas 1853.

——. *The Squatting Question Considered, With A View to its Settlement*. Melbourne: Walker, May and Co. 1861.

Carboni, Raffaello. *The Eureka Stockade*. Melbourne: Melbourne University Press 1975 [1855].

Celebration of the Eightieth Anniversary of the Independence of the United States, by the American Citizens Resident in Melbourne, Australia. Melbourne: 1856.

Celebration of the Eighty-First Anniversary of the Independence of the United States, by the American Citizens Resident in Melbourne, Australia. Melbourne: 1857.

Childers, E. Spencer, ed. *The Life and Correspondence of the Rt. Hon. Hugh C.E. Childers*. London: J. Murray 1901.

Clacy, Ellen. *A Lady's Visit to the Gold Diggings of Australia*. Melbourne: Lansdowne Press 1963 [1853].

——. *Lights and Shadows of Australian Life*. London: Hurst and Blackett 1853.

Clarke, Alfred. *Raw Gold and Sovereigns, Free Trade in Money and No Export Duty on Gold*. Geelong: T. Brown 1855.

Colonus [William a'Beckett]. *Does the Discovery of Gold in Victoria, Viewed in Relation to its Moral and Social Effects, as Hitherto Developed, Deserve to be Considered a National Blessing or a National Curse?* Melbourne: Benjamin Lucas 1852.

Constitution and Laws of the Victorian Institute for the Advancement of Science. Melbourne: 1854.

Cooper, Rev. John. *An Inquiry into the Relation of Christ to the World and of the Church to the State*. Geelong: Thomas Paterson 1856.

Cornwallis, Kinahan. *A Panorama of the New World*. London: T.C. Newby 1859.

Coster, Frederick. *A Land System for Victoria*. Melbourne: James J. Blundell and Co. 1857.

Cumming, Rev. J. *A Lecture on Labor, Rest, and Recreation*. Melbourne: Wilson, Mackinnon and Fairfax 1856.

Dobie, William Wilson. *Recollections of a Visit to Port Phillip Australia, in 1852–55*. Glasgow: T. Murray and Son 1856.

Drummond, G.M. *Three Valedictory Sermons Preached by the Rev. G.M. Drummond on the Occasion of his Resignation of the Cure of Williamstown*. Melbourne: Lucas Brothers 1854.

Duffy, C. Gavan. *The Land Law of Victoria*. London: W. H. Smith 1862.

——. *My Life in Two Hemispheres*. London: T. Fisher Unwin 1898.

Earp, George Butler. *What we did in Australia, being the practical experience of three clerks, in the stockyard and at the goldfields*. London: George Routledge and Co. 1853.

Edwards, J.R. *Essay on Drunkenness*. Melbourne: Wilson, Mackinnon and Fairfax 1859.

Edwards, William. *What Should We Do With Our Criminals?* Melbourne: Edgar Ray and Co. 1857.

Fauchery, Antoine. *Letters from a Miner in Australia*. Melbourne: Georgian House 1965.

Fletcher, Rev. Richard. *Truth and Love*. Melbourne: Wilson, Mackinnon and Fairfax 1856.

Foster, John Fitzgerald Leslie. *The New Colony of Victoria, formerly Port Philip*. London: Trelawney Saunders 1851.

——. *Three Letters to the Speaker of the Legislative Council of Victoria*. Melbourne: James J. Blundell and Co. 1855.

Gerstaecker, F. *Narrative of a Journey Round the World*. 3 vols. London: Hurst and Blackett 1853.

Graham, Sally, ed. *Pioneer Merchant: The Letters of James Graham 1839–54*. Melbourne: Hyland House 1985.

Earl Grey. *The Colonial Policy of Lord John Russell's Administration*. London: Richard Bentley 1853.

Hall, William. *Practical Experience at the Diggings of the Gold Fields of Victoria*. London: Effingham Wilson 1852.

Hamilton, Rev. Robert. *A Sermon and Biographical Sketch delivered on the Occasion of the Death of the Reverend James Ritchie Dalrymple*. Melbourne: Wm. Goodhugh and Co. 1858.

Hardess, George M. *Notes by the Wayside; or, Silent Thoughts for Quiet Hours*. Melbourne: H.T. Dwight 1860.

Hearn, W. A. *Lecture on the Proposed Formation of Adult Educational Classes*. Melbourne: Wilson, Mackinnon and Fairfax 1856.

Higinbotham, George. *Self Education*. Melbourne: Blundell and Ford 1862.

Howitt, William. *A Boy's Adventures in the Wilds of Australia*. London: Arthur Hall, Virtue and Co 1858.

——. *The Rural Life of England.* 3rd ed. London: 1844.

——. *Two Years in Victoria.* London: Longman, Brown, Green and Longmans 1855.

——. *Tallengetta, The Squatter's Home. A Story of Australian Life.* London: Longman, Brown, Green, Longmans and Roberts 1857.

——. *Colonization and Christianity: A Popular History of the Treatment of the Natives by the Europeans in all their Colonies.* London: Longman, Orme, Brown, Green and Longmans 1838.

Jones, Rev. H. Berkeley. *Adventures in Australia in 1852 and 1853.* London: Richard Bentley 1853.

Just, P. *An Appeal to the Government and Colonists of Victoria in Favour of the Employment of the Arts of Painting and Sculpture in Decorating the New Houses of Parliament.* Melbourne: George Robertson 1858.

——. *Australia, or notes taken during a residence in the Colonies from the Gold Discovery in 1851 till 1857.* Dundee: Durham and Thomson 1859.

Kelly, William. *Life in Victoria in 1853, and Victoria in 1858, Showing the March of Improvement made by the Colony within those Periods, In Town and Country, Cities, and the Diggings.* London: Chapman and Hall 1859.

Kentish, N.L. *The Question of Questions.* Melbourne: J.J. Blundell and Co. 1855.

Kilgour, James. *Effect of the Climate of Australia Upon the European Constitution in Health and Disease.* Geelong: William Vale 1855.

Lang, J.D. *Freedom and Independence for the Golden Lands of Australia.* London: Longman, Brown, Green and Longmans 1852.

Lemaitre, S. *Songs of the Gold Fields.* Sandhurst: n.d.

Lindsay, H. Lill. *The Industrial Resources of Victoria.* Melbourne: George Robertson 1856.

McCombie, Thomas. *The History of the Colony of Victoria from its Settlement to the Death of Sir Charles Hotham.* London: Chapman and Hall 1858.

McCoy, F. *On the Formation of Museums in Victoria.* Melbourne: Goodhugh and Hough 1857.

Mackay, M. *Sermon Preached Before the Synod of the Free Presbyterian Church Of Victoria.* Melbourne: G. Robertson 1855.

Mackenna, J. William. *Mortality of Children in Victoria.* Melbourne: W. Fairfax and Co. 1858.

Mackenzie, Rev. David. *The Gold Digger: A Visit to the Gold Fields of Australia in February 1852.* London: W.S. Orr 1852.

Macknight, Charles. *A Review of the report of the Squatting Commission.* Melbourne: Charlwood and Son 1855.

Melbourne Chamber of Commerce. *Reports on the Condition and Progress of the Colony of Victoria since the Discovery of Goldfields.* Edinburgh: Oliver and Boyd 1853.

Melbourne Chamber of Commerce. *Proceedings of the Melbourne Chamber of Commerce and the Special Committee appointed to Consider and Report on the Best Means of Promoting Agriculture and Settling the Waste Lands of the Colony.* Melbourne: Goodhugh and Trembath 1855.

Melbourne Public Library. *Address of the Trustees of the Melbourne Public Library.* Melbourne: 1859.

Meredith, Louisa. *Over the Straits: A Visit to Victoria.* London: Chapman and Hall 1861.

Michie, Archibald. *Readings in Melbourne.* London: Sampson, Low, Marston, Searle and Rivington 1879.

——. *Victoria: Retrospective and Prospective.* Melbourne: W. Fairfax and Co. 1866.

Milton, John. *The Evangelistic, Temperance, Economic, Educational and Model Farm Society, for the Benefit of Soldiers, Policemen, Immigrants, the Uneducated and the Unemployed.* Melbourne: 1855.

Mitchell, Major T.L. *Three Expeditions Into the Interior of Eastern Australia; With Descriptions of the Recently Explored Region of Australia Felix.* London: T. and W. Boone 1839.

Mossman, Samuel. *Emigrants' Letters from Australia.* London: Addey and Co. 1853.

Mossman, Samuel and Thomas Banister. *Australia, Visited and Revisited: A Narrative of Recent Travels and Old Experiences in Victoria and New South Wales.* London: Addey and Co. 1853.

Mueller, F. *Address of the President, Delivered to the Members of the Philosophical Institute.* Melbourne: Mason and Firth 1860.

New, Rev. Isaac. *A Christian Church.* Melbourne: W. Fairfax and Co. 1858.

——. *The Greatness of Man: A Lecture.* Melbourne: W. Fairfax and Co. 1858.

——. *A Memorial of Christian Excellence:The Funeral Address and Discourse Delivered at the Albert Street Baptist Church on the Death of Henry Langlands Esq. by the Rev. Isaac New.* Melbourne: W. B. Stephens 1863.

——. *Religion: All Profit and No Loss.* Melbourne: Herald 1860.

Nixon, Francis H. *The Chinese Puzzle Adjusted.* Beechworth: James Ingram 1857.

Papineau, Peter. *Homesteads for the People.* Melbourne: S. Goode 1855.

Parker, Edward Stone. *The Aborigines of Australia: A Lecture Delivered in the Mechanics Hall, Melbourne.* Melbourne: Hugh McColl 1854.

Peck, George Washington. *Melbourne and the Chincha Islands; with Sketches of Lima, and a voyage around the world.* New York: Charles Scribner 1854.

Perkins, Elizabeth, ed. *The Poetical Works of Charles Harpur.* Sydney: Angus and Robertson 1984.

Perry, Charles. *A Letter on the Financial Position of the Church, To the Few Zealous Members of the United Church of England and Ireland in Victoria.* Melbourne: Lucas Brothers 1857.

——. *The Character of the Writings of the Rev. F.D. Maurice.* Geelong: Heath and Cordell 1859.

——. *The Comparative Position of the Church in England and in Victoria.* Melbourne: Lucas Brothers 1854.

——. *On Divisions in the Church.* Melbourne: William Baker 1851.

——. *On the Church, A Sermon Preached in the Cathedral Church of St James Melbourne.* Melbourne: Lucas Brothers 1851.

——. *A Sermon Preached at the Cathedral Church of St James and the Church of St Peter, Melbourne.* Melbourne: Lucas Brothers 1856.

Perry, Richard. *Contributions to an Amateur Magazine.* London: L. Booth 1857.

Perry, Sarah. *Durable Riches, or A Voice from the Golden Land.* London: 1857.

Philosophical Society of Victoria. *Prospectus of the Philosophical Society of Victoria.* Melbourne: 1854.

Polding, John Bede. *The Eye of Faith: The Pastoral Letters of John Bede Polding.* Kilmore, Vic.: 1978.

Polehampton, Rev. Arthur. *Kangaroo Land.* London: Richard Bentley 1862.

Pollard, N.W. *Homes in Victoria: Or, the British Emigrant's Guide to Victoria.* Melbourne: Walker, May and Co. 1861.

Port Phillip Farmers' Society. *Transactions of the Port Phillip Farmers' Society.* Melbourne: 1857.

Potter, Rev. John. *The Days are Evil: A Sermon.* Ballarat: n.d.

Ramsay, Rev. A.M. *The Voice of the Storm: A Memorial of the Late Flood.* Melbourne: 1850.

Ramsay-Laye, Elizabeth. *Social Life and Manners in Australia.* London: Longman, Green, Longman and Roberts 1861.

A Report of the Inquiry into the Management of the Yarra Bend Lunatic Asylum, as detailed in the Nine Day's Trial of the Action for Libel, Bowie v. Wilson. Melbourne: Wilson and Mackinnon 1862.

Robin, A. de Q., ed. *Australian Sketches: The Journal and Letters of Frances Perry.* Melbourne: Queensberry Hill Press 1984.

Read, C. Rudston. *What I heard, saw, and did at the Australian gold fields.* London: T. and W. Boone 1853.

Rusden, George W. *Gathering Together for the Good of Work and Learning: A Lecture on the Occasion of Opening the Exhibition Building in Melbourne, October 1854.* Melbourne: George Robertson 1857.

——. *The Old Road to Responsible Government.* Melbourne: Herald Office 1856.

Scott, Ernest, ed. *Lord Robert Cecil's Gold Fields Diary.* Melbourne: Melbourne University Press 1935.

Shaw, Dr John. *A Gallop to the Antipodes, Returning Overland through India.* London: J.F. Hope 1858.

Shaw, W. *The Land of Promise; Or, My Impressions of Australia.* London: Simpkin, Marshall and Co. 1854.

Sherer, John. *The Gold Finder of Australia.* Ringwood: Penguin, 1973 [1853].

Sidney, Samuel. *The Three Colonies of Australia.* London: Ingram, Cooke 1852.

Simcox, Howard. *Rustic Rambles in Rhyme, Collected in Various Parts of Victoria.* Ballarat: 1866.

Singleton, John MD. *A Narrative of Incidents in the Eventful Life of a Physician.* Melbourne: Hutchinson 1891.

Smith, John Thomas. *Three Addresses by the Right Worshipful the Mayor of Melbourne.* Melbourne: Lucas Brothers 1858.

Smith, Sidney. *Whether to go and whither? Being a practical view of the whole southern field of settlement.* London: John Kendrick 1852.

Spence, Catherine Helen. *Clara Morison: A Tale of South Australia during the Gold Fever.* London: Parker 1854.

Stawell, Mary. *My Recollections.* London: Richard Clay and Sons 1911.

Stephen, Sir James. 'On Colonisation as a Branch of Social Economy'. In George Hastings, ed., *Transactions of the National Association for the Promotion of Social Science for 1858*, pp.96–109. London: 1859

Stoney, Captain H. Butler. *Victoria: With a Description of its Principal Cities,*

Melbourne and Geelong, and Remarks on the Present State of the Colony. London: Smith, Elder 1856.

Symons, Rev. John C. *The History and Advantages of Young Men's Associations.* Melbourne: George Nicholls 1856.

Taylor, Joseph. *The Church, the State, and the World; Their Duties and Claims.* Melbourne: Wilson, Mackinnon and Fairfax 1856.

Taylor, Rev. Theophilus. *Chapters on the Class Meeting.* Ballarat: T. Taylor 1858.

Thatcher, Chas. R. *Thatcher's Colonial Songster.* Melbourne: Charlwood 1857.

United Church of England and Ireland. *The Seventh Annual Report of the Church Missionary Society of the Diocese of Melbourne.* Melbourne: 1861.

University of Melbourne. *Statutes and Regulations of the University of Melbourne.* Melbourne: 1855.

Verdon, G.F. *The Present and Future of Municipal Government in Victoria.* Melbourne: W. Fairfax and Co. 1858.

Victorian Convention. *Resolutions, Proceedings and Documents.* Melbourne: J.J. Walsh 1857.

Vines, Frederick. *A Glorious Future for Australia; or, the Freeman's Guide Book.* Melbourne: Walker, May and Co., 1856.

——. *The Cue to Prosperity: or, Our Lands and How to Get at Them.* Melbourne: James Caple 1856.

Wathen, George Henry. *The Golden Colony: or, Victoria in 1854.* London: Longman, Green, Brown and Longmans 1855.

Wekey, S. *The Land, Importance of its Culture to the General Prosperity of Victoria.* Melbourne: James J. Blundell 1854.

Westgarth, William. *Personal Recollections of Early Melbourne and Victoria.* Melbourne: George Robertson and Co. 1888.

——. *Victoria; Late Australia Felix, or Port Phillip district of New South Wales.* Edinburgh: Oliver and Boyd 1853.

Wilson, Edward, ed. *An Enquiry into the Principles of Representation.* Melbourne: 1857.

Willson, Rt Rev. R.W. *A Few Observations Relative to the Yarra Bend Lunatic Asylum.* Melbourne: Wm Goodhugh and Co. 1859.

LATER WRITINGS, UNITED STATES

Ahlstrom, Sydney E. 'Religion, Revolution, and the Rise of Modern Nationalism'. *Church History* 44, 1975: pp.492–504.

American Quarterly 37, no.4, fall, 1985. Special issue on republicanism.

Appleby, Joyce. *Capitalism and a New Social Order: The Republican Vision of the 1790s.* New York: New York University Press 1984.

Ashworth, John. *'Agrarians' and 'Aristocrats': Party Political Ideology in the United States.* London: Royal Historical Society 1983.

Bakken, Gordon Morris. *The Development of Law in Frontier California: Civil Law and Society, 1850–1890.* Westport, Conn.: Greenwood 1985.

Bancroft, Hubert Howe. *California Inter Pocula.* San Francisco: The History Company 1888.

——. *Popular Tribunals.* San Francisco: The History Company 1887.

Barnhart, Jacqueline Baker. *The Fair But Frail: Prostitution in San Francisco 1849–1900.* Reno: University of Nevada Press 1986.

Barth, Gunther. *Instant Cities: Urbanization and the Rise of San Francisco and Denver.* New York: Oxford University Press 1975.

Bean, Walton. *California, An Interpretive History.* New York: McGraw-Hill 1968.

Bieber, Ralph. 'California Gold Mania'. *Mississipi Valley Historical Review* 35, no.1, June 1948: pp.3–28.

Billington, Ray Allen. *The Far Western Frontier 1830–1860.* New York: Harper 1956.

Broomall, Robert W. *California Kingdoms.* New York: Fawcett 1992.

Brown, Richard Maxwell. *Strain of Violence: Historical Studies of American Violence and Vigilantism.* New York: Oxford University Press 1975.

Buchanan, A. Russell. *David S. Terry of California: Dueling Judge.* San Marino: Huntington Library 1956.

Burchell, R.A. *The San Francisco Irish: 1848–1880.* Berkeley: University of California Press 1980.

Carter, Clarence E. 'Colonialism in the Continental United States'. *South Atlantic Quarterly* 47, 1948: pp.17–28

Caughey, John Walton. *Gold is the Cornerstone.* Berkeley: University of California Press 1948.

——. *Their Majesties the Mob.* Chicago: University of Chicago Press 1960.

Chiu, Ping. *Chinese Labor in California, 1850–1880: An Economic Study.* Madison: Univ. Wisconsin History Dept 1963.

Cleland, Robert Glass. *From Wilderness to Empire: A History of California.* New York: Knopf 1960.

Coblentz, Stanton. *Villains and Vigilantes.* New York: Wilson-Erickson 1936.

Cook, S.F. *The Conflict Between the California Indian and White Civilization.* Berkeley: University of California Press 1943.

Cott, Nancy. *The Bonds of Womanhood. 'Woman's Sphere' in New England 1780–1835.* New Haven: Yale University Press 1977.

Cunliffe, Marcus. *Soldiers and Civilians: The Martial Spirit in America 1775–1865.* New York: Free Press 1973.

Davis, W.N. 'Research Uses of County Court Records, 1850–1879'. *California Historical Quarterly* 52, no.3 1973: pp.241–66; 52, no.4: pp.338–65.

Dayton, Dello Grimmett. 'The California Militia 1850–1866.' PhD Dissertation, Berkeley: University of California 1951.

Decker, Peter. *Fortunes and Failures: White Collar Mobility in Nineteenth-Century San Francisco.* Cambridge, Mass.: Harvard University Press 1978.

Diggins, John Patrick. *The Lost Soul of American Politics: Virtue, Self-Interest, and the Foundations of Liberalism.* New York: Basic Books 1984.

Drury, Clifford M. *William Anderson Scott, 'No Ordinary Man'.* Glendale, Calif.: H. Clark and Co. 1967.

Elkins, Stanley. *Slavery: A Problem in American Institutional and Intellectual Life.* 2nd ed. Chicago: University of Chicago Press, 1968.

Ellison, Joseph. 'The Mineral Land Question in California, 1848–1866', in Vernon Carstensen ed., *The Public Lands: Studies in the History of the Public Domain.* Madison: University of Wisconsin Press 1963.

Ellison, William H. A Self-Governing Dominion: California, 1849–1860. Berkeley: University of California Press 1950.

Eyring, Rose. 'The Portrayal of the California Gold Rush Period in Imaginative Literature from 1848 to 1875'. PhD Dissertation, Berkeley, University of California 1944.

Field, Stephen J. Personal Reminiscences of Early Days in California with Other Sketches. San Francisco 1893.

Fine, Sidney. Laissez Faire and the General Welfare State: A Study of Conflict in American Thought. Ann Arbor: University of Michigan Press 1956.

Fleming, Sandford. God's Gold: The Story of Baptist Beginnings in California 1849–1860. Philadephia: Judson's Press 1949.

Fox, Richard W. So Far Disordered in Mind: Insanity in California, 1870–1930. Berkeley: University of California Press 1978.

Frankiel, Sandra Sizer. California's Spiritual Frontiers: Religious Alternatives to Anglo-Protestantism, 1850–1910. Berkeley: University of California Press 1988.

Fredrickson, George M. The Inner Civil War: Northern Intellectuals and the Crisis of the Union. New York: Harper and Row 1968.

Gabriel, Ralph Henry. The Course of American Democratic Thought: An Intellectual History Since 1815. New York: The Ronald Press Co. 1940.

Goodykoontz, Colin Brummitt. Home Missions on the American Frontier: with Particular Reference to the American Home Missionary Society. Caldwell, Idaho: Caxton Printers 1939.

Gould, Milton S. A Cast of Hawks. La Jolla, Calif.: Copley Books 1985.

Grant, Jocelyn Maynard. 'The Golden Dream and the Press: Illinois and the California Gold Rush'. Journal of the West 11, no.2, April 1978: pp.17–27.

Grivas, Theodore. Military Governments in California, 1846–1850. Glendale, Calif.: A.H. Clark Co. 1963.

Gunn, L. Ray. The Decline of Authority: Public Economic Policy and Political Development in New York State, 1800–1860. Ithaca: Cornell University Press 1988.

Haggerty, Timothy J. 'The San Francisco Gentleman'. California History 65, no.2, June 1986: pp.97–103.

Hanchett Jr., William Frances. 'Religion and the Gold Rush 1849–1854: The Christian Churches in the California Mines'. PhD dissertation, Berkeley, University of California: 1952.

Hansen, Woodrow James. The Search for Authority in California. Oakland, Calif.: Biobooks 1960.

Heizer, Robert F. and Alan F. Almquist. The Other Californians. Berkeley: University of California Press 1971.

Hittell, Theodore H. History of California, vol.2. San Francisco: Pacific Press 1898.

——. Marshall's Gold Discovery: A Lecture Delivered Before the Society of California Pioneers. San Francisco: B.F. Sterett 1893.

Holliday, J.S. The World Rushed In: The California Gold Rush Experience. New York: Simon and Schuster 1981

Howe, Daniel Walker. The Political Culture of the American Whigs. Chicago: University of Chicago Press 1979.

Hurtado, Albert. Indian Survival on the California Frontier. New Haven: Yale University Press 1988.

Hyde, Anne. *An American Vision: Far Western Landscape and National Culture 1820–1920*. New York: New York University Press 1990.

Issel, William and Robert W. Cherny, *San Francisco 1865–1932: Politics, Power, and Urban Development*. Berkeley: University of California Press 1986.

Johnson, David A. 'Vigilance and the Law: The Moral Authority of Popular Justice in the Far West'. *American Quarterly* 33, no.5, winter 1981: pp. 558–86.

Kammen, Michael. *Selvages and Biases: The Fabric of History in American Culture*. Ithaca: Cornell University Press 1987.

Kelley, Robert. *Battling the Inland Sea: American Political Culture, Public Policy, and the Sacramento Valley, 1850–1986*. Berkeley: University of California Press 1989.

——. *Gold vs Grain: The Hydraulic Mining Controversy in California's Sacramento Valley. A Chapter in the Decline of the Concept of Laissez Faire*. Glendale, Calif.: A.H. Clark and Co. 1959.

Kloppenberg, James T. 'The Virtues of Liberalism: Christianity, Republicanism, and Ethics in Early American Political Discourse'. *Journal of American History* 74, no.1, June 1987: pp. 9–33.

Knoles, George H., ed. *Essays and Assays: California History Reappraised*. San Francisco: California Historical Society 1973.

Kolodny, Annette. *The Land Before Her: Fantasy and Experience of the American Frontiers*. Chapel Hill: University of North Carolina Press 1984.

——. *The Lay of the Land: Metaphor as Experience and History in American Life and Letters*. Chapel Hill: University of North Carolina Press 1975.

——. 'Letting Go of Our Magnificent Obsessions: Notes Toward a New Literary History of the American Frontiers', *American Literature* 64, no.1, March 1992: pp.1–18.

Kramnick, Isaac. 'Republican Revisionism Revisited'. *American Historical Review* 87, no.3, June 1982: pp. 629–64.

Lapp, Rudolph. *Blacks in Gold Rush California*. New Haven: Yale University Press 1977.

Laurie, Bruce. 'Fire Companies and Gangs in Southwark: the 1840s'. In Allen F. Davis and Mark H. Haller, eds. *The Peoples of Philadelphia: A History of Ethnic Groups and Lower-Class Life*. Philadelphia: Temple University Press 1973: pp.71–87.

Laurie, Bruce. *Working People of Philadelphia, 1800–1850*. Philadelphia: Temple University Press 1980.

Leacock, Eleanor Burke and Nancy Oestreich Lurie, eds. *North American Indians in Historical Perspective*. New York: Random House 1971.

Levy, JoAnn. *They Saw The Elephant: Women in the California Gold Rush*. Norman: University of Oklahoma Press 1992.

Limerick, Patricia Nelson. *The Legacy of Conquest: The Unbroken Past of the American West*. New York: Norton 1987.

Limerick, Patricia Nelson, Clyde A. Milner and Charles E. Rankin, eds. *Trails Towards a New Western History*. Lawrence: University Press of Kansas 1991.

Lotchin, Roger. *San Francisco, 1846–56: from Hamlet to City*. New York: Oxford University Press 1974.

McCurdy, Charles. 'Stephen J. Field and the American Judicial Tradition'. In Philip

J. Bergan, Owen M. Fiss and C. McCurdy *The Fields and the Law*. New York: Federal Bar Council 1986.

McGloin, John Bernard. *California's First Archbishop. The Life of Joseph Sadoc Alemany 1814–1888*. New York: Herder and Herder 1966.

——. 'The Catholic Origins of San Francisco'. In *Some California Catholic Reminiscences for the United States Bicentennial*. Francis J. Weber, ed. n.p.: 1976.

McLean, Stuart A. 'Opposition to the California Gold Rush: The Sentimental Argument—1849–1853'. In *American Renaissance and American West*. Laramie: University of Wyoming Press 1982: pp.87–94.

Mann, Ralph. *After the Gold Rush: Society in Grass Valley and Nevada City, California, 1849–1870*. Stanford: Stanford University Press 1982.

——. 'The Americanisation of Arcadia: Images of Hispanic and Gold Rush California'. *American Studies* 19, no. 1, spring 1978: pp. 5–20.

——. 'Frontier Opportunity and the New Social History'. *Pacific Historical Review* 53, no.4, Nov. 1984.

Marx, Leo. *The Machine in the Garden*. New York: Oxford University Press 1964.

Mayer, Carl J. and George A. Riley. *Public Domain, Private Dominion: A History of Public Mineral Policy in America*. San Francisco: Sierra Club 1985.

Merwin, Henry Childs. *The Life of Bret Harte, with Some Account of the California Pioneers*. London: Chatto and Windus 1912.

Monaghan, Jay. *Australians and the Gold Rush*. Berkeley: University of California Press 1966.

Mulvey, Christopher. 'Anglo-American Fictions: National Characteristics in Nineteenth-Century Travel Literature'. In *American Literary Landscapes: The Fiction and the Fact*, Ian F. Bell and D.K. Adams, eds. London: Vision 1988.

Olin, Spencer C. Jr. *California Politics 1846–1920*. San Francisco: Boyd and Fraser 1981.

O'Meara, James. *The Vigilance Committee of 1856*. San Francisco: J.H. Barry 1890.

Paul, Rodman W. *California Gold: The Beginning of Mining in the Far West*. Cambridge, Mass.: Harvard University Press 1947.

——. *Mining Frontiers of the Far West 1848–1880*. New York: Holt, Rinehart and Winston 1963.

——. ' "Old Californians" in British Goldfields'. *Huntington Library Quarterly* 17, no.2, 1954.

Pitt, Leonard, ed. *California Controversies: Major Issues in the History of the State*. Glenview, Ill.: Scott, Foresman 1968.

Pocock, J.G.A. *The Machiavellian Moment: Florentine Political Thought and the Atlantic Republican Tradition*. Princeton: Princeton University Press 1975.

——. 'The Machiavellian Moment Revisited: A Study in History and Ideology'. *Journal of Modern History* 53, March 1981: pp. 49–72.

Pomeroy, Earl. 'California's Legacies from the Pioneers'. In *Essays and Assays: California History Reappraised*, George H. Knoles, ed. San Francisco: 1973.

——. 'California, 1846–1860: Politics of a Representative Frontier State'. *California Historical Society Quarterly* 32, no.4, Dec. 1953: pp.291–302.

Prucha, Francis Paul. *The Great Father: The United States Government and the American Indians*. Lincoln: University of Nebraska Press 1986.

Rawls, James J. *Indians of California: The Changing Image*. Norman, Okla.: University of Oklahoma Press 1984.

Reid, John Phillip. *Law for the Elephant: Property and Social Behaviour on the Overland Trail*. San Marino, Huntington Library 1980.

Robbins, William G. 'Some Perspectives on Law and Order in Frontier Newspapers'. *Journal of the West* 17, no.1, Jan. 1978: pp. 53–61.

Rodgers, Daniel T. *Contested Truths: Keywords in American Politics Since Independence*. New York: Basic Books 1987.

——. 'Republicanism The Career of a Concept'. *Journal of American History* 79, no.1, June 1992: pp.11–38.

——. *The Work Ethic in Industrial America 1850–1920*. Chicago: University of Chicago Press 1978.

Rolle, Andrew. *California: A History*. New York: Crowell 1969.

Rose, Anne C. *Transcendentalism as a Social Movement 1830–1850*. New Haven: Yale University Press 1981.

Rothman, David J. *The Discovery of the Asylum, Social Order and Disorder in the New Republic*. Boston: Little, Brown 1971.

Royce, Josiah. *California, from the Conquest in 1846 to the Second Vigilance Committee in San Francisco*. Boston: Houghton, Mifflin 1886.

Ryan, Mary. *Women in Public: Between Banners and Ballots, 1825–1880*. Baltimore: Johns Hopkins University Press 1990.

Scheiber, Harry N. 'Government and the Economy: Studies of the Commonwealth Policy in Nineteenth Century America'. *Journal of Interdisciplinary History* 3, 1972: pp.135–51.

Senkewicz, Robert M. *Vigilantes in Gold Rush San Francisco*. Stanford: Stanford University Press 1985.

Shi, David E. *The Simple Life: Plain Living and High Thinking in American Culture*. New York: Oxford University Press 1985.

Shinn, Charles Howard. *Mining Camps: A Study in Frontier American Government*. New York: A.A. Knopf 1948 [1885].

Simonds, William Day. *Starr King in California*. San Francisco: Elder and Co. 1917.

Somkin, Fred. *Unquiet Eagle: Memory and Desire in the Idea of American Freedom, 1815–1860*. Ithaca: Cornell University Press 1967.

Starr, Kevin. *Americans and the California Dream*. New York: Oxford University Press 1973.

Swisher, Carl Brent. *Stephen J. Field, Craftsman of the Law*. Washington: Brookings Institution 1930.

Thompson, Gerald. *Edward F. Beale and the American West*. Albuquerque: University of New Mexico Press 1983.

Thorne, Tanis. 'The Almanacs of the San Francisco Bay Region, 1850–1861'. *Journal of the West* 17, no.2, April 1978: pp.37–45.

Tyrrell, Ian. *Sobering Up: From Temperance to Prohibition in Antebellum America 1800–1860*. Westport, Conn.: Greenwood 1979.

Umbeck, John R. *A Theory of Property Rights, with application to the California Gold Rush*. Ames, Iowa: Iowa State University Press 1981.

Wendte, Charles W. *Thomas Starr King: Patriot and Preacher*. Boston: Beacon Press 1921.

Wickson, E.J. *Rural California*. New York: Macmillan 1923.

Williams, Mary F. *History of the San Francisco Committee of Vigilance of 1851*. Berkeley: University of California Press 1921.

Williams, Stephen. *The Chinese in the California Mines 1848–1860*. Stanford: 1930.

Wood, Ellen Rawson. *Californians and Chinese: The First Decade*. Berkeley: 1961.

Wyatt, David. *The Fall into Eden: Landscape and Imagination in California*. Cambridge: Cambridge University Press 1987.

LATER WRITINGS, AUSTRALIA

Adcock, W.E. *The Gold Rushes of the Fifties*. Melbourne: E.W. Cole 1912.

Anderson, Hugh. 'Charles Thatcher: The Bard of Bendigo'. *Victorian Historical Magazine* 42, no.2. May 1971: pp.54–64.

Atkinson, Alan. 'Time, Place and Paternalism: Early Conservative Thinking in New South Wales'. *Australian Historical Studies* 23, no.90, April 1988: pp.1–18.

Baker, Derek. 'Early Mail Communications in Victoria'. *Victorian Historical Magazine* 45, no.3, Aug. 1974: pp. 112–18.

Baker, D.W.A. 'The Origins of Robertson's Land Acts' *Historical Studies Selected Articles, First Series*. Melbourne: 1967.

——. *Days of Wrath: A Life of John Dunmore Lang*. Melbourne: Melbourne University Press 1985.

Bate, Weston. *Lucky City: Ballarat*. Melbourne: Melbourne University Press 1978.

——. *Victorian Gold Rushes*. Melbourne: McPhee Gribble 1988.

Beer, Jane, Charles Fahey, Patricia Grimshaw and Melanie Raymond. *Colonial Frontiers and Family Fortunes*. Melbourne: Melbourne University History Department 1989.

Blainey, Geoffrey. 'Gold and Governors'. *Historical Studies* 9, no.36, May 1961: pp. 337–50.

——. 'The Gold Rushes: The Year of Decision'. *Historical Studies* 10, no.38, May 1962: pp.129–40.

——. *The Rush that Never Ended*. Melbourne: Melbourne University Press 1963.

Bonyhady, Timothy. *Images in Opposition: Australian Landscape Painting 1801–1890*. Melbourne: Oxford University Press 1985.

Bruce, Candice. *Eugene von Guerard*. Canberra: Australian National Gallery 1980.

Burroughs, Peter. *Britain and Australia 1831–55*. Oxford: Oxford University Press 1967.

Butlin, N.G. *Our Original Aggression: Aboriginal Populations of Southeastern Australia 1788–1850*. Sydney: Allen & Unwin, 1983.

Cell, John W. 'The Colonial Office in the 1850s'. *Historical Studies* 12, no.45, Oct. 1965: pp.43–56.

Chambers, Don. *Violet Town, or Honeysuckle in Australia Felix 1836–1908*. Melbourne: Melbourne University Press 1985.

Chase, Malcolm. 'The People's Farm': English Radical Agrarianism 1775–1840*. Oxford: Oxford University Press 1988.

Christie, M.F. *Aborigines in Colonial Victoria 1835–86*. Sydney: Sydney University Press 1979.

Churchward, L.G. *Australia and America 1788–1972: An Alternative History*. Chippendale, NSW: Alternative Publishing 1979.

Clark, C.M.H. *A History of Australia*, vol.4. Melbourne: Melbourne University Press 1978.

Clarke, Patricia. *Pen Portraits: Women Writers and Journalists in Nineteenth Century Australia*. Sydney: Allen & Unwin 1988.

Connell, R.W. and T. Irving. *Class Structure in Australian History*. Melbourne: Longman 1980.

Cronin, Kathryn. *Colonial Casualties: Chinese in Early Victoria*. Melbourne: Melbourne University Press 1982.

Crowley, Frank, ed. *A New History of Australia*. Melbourne: Heinemann 1974.

Davidoff, Leonore and Catherine Hall. *Family Fortunes: Men and Women of the English Middle Class 1780–1850*. London: Hutchinson 1987.

Davison, Graeme. *The Rise and Fall of Marvellous Melbourne*. Melbourne: Melbourne University Press 1978.

——. 'The Use and Abuse of Australian History'. *Australian Historical Studies* 23, no.91, Oct. 1988: pp.55–76.

Davison, Graeme and Chris McConville, eds. *A Heritage Handbook*. Sydney: Allen & Unwin 1991.

de Serville, Paul. *Port Philip Gentlemen and Good Society in Melbourne Before the Gold Rushes*. Melbourne: Oxford University Press 1980.

——. *Pounds and Pedigrees: The Upper Class in Victoria 1850–1880*. Melbourne: Oxford University Press 1991.

Dixon, Robert. *The Course of Empire: Neo-Classical Culture in New South Wales 1788–1860*. Melbourne: Oxford University Press 1986.

Doyle, E.A., ed. *The Golden Years 1851–1951: Published by the Victorian Government to Celebrate the Centenary of the Discovery of Gold in Victoria*. Melbourne: Victorian Government 1951.

Dreams of a Golden Harvest: Gold Seekers in Victoria. An Exhibition in the Irving Benson Hall, La Trobe Library. Melbourne: State Library of Victoria 1982.

Dyson, Edward. *Rhymes from the Mines and Other Lines*. Sydney: Angus and Robertson 1896.

Eureka Supplement: Historical Studies. Melbourne: Melbourne University Press 1954.

Evans, Michael. 'Historical Interpretation at Sovereign Hill'. *Australian Historical Studies* 24, no.96, Apr. 1991: pp.142–52.

Fels, Marie. *Good Men and True: The Aboriginal Police of the Port Phillip District 1837–1853*. Melbourne: Melbourne University Press 1988.

Fitzpatrick, Brian. *The British Empire in Australia: An Economic History 1834–1939*. Melbourne: Macmillan 1949.

Gittins, Jean. *The Diggers from China: The Story of the Chinese on the Goldfields*. Melbourne: Quartet Books 1981.

Gollan, R.A. *Radical and Working Class Politics: A Study of Eastern Australia 1850–1910*. Melbourne: Melbourne University Press 1960.

Goodman, David. 'The Politics of Horticulture'. *Meanjin* 47, no.3, spring 1988: pp.403–12.

——. 'Fear of Circuses: founding the National Museum of Victoria'. *Continuum* 3, no.1, 1990: pp.18–34.

Goodwin, Craufurd D. *The Image of Australia: British Perception of the Australian Economy from the Eighteenth to the Twentieth Century.* Durham, N.C.: Duke University Press 1974.

Griffiths, Tom. *Beechworth: An Australian Country Town and its Past.* Melbourne: Greenhouse 1987.

Haldane, Robert. *The People's Force: A History of the Victoria Police* Melbourne: Melbourne University Press 1986.

Harris, Carole. 'The Respectable Working Class Family and the Labour Movement'. MA thesis, Monash University: 1987.

Hirst, John. *The Strange Birth of Colonial Democracy.* Sydney: Allen & Unwin 1988.

Hoban, Mary. *Fifty One Pieces of Wedding Cake: A Biography of Caroline Chisholm.* Kilmore, Vic.: Lowden Publishing Co. 1973.

Hodge, B.C. 'Goldrush Australia'. *Journal of the Royal Australian Historical Society* 69, part 3, Dec. 1983: pp.161–78.

Howitt, Margaret, ed. *Mary Howitt: An Autobiography.* London: 1889.

Hume, L.J. 'The Labour Movement in NSW and Victoria, 1830–1860'. MEc thesis, University of Sydney 1950.

Inglis, K.S. *The Australian Colonists: An Exploration of Social History 1788–1870.* Melbourne: Melbourne University Press 1974.

Irving, T.H. 'The Development of Liberal Politics in New South Wales, 1843–1855'. PhD thesis, University of Sydney 1968.

Irving, T.H. and Carol Liston. 'State intervention and equality: administration in the New South Wales goldfields 1851–1853', in J.J. Eddy and J.R. Nethercote eds, *From Colony to Coloniser: Studies in Australian Administrative History.* Sydney: Hale and Iremonger 1987.

Kiddle, Margaret. *Caroline Chisholm.* Melbourne: Melbourne University Press 1950.

——. *Men of Yesterday: A Social History of the Western District of Victoria 1834–1890.* Melbourne: Melbourne University Press 1962.

Lake, Marilyn. 'The politics of respectability: Identifying the masculinist context'. *Historical Studies* 22, April 1986: pp.116–131.

La Nauze, J.A. 'The Gold Rushes and Australian Politics'. *Australian Journal of Politics and History* 13, no.1, May 1967: pp.90–4.

——. *Political Economy in Australia: historical studies.* Melbourne: Melbourne University Press 1949.

Lansbury, Coral. *Arcady in Australia: The Evocation of Australia in Nineteenth-Century English Literature.* Melbourne: Melbourne University Press 1970.

Lee, Amice. *Laurels and Rosemary: The Life of William and Mary Howitt.* Oxford: Oxford University Press 1955.

McCombie, Thomas. *Australian Sketches.* Melbourne: The Gazette 1866.

Macdonagh, Oliver. 'The Nineteenth-Century Revolution in Government: A Reappraisal'. In *The Victorian Revolution: Government and Society in Victoria's Britain,* Peter Stansky, ed. New York: New Viewpoints 1973.

Macintyre, Stuart. *A Colonial Liberalism: The Lost World of Three Victorian Visionaries.* Melbourne: Oxford University Press 1991.

McMichael, Philip. *Settlers and the Agrarian Question: Foundations of Capitalism in Colonial Australia.* Cambridge: Cambridge University Press 1984.

McMullin, Ross. 'The Impact of Gold on Lawlessness and Crime in Victoria 1851–1854'. *Victorian Historical Journal* 48, no.2, May 1977: pp.123–37.

McQueen, Humphrey. *A New Britannia: An argument concerning the social origins of Australian radicalism and nationalism*. Ringwood, Vic.: Penguin 1980.

Mayer, Henry, ed. *Marx, Engels and Australia*. Melbourne: Cheshire 1964.

Molony, John. *Eureka*. Ringwood, Vic.: Penguin 1984.

Molony, John and T.J. McKenna. 'All that Glisters'. *Labour History* 32, May 1977: pp.33–45.

Morrell, W.P. *British Colonial Policy in the Age of Peel and Russell*. Oxford: Oxford University Press 1930.

Mulvaney, D.J. and J. Golson, eds. *Aboriginal Man and Environment in Australia*. Canberra: Australian National University Press 1971.

Nadel, George. *Australia's Colonial Culture: Ideas, Men and Institutions in Mid-nineteenth Century Eastern Australia*. Melbourne: Melbourne University Press 1957.

Nance, Beverley. 'The level of violence: Europeans and Aborigines in Port Phillip, 1835–1850'. *Historical Studies* 19, no.77, Oct. 1981: pp.532–52.

Packer, D.R.G. 'Victorian Population Data, 1851–1861'. *Historical Studies* 5, no.20, May 1953: pp. 307–21.

Phillips, Jebbie and Dennis. 'A Black American at the Eureka Stockade'. *Bowyang* 7, Mar. 1982: pp.17–22.

Portus, G.V. 'The Gold Discoveries', in Ernest Scott, ed., *Australia*, vol.VII, part I, *Cambridge History of the British Empire* Cambridge: Cambridge University Press 1933.

Potts, E. Daniel and Annette. 'American Republicanism and the Disturbances on the Goldfields'. *Historical Studies* 13, no.50, Apr. 1968: pp.145–64.

——. *Young America and Australian Gold: Americans and the Gold Rush of the 1850s*. St Lucia: University of Queensland Press 1974.

Powell, J.M., *Mirrors of the New World: Images and Image-Makers in the Settlement Process*. Canberra: Australian National University Press 1978.

——.*The Public Lands of Australia Felix: settlement and land appraisal in Victoria, 1834–91*. Melbourne: Oxford University Press 1970.

Quaife, G.R. 'The Diggers: Democratic Sentiment and Political Apathy'. *Australian Journal of Politics and History* 13, no.2, Aug. 1967: pp. 221–30.

——, ed. *Gold and Colonial Society 1851–1870*. Stanmore, NSW: Cassell 1975.

Reilly, Dianne and Jennifer Carew, eds. *Sun Pictures of Victoria*. Melbourne: Library Council of Victoria 1983.

Renfree, Nancy Swinburne. 'Migrants and Cultural Transference: English Friendly Societies in a Victorian Goldfield Town.' PhD thesis, La Trobe University, 1983.

Reynolds, Henry. *Frontier: Aborigines, settlers and land*. Sydney: Allen & Unwin 1987.

Rusden, G.W. *History of Australia*. London: Chapman and Hall 1883.

Sadleir, J. 'The Early Days of the Victorian Police Force'. *Victorian Historical Magazine* 1, no.3, Sept. 1911: pp.73–9.

Schaffer, Kay. *Women and the Bush: Forces of Desire in the Australian Cultural Tradition*. Melbourne: Cambridge University Press 1987.

Serle, Geoffrey. *The Golden Age: A History of the Colony of Victoria 1851–1861.* Melbourne: Melbourne University Press 1963.
——. 'The Gold Generation'. *Victorian Historical Magazine* 41, no.1, Feb. 1970: pp.265–71.
Smith, Bernard. *European Vision and the South Pacific 1768–1850.* Oxford: Oxford University Press 1969.
Stedman Jones, Gareth. *Languages of Class: Studies in English Working Class History, 1832–1932.* Cambridge: Cambridge University Press 1983.
Thompson, Dorothy. *The Chartists: Popular Politics in the Industrial Revolution.* New York: Pantheon 1984.
Ward, J.M. *Earl Grey and the Australian Colonies 1846–1857: a study of self-government and self-interest.* Melbourne: Melbourne University Press 1958.
——. 'The Responsible Government Question in Victoria, South Australia, and Tasmania 1851–1856'. *Journal of the Royal Australian Historical Society* 63, part 4, Mar. 1978: pp.221–48.
Ward, Russel. *Australia since the coming of man.* Melbourne: Macmillan 1987.
——. *The Australian Legend.* Melbourne: Oxford University Press 1958.
Waterhouse, Richard. *From Minstrel Show to Vaudeville: The Australian Popular Stage, 1788–1914.* Kensington, NSW: University of New South Wales Press 1990.
Wells, Andrew. *Constructing Capitalism: An Economic History of Eastern Australia 1788–1901.* Sydney: Allen & Unwin 1989.
Wesson, A. 'Mechanics' Institutes in Victoria'. *Victorian Historical Magazine* 42, no.3, Aug. 1971: pp.607–17.
White, Richard. *Inventing Australia.* Sydney: Allen & Unwin, 1981.
Woodring, Carl Ray. *Victorian Samplers: William and Mary Howitt.* Lawrence, Kansas: 1952.
Woods, Carole. *Beechworth: A Titan's Field.* Melbourne: Hargreen 1985.

SECONDARY WRITINGS, COMPARATIVE

Alexander, Fred. *Moving Frontiers: An American Theme and its Application to Australian History.* Melbourne: Melbourne University Press 1947.
Allen, H.C. *Bush and Backwoods: A Comparison of the Frontier in Australia and The United States.* East Lansing: Michigan State University Press 1959.
Anderson, Benedict. *Imagined Communities: Reflections on the Origins and Spread of Nationalism.* London: Verso 1983.
Franklin, William. 'Governors, Miners and Institutions'. *California History* 65, no.1, Mar. 1986.
Gerhard, Dietrich. 'The Frontier in Comparative View'. *Comparative Studies in Society and History* 1, 1959: pp.205–29.
Hartz, Louis. *The Founding of New Societies.* New York: Harcourt, Brace and World 1964.
Higham, John. 'Changing Paradigms: The Collapse of Consensus History'. *Journal of American History* 76, Sept. 1989: pp.460–6.
Hirst, John. 'Keeping colonial history colonial: the Hartz thesis revisited'. *Historical Studies* 21, no.82, Apr. 1984: pp.85–104.
Jackson, W. Turrentine. 'A Brief Message for the Young and/or Ambitious: Com-

parative Frontiers as a Field for Investigation'. *Western Historical Quarterly* 9, no.1, Jan. 1978: pp.5–18.

Kirkby, Diane. 'Colonial Policy And Native Depopulation'. *Ethnohistory* 31, no.1, 1984.

Kolodny, Annette. 'Letting Go Our Grand Obsessions: Notes Toward a New Literary History of the American Frontiers', *American Literature* 64, no.1, 1992: pp.1–18

Lamar, Howard and Leonard Thompson, eds. *The Frontier as History: North America and Southern Africa Compared.* New Haven: Yale University Press 1981.

Mangin, J.A. and James Walvin, ed. *Manliness and Morality: Middle-Class Masculinity in Britain and America 1800–1940.* Manchester: Manchester University Press 1987.

Markus, Andrew. *Fear and Hatred: Purifying Australia and California 1850–1901.* Sydney: Hale and Iremonger 1979.

Martin, A.W., J. McCarty, and G. Bolton. *Australian Economic History Review* 12, 1973: pp.131–76.

Miller, David Harry and Jerome O. Steffen, eds. *The Frontier: Comparative Studies.* Norman: University of Oklahoma Press 1977.

Morrell, W.P. *The Gold Rushes.* London: A. and L. Black 1940.

Nicholson, Jan. 'Procedures and Perceptions of Authority: The Gold-Rush Camps of Australia, Canada and the United States'. *Public Administration: The Journal of the Australian Regional Groups of the Royal Institute of Public Administration* 32, no.4, Dec. 1973: pp.392–403.

Pocock, J.G.A. *The Machiavellian Moment: Florentine Political Thought and the Atlantic Republican Tradition.* Princeton: Princeton University Press 1975.

——. *Politics, Language, and Time: essays on political thought and history.* New York: Athenaeum 1971.

——. *Virtue, Commerce and History.* Cambridge: Cambridge University Press 1985.

Sharp, Paul. 'Three Frontiers: Some Comparative Studies of Canadian, American and Australian Settlement'. *Pacific Historical Review* 24, 1955: pp.369–77.

Skocpol, Theda and Margaret Somers. 'The Uses of Comparative History in Macrosocial Inquiry'. *Comparative Studies in Society and History* 22, no.2, Apr. 1980: pp.174–97.

Steffen, Jerome O., ed. *The American West: New Perspectives, New Dimensions.* Norman: University of Oklahoma Press 1979.

——. *Comparative Frontiers: A Proposal for Studying the American West.* Norman: University of Oklahoma Press 1980.

——. 'The Mining Frontiers of California and Australia: A Study in Political Change and Continuity'. *Pacific Historical Review* 52, no.4, Nov. 1983: pp.428–40.

Thelen, David. 'Of Audiences, Borderlands, and Comparisons: Towards the Internationalization of American History', *Journal of American History* 79, no.2, Sept. 1992.

Tyrrell, Ian. 'Comparing Comparative Histories: Australian and American Modes of Comparative Analysis'. *Australasian Journal of American Studies* 9, no.2, Dec. 1990: pp. 1–11.

——. 'American Exceptionalism in an Age of International History', *American Historical Review* 96, no.4, Oct. 1991: pp.1031–55.

Wills, Morris W. 'Sequential Frontiers: The Californian and Victorian Experience, 1850–1900'. *Western Historical Quarterly* 9, no.4, Oct. 1978: pp.483–94.

Winks, Robin W. *The Myth of the American Frontier: Its Relevance to America, Canada and Australia.* Leicester: 1971.

INDEX